DIONYSUS VERSUS THE CRUCIFIED

NIETZSCHE ON CHRISTIANITY

An Anthology
from his Major Works

CONTENTS

"The Church is precisely that against which Jesus inveighed—and against which He taught His disciples to fight. … That which is wrong with Christianity is, that it does none of the things that Christ *commanded.*"
The Will to Power

"The most earnest Christians have always been kindly disposed to me."
Ecce Homo

"I regard Christianity as the most fatal and seductive lie that has ever yet existed—as the greatest and most *impious lie*: I can discern the last sprouts and branches of its ideal beneath every form of disguise, I decline to enter into any compromise or false position in reference to it—
I urge people to declare open war with it."
The Will to Power

INTRODUCTION

Friedrich Nietzsche needs no introduction, having dominated philosophy and the arts for over a hundred years now. All of his books have remained in print since the early 20th century, and more than one university has issued comprehensive editions of his published and unpublished writings. He is the rare philosopher who is read both popularly and scholarly, generation after generation.

In the popular mind, Nietzsche and his philosophy are associated with a few catch phrases: "What does not kill me makes me stronger;" "Beyond good and evil;"[1] and the most famous of all—"God is dead." That the complex views of one of the most intelligent and perceptive men who ever lived would be reduced to a few simple slogans is absurd, but also inevitable, as Nietzsche himself would doubtless have recognized. "The popular consensus amounts to an absurdity," he wrote in *Human, All-Too Human* (sec. 110).

The purpose of this volume is to collect in one place all of Nietzsche's writings on the subject of Christianity. Of all the topics he addressed in his work, this religion, which shaped the destiny of the West for two thousand years, was arguably his chief preoccupation, not least of all because it also shaped him. He returned to it again and again in almost all of his books. What began as a dispassionate reflection on what he regarded as little more than an old superstition grew into an all out assault on what he came to see as "the most fatal and seductive lie that has ever yet existed." Why?

Nietzsche came from a line of Lutheran pastors and was raised in a devout Christian household. He first began to question his religion during adolescence. Most biographers agree that his loss of faith occurred gradually rather than suddenly. It is common for Christian

---

[1] Unfortunately made infamous in the post-sentencing statement of serial killer Richard Ramirez.

critics of Nietzsche to attribute his eventual atheism[2] to the death of his father, but his father died when he was only four, and he remained a Christian—a serious, devout Christian—for at least ten years after. In 1865 when he was 21 years old he wrote, "Do we in our research seek repose, peace, happiness? No, solely the Truth, even if it be exceedingly deterring and ugly … If you wish to aspire to peace of soul and happiness, then believe; if you wish to be the disciple of the Truth, then search."

Nietzsche had a passion and even a fanaticism for truth, at any cost. He saw this devotion to truth as a natural outgrowth of his childhood Christian piety, for the Christian religion teaches that God, in the person of Jesus Christ, is identical with truth: "I am the way, the truth, and the life." (John 14:6) Nietzsche was a master of extrapolating from his personal experiences to broader insights into culture and history.[3] Thus, he saw that Christianity's esteem for truth was a catalyst for the growth of science in Western culture, and that therefore Christianity contained within itself the seed of its own destruction insofar as its account of the natural world would come to conflict with the findings of scientific inquiry. The irony of Nietzsche's devotion to truth is that he came to conclude that absolute Truth, if it exists at all, is unknowable, and even smaller truths are always subject to our perspective.

By the time he began writing for publication, Nietzsche had ceased to be a professing Christian and had come to take the Enlightenment, with its logical positivism and materialism, for granted. (He would later reject both positivism and materialism, for various reasons, one of which was the traces of Christian metaphysical assumptions and morality which he found still present in them.) *The Birth of Tragedy*, as he himself noted in *Ecce Homo*, is silent

---

[2] It could be argued that Nietzsche was not, strictly speaking, an atheist. He did not, to use a phrase of Christopher Hitchens, "deny the numinous," but he did regard all conventional religions as systems of mythology, superstition and social control. He made many distinctions between different types of religions and types of religiosity—see, e.g., *The Will to Power* sec. 145—but he did not endorse any one type as "true."

[3] "Nietzsche was ingenious at applying self-knowledge to social movements, cantilevering out into the remote past from analysis of his own needs for self-assertion, reassurance, revenge, destruction, hero-worship." Ronald Hayman, *Nietzsche: A Critical Life* p.1-2

Introduction

on the topic of Christianity[4]—it isn't until *Human, All-Too Human* that he begins his critique. He does not bother to refute proofs for the existence of God, e.g. Anselm and Aquinas, or to argue about the historicity of the Bible. He regards Christianity as "a protruding bit of antiquity from very remote ages" and marvels that "such things can still be believed" (sec. 113). His critique is not so much of Christianity in particular as of religion and metaphysics in general. Most of it is contained in Book 4, entitled "The Religious Life," which is included here in its entirety.

In his next book, *The Dawn*, he writes

> Formerly it was sought to prove that there was no God—now it is shown how the belief that a God existed could have *originated*, and by what means this belief gained authority and importance: in this way the counterproof that there is no God becomes unnecessary and superfluous.—In former times, when the "evidences of the existence of God" which had been brought forward were refuted, a doubt still remained, viz. whether better proofs could not be found than those which had just been refuted: at that time the atheists did not understand the art of making a *tabula rasa*." (sec. 95)

In *The Dawn* we find Nietzsche's first formulation of one of the main points of his critique of religion: the notion of "another world" which is higher and more important than this one which we inhabit, which is the only one that we perceive and experience. (Sec. 33) He returns to this theme again in *The Gay Science*, where he attributes this notion to "an *error* in the interpretation of certain natural phenomena, a difficulty of the intellect," and again in *The Will to Power*, where he ascribes it to "physiological exhaustion." We see here the progression of Nietzsche's understanding and analysis from the intellect to

---

[4] There is in fact an implicit Buddhism in *The Birth of Tragedy*, since at this time his understanding of the Dionysian is virtually identical with the Buddhist concept of *sunyata* or emptiness. (See sec. 17) This is not surprising since Nietzsche was still very much under the influence of Schopenhauer at this time. It would not be long before he abandoned this conception of the Dionysian, which he calls a "metaphysical comfort" in *The Birth of Tragedy*. He would later take up the concept of the Dionysian again, but this time with a new understanding and a new metaphysic. In the later writings, the Dionysian refers to the ultimate affirmation of life, as opposed to the negation of life that he sees underlying Christianity and also Buddhism. In this new conception, the metaphysic of the Dionysian is no longer the Buddhistic emptiness, but rather the Eternal Return, which he conceived—or which was revealed to him—in 1881.

physiology, from the mind to the *body* as the root of perceptions and evaluations. (Recall that in German the same word, *Geist*, means both "intellect" and "spirit.") Ultimately, Nietzsche concludes that any notion of "another world" is a slander and defamation of *this* world.

The Dawn, according to Nietzsche, is the beginning of his "campaign against morality," which would continue for the rest of his life.[5] What we see in the subsequent works—from *The Gay Science* with its famous passage proclaiming the death of God, to *The Antichrist*, his most sustained polemic on the subject—is a gradual narrowing of focus and an increasing ferocity, as the nature of Christianity and its effects in history become more and more apparent to him. Here, too, Nietzsche's critique of Christianity is rooted in a Christian teaching: "By their fruits, ye shall know them." Nietzsche asks: what have been the fruits, the consequences, of the Christianization of European man?

> The attacks made upon Christianity, hitherto, have been not only timid but false. So long as Christian morality was not felt to be a *capital crime against Life*, its apologists had a good time. The question concerning the mere "truth" of Christianity—whether in regard to the existence of its God, or to the legendary history of its origin, not to speak of its astronomy and natural science—is quite beside the point so long as no inquiry is made into the value of Christian *morality*. Are Christian morals *worth anything*, or are they a profanation and an outrage, despite all the arts of holiness and seduction with which they are enforced? (*The Will to Power* sec. 251)

In 1888 Nietzsche wrote *The Antichrist*, which seems meant to be his final statement on the subject. Typically, when one wishes to understand Nietzsche's views on Christianity, it is to this book that one will turn. But as I hope will become clear here, the arguments and views in *The Antichrist* are largely predicated on what he wrote in his earlier books, and the force of the book is much greater when read as a kind of crescendo rather than as a standalone piece. Because of its singular theme, the entire book is included here, in the superb translation by H.L. Mencken.

*   *   *

---

[5] His most focused and systematic critique of Christian morality is found in *On the Genealogy of Morals* from 1887, of which Book 1 is included here.

Introduction

Nietzsche was trained as a classical philologist at the elite Pforta school near Naumburg. He was proficient in Greek, Latin and Hebrew, as well as numerous contemporary European languages, and read widely on the ancient world and its religions. From very early on, he noted distinctions between the ways that different tribes and ethnic groups conceived of existence and the divine, and what this indicated about their group psychology. The first excerpt here, from *The Birth of Tragedy*, is about the different foundational religious myths of Aryan and Semitic cultures.[6]

Nietzsche was a master psychologist—Freud said that he achieved a level of introspection that no one had ever achieved before, and which no one was likely to ever achieve again. Another key feature of his critique of Christianity is his uncovering of the often less-than-saintly hidden motivations which underly the "good" and "selfless" actions of the religious. In this his predecessor and inspiration was La Rochefoucauld. He also delves into the psychology of asceticism, a discipline for which he has respect when it takes its original form of self-training and self-overcoming, but which he loathes when it is perverted by religious ideas to become self-punishment and self-denial.

Nietzsche understands culture in a biological sense—in science, *to culture* something is to grow it in a controlled environment. Religion informs culture in no small way, and Nietzsche is concerned with how different religious values form different controlled environments which shape and misshape human beings; which either nurture them, or hobble them. Machiavelli evinced a similar perspective when he wrote

> For, as our Religion [Christianity] shows the truth and the true way [of life], it causes us to esteem less the honors of the world: while the Gentiles [Pagans] esteeming them greatly, and having placed the highest good in them, were more ferocious in their actions. ... [T]he ancient Religion did not beatify men except those full of worldly glory, such as were the Captains of armies and Princes of Republics. Our Religion has glorified more humble and contemplative men rather than men of action. It also places the highest good in humility, lowliness, and contempt of human

---

[6] Nietzsche would return to a critique of the mythology and religiosity of the Semites in *The Genealogy of Morals* and *The Antichrist*. He was not, however, a mere partisan of one group over another, for he also saw that the priestly type which he so despised and excoriated was not an invention of the Jews but of the Aryans, and was adopted by the Hebrews later. (See *The Will to Power* sec. 141, 142 and 143)

things: the other places it in the greatness of soul, the strength of body, and all the other things which make men very brave. And, if our Religion requires that there be strength [of soul] in you, it desires that you be more adept at suffering than in achieving great deeds.[7]

Machiavelli clearly felt that ancient paganism was more conducive to the growth of strong and brave men than Christianity. He nonetheless proclaims that he is a Christian, and that the weaker, less manly Christianity which he criticizes here is not "true" Christianity. Nietzsche also contrasts true Christianity to false versions; he takes considerable time to uncover in the Gospels what he regards as the true version, that which was taught by Jesus—a name which, rather remarkably, he calls "holy." However, his intention is not, like a mystic or founder of a new sect, to preach this path, nor, like Machiavelli, to exonerate Christianity as a whole by appealing to a better version of it. Nietzsche distinguishes the original and true Christian path only to reject it just as much as he rejects the subsequent distortions of this path, though he clearly holds some respect for the former and its founder, whereas he has almost none for the latter. (See the sections of *The Will to Power* and *The Antichrist* which lay out what Nietzsche considers to be Jesus' true teaching in considerable detail.)

Nietzsche does leave an opening, however small, for the possibility of a transcendent metaphysical truth embodied in a higher being, of a man who *is* this higher truth. In *Twilight of the Idols* he gives the hypothetical example of "I, Plato, am the truth," which is curious because Plato never said any such thing, but of course Jesus in the Gospels does: "I am the Way, the Truth and the Life." The traditionalist religious scholar Huston Smith notes that among the great prophets and religious figures of history, Jesus and Buddha stand out because when men would encounter them, they would ask not "Who are you?" but rather "*What* are you?"

For Nietzsche, religion grows from the same creative source as art; i.e. a religion is a work of art. Lawgivers like Moses, Jesus, Buddha and Zarathustra are artists and geniuses, men of power who shape human society and human souls the way a sculptor shapes his clay. They are the kind of men who point the way toward the Superman.

---

[7] Cited in https://theamericansun.com/2019/03/25/old-and-new-paganism-by-bap/

But Nietzsche also sees established religion as a kind of crystallized or stagnated art, which exists in opposition to new creation, and so wherever religion is dominant, art is suppressed, and where religion weakens, new art once again becomes ascendent. (*Human, All-Too Human* sec. 150) His fondness for Renaissance Italy was partly for this reason—religious belief had waned, allowing for new art and science. He detested the Reformation as a religious reaction against the Renaissance. (*Human, All-Too Human* sec. 237)

The Superman is Nietzsche's substitute for the religious idols of the past. Just what he meant by it, and what if anything he wanted to replace Christianity in the West, is beyond the scope of this work. On the one hand, he said he did not want to be the founder of a new religion; on the other, he wrote an entire book, *Thus Spoke Zarathustra*,[3] in the form of a religious scripture. He made several predictions about what could or what was likely to happen in the future as far as the religious disposition of European man—for example, that a kind of European Buddhism could arise—but these were not necessarily recommendations or expressions of what he wanted.

*   *   *

Nietzsche began his writing career thinking that Christianity was behind him, only to conclude that it was still very much in front of him and in front of all of us.

> We cannot suppress a certain irony when we contemplate those who think they have overcome Christianity by means of modern natural science. Christian values are by no means overcome by such people. "Christ on the cross" is still the most sublime symbol—even now. (*The Will to Power* sec. 219)

Christians would doubtless agree with this: that Christ stands before you, and like Pilate you must make a choice. Nietzsche did say that "the most earnest Christians have always been kindly disposed to me." The Catholic philosopher Peter Kreeft even called him a prophet.

---

[8] *Zarathustra* is the one book not excerpted in this anthology, because of its stylistic differences from Nietzsche's other works.

Introduction

I hope this book will be useful for both students and critics of Nietzsche. Love him or hate him, agree with him or disagree, this is what he wrote and what he thought about Christianity. Those who think he is wrong, mistakenly or maliciously, can look here to see exactly what they must contend with.

ROGUE SCHOLAR PRESS
AUGUST, 2024

Introduction

A Note on the Text and Selection

Nietzsche seems to have been aware that the fragmentary or fractal nature of his writings made them very amenable to being "remixed," to use a more modern word. Indeed, one of his last books, *Nietzsche Contra Wagner*, was a compendium of passages drawn from his previous books, organized around one theme. It was tempting therefore to do the same here, to carefully select individual passages and painstakingly organize them into a new whole in which one passage follows the next with the same kind of organic link as one would expect to find in a singular tome: *Nietzsche Contra Christianity*. Certainly there would be some advantages to doing this, as it would allow the connection of passages from different volumes which deal more or less with the same point.

We did not opt for this approach, however, for several reasons.[9] First, because Nietzsche's short passages are often so pregnant with information and perspective that they cannot be reduced to simply being about this or that singular subject; BAP noted this when discussing a passage from *Beyond Good & Evil* on his podcast—*how much* Nietzsche gives you to chew on and digest in just one paragraph or page. Secondly, many of Nietzsche's comments about Christianity are already grouped together in his books, usually forming one chapter of the book. This is so in *Human, All-Too Human*, *The Dawn*, *The Gay Science*, and *Beyond Good & Evil*, as well as *The Will to Power*, where they have been grouped together by the editors. *The Antichrist*, of course, is an entire book devoted to only this subject. This means that Nietzsche himself felt that the passages in those books had a certain order to them. So, rather than second guess the author, it seemed more profitable for readers—and easier for the editor—to present them mostly in chronological order and in the sequence in which they appear in the published works, so that one can see both their organization in Nietzsche's mind and the evolution or progress of Nietzsche's thoughts on Christianity.

---

[9] Related passages from different volumes have been noted in footnotes.

Introduction

The translations used, with some minor modifications, are as follows:

1. *The Birth of Tragedy* by Clifton Fadiman

2. *Human, All-Too Human* by Alexander Harvey, Helen Zimmern and Paul Cohn

3. *The Dawn* by J.M. Kennedy

4. *The Gay Science* by Thomas Common

5. *Beyond Good and Evil* by Helen Zimmern

6. *On the Genealogy of Morals* by Horace Samuel

7. *The Case of Wagner* by Anthony Ludovici

8. *The Will to Power* by Anthony Ludovici

9. *Twilight of the Idols* by Anthony Ludovici

10. *The Antichrist* by H.L. Mencken

11. *Ecce Homo* by Anthony Ludovici

from THE BIRTH OF TRAGEDY

9.

Let me now contrast the glory of passivity with the glory of activity which illuminates the *Prometheus* of Aeschylus. What Aeschylus the thinker had to tell us here, but which as a poet he only allows us to surmise through his symbolic picture, the youthful Goethe has known how to reveal to us in the bold words of his Prometheus:—

> Hier sitz' ich, forme Menschen
> Nach meinem Bilde,
> Ein Geschlecht, das mir gleich sei,
> Zu leiden, zu weinen,
> Zu geniessen und zu freuen sich,
> Und dein nicht zu achten,
> Wie ich![10]

Man, rising to the level of the Titans, acquires his culture by himself, and compels the gods to ally themselves with him, because in his self-sufficient wisdom he holds in his hands their existence and their limitations. The most wonderful thing, however, in this Prometheus fable, which according to its fundamental conception is an essential hymn of impiety, is the profound Aeschylean yearning for *justice*. The infinite tragedy of the bold "individual" on the one hand, and the divine necessity and premonition of a twilight of the gods on the other, the force in these two worlds of suffering operating to produce reconciliation, metaphysical oneness—all this strongly suggests the central and main position of the Aeschylean view of the world, which sees Moira as eternal justice enthroned over gods and men.

---

[10] "Here sit I, forming mankind
In my image,
A race resembling me,—
To sorrow, to weep,
To taste, to have pleasure,
And to have no need of thee,
Even as I!"

1

Lest we be surprised at the astounding boldness with which Aeschylus weighs the Olympian world in his scales of justice, we must always keep in mind that the thinking Greek had an immovably firm substratum of metaphysical thought in his mysteries, and that all his fits or skepticism could be vented upon the Olympians. When he thought of these deities, the Greek artist in particular had an obscure feeling of *mutual* dependency: and it is precisely in the Prometheus of Aeschylus that this feeling is symbolized. The Titanic artist discovered in himself a bold confidence in his ability to create men and at least destroy the gods. He might do this by his superior wisdom, for which, to be sure, he had to atone by eternal suffering. The splendid "I can" of the great genius, bought cheaply even at the price of eternal suffering, the stern pride of the artist: this is the essence and soul of Aeschylean poetry, while Sophocles in his Oedipus strikes up as prelude the triumphal chant of the *saint*. But even this interpretation which Aeschylus has given to the myth does not reveal the astounding depth of its terror. As a matter of fact, the artist's delight in unfolding, the gayety of artistic creation bidding defiance to all calamity, is actually a shining stellar and nebular image reflected in a black sea of sadness.

The story of Prometheus is an original possession of the entire Aryan race, and is documentary evidence of its capacity for the profoundly tragic. Indeed, it is not entirely improbable that this myth has the same characteristic significance for the Aryan genius that the myth of the fall of man has for the Semitic, and that the two are related like brother and sister. The presupposition of the Promethean myth is the transcendent value which a naive humanity attaches to *fire* as the true palladium of every rising culture. That man, however, should not receive this fire only as a gift from heaven, in the form of the igniting lightning or the warming sunshine, but should, on the contrary, be able to control it at will—this appeared to the reflective primitive man as sacrilege, as robbery of the divine nature. And thus the first philosophical problem at once causes a painful, irreconcilable antagonism between man and God, and puts as it were a mass of rock at the gate of every culture. The best and highest that men can acquire they must obtain by a crime, and then they must in turn endure its consequences, namely, the whole flood of sufferings and sorrows with which the offended divinities *must* requite the nobly aspiring race of man. It is a bitter thought, which, by the *dignity* it confers on crime, contrasts strangely with the Semitic myth of the fall of man, in which curiosity, deception, weakness in the face of temptation, wantonness,—in short, a whole series of preeminently feminine passions,—were regarded as the origin of evil.

What distinguishes the Aryan conception is the sublime view of *active sin* as the essential Promethean virtue, and the discovery of the ethical basis of pessimistic tragedy in the *justification* of human evil— of human guilt as well as of the suffering incurred thereby. The pain implicit in the very structure of things—which the contemplative Aryan is not disposed to explain away—the antagonism in the heart of the world, manifests itself to him as a medley of different worlds, for instance, a Divine and a human world, both of which are in the right individually, but which, because they exist separately side by side, must suffer for that very individuation. In the heroic effort towards universality made by the individual, in his attempt to penetrate beyond the bounds of individuation and become himself the *one* world-being, he experiences in himself the primordial contradiction concealed in the essence of things, that is, he trespasses and he suffers. Accordingly crime is understood by the Aryans to be masculine, sin by the Semites to be feminine; just as the original crime is committed by man, the original sin by woman. Besides, as the witches' chorus says:

> "Wir nehmen das nicht so genau:
> Mit tausend Schritten macht's die Frau;
> Doch wie sie auch sich eilen kann
> Mit einem Sprunge macht's der Mann."[11]

He who understands this innermost core of the Prometheus myth —namely, the necessity for crime imposed on the titanically striving individual—will at once feel the un-Apollonian element in this pessimistic representation. For Apollo seeks to calm individual beings precisely by drawing boundary lines between them, and by again and again, with his requirements of self-knowledge and self-control,

---

[11] "We do not measure with such care:
Woman in thousand steps is there,
But howsoe'er she hasten may.
Man in one leap has cleared the way."
   Faust, trans. of Bayard Taylor.

recalling these bounds to us as the holiest laws of the universe. However, in order that this Apollonian tendency might not congeal the form to Egyptian rigidity and coldness, in order that the effort to prescribe to the individual wave its path and compass might not ruin the motion of the entire lake, the high tide of the Dionysian tendency destroyed from time to time all those little circles in which the one-sided Apollonian "will" sought to confine the Hellenic world. The suddenly swelling Dionysian tide then takes the separate little wave mountains of individuals on its back, just as the brother of Prometheus, the Titan Atlas, does with the earth. This Titanic impulse, to become as it were the Atlas of all individuals, and on broad shoulders to bear them higher and higher, farther and farther, is what the Promethean and the Dionysian have in common. In this respect the Aeschylean Prometheus is a Dionysian mark, while, in the aforementioned profound yearning for justice, Aeschylus betrays to the intelligent eye his paternal descent from Apollo, the god of individuation, the god who sets the boundaries of justice. And so the double personality of the Aeschylean Prometheus, his conjoint Dionysian and Apollonian nature, might be thus expressed in an abstract formula: "Whatever exists is alike just and unjust, and in both cases equally justified."

"Das ist deine Welt! Das heisst eine Welt!" [12]

17.

Dionysian art, too, wishes to convince us of the eternal joy of existence: only we are to seek this joy not in phenomena, but behind them. We are to recognize that all that comes into being must be ready for a sorrowful end; we are forced to look into the terrors of the individual existence—yet we are not to become rigid with fear; a metaphysical comfort tears us momentarily from the bustle of the transforming figures. We are really for a brief moment Primordial Being itself, feeling its raging desire for existence and joy in existence, the struggle, the pain, the destruction of phenomena, now appear to us as a necessary thing, in view of the surplus of countless forms of

---

[12] "There is thy world, and what a world!"—*Faust*

existence which force and push one another into life, in view of the exuberant fertility of the universal will. We are pierced by the maddening sting of these pains just when we have become, as it were, one with the infinite primordial joy in existence, and when we anticipate, in Dionysian ecstasy, the indestructibility and eternity of this joy. In spite of fear and pity, we are the happy living beings, not as individuals, but as the *one* living being, with whose creative joy we are united.

from HUMAN, ALL-TOO HUMAN

The Religious Life

108.

The Double Contest Against Evil.—If an evil afflicts us we can either so deal with it as to remove its cause or else so deal with it that its effect upon our feeling is changed: hence look upon the evil as a benefit of which the uses will perhaps first become evident in some subsequent period. Religion and art (and also the metaphysical philosophy) strive to effect an alteration of the feeling, partly by an alteration of our judgment respecting the experience (for example, with the aid of the dictum "whom God loves, he chastizes") partly by the awakening of a joy in pain, in emotion especially (whence the art of tragedy had its origin). The more one is disposed to interpret away and justify, the less likely he is to look directly at the causes of evil and eliminate them. An instant alleviation and narcotizing of pain, as is usual in the case of tooth ache, is sufficient for him even in the severest suffering. The more the domination of religions and of all narcotic arts declines, the more searchingly do men look to the elimination of evil itself, which is a rather bad thing for the tragic poets—for there is ever less and less material for tragedy, since the domain of unsparing, immutable destiny grows constantly more circumscribed—and a still worse thing for the priests, for these last have lived heretofore upon the narcoticizing of human ill.

109.

Sorrow is Knowledge.—How willingly would not one exchange the false assertions of the *homines religiosi* that there is a god who commands us to be good, who is the sentinel and witness of every act, every moment, every thought, who loves us, who plans our welfare in every misfortune—how willingly would not one exchange these for truths as healing, beneficial and grateful as those delusions! But there are no such truths. Philosophy can at most set up in opposition to them other metaphysical plausibilities (fundamental untruths as well). The tragedy of it all is that, although one cannot believe these dogmas of religion and metaphysics if one adopts in heart and head the potent methods of truth. one has yet become, through human evolution, so tender, susceptible, sensitive, as to stand in need of the most effective means of rest and consolation. From this state of things arises the danger that, through the perception of truth or, more accurately, seeing through delusion, one may bleed to death. Byron has put this into deathless verse:

> Sorrow is knowledge: they who know the most
> Must mourn the deepest o'er the fatal truth,
> The tree of knowledge is not that of life.

Against such cares there is no better protective than the light fancy of Horace, (at any rate during the darkest hours and sun eclipses of the soul) expressed in the words

> *quid aeternis minorem*
> *consiliis animum fatigas?*
> *cur non sub alta vel platano vel hac*
> *pinu jacentes.*[13]

At any rate, light fancy or heavy heartedness of any degree must be better than a romantic retrogression and desertion of one's flag, an approach to Christianity in any form: for with it, in the present state of knowledge, one can have nothing to do without hopelessly defiling one's intellectual integrity and surrendering it unconditionally. These woes may be painful enough, but without pain one cannot become a leader and guide of humanity: and woe to him who would be such and lacks this pure integrity of the intellect!

110.

The Truth in Religion.—In the ages of enlightenment justice was not done to the importance of religion, of this there can be no doubt. It is also equally certain that in the ensuing reaction of enlightenment, the

---

[13] "Then wherefore should you, who are mortal, outwear
Your soul with a profitless burden of care
Say, why should we not, flung at ease neath this pine,
Or a plane-tree's broad umbrage, quaff gaily our wine?"
  Odes 2.11.12-14
  (Translation of Sir Theodore Martin.)

demands of justice were far exceeded inasmuch as religion was treated with love, even with infatuation and proclaimed as a profound, indeed the most profound knowledge of the world, which science had but to divest of its dogmatic garb in order to possess "truth" in its unmythical form. Religions must therefore—this was the contention of all foes of enlightenment—*sensu allegorico*, with regard for the comprehension of the masses, give expression to that ancient truth which is wisdom in itself, inasmuch as all science of modern times has led up to it instead of away from it. So that between the most ancient wisdom of man and all later wisdom there prevails harmony, even similarity of viewpoint; and the advancement of knowledge—if one be disposed to concede such a thing—has to do not with its nature but with its propagation. This whole conception of religion and science is through and through erroneous, and none would today be hardy enough to countenance it had not Schopenhauer's rhetoric taken it under protection, this high sounding rhetoric which now gains auditors after the lapse of a generation. Much as may be gained from Schopenhauer's religio-ethical human and cosmical oracle as regards the comprehension of Christianity and other religions, it is nevertheless certain that he erred regarding the value of religion to knowledge. He himself was in this but a servile pupil of the scientific teachers of his time who had all taken romanticism under their protection and renounced the spirit of enlightenment. Had he been born in our own time it would have been impossible for him to have spoken of the *sensus allegoricus* of religion. He would instead have done truth the justice to say: never has a religion, directly or indirectly, either as dogma or as allegory, contained a truth. For all religions grew out of dread or necessity, and came into existence through an error of the reason. They have, perhaps, in times of danger from science, incorporated some philosophical doctrine or other into their systems in order to make it possible to continue one's existence within them. But this is but a theological work of art dating from the time in which a religion began to doubt of itself. These theological feats of art, which are most common in Christianity as the religion of a learned age, impregnated with philosophy, have led to this superstition of the *sensus allegoricus*, as has, even more, the habit of the philosophers (namely those half-natures, the poetical philosophers and the philosophising artists) of dealing with their own feelings as if they constituted the fundamental nature of humanity and hence of giving their own religious feelings a predominant influence over the structure of their systems. As the philosophers mostly philosophised under the influence of hereditary religious habits, or at least under the traditional influence of this "metaphysical necessity," they naturally arrived at conclusions closely resembling the Judaic or Christian or Indian religious tenets—resembling, in the way that children are apt to look like their mothers: only in this case the fathers were not certain as to the maternity, as easily happens—but in the innocence of their admiration, they fabled regarding the family likeness of all religion and science. In reality, there exists between religion and true science neither relationship nor friendship, not even enmity: they dwell in different spheres. Every philosophy that lets the religious comet gleam through the darkness of its last outposts renders everything within it that purports to be science, suspicious. It is all probably religion, although it may assume the guise of science.—Moreover, though all the peoples agree concerning certain religious things, for example, the existence of a god (which, by the way, as regards this point, is not the case) this fact would constitute an argument against the thing agreed upon, for example the very existence of a god. The *consensus gentium* and especially *hominum*[14] can probably amount only to an absurdity. Against it there is no *consensus omnium sapientium*[15] whatever, on any point, with the exception of which Goethe's verse speaks:

> All greatest sages to all latest ages
> Will smile, wink and slily agree
> 'Tis folly to wait till a fool's empty pate
> Has learned to be knowing and free.
> So children of wisdom must look upon fools
> As creatures who're never the better for schools.

Stated without rhyme or metre and adapted to our case: the *consensus sapientium* is to the effect that the *consensus gentium* amounts to an absurdity.

---

[14] consensus of peoples and especially of men

[15] consensus of all wise men

111.

Origin of Religious Worship.—Let us transport ourselves back to the times in which religious life flourished most vigorously and we will find a fundamental conviction prevalent which we no longer share and which has resulted in the closing of the door to religious life once for all so far as we are concerned: this conviction has to do with nature and intercourse with her.

In those times nothing is yet known of nature's laws. Neither for earth nor for heaven is there a must. A season, sunshine, rain can come or stay away as it pleases. There is lacking, in particular, all idea of natural causation. If a man rows, it is not the oar that moves the boat, but rowing is a magical ceremony whereby a demon is constrained to move the boat. All illness, death itself, is a consequence of magical influences. In sickness and death nothing natural is conceived. The whole idea of "natural course" is wanting. The idea dawns first upon the ancient Greeks, that is to say in a very late period of humanity, in the conception of a *Moira*[16] ruling over the gods. If any person shoots off a bow, there is always an irrational strength and agency in the act. If the wells suddenly run dry, the first thought is of subterranean demons and their pranks. It must have been the dart of a god beneath whose invisible influence a human being suddenly collapses. In India, the carpenter (according to Lubbock) is in the habit of making devout offerings to his hammer and hatchet. A Brahmin treats the plume with which he writes, a soldier the weapon that he takes into the field, a mason his trowel, a laborer his plow, in the same way. All nature is, in the opinion of religious people, a sum total of the doings of conscious and willing beings, an immense mass of complex volitions. In regard to all that takes place outside of us no conclusion is permissible that anything will result thus and so, must result thus and so, that we are comparatively calculable and certain in our experiences, that man is the rule, nature the ruleless. This view forms the fundamental conviction that dominates crude, religion-producing, early civilizations. We contemporary men feel exactly the opposite: the richer man now feels himself inwardly, the more polyphone the music and the sounding of his soul, the more powerfully does the uniformity of nature impress him. We all, with

---

[16] fate

10

Goethe, recognize in nature the great means of repose for the soul. We listen to the pendulum stroke of this great clock with longing for rest, for absolute calm and quiescence, as if we could drink in the uniformity of nature and thereby arrive first at an enjoyment of oneself. Formerly it was the reverse: if we carry ourselves back to the periods of crude civilization, or if we contemplate contemporary savages, we will find them most strongly influenced by rule, by tradition. The individual is almost automatically bound to rule and tradition and moves with the uniformity of a pendulum. To him nature—the uncomprehended, fearful, mysterious nature—must seem the domain of freedom, of volition, of higher power, indeed as an ultra-human degree of destiny, as god. Every individual in such periods and circumstances feels that his existence, his happiness, the existence and happiness of the family, the state, the success or failure of every undertaking, must depend upon these dispositions of nature. Certain natural events must occur at the proper time and certain others must not occur. How can influence be exercised over this fearful unknown, how can this domain of freedom be brought under subjection? thus he asks himself, thus he worries: Is there no means to render these powers of nature as subject to rule and tradition as you are yourself?—The cogitation of the superstitious and magic-deluded man is upon the theme of imposing a law upon nature: and to put it briefly, religious worship is the result of such cogitation. The problem which is present to every man is closely connected with this one: how can the weaker party dictate laws to the stronger, control its acts in reference to the weaker? At first the most harmless form of influence is recollected, that influence which is acquired when the partiality of anyone has been won. Through beseeching and prayer, through abject humiliation, through obligations to regular gifts and propitiations, through flattering homages, it is possible, therefore, to impose some guidance upon the forces of nature, to the extent that their partiality be won: love binds and is bound. Then agreements can be entered into by means of which certain courses of conduct are mutually concluded, vows are made and authorities prescribed. But far more potent is that species of power exercised by means of magic and incantation. As a man is able to injure a powerful enemy by means of the magician and render him helpless with fear, as the love potion operates at a distance, so can the mighty forces of nature, in the opinion of weaker mankind, be controlled by similar means. The principal means of effecting incantations is to acquire control of something belonging to the party to be influenced, hair, finger nails, food from his table, even his picture or his name. With such apparatus it is possible to act by means of magic, for the basic principle is that to everything spiritual corresponds something corporeal. With the aid of this corporeal element the spirit may be bound, injured or destroyed. The corporeal affords the handle by which the spiritual can be laid hold of. In the same way that man influences mankind does he influence some spirit of nature, for this latter has also its corporeal element that can be grasped. The tree, and on the same basis, the seed from which it grew: this puzzling sequence seems to demonstrate that in both forms the same spirit is embodied, now large, now small. A stone that suddenly rolls, is the body in which the spirit works. Does a huge boulder lie in a lonely moor? It is impossible to think of mortal power having placed it there. The stone must have moved itself there. That is to say some spirit must dominate it. Everything that has a body is subject to magic, including, therefore, the spirits of nature. If a god is directly connected with his portrait, a direct influence (by refraining from devout offerings, by whippings, chainings and the like) can be brought to bear upon him. The lower classes in China tie cords around the picture of their god in order to defy his departing favor, when he has left them in the lurch, and tear the picture to pieces, drag it through the streets into dung heaps and gutters, crying: "You dog of a spirit, we housed you in a beautiful temple, we gilded you prettily, we fed you well, we brought you offerings, and yet how ungrateful you are!" Similar displays of resentment have been made against pictures of the mother of god and pictures of saints in Catholic countries during the present century when such pictures would not do their duty during times of pestilence and drought.

Through all these magical relationships to nature countless ceremonies are occasioned, and finally, when their complexity and confusion grow too great, pains are taken to systematize them, to arrange them so that the favorable course of nature's progress, namely the great yearly circle of the seasons, may be brought about by a corresponding course of the ceremonial progress. The aim of religious worship is to influence nature to human advantage, and hence to instill a subjection to law into her that originally she has not, whereas at present man desires to find out the subjection to law of nature in order to guide himself thereby. In brief, the system of religious worship rests upon the idea of magic between man and man, and the magician is older than the priest. But it rests equally upon other and higher ideas. It brings into prominence the sympathetic relation of man to man, the existence of benevolence, gratitude, prayer, of truces between enemies, of loans upon security, of arrangements for the protection of property. Man, even in very inferior degrees of civilization, does not stand in the presence of nature as a helpless slave, he is not willy-nilly the absolute servant of nature. In the Greek development of religion, especially in the relationship to the Olympian gods, it becomes possible to entertain the idea of an existence side by side of two castes, a higher, more powerful, and a lower, less powerful: but both are bound together in some way, on account of their origin and are one species. They need not be ashamed of one another. This is the element of distinction in Greek religion.

112.

At the Contemplation of Certain Ancient Sacrificial Proceedings.—How many sentiments are lost to us is manifest in the union of the farcical, even of the obscene, with the religious feeling. The feeling that this mixture is possible is becoming extinct. We realize the mixture only historically, in the mysteries of Demeter and Dionysos and in the Christian Easter festivals and religious mysteries. But we still perceive the sublime in connection with the ridiculous, and the like, the emotional with the absurd. Perhaps a later age will be unable to understand even these combinations.

113.

Christianity as Antiquity.—When on a Sunday morning we hear the old bells ringing, we ask ourselves: Is it possible? All this for a Jew crucified two thousand years ago who said he was God's son? The proof of such an assertion is lacking.—Certainly, the Christian religion constitutes in our time a protruding bit of antiquity from very remote ages and that its assertions are still generally believed— although men have become so keen in the scrutiny of claims—

constitutes the oldest relic of this inheritance. A god who begets children by a mortal woman; a sage who demands that no more work be done, that no more justice be administered but that the signs of the approaching end of the world be heeded; a system of justice that accepts an innocent as a vicarious sacrifice in the place of the guilty; a person who bids his disciples drink his blood; prayers for miracles; sins against a god expiated upon a god; fear of a hereafter to which death is the portal; the figure of the cross as a symbol in an age that no longer knows the purpose and the ignominy of the cross—how ghostly all these things flit before us out of the grave of their primitive antiquity! Is one to believe that such things can still be believed?

114.

The Un-Greek in Christianity.—The Greeks did not look upon the Homeric gods above them as lords nor upon themselves beneath as servants, after the fashion of the Jews. They saw but the counterpart as in a mirror of the most perfect specimens of their own caste, hence an ideal, but no contradiction of their own nature. There was a feeling of mutual relationship, resulting in a mutual interest, a sort of alliance. Man thinks well of himself when he gives himself such gods and places himself in a relationship akin to that of the lower nobility with the higher; whereas the Italian races have a decidedly vulgar religion, involving perpetual anxiety because of bad and mischievous powers and soul disturbers. Wherever the Olympian gods receded into the background, there even Greek life became gloomier and more perturbed.—Christianity, on the other hand, oppressed and degraded humanity completely and sank it into deepest mire: into the feeling of utter abasement it suddenly flashed the gleam of divine compassion, so that the amazed and grace-dazzled stupefied one gave a cry of delight and for a moment believed that the whole of heaven was within him. Upon this unhealthy excess of feeling, upon the accompanying corruption of heart and head, Christianity attains all its psychological effects. It wants to annihilate, debase, stupefy, amaze, bedazzle. There is but one thing that it does not want: measure, standard, and therefore is it in the worst sense barbarous, asiatic, vulgar, un-Greek.

115.

Being Religious to Some Purpose.—There are certain insipid, traffic-virtuous people to whom religion is pinned like the hem of some garb of a higher humanity. These people do well to remain religious: it adorns them. All who are not versed in some professional weapon—including tongue and pen as weapons—are servile: to all such the Christian religion is very useful, for then their servility assumes the aspect of Christian virtue and is amazingly adorned.—People whose daily lives are empty and colorless are readily religious. This is comprehensible and pardonable, but they have no right to demand that others, whose daily lives are not empty and colorless, should be religious also.

116.

The Everyday Christian.—If Christianity, with its allegations of an avenging God, universal sinfulness, choice of grace, and the danger of eternal damnation, were true, it would be an indication of weakness of mind and character not to be a priest or an apostle or a hermit, and toil for one's own salvation. It would be irrational to lose sight of one's eternal well being in comparison with temporary advantage: Assuming these dogmas to be generally believed, the every day Christian is a pitiable figure, a man who really cannot count as far as three, and who, for the rest, just because of his intellectual incapacity, does not deserve to be as hard punished as Christianity promises he shall be.

117.

Concerning the Cleverness of Christianity.—It is a master stroke of Christianity to so emphasize the unworthiness, sinfulness and degradation of men in general that contempt of one's fellow creatures becomes impossible. "He may sin as much as he pleases, he is not by nature different from me. It is I who in every way am unworthy and contemptible." So says the Christian to himself. But even this feeling has lost its keenest sting for the Christian does not believe in his individual degradation. He is bad in his general human capacity and he soothes himself a little with the assertion that we are all alike.

118.

Personal Change.—As soon as a religion rules, it has for its opponents those who were its first disciples.

119.

Fate of Christianity.—Christianity arose to lighten the heart, but now it must first make the heart heavy in order to be able to lighten it afterwards. Christianity will consequently go down.

120.

The Testimony of Pleasure.—The agreeable opinion is accepted as true. This is the testimony of pleasure (or as the church says, the evidence of strength) of which all religions are so proud, although they should all be ashamed of it. If a belief did not make blessed it would not be believed. How little it would be worth, then!

121.

Dangerous Play.—Whoever gives religious feeling room, must then also let it grow. He can do nothing else. Then his being gradually changes. The religious element brings with it affinities and kinships. The whole circle of his judgment and feeling is clouded and draped in religious shadows. Feeling cannot stand still. One should be on one's guard.

122.

The Blind Pupil.—As long as one knows very well the strength and the weakness of one's dogma, one's art, one's religion, its strength is still low. The pupil and apostle who has no eye for the weaknesses of a dogma, a religion and so on, dazzled by the aspect of the master and by his own reverence for him, has, on that very account, generally more power than the master. Without blind pupils the influence of a man and his work has never become great. To give victory to knowledge, often amounts to no more than so allying it with stupidity that the brute force of the latter forces triumph for the former.

123.

The Breaking off of Churches.—There is not sufficient religion in the world merely to put an end to the number of religions.

124.

Sinlessness of Men.—If one has understood how "Sin came into the world," namely through errors of the reason, through which men in their intercourse with one another and even individual men looked upon themselves as much blacker and wickeder than was really the case, one's whole feeling is much lightened and man and the world appear together in such a halo of harmlessness that a sentiment of well being is instilled into one's whole nature. Man in the midst of nature is as a child left to its own devices. This child indeed dreams a heavy, anxious dream. But when it opens its eyes it finds itself always in paradise.

125.

Irreligiousness of Artists.—Homer is so much at home among his gods and is as a poet so good natured to them that he must have been profoundly irreligious. That which was brought to him by the popular faith—a mean, crude and partially repulsive superstition—he dealt with as freely as the Sculptor with his clay, therefore with the same freedom that Aeschylus and Aristophanes evinced and with which in later times the great artists of the renaissance, and also Shakespeare and Goethe, drew their pictures.

126.

Art and Strength of False Interpretation.—All the visions, fears, exhaustions and delights of the saint are well known symptoms of sickness, which in him, owing to deep rooted religious and psychological delusions, are explained quite differently, that is not as symptoms of sickness.—So, too, perhaps, the demon of Socrates was nothing but a malady of the ear that he explained, in view of his predominant moral theory, in a manner different from what would be thought rational today. Nor is the case different with the frenzy and the frenzied speeches of the prophets and of the priests of the oracles. It is always the degree of wisdom, imagination, capacity and morality in the heart and mind of the interpreters that got so much out of them. It is among the greatest feats of the men who are called geniuses and saints that they made interpreters for themselves who, fortunately for mankind, did not understand them.

127.

Reverence for Madness.—Because it was perceived that an excitement of some kind often made the head clearer and occasioned fortunate inspirations, it was concluded that the utmost excitement would occasion the most fortunate inspirations. Hence the frenzied being was revered as a sage and an oracle giver. A false conclusion lies at the bottom of all this.[17]

128.

Promises of Wisdom.—Modern science has as its object as little pain as possible, as long a life as possible—hence a sort of eternal blessedness, but of a very limited kind in comparison with the promises of religion.

129.

Forbidden Generosity.—There is not enough of love and goodness in the world to throw any of it away on conceited people.

130.

Survival of Religious Training in the Disposition.—The Catholic Church, and before it all ancient education, controlled the whole domain of means through which man was put into certain unordinary moods and withdrawn from the cold calculation of personal advantage and from calm, rational reflection. A church vibrating with deep tones; gloomy, regular, restraining exhortations from a priestly band, who involuntarily communicate their own tension to their congregation and lead them to listen almost with anxiety as if some miracle were in course of preparation; the awesome pile of architecture which, as the house of a god, rears itself vastly into the

---

[17] This idea is developed further in section 14 of *The Dawn.*

vague and in all its shadowy nooks inspires fear of its nerve-exciting power—who would care to reduce men to the level of these things if the ideas upon which they rest became extinct? But the results of all these things are nevertheless not thrown away: the inner world of exalted, emotional, prophetic, profoundly repentant, hope-blessed moods has become inborn in man largely through cultivation. What still exists in his soul was formerly, as he germinated, grew and bloomed, thoroughly disciplined.

131.

Religious After-Pains.—Though one believe oneself absolutely weaned away from religion, the process has yet not been so thorough as to make impossible a feeling of joy at the presence of religious feelings and dispositions without intelligible content, as, for example, in music; and if a philosophy alleges to us the validity of metaphysical hopes, through the peace of soul therein attainable, and also speaks of "the whole true gospel in the look of Raphael's Madonna," we greet such declarations and innuendoes with a welcome smile. The philosopher has here a matter easy of demonstration. He responds with that which he is glad to give, namely a heart that is glad to accept. Hence it is observable how the less reflective free spirits collide only with dogmas but yield readily to the magic of religious feelings; it is a source of pain to them to let the latter go simply on account of the former.

Scientific philosophy must be very much on its guard lest on account of this necessity—an evolved and hence, also, a transitory necessity—delusions are smuggled in. Even logicians speak of "presentiments" of truth in ethics and in art (for example of the presentiment that the essence of things is unity); a thing which, nevertheless, ought to be prohibited. Between carefully deduced truths and such "foreboded" things there lies the abysmal distinction that the former are products of the intellect and the latter of the necessity. Hunger is no evidence that there is food at hand to appease it. Hunger merely craves food. "Presentiment" does not denote that the existence of a thing is known in any way whatever. It denotes merely that it is deemed possible to the extent that it is desired or feared. The "presentiment" is not one step forward in the domain of certainty.—It is involuntarily believed that the religious tinted sections of a philosophy are better attested than the others, but the case is at bottom just the opposite: there is simply the inner wish that it may be so, that the thing which beautifies may also be true. This wish leads us to accept bad grounds as good.

132.

Of the Christian Need of Salvation.—Careful consideration must render it possible to propound some explanation of that process in the soul of a Christian which is termed need of salvation, and to propound an explanation, too, free from mythology: hence one purely psychological. Heretofore psychological explanations of religious conditions and processes have really been in disrepute, inasmuch as a theology calling itself free gave vent to its unprofitable nature in this domain; for its principal aim, so far as may be judged from the spirit of its creator, Schleier-macher, was the preservation of the Christian religion and the maintenance of the Christian theology. It appeared that in the psychological analysis of religious "facts" a new anchorage and above all a new calling were to be gained. Undisturbed by such predecessors, we venture the following exposition of the phenomena alluded to. Man is conscious of certain acts which are very firmly implanted in the general course of conduct: indeed he discovers in himself a predisposition to such acts that seems to him to be as unalterable as his very being. How gladly he would essay some other kind of acts which in the general estimate of conduct are rated the best and highest, how gladly he would welcome the consciousness of well doing which ought to follow unselfish motive! Unfortunately, however, it goes no further than this longing: the discontent consequent upon being unable to satisfy it is added to all other kinds of discontent which result from his life destiny in particular or which may be due to so called bad acts; so that a deep depression ensues accompanied by a desire for some physician to remove it and all its causes.—This condition would not be found so bitter if the individual but compared himself freely with other men: for then he would have no reason to be discontented with himself in particular as he is merely bearing his share of the general burden of human discontent and incompleteness. But he compares himself with a being who alone must be capable of the conduct that is called unegoistic and of an enduring consciousness of unselfish motive, with God. It is because he gazes into this clear mirror, that his own self seems so extraordinarily distracted and so troubled. Thereupon the thought of that being, in so far as it flits before his fancy as retributive justice, occasions him anxiety. In every conceivable small and great experience he believes he sees the anger of the being, his threats, the very implements and manacles of his judge and prison. What succors him in this danger, which, in the prospect of an eternal duration of punishment, transcends in hideousness all the horrors that can be presented to the imagination?

133.

Before we consider this condition in its further effects, we would admit to ourselves that man is betrayed into this condition not through his "fault" and "sin" but through a series of delusions of the reason; that it was the fault of the mirror if his own self appeared to him in the highest degree dark and hateful, and that that mirror was his own work, the very imperfect work of human imagination and judgment. In the first place a being capable of absolutely unegoistic conduct is as fabulous as the phoenix. Such a being is not even thinkable for the very reason that the whole notion of "unegoistic conduct," when closely examined, vanishes into air. Never yet has a man done anything solely for others and entirely without reference to a personal motive; indeed how could he possibly do anything that had no reference to himself, that is without inward compulsion (which must always have its basis in a personal need)? How could the ego act without ego?—A god, who, on the other hand, is all love, as he is usually represented, would not be capable of a solitary unegoistic act: whence one is reminded of a reflection of Lichtenberg's which is, in truth, taken from a lower sphere: "We cannot possibly feel for others, as the expression goes; we feel only for ourselves. The assertion sounds hard, but it is not, if rightly understood. A man loves neither his father nor his mother nor his wife nor his child, but simply the feelings which they inspire." Or, as La Rochefoucauld says: "If you think you love your mistress for the mere love of her, you are very much mistaken." Why acts of love are more highly prized than others, namely not on account of their nature, but on account of their utility, has already been explained in the section on the origin of moral feelings. But if a man should wish to be all love like the god aforesaid, and want to do all things for others and nothing for himself, the procedure would be fundamentally impossible because he *must* do a great deal for himself before there would be any possibility of doing anything for the love of others. It is also essential that others be sufficiently egoistic to accept always and at all times this self sacrifice and living for others, so that the men of love and self sacrifice have an interest in the survival of unloving and selfish egoists, while the highest morality, in order to maintain itself must formally enforce the existence of immorality (wherein it would be really destroying itself.) —Further: the idea of a god perturbs and discourages as long as it is accepted but as to how it originated can no longer, in the present state of comparative ethnological science, be a matter of doubt, and with the insight into the origin of this belief all faith collapses. What happens to the Christian who compares his nature with that of God is exactly what happened to Don Quixote, who depreciated his own prowess because his head was filled with the wondrous deeds of the heroes of chivalrous romance. The standard of measurement which both employ belongs to the domain of fable.—But if the idea of God collapses, so too, does the feeling of "sin" as a violation of divine rescript, as a stain upon a god-like creation. There still apparently remains that discouragement which is closely allied with fear of the punishment of worldly justice or of the contempt of one's fellow men. The keenest thorn in the sentiment of sin is dulled when it is perceived that one's acts have contravened human tradition, human rules and human laws without having thereby endangered the "eternal salvation of the soul" and its relations with deity. If finally men attain to the conviction of the absolute necessity of all acts and of their utter irresponsibility and then absorb it into their flesh and blood, every relic of conscience pangs will disappear.

134.

If now, as stated, the Christian, through certain delusive feelings, is betrayed into self contempt, that is by a false and unscientific view of his acts and feelings, he must, nevertheless, perceive with the utmost amazement that this state of self contempt, of conscience pangs, of despair in particular, does not last, that there are hours during which all these things are wafted away from the soul and he feels himself once more free and courageous. The truth is that joy in his own being, the fulness of his own powers in connection with the inevitable decline of his profound excitation with the lapse of time, bore off the palm of victory. The man loves himself once more, he feels it—but this very new love, this new self esteem seems to him incredible. He can see in it only the wholly unmerited stream of the light of grace shed down upon him. If he formerly saw in every event merely warnings, threats, punishments and every kind of indication of divine anger, he now reads into his experiences the grace of god. The latter circumstance seems to him full of love, the former as a helpful pointing of the way, and his entirely joyful frame of mind now seems to him to be an absolute proof of the goodness of God. As formerly in his states of discouragement he interpreted his conduct falsely so now he does the same with his experiences. His state of consolation is now regarded as the effect produced by some external power. The love with which, at bottom, he loves himself, seems to be the divine love. That which he calls grace and the preliminary of salvation is in reality self-grace, self-salvation.

135.

Therefore a certain false psychology, a certain kind of imaginativeness in the interpretation of motives and experiences is the essential preliminary to being a Christian and to experiencing the need of salvation. Upon gaining an insight into this wandering of the reason and the imagination, one ceases to be a Christian.

136.

Of Christian Asceticism and Sanctity.—Much as some thinkers have exerted themselves to impart an air of the miraculous to those singular phenomena known as asceticism and sanctity, to question which or to account for which upon a rational basis would be wickedness and sacrilege, the temptation to this wickedness is none the less great. A powerful impulse of nature has in every age led to protest against such phenomena. At any rate science, inasmuch as it is the imitation of nature, permits the casting of doubts upon the inexplicable character and the supernal degree of such phenomena. It is true that heretofore science has not succeeded in its attempts at explanation. The phenomena remain unexplained still, to the great

23

satisfaction of those who revere moral miracles. For, speaking generally, the unexplained must rank as the inexplicable, the inexplicable as the non-natural, supernatural, miraculous—so runs the demand in the souls of all the religious and all the metaphysicians (even the artists if they happen to be thinkers), whereas the scientific man sees in this demand the "evil principle."—The universal, first, apparent truth that is encountered in the contemplation of sanctity and asceticism is that their nature is complicated; for nearly always, within the physical world as well as in the moral, the apparently miraculous may be traced successfully to the complex, the obscure, the multi-conditioned. Let us venture then to isolate a few impulses in the soul of the saint and the ascetic, to consider them separately and then view them as a synthetic development.

137.

There is an obstinacy against oneself, certain sublimated forms of which are included in asceticism. Certain kinds of men are under such a strong necessity of exercising their power and dominating impulses that, if other objects are lacking or if they have not succeeded with other objects they will actually tyrannize over some portions of their own nature or over sections and stages of their own personality. Thus do many thinkers bring themselves to views which are far from likely to increase or improve their fame. Many deliberately bring down the contempt of others upon themselves although they could easily have retained consideration by silence. Others contradict earlier opinions and do not shrink from the ordeal of being deemed inconsistent. On the contrary they strive for this and act like eager riders who enjoy horseback exercise most when the horse is skittish. Thus will men in dangerous paths ascend to the highest steeps in order to laugh to scorn their own fear and their own trembling limbs. Thus will the philosopher embrace the dogmas of asceticism, humility, sanctity, in the light of which his own image appears in its most hideous aspect. This crushing of self, this mockery of one's own nature, this *spernere se sperni*[18] out of which religions have made so much is in reality but a very high development of vanity. The whole ethic of the sermon on the mount belongs in this category: man

---

[18] despise that one is despised

has a true delight in mastering himself through exaggerated pretensions or excessive expedients and later deifying this tyrannically exacting something within him. In every scheme of ascetic ethics, man prays to one part of himself as if it were god and hence it is necessary for him to treat the rest of himself as devil.

138.

Man is not at all hours equally moral; this is established. If one's morality be judged according to one's capacity for great, self sacrificing resolutions and abnegations (which when continual, and made a habit are known as sanctity) one is, in affection, or disposition, the most moral: while higher excitement supplies wholly new impulses which, were one calm and cool as ordinarily, one would not deem oneself even capable of. How comes this? Apparently from the propinquity of all great and lofty emotional states. If a man is brought to an extraordinary pitch of feeling he can resolve upon a fearful revenge or upon a fearful renunciation of his thirst for vengeance indifferently. He craves, under the influences of powerful emotion, the great, the powerful, the immense, and if he chances to perceive that the sacrifice of himself will afford him as much satisfaction as the sacrifice of another, or will afford him more, he will choose self sacrifice. What concerns him particularly is simply the unloading of his emotion. Hence he readily, to relieve his tension, grasps the darts of the enemy and buries them in his own breast. That in self abnegation and not in revenge the element of greatness consisted must have been brought home to mankind only after long habituation. A god who sacrifices himself would be the most powerful and most effective symbol of this sort of greatness. As the conquest of the most hardly conquered enemy, the sudden mastering of a passion —thus does such abnegation *appear*: hence it passes for the summit of morality. In reality all that is involved is the exchange of one idea for another whilst the temperament remained at a like altitude, a like tidal state. Men when coming out of the spell, or resting from such passionate excitation, no longer understand the morality of such instants, but the admiration of all who participated in the occasion sustains them. Pride is their support if the passion and the comprehension of their act weaken. Therefore, at bottom even such acts of self-abnegation are not moral inasmuch as they are not done with a strict regard for others. Rather do others afford the high strung temperament an opportunity to lighten itself through such abnegation.

139.

Even the ascetic seeks to make life easier, and generally by means of absolute subjection to another will or to an all inclusive rule and ritual, pretty much as the Brahmin leaves absolutely nothing to his own volition but is guided in every moment of his life by some holy injunction or other. This subjection is a potent means of acquiring dominion over oneself. One is occupied, hence time does not bang heavy and there is no incitement of the personal will and of the individual passion. The deed once done there is no feeling of responsibility nor the sting of regret. One has given up one's own will once for all and this is easier than to give it up occasionally, as it is also easier wholly to renounce a desire than to yield to it in measured degree. When we consider the present relation of man to the state we perceive unconditional obedience is easier than conditional. The holy person also makes his lot easier through the complete surrender of his life personality and it is all delusion to admire such a phenomenon as the loftiest heroism of morality. It is always more difficult to assert one's personality without shrinking and without hesitation than to give it up altogether in the manner indicated, and it requires moreover more intellect and thought.

140.

After having discovered in many of the less comprehensible actions mere manifestations of pleasure in emotion for its own sake, I fancy I can detect in the self contempt which characterises holy persons, and also in their acts of self torture (through hunger and scourgings, distortions and chaining of the limbs, acts of madness) simply a means whereby such natures may resist the general exhaustion of their will to live (their nerves). They employ the most painful expedients to escape if only for a time from the heaviness and weariness in which they are steeped by their great mental indolence and their subjection to a will other than their own.

141.

The most usual means by which the ascetic and the sanctified individual seeks to make life more endurable comprises certain combats of an inner nature involving alternations of victory and prostration. For this purpose an enemy is necessary and he is found in the so called "inner enemy." That is, the holy individual makes use of his tendency to vanity, domineering and pride, and of his mental longings in order to contemplate his life as a sort of continuous battle and himself as a battlefield, in which good and evil spirits wage war with varying fortune. It is an established fact that the imagination is restrained through the regularity and adequacy of sexual intercourse while on the other hand abstention from or great irregularity in sexual intercourse will cause the imagination to run riot. The imaginations of many of the Christian saints were obscene to a degree; and because of the theory that sexual desires were in reality demons that raged within them, the saints did not feel wholly responsible for them. It is to this conviction that we are indebted for the highly instructive sincerity of their evidence against themselves. It was to their interest that this contest should always be kept up in some fashion because by means of this contest, as already stated, their empty lives gained distraction. In order that the contest might seem sufficiently great to inspire sympathy and admiration in the unsanctified, it was essential that sexual capacity be ever more and more damned and denounced. Indeed the danger of eternal damnation was so closely allied to this capacity that for whole generations Christians showed their children with actual conscience pangs. What evil may not have been done to humanity through this! And yet here the truth is just upside down: an exceedingly unseemly attitude for the truth. Christianity, it is true, had said that every man is conceived and born in sin, and in the intolerable and excessive Christianity of Calderon this thought is again perverted and entangled into the most distorted paradox extant in the well known lines

> The greatest sin of man
> Is the sin of being born.

In all pessimistic religions the act of procreation is looked upon as evil in itself. This is far from being the general human opinion. It is not even the opinion of all pessimists. Empedocles, for example, knows nothing of anything shameful, devilish and sinful in it. He sees rather in the great field of bliss of unholiness simply a healthful and hopeful phenomenon, Aphrodite. She is to him an evidence that strife does not always rage but that some time a gentle demon is to wield the sceptre. The Christian pessimists of practice, had, as stated, a direct interest in the prevalence of an opposite belief. They needed in the loneliness and the spiritual wilderness of their lives an ever living enemy, and a universally known enemy through whose conquest they might appear to the unsanctified as utterly incomprehensible and half unnatural beings. When this enemy at last, as a result of their mode of life and their shattered health, took flight forever, they were able immediately to people their inner selves with new demons. The rise and fall of the balance of cheerfulness and despair maintained their addled brains in a totally new fluctuation of longing and peace of soul. And in that period psychology served not only to cast suspicion on everything human but to wound and scourge it, to crucify it. Man wanted to find himself as base and evil as possible. Man sought to become anxious about the state of his soul, he wished to be doubtful of his own capacity. Everything natural with which man connects the idea of badness and sinfulness (as, for instance, is still customary in regard to the erotic) injures and degrades the imagination, occasions a shamed aspect, leads man to war upon himself and makes him uncertain, distrustful of himself. Even his dreams acquire a tincture of the unclean conscience. And yet this suffering because of the natural element in certain things is wholly superfluous. It is simply the result of opinions regarding the things. It is easy to understand why men become worse than they are if they are brought to look upon the unavoidably natural as bad and later to feel it as of evil origin. It is the master stroke of religions and metaphysics that wish to make man out bad and sinful by nature, to render nature suspicious in his eyes and to so make himself evil, for he learns to feel himself evil when he cannot divest himself of nature. He gradually comes to look upon himself, after a long life lived naturally, so oppressed by a weight of sin that supernatural powers become necessary to relieve him of the burden; and with this notion comes the so called need of salvation, which is the result not of a real but of an imaginary sinfulness. Go through the separate moral expositions in the vouchers of christianity and it will always be found that the demands are excessive in order that it may be impossible for man to satisfy them. The object is not that he may become moral but that he may feel as sinful as possible. If this feeling had not been rendered agreeable to man—why should he have improvised such an ideal and clung to it so long? As in the ancient world an incalculable strength of intellect and capacity for feeling was squandered in order to increase the joy of living through feastful systems of worship, so in the era of Christianity an equally incalculable quantity of intellectual capacity has been sacrificed in another endeavor: that man should in every way feel himself sinful and thereby be moved, inspired, inspirited. To move, to inspire, to inspirit at any cost—is not this the freedom cry of an exhausted, over-ripe, over cultivated age? The circle of all the natural sensations had been gone through a hundred times: the soul had grown weary. Then the saints and the ascetics found a new order of ecstacies. They set themselves before the eyes of all not alone as models for imitation to many, but as fearful and yet delightful spectacles on the boundary line between this world and the next world, where in that period everyone thought he saw at one time rays of heavenly light, at another fearful, threatening tongues of flame. The eye of the saint, directed upon the fearful significance of the shortness of earthly life, upon the imminence of the last judgment, upon eternal life hereafter; this glowering eye in an emaciated body caused men, in the old time world, to tremble to the depths of their being. To look, to look away and shudder, to feel anew the fascination of the spectacle, to yield to it, sate oneself upon it until the soul trembled with ardor and fever— that was the last pleasure left to classical antiquity when its sensibilities had been blunted by the arena and the gladiatorial show.

142.

To sum up all that has been said: that condition of soul at which the saint or expectant saint is rejoiced is a combination of elements which we are all familiar with, except that under other influences than those of mere religious ideation they customarily arouse the censure of men in the same way that when combined with religion itself and regarded as the supreme attainment of sanctity, they are object of admiration and even of prayer—at least in more simple times. Very soon the saint turns upon himself that severity that is so closely allied to the instinct of domination at any price and which inspire even in the most solitary individual the sense of power. Soon his swollen sensitiveness of feeling breaks forth from the longing to restrain his passions within it and is transformed into a longing to master them as if they were wild steeds, the master impulse being ever that of a proud spirit; next he craves a complete cessation of all perturbing, fascinating feelings, a waking sleep, an enduring repose in the lap of a dull, animal, plant-like indolence. Next he seeks the battle and extinguishes it within himself because weariness and boredom confront him. He binds his self-deification with self-contempt. He delights in the wild tumult of his desires and the sharp pain of sin, in the very idea of being lost. He is able to play his very passions, for instance the desire to domineer, a trick so that he goes to the other extreme of abject humiliation and subjection, so that his overwrought soul is without any restraint through this antithesis. And, finally, when indulgence in visions, in talks with the dead or with divine beings overcomes him, this is really but a form of gratification that he craves, perhaps a form of gratification in which all other gratifications are blended. Novalis, one of the authorities in matters of sanctity, because of his experience and instinct, betrays the whole secret with the utmost simplicity when he says: "It is remarkable that the close connection of gratification, religion and cruelty has not long ago made men aware of their inner relationship and common tendency."

143.

Not what the saint is but what he was in the eyes of the non-sanctified gives him his historical importance. Because there existed a delusion respecting the saint, his soul states being falsely viewed and his personality being sundered as much as possible from humanity as a something incomparable and supernatural, because of these things he attained the extraordinary with which he swayed the imaginations of whole nations and whole ages. Even he did not know himself, for even he regarded his dispositions, passions and actions in accordance with a system of interpretation as artificial and exaggerated as the pneumatic interpretation of the bible. The distorted and diseased in his own nature with its blending of spiritual poverty, defective knowledge, ruined health, overwrought nerves, remained as hidden from his view as from the view of his beholders. He was neither a particularly good man nor a particularly bad man but he stood for something that was far above the human standard in wisdom and goodness. Faith in him sustained faith in the divine and miraculous, in a religious significance of all existence, in an impending day of judgment. In the last rays of the setting sun of the ancient world, which fell upon the Christian peoples, the shadowy form of the saint attained enormous proportions—to such enormous proportions, indeed, that down even to our own age, which no longer believes in God, there are thinkers who believe in the saints.

144.

It stands to reason that this sketch of the saint, made upon the model of the whole species, can be confronted with many opposing sketches that would create a more agreeable impression. There are certain exceptions among the species who distinguish themselves either by especial gentleness or especial humanity, and perhaps by the strength of their own personality. Others are in the highest degree fascinating because certain of their delusions shed a particular glow over their whole being, as is the case with the founder of Christianity who took himself for the only begotten son of God and hence felt himself sinless; so that through his imagination—that should not be too harshly judged since the whole of antiquity swarmed with sons of God—he attained the same goal, the sense of complete sinlessness, complete irresponsibility, that can now be attained by every individual through science.—In the same manner I have viewed the saints of India who occupy an intermediate station between the Christian saints and the Greek philosophers and hence are not to be regarded as a pure type. Knowledge and science—as far as they existed—and superiority to the rest of mankind by logical discipline and training of the intellectual powers were insisted upon by the Buddhists as essential to sanctity, just as they were denounced by the Christian world as the indications of sinfulness.

*   *   *   *   *

150.

The Animation of Art.—Art raises its head where creeds relax. It takes over many feelings and moods engendered by religion, lays them

31

to its heart, and itself becomes deeper, more full of soul, so that it is capable of transmitting exultation and enthusiasm, which it previously was not able to do. The abundance of religious feelings which have grown into a stream are always breaking forth again and desire to conquer new kingdoms, but the growing enlightenment has shaken the dogmas of religion and inspired a deep mistrust,—thus the feeling, thrust by enlightenment out of the religious sphere, throws itself upon art, in a few cases into political life, even straight into science. Everywhere where human endeavour wears a loftier, gloomier aspect, it may be assumed that the fear of spirits, incense, and church-shadows have remained attached to it.

153.

Art Makes Heavy the Heart of the Thinker.—How strong metaphysical need is and how difficult nature renders our departure from it may be seen from the fact that even in the free spirit, when he has cast off everything metaphysical, the loftiest effects of art can easily produce a resounding of the long silent, even broken, metaphysical string,—it may be, for instance, that at a passage in Beethoven's Ninth Symphony he feels himself floating above the earth in a starry dome with the dream of *immortality* in his heart; all the stars seem to shine round him, and the earth to sink farther and farther away.—If he becomes conscious of this state, he feels a deep pain at his heart, and sighs for the man who will lead back to him his lost darling, be it called religion or metaphysics. In such moments his intellectual character is put to the test.

162.

The Cult of Genius For the Sake of Vanity.—Because we think well of ourselves, but nevertheless do not imagine that we are capable of the conception of one of Raphael's pictures or of a scene such as those of one of Shakespeare's dramas, we persuade ourselves that the faculty for doing this is quite extraordinarily wonderful, a very rare case, or, if we are religiously inclined, a grace from above. Thus the cult of genius fosters our vanity, our self-love, for it is only when we think of it as very far removed from us, as a *miraculum*, that it does not wound us
...

220.

The Beyond in Art.—It is not without deep pain that we acknowledge the fact that in their loftiest soarings, artists of all ages have exalted and divinely transfigured precisely those ideas which we now recognise as false; they are the glorifiers of humanity's religious and philosophical errors, and they could not have been this without belief in the absolute truth of these errors. But if the belief in such truth diminishes at all, if the rainbow colours at the farthest ends of human knowledge and imagination fade, then this kind of art can never re-flourish, for, like the *Divina Commedia,* Raphael's paintings, Michelangelo's frescoes, and Gothic cathedrals, they indicate not only a cosmic but also a metaphysical meaning in the work of art. Out of all this will grow a touching legend that such an art and such an artistic faith once existed.

226.

The Origin of Faith.—The fettered spirit does not take up his position from conviction, but from habit; he is a Christian, for instance, not because he had a comprehension of different creeds and could take his choice; he is an Englishman, not because he decided for England, but he found Christianity and England ready-made and accepted them without any reason, just as one who is born in a wine-country becomes a wine-drinker. Later on, perhaps, as he was a Christian and an Englishman, he discovered a few reasons in favour of his habit; these reasons may be upset, but he is not therefore upset in his whole position. For instance, let a fettered spirit be obliged to bring forward his reasons against bigamy and then it will be seen whether his holy zeal in favour of monogamy is based upon reason or upon custom. The adoption of guiding principles without reasons is called *faith.*

227.

Conclusions Drawn from the Consequences and Traced Back to Reason and Un-reason.—All states and orders of society, professions, matrimony, education, law: all these find strength and duration only in the faith which the fettered spirits repose in them,—that is, in the absence of reasons, or at least in the averting of inquiries as to reasons. The restricted spirits do not willingly acknowledge this, and feel that it is a *pudendum*. Christianity, however, which was very simple in its intellectual ideas, remarked nothing of this *pudendum*, required faith and nothing but faith, and passionately repulsed the demand for reasons; it pointed to the success of faith: "You will soon feel the advantages of faith," it suggested, "and through faith shall ye be saved." As an actual fact, the State pursues the same course, and every father brings up his son in the same way: "Only believe this," he says, "and you will soon feel the good it does." This implies, however, that the truth of an opinion is proved by its personal usefulness; the wholesomeness of a doctrine must be a guarantee for its intellectual surety and solidity. It is exactly as if an accused person in a court of law were to say, "My counsel speaks the whole truth, for only see what is the result of his speech: I shall be acquitted." Because the fettered spirits retain their principles on account of their usefulness, they suppose that the free spirit also seeks his own advantage in his views and only holds that to be true which is profitable to him. But as he appears to find profitable just the contrary of that which his compatriots or equals find profitable, these latter assume that his principles are dangerous to them; they say or feel, "He must not be right, for he is injurious to us."

237.

Renaissance and Reformation.—The Italian Renaissance contained within itself all the positive forces to which we owe modern culture. Such were the liberation of thought, the disregard of authorities, the triumph of education over the darkness of tradition, enthusiasm for science and the scientific past of mankind, the unfettering of the Individual, an ardour for truthfulness and a dislike of delusion and mere effect (which ardour blazed forth in an entire company of artistic characters, who with the greatest moral purity required from themselves perfection in their works, and nothing but perfection); yes, the Renaissance had positive forces, which have, *as yet*, never become so mighty again in our modern culture. It was the Golden Age of the last thousand years, in spite of all its blemishes and vices. On the other hand, the German Reformation stands out as an energetic protest of antiquated spirits, who were by no means tired of mediæval views of life, and who received the signs of its dissolution, the extraordinary flatness and alienation of the religious life, with deep dejection instead of with the rejoicing that would have been seemly. With their northern strength and stiff-neckedness they threw mankind back again, brought about the counter-reformation, that is, a Catholic Christianity of self-defence, with all the violences of a state of siege, and delayed for two or three centuries the complete awakening and mastery of the sciences; just as they probably made for ever impossible the complete inter-growth of the antique and the modern spirit. The great task of the Renaissance could not be brought to a termination, this was prevented by the protest of the contemporary backward German spirit (which, for its salvation, had had sufficient sense in the Middle Ages to cross the Alps again and again). It was the chance of an extraordinary constellation of politics that Luther was preserved, and that his protest; gained strength, for the Emperor protected him in order to employ him as a weapon against the Pope, and in the same way he was secretly favoured by the Pope in order to use the Protestant princes as a counter-weight against the Emperor. Without this curious counter-play of intentions, Luther would have been burnt like Huss,—and the morning sun of enlightenment would probably have risen somewhat earlier, and with a splendour more beauteous than we can now imagine.

244.

In the Neighbourhood of Insanity.—The sum of sensations, knowledge and experiences, the whole burden of culture, therefore, has become so great that an overstraining of nerves and powers of thought is a common danger, indeed the cultivated classes of European countries are throughout neurotic, and almost every one of their great families is on the verge of insanity in one of their branches. True, health is now sought in every possible way; but in the main a diminution of that tension of feeling, of that oppressive burden of culture, is needful, which, even though it might be bought at a heavy sacrifice, would at least give us room for the great hope of a *new Renaissance*. To Christianity, to the philosophers, poets, and musicians we owe an abundance of deeply emotional sensations; in order that these may not get beyond our control we must invoke the spirit of science, which on the whole makes us somewhat colder and more sceptical, and in particular cools the faith in final and absolute truths; it is chiefly through Christianity that it has grown so wild.

280.

Aggravation As Relief, and vice versa.—Much that makes life more difficult in certain grades of mankind serves to lighten it in a higher grade, because such people have become familiar with greater aggravations of life. The contrary also happens; for instance, religion has a double face, according to whether a man looks up to it to relieve him of his burden and need, or looks down upon it as-upon fetters laid on him to prevent him from soaring too high into the air.

281.

The Higher Culture Is Necessarily Misunderstood.—He who has strung his instrument with only two strings, like the scholars who, besides the *instinct of knowledge* possess only an acquired *religious* instinct, does not understand people who can play upon more strings. It lies in the nature of the higher, *many-stringed* culture that it should always be falsely interpreted by the lower; an example of this is when art appears as a disguised form of the religious. People who are only religious understand even science as a searching after the religious sentiment, just as deaf mutes do not know what music is, unless it be visible movement.

292.

Forward.—And thus forward upon the path of wisdom, with a firm step and good confidence! However you may be situated, serve yourself as a source of experience! Throw off the displeasure at your nature, forgive yourself your own individuality, for in any case you have in yourself a ladder with a hundred steps upon which you can mount to knowledge. The age into which with grief you feel yourself thrown thinks you happy because of this good fortune; it calls out to you that you shall still have experiences which men of later ages will perhaps be obliged to forego. Do not despise the fact of having been religious; consider fully how you have had a genuine access to art. Can you not, with the help of these experiences, follow immense stretches of former humanity with a clearer understanding? Is not that ground which sometimes displeases you so greatly, that ground of clouded thought, precisely the one upon which have grown many of the most glorious fruits of older civilisations? You must have loved religion and art as you loved mother and nurse,—otherwise you cannot be wise. But you must be able to see beyond them, to outgrow them; if you, remain under their ban you do not understand them. You must also be familiar with history and that cautious play with the balances: "On the one hand—on the other hand." Go back, treading in the footsteps made by mankind in its great and painful journey through the desert of the past, and you will learn most surely whither it is that all later humanity never can or may go again. And inasmuch as you wish with all your strength to see in advance how the knots of the future are tied, your own life acquires the value of an instrument and means of knowledge. It is within your power to see that all you have experienced, trials, errors, faults, deceptions, passions, your love and your hope, shall be merged wholly in your aim. This aim is to become a necessary chain of culture-links yourself, and from this necessity to draw a conclusion as to the necessity in the progress of general culture. When your sight has become strong enough to see to the bottom of the dark well of your nature and your knowledge, it is possible that in its mirror you may also behold the far-away visions of future civilisations. Do you think that such a life with such an aim is too wearisome, too empty of all that is agreeable? Then you have still to learn that no honey is sweeter than that of knowledge, and that the overhanging clouds of trouble must be to you as an udder from which you shall draw milk for your refreshment. And only when old age approaches will you rightly perceive how you listened to the voice of nature, that nature which rules the whole world through pleasure; the same life which has its zenith in age has also its zenith in wisdom, in that mild sunshine of a constant mental joyfulness; you meet them both, old age and wisdom, upon one ridge of life,—it was thus intended by Nature. Then it is time, and no cause for anger, that the mists of death approach. Towards the light is your last movement; a joyful cry of knowledge is your last sound.

396.

Wanting to Be in Love.—Betrothed couples who have been matched by convenience often exert themselves *to fall in love*, to avoid the reproach of cold, calculating expediency. In the same manner those who become converts to Christianity for their advantage exert themselves to become genuinely pious; because the religious cast of countenance then becomes easier to them.

472.

Religion and Government.—So long as the State, or, more properly, the Government, regards itself as the appointed guardian of a number of minors, and on their account considers the question whether religion should be preserved or abolished, it is highly probable that it will always decide for the preservation thereof. For religion satisfies the nature of the individual in times of loss, destitution, terror, and distrust, in cases, therefore, where the Government feels itself incapable of doing anything directly for the mitigation of the spiritual sufferings of the individual; indeed, even in general unavoidable and next to inevitable evils (famines, financial crises, and wars) religion gives to the masses an attitude of tranquillity and confiding expectancy.

Whenever the necessary or accidental deficiencies of the State Government, or the dangerous consequences of dynastic interests, strike the eyes of the intelligent and make them refractory, the unintelligent will only think they see the finger of God therein and will submit with patience to the dispensations from *on high* (a conception in which divine and human modes of government usually coalesce); thus internal civil peace and continuity of development will be preserved. The power, which lies in the unity of popular feeling, in the existence of the same opinions and aims for all, is protected and confirmed by religion,—the rare cases excepted in which a priesthood cannot agree with the State about the price, and therefore comes into conflict with it. As a rule the State will know how to win over the priests, because it needs their most private and secret system for educating souls, and knows how to value servants who apparently, and outwardly, represent quite other interests. Even at present no power can become "legitimate" without the assistance of the priests; a fact which Napoleon understood. Thus, absolutely paternal government and the careful preservation of religion necessarily go hand-in-hand.

In this connection it must be taken for granted that the rulers and governing classes are enlightened concerning the advantages which religion affords, and consequently feel themselves to a certain extent superior to it, inasmuch as they use it as a means; thus freedom of spirit has its origin here. But how will it be when the totally different interpretation of the idea of Government, such as is taught in *democratic* States, begins to prevail? When one sees in it nothing but the instrument of the popular will, no "upper" in contrast to an "under," but merely a function of the sole sovereign, the people? Here also only the same attitude which the people assume towards religion can be assumed by the Government; every diffusion of enlightenment will have to find an echo even in the representatives, and the utilising and exploiting of religious impulses and consolations for State purposes will not be so easy (unless powerful party leaders occasionally exercise an influence resembling that of enlightened despotism). When, however, the State is not permitted to derive any further advantage from religion, or when people think far too variously on religious matters to allow the State to adopt a consistent and uniform procedure with respect to them, the way out of the difficulty will necessarily present itself, namely to treat religion as a private affair and leave it to the conscience and custom of each single individual.

The first result of all is that religious feeling seems to be strengthened, inasmuch as hidden and suppressed impulses thereof, which the State had unintentionally or intentionally stifled, now break forth and rush to extremes; later on, however, it is found that religion is over-grown with sects, and that an abundance of dragon's teeth were sown as soon as religion was made a private affair. The spectacle of strife, and the hostile laying bare of all the weaknesses of religious confessions, admit finally of no other expedient except that every better and more talented person should make irreligiousness his private affair, a sentiment which now obtains the upper hand even in the minds of the governing classes, and, almost against their will, gives an anti-religious character to their measures. As soon as this happens, the sentiment of persons still religiously disposed, who formerly adored the State as something half sacred or wholly sacred, changes into decided *hostility to the State;* they lie in wait for governmental measures, seeking to hinder, thwart, and disturb as much as they can, and, by the fury of their contradiction, drive the opposing parties, the irreligious ones, into an almost fanatical enthusiasm *for* the State; in connection with which there is also the silently co-operating influence, that since their separation from religion the hearts of persons in these circles are conscious of a void, and seek by devotion to the State to provide themselves provisionally with a substitute for religion, a kind of stuffing for the void.

After these perhaps lengthy transitional struggles, it is finally decided whether the religious parties are still strong enough to revive an old condition of things, and turn the wheel backwards: in which case enlightened despotism (perhaps less enlightened and more timorous than formerly), inevitably gets the State into its hands,—or whether the non-religious parties achieve their purpose, and, possibly through schools and education, check the increase of their opponents during several generations, and finally make them no longer possible. Then, however, their enthusiasm for the State also abates: it always becomes more obvious that along with the religious adoration which regards the State as a mystery and a supernatural institution, the reverent and pious relation to it has also been convulsed. Henceforth individuals see only that side of the State which may be useful or injurious to them, and press forward by all means to obtain an influence over it. But this rivalry soon becomes too great; men and parties change too rapidly, and throw each other down again too furiously from the mountain when they have only just succeeded in getting aloft. All the measures which such a Government carries out lack the guarantee of permanence; people then fight shy of undertakings which would require the silent growth of future decades or centuries to produce ripe fruit. Nobody henceforth feels any other obligation to a law than to submit for the moment to the power which introduced the law; people immediately set to work, however, to undermine it by a new power, a newly-formed majority. Finally—it may be confidently asserted—the distrust of all government, the insight into the useless and harassing nature of these short-winded struggles, must drive men to an entirely new resolution: to the abrogation of the conception of the State and the abolition of the contrast of "private and public." Private concerns gradually absorb the business of the State; even the toughest residue which is left over from the old work of governing (the business, for instance, which is meant to protect private persons from private persons) will at last some day be managed by private enterprise.

The neglect, decline, and *death of the State*, the liberation of the private person (I am careful not to say the individual), are the consequences of the democratic conception of the State; that is its mission. When it has accomplished its task,—which, like everything human, involves much rationality and irrationality,—and when all relapses into the old malady have been overcome, then a new leaf in the story-book of humanity will be unrolled, on which readers will find all kinds of strange tales and perhaps also some amount of good. To repeat shortly what has been said: the interests of the tutelary Government and the interests of religion go hand-in-hand, so that when the latter begins to decay the foundations of the State are also shaken. The belief in a divine regulation of political affairs, in a mystery in the existence of the State, is of religious origin: if religion disappears, the State will inevitably lose its old veil of Isis, and will no longer arouse veneration. The sovereignty of the people, looked at closely, serves also to dispel the final fascination and superstition in the realm of these sentiments; modern democracy is the historical form of the *decay of the State*.

The outlook which results from this certain decay is not, however, unfortunate in every respect; the wisdom and the selfishness of men are the best developed of all their qualities; when the State no longer meets the demands of these impulses, chaos will least of all result, but a still more appropriate expedient than the State will get the mastery over the State. How many organising forces have already been seen to die out! For example, that of the *gens* or clan which for millennia was far mightier than the power of the family, and indeed already ruled and regulated long before the latter existed. We ourselves see the important notions of the right and might of the family, which once possessed the supremacy as far as the Roman system extended, always becoming paler and feebler. In the same way a later generation will also see the State become meaningless in certain parts of the world,— an idea which many contemporaries can hardly contemplate without alarm and horror. To *labour* for the propagation and realisation of this idea is, certainly, another thing; one must think very presumptuously of one's reason, and only half understand history, to set one's hand to the plough at present—when as yet no one can show us the seeds that are afterwards to be sown upon the broken soil. Let us, therefore, trust to the "wisdom and selfishness of men" that the State may *yet* exist a good while longer, and that the destructive attempts of over-zealous, too hasty sciolists may be in vain!

476.

Apparent Superiority of the Middle Ages.—The Middle Ages present in the Church an institution with an absolutely universal aim, involving the whole of humanity—an aim, moreover, which, presumedly, concerned man's highest interests. In comparison therewith the aims of the States and nations which modern history exhibits make a painful impression; they seem petty, base, material, and restricted in extent. But this different impression on our imagination should certainly not determine our judgment; for that universal institution corresponded to feigned and fictitiously fostered needs, such as the need of salvation, which, wherever they did not already exist, it had first of all to create: the new institutions, however, relieve actual distresses; and the time is coming when institutions will arise to minister to the common, genuine needs of all men, and to cast that fantastic prototype, the Catholic Church, into shade and oblivion.

from Volume Two

ASSORTED OPINIONS AND MAXIMS

95.

"Love."—The finest artistic conception wherein Christianity had the advantage over other religious systems lay in one word—Love. Hence it became the *lyric* religion (whereas in its two other creations Semitism bestowed heroico-epical religions upon the world). In the word "love" there is so much meaning, so much that stimulates and appeals to memory and hope, that even the meanest intelligence and the coldest heart feel some glimmering of its sense. The cleverest woman and the lowest man think of the comparatively unselfish moments of their whole life, even if with them Eros never soared high: and the vast number of beings who *miss* love from their parents

or children or sweethearts, especially those whose sexual instincts have been refined away, have found their heart's desire in Christianity.

96.

The Fulfilment of Christianity.—In Christianity there is also an Epicurean trend of thought, starting from the idea that God can only demand of man, his creation and his image, what it is possible for man to fulfil, and accordingly that Christian virtue and perfection are attainable and often attained. Now, for instance, the belief in loving one's enemies—even if it is only a belief or fancy, and by no means a psychological reality (a real love)—gives unalloyed happiness, so long as it is genuinely believed. (As to the reason of this, psychologist and Christian might well differ.) Hence earthly life, through the belief, I mean the fancy, that it satisfies not only the injunction to love our enemies, but all the other injunctions of Christianity, and that it has really assimilated and embodied in itself the Divine perfection according to the command, "Be perfect as your Father in heaven is perfect," might actually become a holy life. Thus error can make Christ's promise come true.

97.

Of the Future of Christianity.—We may be allowed to form a conjecture as to the disappearance of Christianity and as to the places where it will be the slowest to retreat, if we consider where and for what reasons Protestantism spread with such startling rapidity. As is well known, Protestantism promised to do far more cheaply all that the old Church did, without costly masses, pilgrimages, and priestly pomp and circumstance. It spread particularly among the Northern nations, which were not so deeply rooted as those of the South in the old Church's symbolism and love of ritual. In the South the more powerful pagan religion survived in Christianity, whereas in the North Christianity meant an opposition to and a break with the old-time creed, and hence was from the first more thoughtful and less sensual, but for that very reason, in times of peril, more fanatical and more obstinate. If from the standpoint of *thought* we succeed in uprooting Christianity, we can at once know the point where it will begin to disappear—the very point at which it will be most stubborn in defence. In other places it will bend but not break, lose its leaves but burst into leaf afresh, because the senses, and not thought, have gone over to its side. But it is the senses that maintain the belief that with all its expensive outlay the Church is more cheaply and conveniently managed than under the stern conditions of work and wages. Yet what does one hold leisure (or semi-idleness) to be worth, when once one has become accustomed to it? The senses plead against a dechristianised world, saying that there would be too much work to do in it and an insufficient supply of leisure. They take the part of magic —that is, they let God work himself (*oremus nos, Deus laboret*).[19]

98.

Theatricality and Honesty of Unbelievers.—There is no book that contains in such abundance or expresses so faithfully all that man occasionally finds salutary—ecstatic inward happiness, ready for sacrifice or death in the belief in and contemplation of *his* truth—as the book that tells of Christ. From that book a clever man may learn all the means whereby a book can be made into a world-book, a *vade mecum*[20] for all, and especially that master-means of representing everything as discovered, nothing as future and uncertain. All influential books try to leave the same impression, as if the widest intellectual horizon were circumscribed here and as if about the sun that shines here every constellation visible at present or in the future must revolve.—Must not then all purely scientific books be poor in influence on the same grounds as such books are rich in influence? Is not the book fated to live humble and among humble folk, in order to be crucified in the end and never resurrected? In relation to what the religious inform us of their "knowledge" and their "holy spirit," are not all upright men of science "poor in spirit"? Can any religion demand more self-denial and draw the selfish out of themselves more inexorably than science?—This and similar things we may say, in any case with a certain theatricality, when we have to defend ourselves against believers, for it is impossible to conduct a defence without a

---

[19] "We pray, God will work"

[20] Literally "go with me"; used to mean a manual or guidebook which can be carried on one's person.

certain amount of theatricality. But between ourselves our language must be more honest, and we employ a freedom that those believers are not even allowed, in their own interests, to understand. Away, then, with the monastic cowl of self-denial, with the appearance of humility! Much more and much better—so rings our truth! If science were not linked with the pleasure of knowledge, the utility of the thing known, what should we care for science? If a little faith, love, and hope did not lead our souls to knowledge, what would attract us to science? And if in science the ego means nothing, still the inventive, happy ego, every upright and industrious ego, means a great deal in the republic of the men of science. The homage of those who pay homage, the joy of those whom we wish well or honour, in some cases glory and a fair share of immortality, is the personal reward for every suppression of personality: to say nothing here of meaner views and rewards, although it is just on this account that the majority have sworn and always continue to swear fidelity to the laws of the republic and of science. If we had not remained in some degree unscientific, what would science matter to us? Taking everything together and speaking in plain language: "To a purely knowing being knowledge would be indifferent."—Not the quality but the quantity of faith and devoutness distinguishes us from the pious, the believers. We are content with less. But should one of them cry out to us: "Be content and show yourselves contented!" we could easily answer: "As a matter of fact, we do not belong to the most discontented class. But you, if your faith makes you happy, show yourselves to be happy. Your faces have always done more harm to your faith than our reasons! If that glad message of your Bible were written in your faces, you would not need to demand belief in the authority of that book in such stiff-necked fashion. Your words, your actions should continually make the Bible superfluous—in fact, through you a new Bible should continually come into being. As it is, your apologia for Christianity is rooted in your unchristianity, and with your defence you write your own condemnation. If you, however, should wish to emerge from your dissatisfaction with Christianity, you should ponder over the experience of two thousand years, which, clothed in the modest form of a question, may be voiced as follows: 'If Christ really intended to redeem the world, may he not be said to have failed?' "

176.

The Mouthpiece of the Gods.—The poet expresses the universal higher opinions of the nation, he is its mouthpiece and flute; but by virtue of metre and all other artistic means he so expresses them that the nation regards them as something quite new and wonderful, and believes in all seriousness that he is the mouthpiece of the Gods. Yes, under the clouds of creation the poet himself forgets whence he derives all his intellectual wisdom—from father and mother, from teachers and books of all kinds, from the street and particularly from the priest. He is deceived by his own art, and really believes, in a naïve period, that a God is speaking through him, that he is creating in a state of religious inspiration. As a matter of fact, he is only saying what he has learnt, a medley of popular wisdom and popular foolishness. Hence, so far as a poet is really *vox populi* he is held to be *vox dei.*

224.

Balm and Poison.—We cannot ponder too deeply on this fact: Christianity is the religion of antiquity grown old; it presupposes degenerate old culture-stocks, and on them it had, and still has, power to work like balm. There are periods when ears and eyes are full of slime, so that they can no longer hear the voice of reason and philosophy or see the wisdom that walks in bodily shape, whether it bears the name of Epictetus or of Epicurus. Then, perhaps, the erection of the martyr's cross and the "trumpet of the last judgment" may have the effect of still inspiring such races to end their lives decently. If we think of Juvenal's Rome, of that poisonous toad with the eyes of Venus, we understand what it means to make the sign of the Cross before the world, we honour the silent Christian community and are grateful for its having stifled the Greco-Roman Empire. If, indeed, most men were then born in spiritual slavery, with the sensuality of old men, what a pleasure to meet beings who were more soul than body, and who seemed to realise the Greek idea of the shades of the under-world—shy, scurrying, chirping, kindly creatures, with a reversion on the "better life," and therefore so unassuming, so secretly scornful, so proudly patient!—This Christianity, as the evening chime of the *good* antiquity, with cracked, weary and yet melodious bell, is balm in the ears even to one who only now traverses those centuries historically. What must it have been to those men themselves!—To young and fresh barbarian nations, on the other hand, Christianity is a poison. For to implant the teaching of sinfulness and damnation in the heroic, childlike, and animal soul of the old Germans is nothing but poisoning. An enormous chemical fermentation and decomposition, a medley of sentiments and judgments, a rank growth of adventurous legend, and hence in the long run a fundamental weakening of such barbarian peoples, was the inevitable result. True, without this weakening what should we have left of Greek culture, of the whole cultured past of the human race? For the barbarians untouched by Christianity knew very well how to make a clean sweep of old cultures, as was only too clearly shown by the heathen conquerors of Romanised Britain. Thus Christianity, against its will, was compelled to aid in making "the antique world" immortal.—There remains, however, a counter-question and the possibility of a counter-reckoning. Without this weakening through the poisoning referred to, would any of those fresh stocks—the Germans, for instance—have been in a position gradually to find by themselves a higher, a peculiar, a new culture, of which the most distant conception would therefore have been lost to humanity?—In this, as in every case, we do not know, Christianly speaking, whether God owes the devil or the devil God more thanks for everything having turned out as it has.

225.

Faith makes Holy and Condemns.—A Christian who happened upon forbidden paths of thought might well ask himself on some occasion whether it is really necessary that there should be a God, side by side with a representative Lamb, if faith in the existence of these beings suffices to produce the same influences? If they do exist after all, are they not superfluous beings? For all that is given by the Christian religion to the human soul, all that is beneficent, consoling, and edifying, just as much as all that depresses and crushes, emanates from that faith and not from the objects of that faith. It is here as in another well-known case—there were indeed no witches, but the terrible effects of the belief in witches were the same as if they really had existed. For all occasions where the Christian awaits the immediate intervention of a God, though in vain (for there is no

God), his religion is inventive enough to find subterfuges and reasons for tranquillity. In so far Christianity is an ingenious religion.—Faith, indeed, has up to the present not been able to move real mountains, although I do not know who assumed that it could. But it can put mountains where there are none.

THE WANDERER AND HIS SHADOW

57.

Interactions with Animals.—The origin of our morality may still be observed in our relations with animals. Where advantage or the reverse do not come into play, we have a feeling of complete irresponsibility. For example, we kill or wound insects or let them live, and as a rule think no more about it. We are so clumsy that even our gracious acts towards flowers and small animals are almost always murderous: this does not in the least detract from our pleasure in them.—Today is the festival of the small animals, the most sultry day of the year. There is a swarming and crawling around us, and we, without intention, but also without reflection, crush here and there a little fly or winged beetle.—If animals do us harm, we strive to *annihilate* them in every possible way. The means are often cruel enough, even without our really intending them to be so—it is the cruelty of thoughtlessness. If they are useful, we turn them to advantage, until a more refined wisdom teaches us that certain animals amply reward a different mode of treatment, that of tending and breeding. Here responsibility first arises. Torturing is avoided in the case of the domestic animal. One man is indignant if another is cruel to his cow, quite in accordance with the primitive communal morality, which sees the commonwealth in danger whenever an individual does wrong. He who perceives any transgression in the community fears indirect harm to himself. Thus we fear in this case for the quality of meat, agriculture, and means of communication if we see the domestic animals ill-treated. Moreover, he who is harsh to animals awakens a suspicion that he is also harsh to men who are weak, inferior, and incapable of revenge. He is held to be ignoble and deficient in the finer form of pride. Thus arises a foundation of moral judgments and sentiments, but the greatest contribution is made by superstition. Many animals incite men by glances, tones, and gestures to transfer themselves into them in imagination, and some religions teach us, under certain circumstances, to see in animals the dwelling-place of human and divine souls: whence they recommend a nobler caution or even a reverential awe in interactions with animals. Even after the disappearance of this superstition the sentiments awakened by it continue to exercise their influence, to ripen and to blossom.— Christianity, as is well known, has shown itself in this respect a poor and retrograde religion.

74.

Prayer.—On two hypotheses alone is there any sense in prayer, that not quite extinct custom of olden times. It would have to be possible either to fix or alter the will of the godhead, and the devotee would have to know best himself what he needs and should really desire. Both hypotheses, axiomatic and traditional in all other religions, are denied by Christianity. If Christianity nevertheless maintained prayer side by side with its belief in the all-wise and all-provident divine reason (a belief that makes prayer really senseless and even blasphemous), it showed here once more its admirable "wisdom of the serpent." For an outspoken command, "Thou shalt not pray," would have led Christians by way of boredom to the denial of Christianity. In the Christian *ora et labora,*[21] *ora* plays the role of pleasure. Without *ora* what could those unlucky saints who renounced *labora* have done? But to have a chat with God, to ask him for all kinds of pleasant things, to feel a slight amusement at one's own folly in still having any wishes at all, in spite of so excellent a father—all that was an admirable invention for saints.

78.

The Belief in Disease qua *Disease.*—Christianity first painted the devil on the wall of the world. Christianity first brought the idea of sin into the world. The belief in the remedies, which is offered as an antidote, has gradually been shaken to its very foundations. But the

----

[21] pray and work

FRIEDRICH NIETZSCHE

belief in the disease, which Christianity has taught and propagated, still exists.

80.

The Danger in Personality.—The more God has been regarded as a personality in himself, the less loyal have we been to him. Men are far more attached to their thought-images than to their best beloved. That is why they sacrifice themselves for State, Church, and even for God—so far as he remains *their* creation, their thought, and is not too much looked upon as a personality. In the latter case they almost always quarrel with him. After all, it was the most pious of men who let slip that bitter cry: "My God, why hast thou forsaken me?"

81.

Worldly Justice.—It is possible to unhinge worldly justice with the doctrine of the complete non-responsibility and innocence of every man. An attempt has been made in the same direction on the basis of the opposite doctrine of the full responsibility and guilt of every man. It was the founder of Christianity who wished to abolish worldly justice and banish judgment and punishment from the world. For he understood all guilt as "sin"—that is, an outrage against God and not against the world. On the other hand, he considered every man in a broad sense, and almost in every sense, a sinner. The guilty, however, are not to be the judges of their peers—so his rules of equity decided. Thus all dispensers of worldly justice were in his eyes as culpable as those they condemned, and their air of guiltlessness appeared to him hypocritical and pharisaical. Moreover, he looked to the motives and not to the results of actions, and thought that only one was keen-sighted enough to give a verdict on motives—himself or, as he expressed it, God.

83.

Saviour and Physician.—In his knowledge of the human soul the founder of Christianity was, as is natural, not without many great deficiencies and prejudices, and, as physician of the soul, was addicted to that disreputable, laical belief in a universal medicine. In his methods he sometimes resembles that dentist who wishes to heal all pain by extracting the tooth. Thus, for example, he assails sensuality with the advice: "If thine eye offend thee, pluck it out."—Yet there still remains the distinction that the dentist at least attains his object—painlessness for the patient—although in so clumsy a fashion that he becomes ridiculous; whereas the Christian who follows that advice and thinks he has killed his sensuality, is wrong, for his sensuality still lives in an uncanny, vampire form, and torments him in hideous disguises.

85.

The Persecutors of God.—Paul conceived and Calvin followed up the idea that countless creatures have been predestined to damnation from time immemorial, and that this fair world was made in order that the glory of God might be manifested therein. So heaven and hell and mankind merely exist to satisfy the vanity of God! What a cruel, insatiable vanity must have smouldered in the soul of the first or second thinker of such a thought!—Paul, then, after all, remained Saul—the persecutor of God.

FRIEDRICH NIETZSCHE

from THE DAWN

3.

So far it is on Good and Evil that we have meditated least profoundly: this was always too dangerous a subject. Conscience, a good reputation, hell, and at times even the police, have not allowed and do not allow of impartiality; in the presence of morality, as before all authority, we *must* not even think, much less speak: here we must obey! Ever since the beginning of the world, no authority has permitted itself to be made the subject of criticism; and to criticise morals—to look upon morality as a problem, as problematic—what! was that not—*is* that not—immoral?—But morality has at its disposal not only every means of intimidation wherewith to keep itself free from critical hands and instruments of torture: its security lies rather in a certain art of enchantment, in which it is a past master—it knows how to "enrapture." It can often paralyse the critical will with a single look, or even seduce it to itself: yea, there are even cases where morality can turn the critical will against itself; so that then, like the scorpion, it thrusts the sting into its own body. Morality has for ages been an expert in all kinds of devilry in the art of convincing: even at the present day there is no orator who would not turn to it for assistance (only hearken to our anarchists, for instance: how morally they speak when they would fain convince! In the end they even call themselves "the good and the just").

Morality has shown herself to be the greatest mistress of seduction ever since men began to discourse and persuade on earth— and, what concerns us philosophers even more, she is the veritable *Circe of philosophers*. For, to what is it due that, from Plato onwards, all the philosophic architects in Europe have built in vain? that everything which they themselves honestly believed to be *aere perennius*[22] threatens to subside or is already laid in ruins? Oh, how wrong is the answer which, even in our own day, rolls glibly off the tongue when this question is asked: "Because they have all neglected

---

[22] eternal

52

the prerequisite, the examination of the foundation, a critique of all reason"—that fatal answer made by Kant, who has certainly not thereby attracted us modern philosophers to firmer and less treacherous ground! (and, one may ask apropos of this, was it not rather strange to demand that an instrument should criticise its own value and effectiveness? that the intellect itself should "recognise" its own worth, power, and limits? was it not even just a little ridiculous?) The right answer would rather have been, that all philosophers, including Kant himself were building under the seductive influence of morality—that they aimed at certainty and "truth" only in appearance; but that in reality their attention was directed towards "*majestic moral edifices*," to use once more Kant's innocent mode of expression, who deems it his "less brilliant, but not undeserving" task and work "to level the ground and prepare a solid foundation for the erection of those majestic moral edifices" (*Critique of Pure Reason*, ii. 257).

Alas! He did not succeed in his aim, quite the contrary—as we must acknowledge today. With this exalted aim, Kant was merely a true son of his century, which more than any other may justly be called the century of exaltation: and this he fortunately continued to be in respect to the more valuable side of this century (with that solid piece of sensuality, for example, which he introduced into his theory of knowledge). He, too, had been bitten by the moral tarantula, Rousseau; he, too, felt weighing on his soul that moral fanaticism of which another disciple of Rousseau's, Robespierre, felt and proclaimed himself to be the executor: *de fonder sur la terre l'empire de la sagesse, de la justice, et de la vertu.*[23] (Speech of June 4th, 1794.)

On the other hand, with such a French fanaticism in his heart, no one could have cultivated it in a less French, more deep, more thorough and more German manner—if the word German is still permissible in this sense—than Kant did: in order to make room for *his* "moral kingdom," he found himself compelled to add to it an indemonstrable world, a logical "beyond"—that was why he required his critique of pure reason! In other words, *he would not have wanted it*, if he had not deemed one thing to be more important than all the others: to render his moral kingdom unassailable by—or, better still,

---

[23] "to establish on Earth the empire of wisdom, justice and virtue"

invisible to, reason—for he felt too strongly the vulnerability of a moral order of things in the face of reason. For, when confronted with nature and history, when confronted with the ingrained *immorality* of nature and history, Kant was, like all good Germans from the earliest times, a pessimist: he believed in morality, not because it is demonstrated through nature and history, but *despite* its being steadily contradicted by them.

To understand this "despite," we should perhaps recall a somewhat similar trait in Luther, that other great pessimist, who once urged it upon his friends with true Lutheran audacity: "If we could conceive by reason alone how that God who shows so much wrath and malignity could be merciful and just, what use should we have for faith?" For, from the earliest times, nothing has ever made a deeper impression upon the German soul, nothing has ever "tempted" it more, than that deduction, the most dangerous of all, which for every true Latin is a sin against the intellect: *credo quia absurdum est.*[24]—With it German logic enters for the first time into the history of Christian dogma; but even today, a thousand years later, we Germans of the present, late Germans in every way, catch the scent of truth, a *possibility* of truth, at the back of the famous fundamental principle of dialectics with which Hegel secured the victory of the German spirit over Europe—"contradiction moves the world; all things contradict themselves." We are pessimists—even in logic.

9.

Conception of the Morality of Custom.—In comparison with the mode of life which prevailed among men for thousands of years, we men of the present day are living in a very immoral age: the power of custom has been weakened to a remarkable degree, and the sense of morality is so refined and elevated that we might almost describe it as volatilised. That is why we late comers experience such difficulty in obtaining a fundamental conception of the origin of morality: and even if we do obtain it, our words of explanation stick in our throats, so coarse would they sound if we uttered them! or to so great an extent would they seem to be a slander upon morality! Thus, for

---

[24] "I believe because it is absurd" Originally misattributed to Tertullian, it appears to be a paraphrase of another of his sayings.

example, the fundamental clause: morality is nothing else (and, above all, nothing more) than obedience to customs, of whatsoever nature they may be. But customs are simply the traditional way of acting and valuing. Where there is no tradition there is no morality; and the less life is governed by tradition, the narrower the circle of morality. The free man is immoral, because it is his *will* to depend upon himself and not upon tradition: in all the primitive states of humanity "evil" is equivalent to "individual," "free," "arbitrary," "unaccustomed," "unforeseen," "incalculable." In such primitive conditions, always measured by this standard, any action performed—*not* because tradition commands it, but for other reasons (*e.g* on account of its individual utility), even for the same reasons as had been formerly established by custom—is termed immoral, and is felt to be so even by the very man who performs it, for it has not been done out of obedience to the tradition.

What is tradition? A higher authority, which is obeyed, not because it commands what is useful to us, but merely because it commands. And in what way can this feeling for tradition be distinguished from a general feeling of fear? It is the fear of a higher intelligence which commands, the fear of an incomprehensible power, of something that is more than personal—there is *superstition* in this fear. In primitive times the domain of morality included education and hygienics, marriage, medicine, agriculture, war, speech and silence, the relationship between man and man, and between man and the gods—morality required that a man should observe her prescriptions without thinking of *himself* as individual. Everything, therefore, was originally custom, and whoever wished to raise himself above it, had first of all to make himself a kind of lawgiver and medicine-man, a sort of demi-god—in other words, he had to create customs, a dangerous and fearful thing to do!—Who is the most moral man? On the one hand, he who most frequently obeys the law: *e.g* he who, like the Brahmins, carries a consciousness of the law about with him wherever he may go, and introduces it into the smallest divisions of time, continually exercising his mind in finding opportunities for obeying the law. On the other hand, he who obeys the law in the most difficult cases. The most moral man is he who makes the greatest *sacrifices* to morality; but what are the greatest sacrifices? In answering this question several different kinds of morality will be developed: but the distinction between the morality of the *most frequent obedience* and the morality of the *most difficult obedience* is of the greatest importance. Let us not be deceived as to the motives of that moral law which requires, as an indication of morality, obedience to custom in the most difficult cases! Self-conquest is required, not by reason of its useful consequences for the individual; but that custom and tradition may appear to be dominant, in spite of all individual counter desires and advantages. The individual shall sacrifice himself—so demands the morality of custom.

On the other hand, those moralists who, like the followers of Socrates, recommend self-control and sobriety to the *individual* as his greatest possible advantage and the key to his greatest personal happiness, are *exceptions*—and if we ourselves do not think so, this is simply due to our having been brought up under their influence. They all take a new path, and thereby bring down upon themselves the utmost disapproval of all the representatives of the morality of custom. They sever their connection with the community, as immoralists, and are, in the fullest sense of the word, evil ones. In the same way, every Christian who "sought, above all things, his *own* salvation," must have seemed evil to a virtuous Roman of the old school. Wherever a community exists, and consequently also a morality of custom, the feeling prevails that any punishment for the violation of a custom is inflicted, above all, on the community: this punishment is a supernatural punishment, the manifestations and limits of which are so difficult to understand, and are investigated with such superstitious fear. The community can compel any one member of it to make good, either to an individual or to the community itself, any ill consequences which may have followed upon such a member's action. It can also call down a sort of vengeance upon the head of the individual by endeavouring to show that, as the result of his action, a storm of divine anger has burst over the community,—but, above all, it regards the guilt of the individual more particularly as *its own* guilt, and bears the punishment of the isolated individual as its own punishment—"Morals," they bewail in their innermost heart, "morals have grown lax, if such deeds as these are possible." And every individual action, every individual mode of thinking, causes dread. It is impossible to determine how much the more select, rare, and original minds must have suffered in the course of time by being considered as evil and dangerous, *yea, because they even looked upon themselves as such*. Under the dominating influence of the morality of custom, originality of every kind came to acquire a bad conscience; and even now the sky of the best minds seems to be more overcast by this thought than it need be.

22.

Works and Faith.[25]—Protestant teachers are still spreading the fundamental error that faith only is of consequence, and that works must follow naturally upon faith. This doctrine is certainly not true, but it is so seductive in appearance that it has succeeded in fascinating quite other intellects than that of Luther (*e.g* the minds of Socrates and Plato): though the plain evidence and experience of our daily life prove the contrary. The most assured knowledge and faith cannot give us either the strength or the dexterity required for action, or the practice in that subtle and complicated mechanism which is a prerequisite for anything to be changed from an idea into action. Then, I say, let us first and foremost have works! and this means practice! practice! practice! The necessary faith will come later—be certain of that!

29.

Actors of Virtue and Sin.—Among the ancients who became celebrated for their virtue there were many, it would seem, *who acted to themselves*, especially the Greeks, who, being actors by nature, must have acted quite unconsciously, seeing no reason why they should not do so. In addition, every one was striving to outdo some one else's virtue with his own, so why should they not have made use of every artifice to show off their virtues, especially among themselves, if only for the sake of practice! Of what use was a virtue which one could not display, and which did not know how to display itself!—Christianity put an end to the career of these actors of virtue; instead it devised the disgusting ostentation and parading of sins: it brought into the world a state of *mendacious sinfulness* (even at the present day this is considered as *bon ton* among orthodox Christians).

---

[25] See also *The Will to Power* section 192.

33.

The Contempt of Causes, Consequences, and Reality.—Those unfortunate occurrences which take place at times in the community, such as sudden storms, bad harvests, or plagues, lead members of the community to suspect that offences against custom have been committed, or that new customs must be invented to appease a new demoniac power and caprice. Suspicion and reasoning of this kind, however, evade an inquiry into the real and natural causes, and take the demoniac cause for granted. This is one source of the hereditary perversion of the human intellect; and the other one follows in its train, for, proceeding on the same principle, people paid much less attention to the real and natural consequences of an action than to the supernatural consequences (the so-called punishments and mercies of the Divinity). It is commanded, for instance, that certain baths are to be taken at certain times: and the baths are taken, not for the sake of cleanliness, but because the command has been made. We are not taught to avoid the real consequences of dirt, but merely the supposed displeasure of the gods because a bath has been omitted. Under the pressure of superstitious fear, people began to suspect that these ablutions were of much greater importance than they seemed; they ascribed inner and supplementary meanings to them, gradually lost their sense of and pleasure in reality, and finally reality is considered as valuable *only to the extent that it is a symbol.* Hence a man who is under the influence of the morality of custom comes to despise causes first of all, secondly consequences, and thirdly reality, and weaves all his higher feelings (reverence, sublimity, pride, gratitude, love) *into an imaginary world*: the so-called higher world.[26] And even today we can see the consequences of this: wherever, and in whatever fashion, man's feelings are raised, that imaginary world is in evidence. It is sad to have to say it; but for the time being *all higher sentiments* must be looked upon with suspicion by the man of science, to so great an extent are they intermingled with illusion and extravagance. Not that they need necessarily be suspected *per se* and for ever; but there is no doubt that, of all the gradual *purifications* which await humanity, the purification of the higher feelings will be one of the slowest.

---

[26] See *The Will to Power* sec. 230 and *Twilight of the Idols* "How the 'True World' Ultimately Became A Fable."

39.

The Prejudice concerning "Pure Spirit."—Wherever the doctrine of *pure spirituality* has prevailed, its excesses have resulted in the destruction of the tone of the nerves: it taught that the body should be despised, neglected, or tormented, and that, on account of his impulses, man himself should be tortured and regarded with contempt. It gave rise to gloomy, strained, and downcast souls—who, besides, thought they knew the reason of their misery and how it might possibly be relieved! "It *must* be in the body! For it still *thrives* too well!"—such was their conclusion, whilst the fact was that the body, through its agonies, protested time after time against this never-ending mockery. Finally, a universal and chronic hyper-nervousness seized upon those virtuous representatives of the pure spirit: they learned to recognise joy only in the shape of ecstasies and other preliminary symptoms of insanity—and their system reached its climax when it came to look upon ecstasy as the highest aim of life, and as the standard by which all earthly things must be *condemned*.

42.

Origin of the *Vita Contemplativa*.—During barbarous ages, when pessimistic judgments held sway over men and the world, the individual, in the consciousness of his full power, always endeavoured to act in conformity with such judgments, that is to say, he put his ideas into action by means of hunting, robbery, surprise attacks, brutality, and murder: including the weaker forms of such acts, as far as they are tolerated within the community. When his strength declines, however, and he feels tired, ill, melancholy, or satiated— consequently becoming temporarily void of wishes or desires—he is a relatively better man, that is to say, less dangerous; and his pessimistic ideas will now discharge themselves only in words and reflections— upon his companions, for example, or his wife, his life, his gods,—his judgments will be *evil* ones. In this frame of mind he develops into a thinker and prophet, or he adds to his superstitions and invents new observances, or mocks his enemies. Whatever he may devise, however, all the productions of his brain will necessarily reflect his frame of mind, such as the increase of fear and weariness, and the lower value he attributes to action and enjoyment. The substance of these productions must correspond to the substance of these poetic, thoughtful, and priestly moods; the evil judgment must be supreme.

In later years, all those who acted continuously as this man did in those special circumstances—*i.e.* those who gave out pessimistic judgments, and lived a melancholy life, poor in action—were called poets, thinkers, priests, or "medicine-men." The general body of men would have liked to disregard such people, because they were not active enough, and to turn them out of the community; but there was a certain risk in doing so: these inactive men had found out and were following the tracks of superstition and divine power, and no one doubted that they had unknown means of power at their disposal. This was the value which was set upon *the ancient race of contemplative natures*—despised as they were in just the same degree as they were not dreaded! In such a masked form, in such an ambiguous aspect, with an evil heart and often with a troubled head, did Contemplation make its first appearance on earth: both weak and terrible at the same time, despised in secret, and covered in public with every mark of superstitious veneration. Here, as always, we must say: *pudenda origo!*[27]

50.

Belief in Inebriation.—Those men who have moments of sublime ecstasy, and who, on ordinary occasions, on account of the contrast and the excessive wearing away of their nervous forces, usually feel miserable and desolate, come to consider such moments as the true manifestation of their real selves, of their "ego," and their misery and dejection, on the other hand, as the *effect of the "non-ego"*. This is why they think of their environment, the age in which they live, and the whole world in which they have their being, with feelings of vindictiveness. This intoxication appears to them as their true life, their actual ego; and everywhere else they see only those who strive to oppose and prevent this intoxication, whether of an intellectual, moral, religious, or artistic nature.

Humanity owes no small part of its evils to these fantastic enthusiasts; for they are the insatiable sowers of the weed of discontent with one's self and one's neighbour, of contempt for the

---

[27] shameful origin

world and the age, and, above all, of world-lassitude. An entire hell of criminals could not, perhaps, bring about such unfortunate and far-reaching consequences, such heavy and disquieting effects that corrupt earth and sky, as are brought about by that "noble" little community of unbridled, fantastic, half-mad people—of geniuses, too—who cannot control themselves, or experience any inward joy, until they have lost themselves completely: while, on the other hand, the criminal often gives a proof of his admirable self-control, sacrifice, and wisdom, and thus maintains these qualities in those who fear him. Through him life's sky may at times seem overcast and threatening, but the atmosphere ever remains brisk and vigorous.—Furthermore, these enthusiasts bring their entire strength to bear on the task of imbuing mankind with belief in inebriation as in life itself: a dreadful belief! As savages are now quickly corrupted and ruined by "fire-water," so likewise has mankind in general been slowly though thoroughly corrupted by these spiritual "fire-waters" of intoxicating feelings and by those who keep alive the craving for them. It may yet be ruined thereby.

53.

Abuse of the Conscientious Ones.—It is the conscientious, and not the unscrupulous, who have suffered so greatly from exhortations to penitence and the fear of hell, especially if they happened to be men of imagination. In other words, a gloom has been cast over the lives of those who had the greatest need of cheerfulness and agreeable images—not only for the sake of their own consolation and recovery from themselves, but that humanity itself might take delight in them and absorb a ray of their beauty. Alas, how much superfluous cruelty and torment have been brought about by those religions which invented sin! and by those men who, by means of such religions, desired to reach the highest enjoyment of their power!

57.

Other Fears, other Safeties.—Christianity overspread life with a new and unlimited *insecurity*, thereby creating new safeties, enjoyments and recreations, and new valuations of all things. Our own century denies the existence of this insecurity, and does so with a good conscience, yet it clings to the old habit of Christian certainties, enjoyments, recreations, and valuations!—even in its noblest arts and philosophies. How feeble and worn out must all this now seem, how imperfect and clumsy, how arbitrarily fanatical, and, above all, how uncertain: now that its horrible contrast has been taken away—the ever-present fear of the Christian for his *eternal* salvation!

58.

Christianity and the Emotions.—In Christianity we may see a great popular protest against philosophy: the reasoning of the sages of antiquity had withdrawn men from the influence of the emotions, but Christianity would fain give men their emotions back again. With this aim in view, it denies any moral value to virtue such as philosophers understood it—as a victory of the reason over the passions—generally condemns every kind of goodness, and calls upon the passions to manifest themselves in their full power and glory: as *love* of God, *fear* of God, fanatic *belief* in God, blind *hope* in God.

59.

Error as a Cordial.—Let people say what they will, it is nevertheless certain that it was the aim of Christianity to deliver mankind from the yoke of moral engagements by indicating what it believed to be the *shortest way to perfection*: exactly in the same manner as a few philosophers thought they could dispense with tedious and laborious dialectics, and the collection of strictly-proved facts, and point out a royal road to truth. It was an error in both cases, but nevertheless a great cordial for those who were worn out and despairing in the wilderness.

60.

All Spirit finally becomes Visible.—Christianity has assimilated the entire spirituality of an incalculable number of men who were by nature submissive, all those enthusiasts of humiliation and reverence, both refined and coarse. It has in this way freed itself from its own original rustic coarseness—of which we are vividly reminded when we look at the oldest image of St. Peter the Apostle—and has become a very intellectual religion, with thousands of wrinkles, *arrière-pensées*,[28] and masks on its face. It has made European humanity more clever, and not only cunning from a theological standpoint. By the spirit which it has thus given to European humanity—in conjunction with the power of abnegation, and very often in conjunction with the profound conviction and loyalty of that abnegation—it has perhaps chiselled and shaped the most subtle individualities which have ever existed in human society: the individualities of the higher ranks of the Catholic clergy, especially when these priests have sprung from a noble family, and have brought to their work, from the very beginning, the innate grace of gesture, the dominating glance of the eye, and beautiful hands and feet. Here the human face acquires that spiritualisation brought about by the continual ebb and flow of two kinds of happiness (the feeling of power and the feeling of submission) after a carefully-planned manner of living has conquered the beast in man. Here an activity, which consists in blessing, forgiving sins, and representing the Almighty, ever keeps alive in the soul, *and even in the body*, the consciousness of a supreme mission; here we find that noble contempt concerning the perishable nature of the body, of well-being, and of happiness, peculiar to born soldiers: their *pride* lies in obedience, a distinctly aristocratic trait; their excuse and their idealism arise from the enormous impossibility of their task. The surpassing beauty and subtleties of these princes of the Church have always proved to the people the truth of the Church; a momentary brutalisation of the clergy (such as came about in Luther's time) always tended to encourage the contrary belief. And would it be maintained that this result of beauty and human subtlety, shown in harmony of figure, intellect, and task, would come to an end with religions? and that nothing higher could be obtained, or even conceived?

61.

The Needful Sacrifice.—Those earnest, able, and just men of profound feelings, who are still Christians at heart, owe it to themselves to make one attempt to live for a certain space of time without Christianity! they owe it *to their faith* that they should thus for

---

[28] afterthoughts

once take up their abode "in the wilderness"—if for no other reason than that of being able to pronounce on the question as to whether Christianity is needful. So far, however, they have confined themselves to their own narrow domain and insulted every one who happened to be outside of it: yea, they even become highly irritated when it is suggested to them that beyond this little domain of theirs lies the great world, and that Christianity is, after all, only a corner of it! No; your evidence on the question will be valueless until you have lived year after year without Christianity, and with the inmost desire to continue to exist without it: until, indeed, you have withdrawn far, far away from it. It is not when your nostalgia urges you back again, but when your judgment, based on a strict comparison, drives you back, that your homecoming has any significance!—Men of coming generations will deal in this manner with all the valuations of the past; they must be voluntarily *lived* over again, together with their contraries, in order that such men may finally acquire the right of shifting them.

62.

On the Origin of Religions.—How can any one regard his own opinion of things as a revelation? This is the problem of the formation of religions: there has always been some man in whom this phenomenon was possible. A postulate is that such a man already believed in revelations. Suddenly, however, a new idea occurs to him one day, *his* idea; and the entire blessedness of a great personal hypothesis, which embraces all existence and the whole world, penetrates with such force into his conscience that he dare not think himself the creator of such blessedness, and he therefore attributes to his God the cause of this new idea and likewise the cause of the cause, believing it to be the revelation of his God. How could a man be the author of so great a happiness? ask his pessimistic doubts. But other levers are secretly at work: an opinion may be strengthened by one's self if it be considered as a revelation; and in this way all its hypothetic nature is removed; the matter is set beyond criticism and even beyond doubt: it is sanctified. It is true that, in this way, a man lowers himself to playing the role of "mouthpiece," but his thought will end by being victorious as a divine thought—the feeling of finally gaining the victory conquers the feeling of degradation. There is also another feeling in the background: if a man raises his products above himself, and thus apparently detracts from his own worth, there nevertheless remains a kind of joyfulness, paternal love, and paternal pride, which compensates man—more than compensates man—for everything.

63.

Hatred of One's Neighbour.—Supposing that we felt towards our neighbour as he does himself—Schopenhauer calls this compassion, though it would be more correct to call it auto-passion, fellow-feeling —we should be compelled to hate him, if, like Pascal, he thought himself hateful. And this was probably the general feeling of Pascal regarding mankind, and also that of ancient Christianity, which, under Nero, was "convicted" of *odium generis humani*,[29] as Tacitus has recorded.

64.

The Broken-Hearted Ones.—Christianity has the instinct of a hunter for finding out all those who may by hook or by crook be driven to despair—only a very small number of men can be brought to this despair. Christianity lies in wait for such as those, and pursues them. Pascal made an attempt to find out whether it was not possible, with the help of the very subtlest knowledge, to drive everybody into despair. He failed: to his second despair.

65.

Brahminism and Christianity.—There are certain precepts for obtaining a consciousness of power: on the one hand, for those who already know how to control themselves, and who are therefore already quite used to the feeling of power; and, on the other hand, for those who cannot control themselves. Brahminism has given its care to the former type of man; Christianity to the latter.

---

[29] hatred of humanity

66.

The Faculty of Vision.—During the whole of the Middle Ages it was believed that the real distinguishing trait of higher men was the faculty of having visions—that is to say, of having a grave mental trouble. And, in fact, the rules of life of all the higher natures of the Middle Ages (the *religiosi*) were drawn up with the object of making man capable of vision! Little wonder, then, that the exaggerated esteem for these half-mad fanatics, so-called men of genius, has continued even to our own days. "They have seen things that others do not see"—no doubt! and this fact should inspire us with caution where they are concerned, and not with belief!

67.

The Price of Believers.—He who sets such a value on being believed in has to promise heaven in recompense for this belief: and every one, even a thief on the Cross, must have suffered from a terrible doubt and experienced crucifixion in every form: otherwise he would not buy his followers so dearly.

68.

The First Christian.—The whole world still believes in the literary career of the "Holy Ghost," or is still influenced by the effects of this belief: when we look into our Bibles we do so for the purpose of "edifying ourselves," to find a few words of comfort for our misery, be it great or small—in short, we read ourselves into it and out of it. But who—apart from a few learned men—know that it likewise records the history of one of the most ambitious and importunate souls that ever existed, of a mind full of superstition and cunning: the history of the Apostle Paul? Nevertheless, without this singular history, without the tribulations and passions of such a mind, and of such a soul, there would have been no Christian kingdom; we should have scarcely have even heard of a little Jewish sect, the founder of which died on the Cross. It is true that, if this history had been understood in time, if we had read, *really read*, the writings of St. Paul, not as the revelations of the "Holy Ghost," but with honest and independent minds, oblivious of all our personal troubles—there were no such readers for fifteen centuries—it would have been all up with Christianity long ago: so searchingly do these writings of the Jewish Pascal lay bare the origins of Christianity, just as the French Pascal let us see its destiny and how it will ultimately perish. That the ship of Christianity threw overboard no inconsiderable part of its Jewish ballast, that it was able to sail into the waters of the heathen and actually did do so: this is due to the history of one single man, this apostle who was so greatly troubled in mind and so worthy of pity, but who was also very disagreeable to himself and to others.

This man suffered from a fixed idea, or rather a fixed question, an ever-present and ever-burning question: what was the *meaning* of the Jewish Law? and, more especially, *the fulfilment of this Law*? In his youth he had done his best to satisfy it, thirsting as he did for that highest distinction which the Jews could imagine—this people, which raised the imagination of moral loftiness to a greater elevation than any other people, and which alone succeeded in uniting the conception of a holy God with the idea of sin considered as an offence against this holiness. St. Paul became at once the fanatic defender and guard-of-honour of this God and His Law. Ceaselessly battling against and lying in wait for all transgressors of this Law and those who presumed to doubt it, he was pitiless and cruel towards all evil-doers, whom he would fain have punished in the most rigorous fashion possible.

Now, however, he was aware in his own person of the fact that such a man as himself—violent, sensual, melancholy, and malicious in his hatred—*could* not fulfil the Law; and furthermore, what seemed strangest of all to him, he saw that his boundless craving for power was continually provoked to break it, and that he could not help yielding to this impulse. Was it really "the flesh" which made him a trespasser time and again? Was it not rather, as it afterwards occurred to him, the Law itself, which continually showed itself to be impossible to fulfil, and seduced men into transgression with an irresistible charm? But at that time he had not thought of this means of escape. As he suggests here and there, he had many things on his conscience—hatred, murder, sorcery, idolatry, debauchery, drunkenness, and orgiastic revelry,—and to however great an extent he tried to soothe his conscience, and, even more, his desire for power, by the extreme fanaticism of his worship for and defence of the Law, there were times when the thought struck him: "It is all in vain! The anguish of the unfulfilled Law cannot be overcome." Luther must have experienced similar feelings, when, in his cloister, he endeavoured to become the ideal man of his imagination; and, as Luther one day began to hate the ecclesiastical ideal, and the Pope, and the saints, and the whole clergy, with a hatred which was all the more deadly as he could not avow it even to himself, an analogous feeling took possession of St. Paul. The Law was the Cross on which he felt himself crucified. How he hated it! What a grudge he owed it! How he began to look round on all sides to find a means for its total annihilation, that he might no longer be obliged to fulfil it himself! And at last a liberating thought, together with a vision—which was only to be expected in the case of an epileptic like himself—flashed into his mind: to him, the stern upholder of the Law—who, in his innermost heart, was tired to death of it—there appeared on the lonely path that Christ, with the divine effulgence on His countenance, and Paul heard the words: "Why persecutest thou Me?"

What actually took place, then, was this: his mind was suddenly enlightened, and he said to himself: "It is unreasonable to persecute this Jesus Christ! Here is my means of escape, here is my complete vengeance, here and nowhere else have I the destroyer of the Law in my hands!" The sufferer from anguished pride felt himself restored to health all at once, his moral despair disappeared in the air; for morality itself was blown away, annihilated—that is to say, *fulfilled*, there on the Cross! Up to that time that ignominious death had seemed to him to be the principal argument against the "Messiahship" proclaimed by the followers of the new doctrine: but what if it were necessary for doing away with the Law? The enormous consequences of this thought, of this solution of the enigma, danced before his eyes, and he at once became the happiest of men. The destiny of the Jews, yea, of all mankind, seemed to him to be intertwined with this instantaneous flash of enlightenment: he held the thought of thoughts, the key of keys, the light of lights; history would henceforth revolve round him! For from that time forward he would be the apostle of the *annihilation of the Law*! To be dead to sin—that meant to be dead to the Law also; to be in the flesh —that meant to be under the Law! To be one with Christ—that meant to have become, like Him, the destroyer of the Law; to be dead with Him—that meant likewise to be dead to the Law. Even if it were still possible to sin, it would not at any rate be possible to sin against the Law: "I am above the Law," thinks Paul; adding, "If I were now to acknowledge the Law again and to submit to it, I should make Christ an accomplice in the sin"; for the Law was there for the purpose of producing sin and setting it in the foreground, as an emetic produces sickness. God could not have decided upon the death of Christ had it been possible to fulfil the Law without it; henceforth, not only are all sins expiated, but sin itself is abolished; henceforth the Law is dead; henceforth "the flesh" in which it dwelt is dead—or at all events dying, gradually wasting away. To live for a short time longer amid this decay!—this is the Christian's fate, until the time when, having become one with Christ, he arises with Him, sharing with Christ the divine glory, and becoming, like Christ, a "Son of God." Then Paul's exaltation was at its height, and with it the importunity of his soul—the thought of union with Christ made him lose all shame, all submission, all constraint, and his ungovernable ambition was shown to be revelling in the expectation of divine glories.

Such was the first Christian, the inventor of Christianity! before him there were only a few Jewish sectaries.[30]

69.

Inimitable.—There is an enormous strain and distance between envy and friendship, between self-contempt and pride: the Greek lived in the former, the Christian in the latter.

70.

The Use of a Coarse Intellect.—The Christian Church is an encyclopædia of primitive cults and views of the most varied origin; and is, in consequence, well adapted to missionary work: in former times she could—and still does—go wherever she would, and in doing so always found something resembling herself, to which she could assimilate herself and gradually substitute her own spirit for it. It is not to what is Christian in her usages, but to what is universally pagan in them, that we have to attribute the development of this universal religion. Her thoughts, which have their origin at once in the Judaic

---

[30] This is Nietzsche's first extensive discussion of Paul, a subject to which he would return in *The Will to Power* (sec. 167, 171, 173, 175) and *The Antichrist* (sec. 42, 44, 47).

and in the Hellenic spirit, were able from the very beginning to raise themselves above the exclusiveness and subtleties of races and nations, as above prejudices. Although we may admire the power which makes even the most difficult things coalesce, we must nevertheless not overlook the contemptible qualities of this power—the astonishing coarseness and narrowness of the Church's intellect when it was in process of formation, a coarseness which permitted it to accommodate itself to any diet, and to digest contradictions like pebbles.

71.

The Christian Vengeance against Rome.—Perhaps nothing is more fatiguing than the sight of a continual conqueror: for more than two hundred years the world had seen Rome overcoming one nation after another, the circle was closed, all future seemed to be at an end, everything was done with a view to its lasting for all time—yea, when the Empire built anything it was erected with a view to being *aere perennius*. We, who know only the "melancholy of ruins," can scarcely understand that totally different *melancholy of eternal buildings*, from which men endeavoured to save themselves as best they could—with the light-hearted fancy of a Horace, for example. Others sought different consolations for the weariness which was closely akin to despair, against the deadening knowledge that from henceforth all progress of thought and heart would be hopeless, that the huge spider sat everywhere and mercilessly continued to drink all the blood within its reach, no matter where it might spring forth. This mute, century-old hatred of the wearied spectators against Rome, wherever Rome's domination extended, was at length vented in Christianity, which united Rome, "the world," and "sin" into a single conception. The Christians took their revenge on Rome by proclaiming the immediate and sudden destruction of the world; by once more introducing a future—for Rome had been able to transform everything into the history of its *own* past and present—a future in which Rome was no longer the most important factor; and by dreaming of the last judgment—while the crucified Jew, as the symbol of salvation, was the greatest derision on the superb Roman prætors in the provinces; for now they seemed to be only the symbols of ruin and a "world" ready to perish.[31]

72.

The "Life after Death."—Christianity found the idea of punishment in hell in the entire Roman Empire: for the numerous mystic cults have hatched this idea with particular satisfaction as being the most fecund egg of their power. Epicurus thought he could do nothing better for his followers than to tear this belief up by the roots: his triumph found its finest echo in the mouth of one of his disciples, the Roman Lucretius, a poet of a gloomy, though afterwards enlightened, temperament. Alas! his triumph had come too soon: Christianity took under its special protection this belief in subterranean horrors, which was already beginning to die away in the minds of men; and that was clever of it. For, without this audacious leap into the most complete paganism, how could it have proved itself victorious over the popularity of Mithras and Isis? In this way it managed to bring timorous folk over to its side—the most enthusiastic adherents of a new faith! The Jews, being a people which, like the Greeks, and even in a greater degree than the Greeks, loved and still love life, had not cultivated that idea to any great extent: the thought of final death as the punishment of the sinner, death without resurrection as an extreme menace: this was sufficient to impress these peculiar men, who did not wish to get rid of their bodies, but hoped, with their refined Egypticism, to preserve them for ever. (A Jewish martyr, about whom we may read in the Second Book of the Maccabees, would not think of giving up his intestines, which had been torn out: he wanted to have them at the resurrection: quite a Jewish characteristic!)

Thoughts of eternal damnation were far from the minds of the early Christians: they thought they were *delivered* from death, and awaited a transformation from day to day, but not death. (What a curious effect the first death must have produced on these expectant people! How many different feelings must have been mingled together —astonishment, exultation, doubt, shame, and passion! Verily, a subject worthy of a great artist!) St. Paul could say nothing better in praise of his Saviour than that he had opened the gates of

---

[31] This idea is developed fully in Book 1 of *On The Genealogy of Morals.*

immortality to everybody—he did not believe in the resurrection of those who had not been saved: more than this, by reason of his doctrine of the impossibility of carrying out the Law, and of death considered as a consequence of sin, he even suspected that, up to that time, no one had become immortal (or at all events only a very few, solely owing to special grace and not to any merits of their own): it was only in his time that immortality had begun to open its gates—and only a few of the elect would finally gain admittance, as the pride of the elect cannot help saying.

In other places, where the impulse towards life was not so strong as among the Jews and the Christian Jews, and where the prospect of immortality did not appear to be more valuable than the prospect of a final death, that pagan, yet not altogether un-Jewish addition of Hell became a very useful tool in the hands of the missionaries: then arose the new doctrine that even the sinners and the unsaved are immortal, the doctrine of eternal damnation, which was more powerful than the idea of a *final death*, which thereafter began to fade away. It was science alone which could overcome this idea, at the same time brushing aside all other ideas about death and an after-life. We are poorer in one particular: the "life after death" has no further interest for us! an indescribable blessing, which is as yet too recent to be considered as such throughout the world. And Epicurus is once more triumphant.

73.

For the "Truth"!—"The truth of Christianity was attested by the virtuous lives of the Christians, their firmness in suffering, their unshakable belief and above all by the spread and increase of the faith in spite of all calamities."—That's how you talk even now. The more's the pity. Learn, then, that all this proves nothing either in favour of truth or against it; that truth must be demonstrated differently from conscientiousness, and that the latter is in no respect whatever an argument in favour of the former.

74.

A Christian *Arrière-pensée.*—Would not this have been a general reservation among Christians of the first century: "It is better to persuade ourselves into the belief that we are guilty rather than that we are innocent; for it is impossible to ascertain the disposition of so powerful a judge—but it is to be feared that he is looking out only for those who are conscious of guilt. Bearing in mind his great power, it is more likely that he will pardon a guilty person than admit that any one is innocent, in his presence." This was the feeling of poor provincial folk in the presence of the Roman prætor: "He is too proud for us to dare to be innocent." And may not this very sentiment have made its influence felt when the Christians endeavoured to picture to themselves the aspect of the Supreme Judge?

75.

Neither European nor Noble.—There is something Oriental and feminine in Christianity, and this is shown in the thought, "Whom the Lord loveth, He chasteneth"; for women in the Orient consider castigations and the strict seclusion of their persons from the world as a sign of their husband's love, and complain if these signs of love cease.

76.

If you think it Evil, you make it Evil.—The passions become evil and malignant when regarded with evil and malignant eyes. It is in this way that Christianity has succeeded in transforming Eros and Aphrodite—sublime powers, capable of idealisation—into hellish genii and phantom goblins, by means of the pangs which every sexual impulse was made to raise in the conscience of the believers. Is it not a dreadful thing to transform necessary and regular sensations into a source of inward misery, and thus arbitrarily to render interior misery necessary and regular *in the case of every man*! Furthermore, this misery remains secret with the result that it is all the more deeply rooted, for it is not all men who have the courage, which Shakespeare shows in his sonnets, of making public their Christian gloom on this point.

Must a feeling, then, always be called evil against which we are forced to struggle, which we must restrain even within certain limits, or, in given cases, banish entirely from our minds? Is it not the habit of vulgar souls always to call an *enemy* evil! and must we call Eros an enemy? The sexual feelings, like the feelings of pity and adoration, possess the particular characteristic that, in their case, one being gratifies another by the pleasure he enjoys—it is but rarely that we meet with such a benevolent arrangement in nature. And yet we calumniate and corrupt it all by our bad conscience! We connect the procreation of man with a bad conscience!

But the outcome of this diabolisation of Eros is a mere farce: the "demon" Eros becomes an object of greater interest to mankind than all the angels and saints put together, thanks to the mysterious Mumbo-Jumboism of the Church in all things erotic: it is due to the Church that love stories, even in our own time, have become the one common interest which appeals to all classes of people—with an exaggeration which would be incomprehensible to antiquity, and which will not fail to provoke roars of laughter in coming generations. All our poetising and thinking, from the highest to the lowest, is marked, and more than marked, by the exaggerated importance bestowed upon the love story as the principal item of our existence. Posterity may perhaps, on this account, come to the conclusion that its entire legacy of Christian culture is tainted with narrowness and insanity.[32]

77.

The Tortures of the Soul.—The whole world raises a shout of horror at the present day if one man presumes to torture the body of another: the indignation against such a being bursts forth almost spontaneously. Nay; we tremble even at the very thought of torture being inflicted on a man or an animal, and we undergo unspeakable misery when we hear of such an act having been accomplished. But the same feeling is experienced in a very much lesser degree and extent when it is a question of the tortures of the soul and the dreadfulness of their infliction. Christianity has introduced such tortures on an unprecedented scale, and still continues to preach this kind of martyrdom—yea, it even complains innocently of backsliding and indifference when it meets with a state of soul which is free from such agonies. From all this it now results that humanity, in the face of spiritual racks, tortures of the mind, and instruments of punishment, behaves even today with the same awesome patience and indecision

---

[32] See *Beyond Good & Evil* 168

which it exhibited in former times in the presence of the cruelties practised on the bodies of men or animals. Hell has certainly not remained merely an empty sound; and a new kind of pity has been devised to correspond to the newly-created fears of hell—a horrible and ponderous compassion, hitherto unknown; with people "irrevocably condemned to hell," as, for example, the Stony Guest gave Don Juan to understand, and which, during the Christian era, should often have made the very stones weep.

Plutarch presents us with a gloomy picture of the state of mind of a superstitious man in pagan times: but this picture pales when compared with that of a Christian of the Middle Ages, who *supposes* that nothing can save him from "torments everlasting." Dreadful omens appear to him: perhaps he sees a stork holding a snake in his beak and hesitating to swallow it. Or all nature suddenly becomes pale; or bright, fiery colours appear across the surface of the earth. Or the ghosts of his dead relations approach him, with features showing traces of dreadful sufferings. Or the dark walls of the room in which the man is sleeping are suddenly lighted up, and there, amidst a yellow flame, he perceives instruments of torture and a motley horde of snakes and devils. Christianity has surely turned this world of ours into a fearful habitation by raising the crucifix in all parts and thereby proclaiming the earth to be a place "where the just man is tortured to death!" And when the ardour of some great preacher for once disclosed to the public the secret sufferings of the individual, the agonies of the lonely souls, when, for example, Whitefield preached "like a dying man to the dying," now bitterly weeping, now violently stamping his feet, speaking passionately, in abrupt and incisive tones, without fearing to turn the whole force of his attack upon any one individual present, excluding him from the assembly with excessive harshness—then indeed did it seem as if the earth were being transformed into a "field of evil." The huge crowds were then seen to act as if seized with a sudden attack of madness: many were in fits of anguish; others lay unconscious and motionless; others, again, trembled or rent the air with their piercing shrieks. Everywhere there was a loud breathing, as of half-choked people who were gasping for the breath of life. "Indeed," said an eye-witness once, "almost all the noises appeared to come from people who were dying in the bitterest agony."

Let us never forget that it was Christianity which first turned the death-bed into a bed of agony, and that, by the scenes which took place there, and the terrifying sounds which were made possible there for the first time, it has poisoned the senses and the blood of innumerable witnesses and their children. Imagine the ordinary man who can never efface the recollection of words like these: "Oh, eternity! Would that I had no soul! Would that I had never been born! My soul is damned, damned; lost for ever! Six days ago you might have helped me. But now all is over. I belong to the devil, and with him I will go down to hell. Break, break, ye poor hearts of stone! Ye will not break? What more can be done for hearts of stone? I am damned that ye may be saved! There he is! Yea; there he is! Come, good devil! Come!"

78.

Avenging Justice.—Misfortune and guilt: these two things have been put on one scale by Christianity; so that, when the misfortune which follows a fault is a serious one, this fault is always judged accordingly to be a very heinous one. But this was not the valuation of antiquity, and that is why Greek tragedy—in which misfortune and punishment are discussed at length, and yet in another sense—forms part of the great liberators of the mind to an extent which even the ancients themselves could not realise. They remained ingenuous enough not to set up an "adequate relation" between guilt and misfortune. The guilt of their tragic heroes is, indeed, the little pebble that makes them stumble, and on which account they sometimes happen to break an arm or knock out an eye. Upon this the feeling of antiquity made the comment, "Well, he should have gone his way with more caution and less pride." It was reserved for Christianity, however, to say: "Here we have a great misfortune, and behind this great misfortune there must lie a great fault, an equally *serious fault*, though we cannot clearly see it! If, wretched man, you do not feel it, it is because your heart is hardened—and worse than this will happen to you!"

Besides this, antiquity could point to examples of real misfortunes, misfortunes that were pure and innocent; it was only with the advent of Christianity that all punishment became well-merited punishment: in addition to this it renders the imagination of the sufferer still more suffering, so that the victim, in the midst of his distress, is seized with the feeling that he has been morally reproved and cast away. Poor humanity! The Greeks had a special word to stand for the feeling of indignation which was experienced at the misfortune of another: among Christian peoples this feeling was prohibited and was not permitted to develop; hence the reason why they have no name for this *more virile* brother of pity.

79.

A Proposal.—If, according to the arguments of Pascal and Christianity, our ego is always hateful, how can we permit and suppose other people, whether God or men, to love it? It would be contrary to all good principles to let ourselves be loved when we know very well that we deserve nothing but hatred—not to speak of other repugnant feelings. "But this is the very Kingdom of Grace." Then you look upon your love for your neighbour as a grace? Your pity as a grace? Well, then, if you can do all this, there is no reason why you should not go a step further: love yourselves through grace, and then you will no longer find your God necessary, and the entire drama of the Fall and Redemption of mankind will reach its last act in yourselves!

80.

The Compassionate Christian.—A Christian's compassion in the presence of his neighbour's suffering has another side to it: viz. his profound suspicion of all the joy of his neighbour, of his neighbour's joy in everything that he wills and is able to do.

81.

The Saint's Humanity.—A saint had fallen into the company of believers, and could no longer stand their continually expressed hatred for sin. At last he said to them: "God created all things, except sin: therefore it is no wonder that He does not like it. But man has created sin, and why, then, should he disown this only child of his merely because it is not regarded with a friendly eye by God, its grandfather? Is that human? Honour to whom honour is due—but one's heart and duty must speak, above all, in favour of the child—and only in the second place for the honour of the grandfather!"

82.

The Theological Attack.—"You must arrange that with yourself; for your life is at stake!"—Luther it is who suddenly springs upon us with these words and imagines that we feel the knife at our throats. But we throw him off with the words of one higher and more considerate than he: "We need form no opinion in regard to this or that matter, and thus save our souls from trouble. For, by their very nature, the things themselves cannot compel us to express an opinion."

83.

Poor Humanity!—A single drop of blood too much or too little in the brain may render our life unspeakably miserable and difficult, and we may suffer more from this single drop of blood than Prometheus from his vulture. But the worst is when we do not know that this drop is causing our sufferings—and we think it is "the devil!" Or "sin!"

84.

The Philology of Christianity.—How little Christianity cultivates the sense of honesty can be inferred from the character of the writings of its learned men. They set out their conjectures as audaciously as if they were dogmas, and are but seldom at a disadvantage in regard to the interpretation of Scripture. Their continual cry is: "I am right, for it is written"—and then follows an explanation so shameless and capricious that a philologist, when he hears it, must stand stock-still between anger and laughter, asking himself again and again: Is it possible? Is it honest? Is it even decent?

It is only those who never—or always—attend church that underestimate the dishonesty with which this subject is still dealt in Protestant pulpits; in what a clumsy fashion the preacher takes advantage of his security from interruption; how the Bible is pinched and squeezed; and how the people are made acquainted with every form of *the art of false reading.*

When all is said and done, however, what can be expected from the effects of a religion which, during the centuries when it was being firmly established, enacted that huge philological farce concerning the Old Testament? I refer to that attempt to tear the Old Testament from the hands of the Jews under the pretext that it contained only

Christian doctrines and *belonged* to the Christians as the true people of Israel, while the Jews had merely arrogated it to themselves without authority. This was followed by a mania of would-be interpretation and falsification, which could not under any circumstances have been allied with a good conscience. However strongly Jewish savants protested, it was everywhere sedulously asserted that the Old Testament alluded everywhere to Christ, and nothing but Christ, more especially His Cross, and thus, wherever reference was made to wood, a rod, a ladder, a twig, a tree, a willow, or a staff, such a reference could not but be a prophecy relating to the wood of the Cross: even the setting-up of the Unicorn and the Brazen Serpent, even Moses stretching forth his hands in prayer—yea, the very spits on which the Easter lambs were roasted: all these were allusions to the Cross, and, as it were, preludes to it! Did any one who kept on asserting these things ever *believe* in them? Let it not be forgotten that the Church did not shrink from putting interpolations in the text of the Septuagint (*e.g.* Ps. xcvi. 10), in order that she might later on make use of these interpolated passages as Christian prophecies. They were engaged in a struggle, and thought of their foes rather than of honesty.

85.

Subtlety in Penury.—Take care not to laugh at the mythology of the Greeks merely because it so little resembles your own profound metaphysics! You should admire a people who checked their quick intellect at this point, and for a long time afterwards had tact enough to avoid the danger of scholasticism and hair-splitting superstition.

86.

The Christian Interpreters of the Body.—Whatever originates in the stomach, the intestines, the beating of the heart, the nerves, the bile, the seed—all those indispositions, debilities, irritations, and the whole contingency of that machine about which we know so little—a Christian like Pascal considers it all as a moral and religious phenomenon, asking himself whether God or the devil, good or evil, salvation or damnation, is the cause. Alas for the unfortunate interpreter! How he must distort and worry his system! How he must distort and worry himself in order to gain his point!

87.

The Moral Miracle.—In the domain of morality, Christianity knows of nothing but the miracle; the sudden change in all valuations, the sudden renouncement of all habits, the sudden and irresistible predilection for new things and persons. Christianity looks upon this phenomenon as the work of God, and calls it the act of regeneration, thus giving it a unique and incomparable value. Everything else which is called morality, and which bears no relation to this miracle, becomes in consequence a matter of indifference to the Christian, and indeed, so far as it is a feeling of well-being and pride, an object of fear. The canon of virtue, of the fulfilled law, is established in the New Testament, but in such a way as to be the canon of *impossible virtue*: men who still aspire to moral perfections must come to understand, in the face of this canon, that they are further and further *removed* from their aim; they must *despair* of virtue, and end by throwing themselves at the feet of the Merciful One.

It is only in reaching a conclusion like this that moral efforts on the part of the Christian can still be regarded as possessing any value: the condition that these efforts shall always remain sterile, painful, and melancholy is therefore indispensable; and it is in this way that those efforts could still avail to bring about that moment of ecstasy when man experiences the "overflow of grace" and the moral miracle. This struggle for morality is, however, not *necessary*; for it is by no means uncommon for this miracle to happen to the sinner at the very moment when he is, so to speak, wallowing in the mire of sin: yea, the leap from the deepest and most abandoned sinfulness into its contrary seems easier, and, as a clear proof of the miracle, even more desirable.

What, for the rest, may be the signification of such a sudden, unreasonable, and irresistible revolution, such a change from the depths of misery into the heights of happiness? (might it be a disguised epilepsy?) This should at all events be considered by alienists, who have frequent opportunities of observing similar "miracles"—for example, the mania of murder or suicide. The relatively "more pleasant consequences" in the case of the Christian make no important difference.

88.

Luther, the Great Benefactor.—Luther's most important result is the suspicion which he awakened against the saints and the entire Christian *vita contemplativa*; only since his day has an un-Christian *vita contemplativa* again become possible in Europe, only since then has contempt for laymen and worldly activity ceased. Luther continued to be an honest miner's son even after he had been shut up in a monastery, and there, for lack of other depths and "borings," he descended into himself, and bored terrifying and dark passages through his own depths—finally coming to recognise that an introspective and saintly life was impossible to him, and that his innate "activity" in body and soul would end by being his ruin. For a long time, too long, indeed, he endeavoured to find the way to holiness through castigations; but at length he made up his mind, and said to himself: "There is no real *vita contemplativa*! We have been deceived. The saints were no better than the rest of us." This was truly a rustic way of gaining one's case; but for the Germans of that period it was the only proper way. How edified they felt when they could read in their Lutheran catechism: "Apart from the Ten Commandments there is no work which could find favour in the eyes of God—these much-boasted spiritual works of the saints are purely imaginary!"

89.

Doubt As Sin.—Christianity has done all it possibly could to draw a circle round itself, and has even gone so far as to declare doubt itself to be a sin. We are to be precipitated into faith by a miracle, without the help of reason, after which we are to float in it as the clearest and least equivocal of elements—a mere glance at some solid ground, the thought that we exist for some purpose other than floating, the least movement of our amphibious nature: all this is a sin! Let it be noted that, following this decision, the proofs and demonstration of the faith, and all meditations upon its origin, are prohibited as sinful. Christianity wants blindness and frenzy and an eternal swan-song above the waves under which reason has been drowned!

90.

Egoism versus Egoism.—How many are there who still come to the conclusion: "Life would be intolerable were there no God!" Or, as is said in idealistic circles: "Life would be intolerable if its ethical signification were lacking." Hence there must be a God—or an ethical signification of existence! In reality the case stands thus: He who is accustomed to conceptions of this sort does not desire a life without them, hence these conceptions are necessary for him and his preservation—but what a presumption it is to assert that everything necessary for my preservation must exist *in reality*! As if my preservation were really necessary! What if others held the contrary opinion? if they did not care to live under the conditions of these two articles of faith, and did not regard life as worth living if they were realised!—And that is the present position of affairs.

91.

The Honesty of God.—An omniscient and omnipotent God who does not even take care that His intentions shall be understood by His creatures—could He be a God of goodness? A God, who, for thousands of years, has permitted innumerable doubts and scruples to continue unchecked as if they were of no importance in the salvation of mankind, and who, nevertheless, announces the most dreadful consequences for any one who mistakes his truth? Would he not be a cruel god if, being himself in possession of the truth, he could calmly contemplate mankind, in a state of miserable torment, worrying its mind as to what was truth?

Perhaps, however, he really is a God of goodness, and was unable to express Himself more clearly? Perhaps he lacked intelligence enough for this? Or eloquence? All the worse! For in such a case he may have been deceived himself in regard to what he calls his "truth," and may not be far from being another "poor, deceived devil!" Must he not therefore experience all the torments of hell at seeing His creatures suffering so much here below—and even more, suffering through all eternity—when he himself can neither advise nor help them, except as a deaf and dumb person, who makes all kinds of equivocal signs when his child or his dog is threatened with the most fearful danger? A distressed believer who argues thus might be pardoned if his pity for the suffering God were greater than his pity for his "neighbours"; for they are his neighbours no longer if that most solitary and primeval being is also the greatest sufferer and stands most in need of consolation.

Every religion shows some traits of the fact that it owes its origin to a state of human intellectuality which was as yet too young and immature: they all make light of the necessity for speaking the truth: as yet they know nothing of the *duty of God*, the duty of being clear and truthful in His communications with men. No one was more eloquent than Pascal in speaking of the "hidden God" and the reasons why He had to keep Himself hidden, all of which indicates clearly enough that Pascal himself could never make his mind easy on this point: but he speaks with such confidence that one is led to imagine that he must have been let into the secret at some time or other. He seemed to have some idea that the *deus absconditus* bore a few slight traces of immorality; and he felt too much ashamed and afraid of acknowledging this to himself: consequently, like a man who is afraid, he spoke as loudly as he could.

92.

At the Death-bed of Christianity.—All truly active men now do without inward Christianity, and the most moderate and thoughtful men of the intellectual middle classes possess only a kind of modified Christianity; that is, a peculiarly simplified Christianity. A God who, in his love, ordains everything so that it may be best for us, a God who gives us our virtue and our happiness and then takes them away from us, so that everything at length goes on smoothly and there is no reason left why we should take life ill or grumble about it: in short, resignation and modesty raised to the rank of divinities—that is the best and most lifelike remnant of Christianity now left to us. It must be remembered, however, that in this way Christianity has developed into a soft *moralism*: instead of "God, freedom, and immortality," we have now a kind of benevolence and honest sentiments, and the belief that, in the entire universe, benevolence and honest sentiments will finally prevail: this is the euthanasia of Christianity.

93.

What is Truth?—Who will not be pleased with the conclusions which the faithful take such delight in coming to?—"Science cannot be true; for it denies God. Hence it does not come from God; and consequently it cannot be true—for God is truth." It is not the deduction but the premise which is fallacious. What if God were not exactly truth, and if this were proved? And if he were instead the vanity, the desire for power, the ambitions, the fear, and the enraptured and terrified folly of mankind?

94.

Remedy for the Displeased.—Even Paul already believed that some sacrifice was necessary to take away the deep displeasure which God experienced concerning sin: and ever since then Christians have never ceased to vent the ill-humour which they felt with themselves upon some victim or another—whether it was "the world," or "history," or "reason," or joy, or the tranquillity of other men—something good, no matter what, had to die for *their* sins (even if only *in effigie*)!

95.

The Historical Refutation as the Decisive One.—Formerly it was sought to prove that there was no God—now it is shown how the belief that a God existed could have *originated*, and by what means this belief gained authority and importance: in this way the counterproof that there is no God becomes unnecessary and superfluous.—In former times, when the "evidences of the existence of God" which had been brought forward were refuted, a doubt still remained, viz. whether better proofs could not be found than those which had just been refuted: at that time the atheists did not understand the art of making a *tabula rasa*.

96.

"In hoc signo vinces."—To whatever degree of progress Europe may have attained in other respects, where religious affairs are concerned it has not yet reached the liberal naïveté of the ancient Brahmins, which proves that, in India, four thousand years ago, people meditated more profoundly and transmitted to their descendants more pleasure in

meditating than is the case in our own days. For those Brahmins believed in the first place that the priests were more powerful than the gods, and in the second place that it was observances which constituted the power of the priests: as a result of which their poets were never tired of glorifying those observances (prayers, ceremonies, sacrifices, chants, improvised melodies) as the real dispensers of all benefits. Although a certain amount of superstition and poetry was mingled with all this, the principles were *true*! A step further, and the gods were cast aside—which Europe likewise will have to do before very long! One more step further, and priests and intermediaries could also be dispensed with—and then Buddha, the teacher of the religion of self-redemption, appeared. How far Europe is still removed from this degree of culture! When at length all the customs and observances, upon which rests the power of gods, priests, and saviours, shall have been destroyed, when as a consequence morality, in the old sense, will be dead, then there will come ... yea, what will come then? But let us refrain from speculating; let us rather make certain that Europe will retrieve that which, in India, amidst this people of thinkers, was carried out thousands of years ago as a commandment of thought!

Scattered among the different nations of Europe there are now from ten to twenty millions of men who no longer "believe in God"—is it too much to ask that they should give each other some indication or password? As soon as they recognise each other in this way, they will also make themselves known to each other; and they will immediately become a power in Europe, and, happily, a power *among* the nations! among the classes! between rich and poor! between those who command, and those who obey! between the most restless and the most tranquil, tranquillising people!

132.

The Last Echoes of Christianity In Morals.—"On n'est bon que par la pitié: il faut donc qu'il y ait quelque pitié dans tous nos sentiments"[33]—so says morality nowadays. And how does this come about? The fact that the man who performs social, sympathetic,

---

[33] "We are only good through pity: there must therefore be some pity in all our feelings."

disinterested, and benevolent actions is now considered as the moral man: this is perhaps the most general effect, the most complete transformation, that Christianity has produced in Europe; perhaps in spite of itself, and not by any means because this was part of its essential doctrine. But this was the residuum of those Christian feelings that prevailed at the time when the contrary and thoroughly selfish faith in the "one thing needful," the absolute importance of eternal and personal salvation, together with the dogmas upon which this belief had rested, were gradually receding, and when the auxiliary beliefs in "love" and "love of one's neighbour," harmonising with the extraordinary practice of charity by the Church, were thereby coming to the front. The more people gradually became separated from the dogmas, the more did they seek some sort of justification for this separation in a cult of the love of humanity: not to fall short in this respect of the Christian ideal, but to excel it if possible, was the secret stimulus of all the French free-thinkers from Voltaire to Auguste Comte; and this latter with his famous moral formula "vivre pour autrui"[34] has indeed out-christianised even Christianity!

160.

Vain, Greedy, and not very Wise.—Your desires are greater than your understanding, and your vanity is even greater than your desires,—to people of your type a great deal of Christian practice and a little Schopenhauerian theory may be strongly recommended.

211.

To those who Dream of Immortality.—So you desire the everlasting perpetuity of this beautiful consciousness of yourselves? Is it not shameful? Do you forget all those other things which would in their turn have to support *you* for all eternity, just as they have borne with you up to the present with more than Christian patience? Or do you think that you can inspire them with an eternally pleasant feeling towards yourself? A single immortal man on earth would imbue everyone around him with such a disgust for him that a general epidemic of murder and suicide would be brought about. And yet, ye

---

[34] "Live for others"

petty dwellers on earth, with your narrow conceptions of a few thousand little minutes of time, ye would wish to be an everlasting burden on this everlasting universal existence! Could anything be more impertinent? After all, however, let us be indulgent towards a being of seventy years: he has not been able to exercise his imagination in conceiving his own "eternal tediousness"—he had not time enough for that!

262.

The Demon of Power.—Neither necessity nor desire, but the love of power, is the demon of mankind. You may give men everything possible—health, food, shelter, enjoyment—but they are and remain unhappy and capricious, for the demon waits and waits; and must be satisfied. Let everything else be taken away from men, and let this demon be satisfied, and then they will nearly be happy—as happy as men and demons can be; but why do I repeat this? Luther has already said it, and better than I have done, in the verses:

> "And though they take our life,
> Goods, honour, children, wife,
> Yet is their profit small,
> These things shall vanish all,
> The Kingdom it remaineth."

The Kingdom![35] there it is again!

321.

… Christianity, with its contempt for the world, has made ignorance a virtue—innocence, perhaps because the most frequent result of this innocence is precisely, as I have indicated above, guilt, the sense of guilt, and despair: In other words, a virtue which leads to Heaven by the circuitous route of Hell; for only then can the gloomy propylæa of Christian salvation be thrown open, and only then is the promise of a posthumous second innocence effective. This is one of the finest inventions of Christianity!

---

[35] German: *Reich* — Nietzsche alludes to the similarity between the worldly and otherworldly pursuits of power.

411.

Without Hatred.—You wish to bid farewell to your passion? Very well, but do so without hatred against it! Otherwise you have a second passion.—The soul of the Christian who has freed himself from sin is generally ruined afterwards by the hatred for sin. Just look at the faces of the great Christians! they are the faces of great haters.

456.

A Virtue in Process of Becoming.—Such assertions and promises as those of the ancient philosophers on the unity of virtue and felicity, or that of Christianity, "Seek ye first the Kingdom of God and His righteousness, and all these things shall be added unto you," have never been made with absolute sincerity, but always without a bad conscience nevertheless. People were in the habit of boldly laying down principles—which they wished to be true—exactly as if they were truth itself, in spite of all appearances to the contrary, and in doing this they felt neither religious nor moral compunction; for it was *in honorem maiorem*[36] of virtue or of God that one had gone beyond truth, without, however, any selfish intention!

Many good people still act up to this degree of truthfulness: when they feel unselfish they think it permissible to treat truth more lightly. Let it be remembered that the word honesty is neither to be found among the Socratic nor the Christian virtues: it is one of our most recent virtues, not yet quite mature, frequently misconstrued and misunderstood, scarcely conscious of itself—something in embryo, which we may either promote or check according to our inclination.

546.

Slave and Idealist.—The followers of Epictetus would doubtless not be to the taste of those who are now striving after the ideal. The constant tension of his being, the indefatigable inward glance, the prudent and reserved incommunicativeness of his eye whenever it happens to gaze upon the outer world, and above all, his silence or laconic speech: all these are characteristics of the strictest fortitude,— and what would our idealists, who above all else are desirous of

---

[36] in greater honor

expansion, care for this? But in spite of all this the Stoic is not fanatical. He detests the display and boasting of our idealists: his pride, however great it may be, is not eager to disturb others. It permits of a certain gentle approach, and has no desire to spoil anybody's good humour—nay, it can even smile. A great deal of ancient humanity is to be seen exemplified in this ideal. The most excellent feature about it, however, is that the thinker is completely free from the fear of God, strictly believes in reason, and is no preacher of penitence.

Epictetus was a slave: his ideal man is without any particular rank, and may exist in any grade of society, but above all he is to be sought in the deepest and lowest social classes, as the silent and self-sufficient man in the midst of a general state of servitude, a man who defends himself alone against the outer world, and is constantly living in a state of the highest fortitude. He is distinguished from the Christian especially, because the latter lives in hope in the promise of "unspeakable glory," permits presents to be made to him, and expects and accepts the best things from divine love and grace, and not from himself. Epictetus, on the other hand, neither hopes nor allows his best treasure to be given him—he possesses it already, holds it bravely in his hand, and defies the world to take it away from him. Christianity was devised for another class of ancient slaves, for those who had a weak will and weak reason—that is to say, for the majority of slaves.

from THE GAY SCIENCE

4.

... "Is it true that the good God is everywhere present?" asked a little girl of her mother: "I think that is indecent":—a hint to philosophers! ...

108.

New Struggles.—After Buddha was dead people showed his shadow for centuries afterwards in a cave,—an immense frightful shadow. God is dead:—but as the human race is constituted, there will perhaps be caves for millenniums yet, in which people will show his shadow.— And we—we have still to overcome his shadow!

122.

The Element of Moral Scepticism in Christianity.—Christianity also has made a great contribution to enlightenment, and has taught moral scepticism —in a very impressive and effective manner, accusing and embittering, but with untiring patience and subtlety; it annihilated in every individual the belief in his virtues: it made the great virtuous ones, of whom antiquity had no lack, vanish for ever from the earth, those popular men, who, in the belief in their perfection, walked about with the dignity of a hero of the bull-fight. When, trained in this Christian school of scepticism, we now read the moral books of the ancients, for example those of Seneca and Epictetus, we feel a pleasurable superiority, and are full of secret insight and penetration, —it seems to us as if a child talked before an old man, or a pretty, gushing girl before La Rochefoucauld:—we know better what virtue is! After all, however, we have applied the same scepticism to all *religious* states and processes, such as sin, repentance, grace, sanctification, &c., and have allowed the worm to burrow so well, that we have now the same feeling of subtle superiority and insight even in reading all Christian books:—we know also the religious feelings better! And it is time to know them well and describe them well, for the pious ones of the old belief die out also; let us save their likeness and type, at least for the sake of knowledge.

125.

The Madman.—Have you ever heard of the madman who on a bright morning lighted a lantern and ran to the market-place calling out unceasingly: "I seek God! I seek God!"—As there were many people standing about who did not believe in God, he caused a great deal of amusement. Why! is he lost? said one. Has he strayed away like a child? said another. Or does he keep himself hidden? Is he afraid of us? Has he taken a sea-voyage? Has he emigrated?—the people cried out laughingly, all in a hubbub. The insane man jumped into their midst and transfixed them with his glances. "Where is God gone?" he called out. "I mean to tell you! *We have killed him,*—you and I! We are all his murderers! But how have we done it? How were we able to drink up the sea? Who gave us the sponge to wipe away the whole horizon? What did we do when we loosened this earth from its sun? Whither does it now move? Whither do we move? Away from all suns? Do we not dash on unceasingly? Backwards, sideways, forewards, in all directions? Is there still an above and below? Do we not stray, as through infinite nothingness? Does not empty space breathe upon us? Has it not become colder? Does not night come on continually, darker and darker? Shall we not have to light lanterns in the morning? Do we not hear the noise of the grave-diggers who are burying God? Do we not smell the divine putrefaction?—for even Gods putrefy! God is dead. God remains dead! And we have killed him! How shall we console ourselves, the most murderous of all murderers? The holiest and the mightiest that the world has hitherto possessed, has bled to death under our knife,—who will wipe the blood from us? With what water could we cleanse ourselves? What lustrums, what sacred games shall we have to devise? Is not the magnitude of this deed too great for us? Shall we not ourselves have to become Gods, merely to seem worthy of it? There never was a greater event,—and on account of it, all who are born after us belong to a higher history than any history hitherto!"—Here the madman was silent and looked again at his hearers; they also were silent and looked at him in surprise. At last he threw his lantern on the ground, so that it broke in pieces and was extinguished. "I come too early," he then said, "I am not yet at the right time. This prodigious event is still on its way, and is travelling,—it has not yet reached men's ears. Lightning and thunder need time, the light of the stars needs time, deeds need time, even after they are done, to be seen and heard. This deed is as yet further from them than the furthest star,—*and yet they have done it!*"—It is further stated that the madman made his way into different churches on the same day, and there intoned his *Requiem æternam deo.* When led out and called to account, he always gave the reply: "What are these churches now, if they are not the tombs and monuments of God?"—

126.

Mystical Explanations.—Mystical explanations are regarded as profound; the truth is that they do not even go the length of being superficial.

128.

The Value of Prayer.—Prayer has been devised for such men as have never any thoughts of their own, and to whom an elevation of the soul is unknown, or passes unnoticed; what shall these people do in holy places and in all important situations in life which require repose and some kind of dignity? In order at least that they may not *disturb,* the wisdom of all the founders of religions, the small as well as the great, has commended to them the formula of prayer, as a long mechanical labour of the lips, united with an effort of the memory, and with a uniform, prescribed attitude of hands and feet—*and* eyes! They may then, like the Tibetans, chew the cud of their *"om mane padme hum,"* innumerable times, or, as in Benares, count the name of the God Ram-Ram-Ram (etc., with or without grace) on their fingers; or honour Vishnu with his thousand names of invocation, Allah with his ninety-nine; or they may make use of the prayer-wheels and the rosary: the main thing is that they are settled down for a time at this work, and present a tolerable appearance; their mode of prayer is devised for the advantage of the pious who have thought and elevation of their own. But even these have their weary hours when a series of venerable words and sounds, and a mechanical, pious ritual does them good. But supposing that these rare men—in every religion the religious man is an exception—know how to help themselves, the poor in spirit do not know, and to forbid them the prayer-babbling would mean to take their religion from them, a fact which Protestantism brings more and more to light. All that religion wants with such persons is that they should *keep still* with their eyes, hands, legs, and all their organs: they thereby become temporarily beautified and—more human-looking!

129.

The Conditions for God.—"God himself cannot subsist without wise men," said Luther, and with good reason; but "God can still less subsist without unwise men,"—good Luther did not say that!

130.

A Dangerous Resolution.—The Christian resolution to find the world ugly and bad, has made the world ugly and bad.

131.

Christianity and Suicide.—Christianity made use of the excessive longing for suicide at the time of its origin as a lever for its power: it left only two forms of suicide, invested them with the highest dignity and the highest hopes, and forbade all others with dreadful threatenings. But martyrdom and the slow self-annihilation of the ascetic were permitted.

132.

Against Christianity.—It is now no longer our reason, but our taste that decides against Christianity.

133.

Axioms.—An unavoidable hypothesis on which mankind must always fall back again, is in the long run *more powerful* than the most firmly believed belief in something untrue (like the Christian belief). In the long run: that means a hundred thousand years hence.

135.

Origin of Sin—Sin, as it is at present felt wherever Christianity prevails or has prevailed, is a Jewish feeling and a Jewish invention; and in respect to this background of all Christian morality Christianity has in fact aimed at "Judaising" the whole world. To what an extent this has succeeded in Europe is traced most accurately in our remarkable alienness to Greek antiquity—a world without the feeling of sin—in our sentiments even at present; in spite of all the good will to approximation and assimilation, which whole generations and many distinguished individuals have not failed to display. "Only when thou *repentest* is God gracious to thee"—that would arouse the laughter or the wrath of a Greek: he would say, "Slaves may have such sentiments." Here a mighty being, an almighty being, and yet a revengeful being, is presupposed; his power is so great that no injury whatever can be done to him except in the point of honour. Every sin is an infringement of respect, a *crimen laesae majestatis divinae*[37]—and nothing more! Contrition, degradation, rolling-in-the-dust,—these are the first and last conditions on which his favour depends: the restoration, therefore, of his divine honour! If injury be caused otherwise by sin, if a profound, spreading evil be propagated by it, an evil which, like a disease, attacks and strangles one man after another —that does not trouble this honour-craving Oriental in heaven; sin is an offence against him, not against mankind!—to him on whom he has bestowed his favour he bestows also this indifference to the natural consequences of sin. God and mankind are here thought of as separated as so antithetical that sin against the latter cannot be at all possible,—all deeds are to be looked upon *solely with respect to their supernatural consequences,* and not with respect to their natural results: it is thus that the Jewish feeling, to which all that is natural seems unworthy in itself, would have things. The *Greeks,* on the other hand, were more familiar with the thought that transgression also may have dignity,—even theft, as in the case of Prometheus,[38] even the slaughtering of cattle as the expression of frantic jealousy, as in the case of Ajax; in their need to attribute dignity to transgression and embody it therein, they invented *tragedy,*—an art and a delight, which

---

[37] crime of injuring the divine majesty

[38] See the excerpt from *The Birth of Tragedy* in Section 1.

in its profoundest essence has remained alien to the Jew, in spite of all his poetic endowment and taste for the sublime.

136.

The Chosen People.—The Jews, who regard themselves as the chosen people among the nations, and that too because they are the moral genius among the nations (in virtue of their capacity for *despising* the human in themselves *more* than any other people)—the Jews have a pleasure in their divine monarch and saint similar to that which the French nobility had in Louis XIV. This nobility had allowed its power and autocracy to be taken from it, and had become contemptible: in order not to feel this, in order to be able to forget it, an *unequalled* royal magnificence, royal authority and plenitude of power was needed, to which there was access only for the nobility. As in accordance with this privilege they raised themselves to the elevation of the court, and from that elevation saw everything under them,—saw everything contemptible,—they got beyond all uneasiness of conscience. They thus elevated intentionally the tower of the royal power more and more into the clouds, and set the final coping-stone of their own power thereon.

137.

Spoken in Parable.—A Jesus Christ was only possible in a Jewish landscape—I mean in one over which the gloomy and sublime thunder-cloud of the angry Jehovah hung continually. Here only was the rare, sudden flashing of a single sunbeam through the dreadful, universal and continuous nocturnal-day regarded as a miracle of "love," as a beam of the most unmerited "grace." Here only could Christ dream of his rainbow and celestial ladder on which God descended to man; everywhere else the clear weather and the sun were considered the rule and the commonplace.

138.

The Error of Christ.—The founder of Christianity thought there was nothing from which men suffered so much as from their sins:—it was his error, the error of him who felt himself without sin, to whom experience was lacking in this respect! It was thus that his soul filled with that marvellous, fantastic pity which had reference to a trouble that even among his own people, the inventors of sin, was rarely a great trouble! But Christians understood subsequently how to do justice to their master, and how to sanctify his error into a "truth."

139.

Colour of the Passions.—Natures such as the apostle Paul, have an evil eye for the passions; they learn to know only the filthy, the distorting, and the heart-breaking in them,—their ideal aim, therefore, is the annihilation of the passions; in the divine they see complete purification from passion. The Greeks, quite otherwise than Paul and the Jews, directed their ideal aim precisely to the passions, and loved, elevated, embellished and deified them: in passion they evidently not only felt themselves happier, but also purer and diviner than otherwise.—And now the Christians? Have they wished to become Jews in this respect? Have they perhaps become Jews?

140.

Too Jewish.—If God had wanted to become an object of love, he would first of all have had to forgo judging and justice; a judge, and even a gracious judge, is no object of love. The founder of Christianity showed too little of the finer feelings in this respect—being a Jew.

141.

Too Oriental.—What? A God who loves men provided that they believe in him, and who hurls frightful glances and threatenings at him who does not believe in this love! What? A conditioned love as the feeling of an almighty God! A love which has not even become master of the sentiment of honour and of the irritable desire for vengeance! How Oriental is all that! "If I love thee, what does it concern thee?" is already a sufficient criticism of the whole of Christianity.

142.

Frankincense.—Buddha says: "Do not flatter thy benefactor!" Let one repeat this saying in a Christian church:—it immediately purifies the air.

143.

The Greatest Utility of Polytheism.—For the individual to set up his *own* ideal and derive from it his laws, his pleasures and his rights—*that* has perhaps been hitherto regarded as the most monstrous of all human aberrations, and as idolatry in itself; in fact, the few who have ventured to do this have always needed to apologise to themselves, usually in this wise: "Not I! not I! but *a God*, through my instrumentality!" It was in the marvellous art and capacity for creating Gods—in polytheism—that this impulse was permitted to discharge itself, it was here that it became purified, perfected, and ennobled; for it was originally a commonplace and unimportant impulse, akin to stubbornness, disobedience and envy. To be *hostile* to this impulse towards the individual ideal,—that was formerly the law of every morality. There was then only one norm, "the man"—and every people believed that it *had* this one and ultimate norm. But above himself, and outside of himself, in a distant over-world, a person could see a *multitude of norms:* the one God was not the denial or blasphemy of the other Gods! It was here that individuals were first permitted, it was here that the right of individuals was first respected. The inventing of Gods, heroes, and supermen of all kinds, as well as co-ordinate men and undermen—dwarfs, fairies, centaurs, satyrs, demons, devils—was the inestimable preliminary to the justification of the selfishness and sovereignty of the individual: the freedom which was granted to one God in respect to other Gods, was at last given to the individual himself in respect to laws, customs and neighbours. Monotheism, on the contrary, the rigid consequence of the doctrine of one normal human being—consequently the belief in a normal God, beside whom there are only false, spurious Gods—has perhaps been the greatest danger of mankind in the past: man was then threatened by that premature state of inertia, which, so far as we can see, most of the other species of animals reached long ago, as creatures who all believed in one normal animal and ideal in their species, and definitely translated their morality of custom into flesh and blood. In polytheism man's free-thinking and many-sided thinking had a prototype set up: the power to create for himself new and individual eyes, always newer and more individualised: so that these are no *eternal* horizons and perspectives.

148.

Where Reformations Originate.—At the time of the great corruption of the church it was least of all corrupt in Germany: it was on that account that the Reformation originated *here*, as a sign that even the beginnings of corruption were felt to be unendurable. For, comparatively speaking, no people was ever more Christian than the Germans at the time of Luther; their Christian culture was just about to burst into bloom with a hundred-fold splendour,—one night only was still lacking; but that night brought the storm which put an end to all.

149.

The Failure of Reformations.—It testifies to the higher culture of the Greeks, even in rather early ages, that attempts to establish new Grecian religions frequently failed; it testifies that quite early there must have been a multitude of dissimilar individuals in Greece, whose dissimilar troubles were not cured by a single recipe of faith and hope. Pythagoras and Plato, perhaps also Empedocles, and already much earlier the Orphic enthusiasts, aimed at founding new religions; and the two first-named were so endowed with the qualifications for founding religions, that one cannot be sufficiently astonished at their failure: they just reached the point of founding sects. Every time that the Reformation of an entire people fails and only sects raise their heads, one may conclude that the people already contains many types, and has begun to free itself from the gross herding instincts and the morality of custom—a momentous state of suspense, which one is accustomed to disparage as decay of morals and corruption, while it announces the maturing of the egg and the early rupture of the shell. That Luther's Reformation succeeded in the north is a sign that the north had remained backward in comparison with the south of Europe, and still had requirements tolerably uniform in colour and kind; and there would have been no Christianising of Europe at all, if the culture of the old world of the south had not been gradually barbarized by an excessive admixture of the blood of German barbarians, and thus lost its ascendency. The more universally and unconditionally an individual, or the thought of an individual, can operate, so much more homogeneous and so much lower must be the mass that is there operated upon; while counter-strivings betray internal counter-requirements, which also want to gratify and realise themselves. Reversely, one may always conclude with regard to an actual elevation of culture, when powerful and ambitious natures only produce a limited and sectarian effect: this is true also for the separate arts, and for the provinces of knowledge. Where there is ruling there are masses: where there are masses there is need of slavery. Where there is slavery the individuals are but few, and have the instincts and conscience of the herd opposed to them.

150.

Criticism of Saints.—Must one then, in order to have a virtue, be desirous of having it precisely in its most brutal form?—as the Christian saints desired and needed;—those who only *endured* life with the thought that at the sight of their virtue self-contempt might seize every man. A virtue with such an effect I call brutal.

151.

The Origin of Religion.—The metaphysical requirement is not the origin of religions, as Schopenhauer claims, but only a *later sprout* from them. Under the dominance of religious thoughts we have accustomed ourselves to the idea of "another (back, under, or upper) world," and feel an uncomfortable void and privation through the annihilation of the religious illusion;—and then "another world" grows out of this feeling once more, but now it is only a metaphysical world, and no longer a religious one. That however which in general led to the assumption of "another world" in primitive times, was *not* an impulse or requirement, but an *error* in the interpretation of certain natural phenomena, a difficulty of the intellect.[39]

---

[39] See *The Dawn* sec. 33, *The Will to Power* sec. 230 and "How The 'True World' Ultimately Became A Fable" from *Twilight of the Idols*

214.

Faith Saves.—Virtue gives happiness and a state of blessedness only to those who have a strong faith in their virtue:—not, however, to the more refined souls whose virtue consists of a profound distrust of themselves and of all virtue. After all, therefore, it is "faith that saves" here also!—and be it well observed, *not* virtue!

285.

Excelsior!—"Thou wilt never more pray, never more worship, never more repose in infinite trust—thou refusest to stand still and dismiss thy thoughts before an ultimate wisdom, an ultimate virtue, an ultimate power,—thou hast no constant guardian and friend in thy seven solitudes—thou livest without the outlook on a mountain that has snow on its head and fire in its heart—there is no longer any requiter for thee, nor any amender with, his finishing touch—there is no longer any reason in that which happens, or any love in that which will happen to thee—there is no longer any resting-place for thy weary heart, where it has only to find and no longer to seek, thou art opposed to any kind of ultimate peace, thou desirest the eternal recurrence of war and peace:—man of renunciation, wilt thou renounce in all these things? Who will give thee the strength to do so? No one has yet had this strength!"—There is a lake which one day refused to flow away, and threw up a dam at the place where it had hitherto discharged: since then this lake has always risen higher and higher. Perhaps the very renunciation will also furnish us with the strength with which the renunciation itself can be borne; perhaps man will ever rise higher and higher from that point onward, when he no longer *flows out* into a God.

292.

To the Preachers of Morality.—I do not mean to moralise, but to those who do, I would give this advice: if you mean ultimately to deprive the best things and the best conditions of all honour and worth, continue to speak of them in the same way as heretofore! Put them at the head of your morality, and speak from morning till night of the happiness of virtue, of repose of soul, of righteousness, and of reward and punishment in the nature of things: according as you go on in this manner, all these good things will finally acquire a popularity and a street-cry for themselves: but then all the gold on them will also be worn off, and more besides: all the gold *in them* will have changed into lead. Truly, you understand the reverse art of alchemy, the depreciating of the most valuable things! Try, just for once, another recipe, in order not to realise as hitherto the opposite of what you mean to attain: *deny* those good things, withdraw from them the applause of the populace and discourage the spread of them, make them once more the concealed chastities of solitary souls, and say: *morality is something forbidden!* Perhaps you will thus attract to your cause the sort of men who are only of any account, I mean the *heroic*. But then there must be something formidable in it, and not as hitherto something disgusting. Might one not be inclined to say at present with reference to morality what Meister Eckhart says: "I pray God to deliver me from God!"

319.

As Interpreters of our Experiences.—One form of honesty has always been lacking among founders of religions and their kin:—they have never made their experiences a matter of the intellectual conscience. "What did I really experience? What then took place in me and around me? Was my understanding clear enough? Was my will directly opposed to all deception of the senses, and courageous in its defence against fantastic notions?"—None of them ever asked these questions, nor to this day do any of the good religious people ask them. They have rather a thirst for things which are *contrary to reason*, and they don't want to have too much difficulty in satisfying this thirst, —so they experience "miracles" and "regenerations," and hear the voices of angels! But we who are different, who are thirsty for reason, want to look as carefully into our experiences as in the case of a scientific experiment, hour by hour, day by day! We ourselves want to be our own experiments, and our own subjects of experiment.

347.

Believers and their Need of Belief.—How much *faith* a person requires in order to flourish, how much "fixed opinion" he requires which he does not wish to have shaken, because he *holds* himself thereby—is a measure of his power (or more plainly speaking, of his weakness). Most people in old Europe, as it seems to me, still need Christianity at present, and on that account it still finds belief. For such is man: a theological dogma might be refuted to him a thousand times,— provided, however, that he had need of it, he would again and again accept it as "true,"—according to the famous "proof of power" of which the Bible speaks. Some have still need of metaphysics; but also the impatient *longing for certainty* which at present discharges itself in scientific, positivist fashion among large numbers of the people, the longing by all means to get at something stable (while on account of the warmth of the longing the establishing of the certainty is more leisurely and negligently undertaken):—even this is still the longing for a hold, a support; in short, the *instinct of weakness*, which, while not actually creating religions, metaphysics, and convictions of all kinds, nevertheless—preserves them.

In fact, around all these positivist systems there fume the vapours of a certain pessimistic gloom, something of weariness, fatalism, disillusionment, and fear of new disillusionment—or else manifest animosity, ill-humour, anarchic exasperation, and whatever there is of symptom or masquerade of the feeling of weakness. Even the readiness with which our cleverest contemporaries get lost in wretched corners and alleys, for example, in Vaterländerei (so I designate Jingoism, called *chauvinisme* in France, and "*deutsch*" in Germany), or in petty æsthetic creeds in the manner of Parisian *naturalisme* (which only brings into prominence and uncovers—*that* aspect of nature which excites simultaneously disgust and astonishment—they like at present to call this aspect *la vérité vraie*), or in Nihilism in the St Petersburg style (that is to say, in the *belief in unbelief*, even to martyrdom for it):—this shows always and above all the need of belief, support, backbone, and buttress.

Belief is always most desired, most pressingly needed, where there is a lack of will: for the will, as emotion of command, is the distinguishing characteristic of sovereignty and power. That is to say, the less a person knows how to command, the more urgent is his desire for that; which commands, and commands sternly,—a God, a prince, a caste, a physician, a confessor, a dogma, a party conscience. From whence perhaps it could be inferred that the two world-religions, Buddhism and Christianity, might well have had the cause of their rise, and especially of their rapid extension, in an extraordinary *malady of the will.* And in truth it has been so: both religions lighted upon a longing, monstrously exaggerated by malady of the will, for an imperative, a "Thou-shalt," a longing going the length of despair; both religions were teachers of fanaticism in times of slackness of will-power, and thereby offered to innumerable persons a support, a new possibility of exercising will, an enjoyment in willing. For in fact fanaticism is the sole "volitional strength" to which the weak and irresolute can be excited, as a sort of hypnotising of the entire sensory-intellectual system, in favour of the over-abundant nutrition (hypertrophy) of a particular point of view and a particular sentiment, which then dominates—the Christian calls it his *faith.* When a man arrives at the fundamental conviction that he *requires* to be commanded, he becomes "a believer." Reversely, one could imagine a delight and a power of self-determining, and a *freedom* of will, whereby a spirit could bid farewell to every belief, to every wish for certainty, accustomed as it would be to support itself on slender cords and possibilities, and to dance even on the verge of abysses. Such a spirit would be the *free spirit par excellence.*

350.

In Honour of Homines Religiosi.—The struggle against the church is certainly (among other things—for it has a manifold significance) the struggle of the more ordinary, cheerful, confiding, superficial natures against the rule of the graver, profounder, more contemplative natures, that is to say, the more malign and suspicious men, who with long continued distrust in the worth of life, brood also over their own worth:—the ordinary instinct of the people, its sensual gaiety, its "good heart," revolts against them. The entire Roman Church rests on a Southern suspicion of the nature of man (always misunderstood in the North), a suspicion whereby the European South has succeeded, to the inheritance of the profound Orient—the mysterious, venerable Asia—and its contemplative spirit. Protestantism was a popular insurrection in favour of the simple, the respectable, the superficial (the North has always been more good-natured and more shallow than the South), but it was the French Revolution that first gave the sceptre wholly and solemnly into the hands of the "good man" (the sheep, the ass, the goose, and everything incurably shallow, bawling, and fit for the Bedlam of "modern ideas").

351.

In Honour of Priestly Natures.—I think that philosophers have always felt themselves very remote from that which the people (in all classes of society nowadays) take for wisdom: the prudent, bovine placidity, piety, and country-parson meekness, which lies in the meadow and *gazes at* life seriously and ruminatingly:—this is probably because philosophers have not had sufficiently the taste of the "people," or of the country-parson, for that kind of wisdom. Philosophers will also perhaps be the last to acknowledge that the people *should* understand something of that which lies furthest from them, something of the great *passion* of the thinker, who lives and must live continually in the storm-cloud of the highest problems and the heaviest responsibilities (consequently, not gazing at all, to say nothing of doing so indifferently, securely, objectively). The people venerate an entirely different type of men when on their part they form the ideal of a "sage," and they are a thousand times justified in rendering homage with the highest eulogies and honours to precisely that type of men— namely, the gentle, serious, simple, chaste, priestly natures and those related to them—it is to them that the praise falls due in the popular veneration of wisdom. And to whom should the multitude have more reason to be grateful than to these men who pertain to its class and rise from its ranks, but are persons consecrated, chosen, and *sacrificed* for its good—they themselves believe themselves sacrificed to God— before whom every one can pour forth his heart with impunity, by whom he can *get rid* of his secrets, cares, and worse things (for the man who "communicates himself" gets rid of himself, and he who has "confessed" forgets). Here there exists a great need: for sewers and pure cleansing waters are required also for spiritual filth, and rapid currents of love are needed, and strong, lowly, pure hearts, who qualify and sacrifice themselves for such service of the non-public health-department—for it *is* a sacrificing, the priest is, and continues to be, a human sacrifice.

The people regard such sacrificed, silent, serious men of "faith" as *"wise,"* that is to say, as men who have become sages, as "reliable" in relation to their own unreliability. Who would desire to deprive the people of that expression and that veneration?—But as is fair on the other side, among philosophers the priest also is still held to belong to the "people," and is *not* regarded as a sage, because, above all, they themselves do not believe in "sages," and they already scent "the people" in this very belief and superstition. It was *modesty* which invented in Greece the word "philosopher," and left to the play-actors of the spirit the superb arrogance of assuming the name "wise"—the modesty of such monsters of pride and self-glorification as Pythagoras and Plato.—

353.

The Origin of Religions.—The real inventions of founders of religions are, on the one hand, to establish a definite mode of life and everyday custom, which operates as *disciplina voluntatis*,[40] and at the same time does away with ennui; and on the other hand, to give to that very mode of life an *interpretation*, by virtue of which it appears illumined with the highest value; so that it henceforth becomes a good for which people struggle, and under certain circumstances lay down their lives. In truth, the second of these inventions is the more essential: the first, the mode of life, has usually been there already, side by side, however, with other modes of life, and still unconscious of the value which it embodies. The import, the originality of the founder of a religion, discloses itself usually in the fact that he *sees* the mode of life, *selects* it, and *divines* for the first time the purpose for which it can be used, how it can be interpreted. Jesus (or Paul) for example, found around him the life of the common people in the Roman province, a modest, virtuous, oppressed life: he interpreted it, he put the highest significance and value into it—and thereby the courage to despise every other mode of life, the calm fanaticism of the Moravians, the secret, subterranean self-confidence which goes on increasing, and is at last ready "to overcome the world" (that is to say,

---

40 discipline of the will

Rome, and the upper classes throughout the empire).[41] Buddha, in like manner, found the same type of man,—he found it in fact dispersed among all the classes and social ranks of a people who were good and kind (and above all inoffensive), owing to indolence, and who likewise owing to indolence, lived abstemiously, almost without requirements. He understood that such a type of man, with all its *vis inertiæ*,[42] had inevitably to glide into a belief which promises *to avoid* the return of earthly ill (that is to say, labour and activity generally),— this "understanding" was his genius. The founder of a religion possesses psychological infallibility in the knowledge of a definite, average type of souls, who have not yet *recognised* themselves as akin. It is he who brings them together: the founding of a religion, therefore, always becomes a long ceremony of recognition.—

357.

... A fourth question would be whether also *Schopenhauer* with his Pessimism, that is to say, the problem of *the worth of existence*, had to be a German. I think not. The event *after* which this problem was to be expected with certainty, so that an astronomer of the soul could have calculated the day and the hour for it—namely, the decay of the belief in the Christian God, the victory of scientific atheism,—is a universal European event, in which all races are to have their share of service and honour. On the contrary, it has to be ascribed precisely to the Germans—those with whom Schopenhauer was contemporary,— that they delayed this victory of atheism longest, and endangered it most. Hegel especially was its retarder *par excellence*, in virtue of the grandiose attempt which he made to persuade us at the very last of the divinity of existence, with the help of our sixth sense, "the historical sense." As philosopher, Schopenhauer was the *first* avowed and inflexible atheist we Germans have had: his hostility to Hegel had here its motive. The non-divinity of existence was regarded by him as something understood, palpable, indisputable; he always lost his philosophical composure and got into a passion when he saw anyone hesitate and beat about the bush here. It is at this point that his

---

[41] See *On The Genealogy of Morals* for an elaboration of this.

[42] force of inertia

thorough uprightness of character comes in: unconditional, honest atheism is precisely the *preliminary condition* for his raising the problem, as a final and hard won victory of the European conscience, as the most prolific act of two thousand years' discipline to truth, which in the end no longer tolerates the *lie* of the belief in a God.

One sees what has really gained the victory over the Christian God—, Christian morality itself, the conception of veracity, taken ever more strictly, the confessional subtlety of the Christian conscience, translated and sublimated to the scientific conscience, to intellectual purity at any price. To look upon nature as if it were a proof of the goodness and care of a God; to interpret history in honour of a divine reason, as a constant testimony to a moral order in the world and a moral final purpose; to explain personal experiences as pious men have long enough explained them, as if everything were a dispensation or intimation of Providence, something planned and sent on behalf of the salvation of the soul: all that is now *past*, it has conscience *against* it, it is regarded by all the more acute consciences as disreputable and dishonourable, as mendaciousness, feminism, weakness, and cowardice,—by virtue of this severity, if by anything, we are *good* Europeans, the heirs of Europe's longest and bravest self-conquest. When we thus reject the Christian interpretation, and condemn its "significance" as a forgery, we are immediately confronted in a striking manner with the *Schopenhauerian* question: *Has existence then a significance at all?*—the question which will require a couple of centuries even to be completely heard in all its profundity. Schopenhauer's own answer to this question was—if I may be forgiven for saying so—a premature, juvenile reply, a mere compromise, a stoppage and sticking in the very same Christian-ascetic, moral perspectives, *the belief in which had got notice to quit* along with the belief in God. ... But he *raised* the question—as a good European, as we have said, and *not* as a German.—

358.

The Peasant Revolt of the Spirit.—We Europeans find ourselves in view of an immense world of ruins, where some things still tower aloft, while other objects stand mouldering and dismal, where most things however already lie on the ground, picturesque enough—where were there ever finer ruins?—overgrown with weeds, large and small.

It is the Church which is this city of decay: we see the religious organisation of Christianity shaken to its deepest foundations. The belief in God is overthrown, the belief in the Christian ascetic ideal is now fighting its last fight. Such a long and solidly built work as Christianity—it was the last construction of the Romans!—could not of course be demolished all at once; every sort of earthquake had to shake it, every sort of spirit which perforates, digs, gnaws and moulders had to assist in the work of destruction. But that which is strangest is that those who have exerted themselves most to retain and preserve Christianity, have been precisely those who did most to destroy it,—the Germans. It seems that the Germans do not understand the essence of a Church. Are they not spiritual enough, or not distrustful enough to do so? In any case the structure of the Church rests on a *southern* freedom and liberality of spirit, and similarly on a southern suspicion of nature, man, and spirit,—it rests on a knowledge of man, an experience of man, entirely different from what the north has had. The Lutheran Reformation in all its length and breadth was the indignation of the simple against something "complicated." To speak cautiously, it was a coarse, honest misunderstanding, in which much is to be forgiven,—people did not understand the mode of expression of a *victorious* Church, and only saw corruption; they misunderstood the noble scepticism, the *luxury* of scepticism and toleration which every victorious, self-confident power permits.

One overlooks the fact readily enough at present that as regards all cardinal questions concerning power Luther was badly endowed; he was fatally short-sighted, superficial and imprudent—and above all, as a man sprung from the people, he lacked all the hereditary qualities of a ruling caste, and all the instincts for power; so that his work, his intention to restore the work of the Romans, merely became involuntarily and unconsciously the commencement of a work of destruction. He unravelled, he tore asunder with honest rage, where the old spider had woven longest and most carefully. He gave the sacred books into the hands of everyone,—they thereby got at last into the hands of the philologists, that is to say, the annihilators of every belief based upon books. He demolished the conception of "the Church" in that he repudiated the belief in the inspiration of the Councils: for only under the supposition that the inspiring spirit which had founded the Church still lives in it, still builds it, still goes on building its house, does the conception of "the Church" retain its power. He gave back to the priest sexual intercourse: but three-fourths of the reverence of which the people (and above all the women of the people) are capable, rests on the belief that an exceptional man in this respect will also be an exceptional man in other respects. It is precisely here that the popular belief in something superhuman in man, in a miracle, in the saving God in man, has its most subtle and insidious advocate. After Luther had given a wife to the priest, he had *to take from him* auricular confession; that was psychologically right: but thereby he practically did away with the Christian priest himself, whose profoundest utility has ever consisted in his being a sacred ear, a silent well, and a grave for secrets. "Every man his own priest"— behind such formulæ and their bucolic slyness, there was concealed in Luther the profoundest hatred of "higher men," and of the rule of "higher men," as the Church had conceived them. Luther disowned an ideal which he did not know how to attain, while he seemed to combat and detest the degeneration thereof. As a matter of fact, he, the impossible monk, repudiated the *rule* of the *homines religiosi*; he consequently brought about precisely the same thing within the ecclesiastical social order that he combated so impatiently in the civic order,—namely a "peasant insurrection."

As to all that grew out of his Reformation afterwards, good and bad, which can at present be almost counted up—who would be naïve enough to praise or blame Luther simply on account of these results? He is innocent of all; he knew not what he did. The art of making the European spirit shallower especially in the north, or more *good-natured,* if people would rather hear it designated by a moral expression, undoubtedly took a clever step in advance in the Lutheran Reformation; and similarly there grew out of it the mobility and disquietude of the spirit, its thirst for independence, its belief in the right to freedom, and its "naturalness." If people wish to ascribe to the Reformation in the last instance the merit of having prepared and favoured that which we at present honour as "modern science," they must of course add that it is also accessory to bringing about the degeneration of the modern scholar, with his lack of reverence, of shame and of profundity; and that it is also responsible for all naïve candour and plain-dealing in matters of knowledge, in short for the *plebeianism of the spirit* which is peculiar to the last two centuries, and from which even pessimism hitherto, has not in any way delivered us. "Modern ideas" also belong to this peasant insurrection of the north against the colder, more ambiguous, more suspicious spirit of the south, which has built itself its greatest monument in the Christian Church. Let us not forget in the end what a Church is, and especially in contrast to every "State": a Church is above all an authoritative organisation which secures to the *most spiritual* men the highest rank, and *believes* in the power of spirituality so far as to forbid all grosser appliances of authority. Through this alone the Church is under all circumstances a *nobler* institution than the State.—

from BEYOND GOOD AND EVIL

Preface

Supposing that Truth is a woman—what then? Is there not ground for suspecting that all philosophers, in so far as they have been dogmatists, have failed to understand women—that the terrible seriousness and clumsy importunity with which they have usually paid their addresses to Truth, have been unskilled and unseemly methods for winning a woman? Certainly she has never allowed herself to be won; and at present every kind of dogma stands with sad and discouraged mien—*if*, indeed, it stands at all! For there are scoffers who maintain that it has fallen, that all dogma lies on the ground— nay more, that it is at its last gasp. But to speak seriously, there are good grounds for hoping that all dogmatizing in philosophy, whatever solemn, whatever conclusive and decided airs it has assumed, may have been only a noble puerilism and tyronism; and probably the time is at hand when it will be once and again understood *what* has actually sufficed for the basis of such imposing and absolute philosophical edifices as the dogmatists have hitherto reared: perhaps some popular superstition of immemorial time (such as the soul-superstition, which, in the form of subject- and ego-superstition, has not yet ceased doing mischief): perhaps some play upon words, a deception on the part of grammar, or an audacious generalization of very restricted, very personal, very human—all-too-human facts. The philosophy of the dogmatists, it is to be hoped, was only a promise for thousands of years afterwards, as was astrology in still earlier times, in the service of which probably more labour, gold, acuteness, and patience have been spent than on any actual science hitherto: we owe to it, and to its "super-terrestrial" pretensions in Asia and Egypt, the grand style of architecture. It seems that in order to inscribe themselves upon the heart of humanity with everlasting claims, all great things have first to wander about the earth as enormous and awe-inspiring caricatures: dogmatic philosophy has been a caricature of this kind—for instance, the Vedanta doctrine in Asia, and Platonism in Europe. Let us not be ungrateful to it, although it must certainly be confessed that the worst, the most tiresome, and the most dangerous of errors hitherto has been a dogmatist error—namely, Plato's invention of Pure Spirit and the Good in Itself. But now when it has been surmounted, when Europe, rid of this nightmare, can again draw breath freely and at least enjoy a healthier—sleep, we, *whose duty is wakefulness itself,* are the heirs of all the strength which the struggle against this error has fostered. It amounted to the very inversion of truth, and the denial of the *perspective*—the fundamental condition—of life, to speak of Spirit and the Good as Plato spoke of them; indeed one might ask, as a physician: "How did such a malady attack that finest product of antiquity, Plato? Had the wicked Socrates really corrupted him? Was Socrates after all a corrupter of youths, and deserved his hemlock?" But the struggle against Plato, or—to speak plainer, and for the "people"—the struggle against the ecclesiastical oppression of millenniums of Christianity (for Christianity is Platonism for the "people"), produced in Europe a magnificent tension of soul, such as had not existed anywhere previously; with such a tensely strained bow one can now aim at the furthest goals. As a matter of fact, the European feels this tension as a state of distress, and twice attempts have been made in grand style to unbend the bow: once by means of Jesuitism, and the second time by means of democratic enlightenment —which, with the aid of liberty of the press and newspaper-reading, might, in fact, bring it about that the spirit would not so easily find itself in "distress"! (The Germans invented gunpowder—all credit to them! but they again made things square—they invented printing.) But we, who are neither Jesuits, nor democrats, nor even sufficiently Germans, we *good Europeans,* and free, *very* free spirits—we have it still, all the distress of spirit and all the tension of its bow! And perhaps also the arrow, the duty, and, who knows? *the goal to aim at ...*

The Religious Mood

45.

The human soul and its limits, the range of man's inner experiences hitherto attained, the heights, depths and distances of these experiences, the entire history of the soul *up to the present time,* and its still unexhausted possibilities: this is the preordained hunting-domain for a born psychologist and lover of a "big hunt." But how often must he say despairingly to himself: "A single individual I alas, only a single individual! and this great forest, this virgin forest!" So he would like to have some hundreds of hunting assistants, and fine trained hounds, which he could send into the history of the human soul, to drive *his* game together. In vain: again and again he experiences, profoundly and bitterly, how difficult it is to find assistants and dogs for all the things that directly excite his curiosity. The evil of sending scholars into new and dangerous hunting-domains, where courage, sagacity, and subtlety in every sense are required, is that they are no longer serviceable just when the "*big* hunt," and also the great danger commences,—it is precisely then that they lose their keen eye and nose. In order, for instance, to divine and determine what sort of history the problem of *knowledge and conscience* has hitherto had in the souls of *homines religiosi*, a person would perhaps himself have to possess as profound, as bruised, as immense an experience as the intellectual conscience of Pascal; and then he would still require that wide-spread heaven of clear, wicked spirituality, which, from above, would be able to oversee, arrange, and effectively formulise this mass of dangerous and painful experiences.—But who could do me this service! And who would have time to wait for such servants!—they evidently appear too rarely, they are so improbable at all times! Eventually one must do everything *oneself* in order to know something; which means that one has *much* to do! —But a curiosity like mine is once for all the most agreeable of vices—pardon me! I mean to say that the love of truth has its reward in heaven, and already upon earth.

46.

Faith, such as early Christianity desired, and not infrequently achieved in the midst of a sceptical and southernly free-spirited world, which had centuries of struggle between philosophical schools behind it and in it, counting besides the education in tolerance which the *imperium Romanum* gave—this faith is *not* that sincere, austere slave-faith by which perhaps a Luther or a Cromwell, or some other northern barbarian of the spirit remained attached to his God and Christianity; it is much rather the faith of Pascal, which resembles in a terrible manner a continuous suicide of reason—a tough, long-lived, wormlike reason, which is not to be slain at once and with a single blow. The Christian faith from the beginning, is sacrifice: the sacrifice of all freedom, all pride, all self-confidence of spirit; it is at the same time subjection, self-derision, and self-mutilation. There is cruelty and religious Phoenicianism in this faith, which is adapted to a tender, many-sided, and very fastidious conscience; it takes for granted that the subjection of the spirit is indescribably *painful*, that all the past and all the habits of such a spirit resist the *absurdissimum*,[43] in the form of which "faith" comes to it. Modern men, with their obtuseness as regards all Christian nomenclature, have no longer the sense for the terribly superlative conception which was implied to an antique taste by the paradox of the formula, "God on the Cross." Hitherto there had never and nowhere been such boldness in inversion, nor anything at once so dreadful, questioning, and questionable as this formula: it promised a transvaluation of all ancient values.—It was the Orient, the *profound* Orient, it was the Oriental slave who thus took revenge on Rome and its noble, light-minded toleration, on the Roman "Catholicism" of non-faith; and it was always, not the faith, but the freedom from the faith, the half-stoical and smiling indifference to the seriousness of the faith, which made the slaves indignant at their masters and revolt against them. "Enlightenment" causes revolt: for the slave desires the unconditioned, he understands nothing but the tyrannous, even in morals; he loves as he hates, without *nuance*, to the very depths, to the point of pain, to the point of sickness—his many *hidden* sufferings make him revolt against the noble taste which seems to *deny* suffering. The scepticism with regard to suffering, fundamentally only an attitude of aristocratic morality, was not the least of the causes, also, of the last great slave-insurrection which began with the French Revolution.

47.

Wherever the religious neurosis has appeared on the earth so far, we find it connected with three dangerous prescriptions as to regimen: solitude, fasting, and sexual abstinence—but without it being possible to determine with certainty which is cause and which is effect, or *if* any relation at all of cause and effect exists there. This latter doubt is

---

[43] "Height of absurdity"

justified by the fact that one of the most regular symptoms among savage as well as among civilised peoples is the most sudden and excessive sensuality; which then with equal suddenness transforms into penitential paroxysms, world-renunciation, and will-renunciation: both symptoms perhaps explainable as disguised epilepsy? But nowhere is it *more* obligatory to put aside explanations: around no other type has there grown such a mass of absurdity and superstition, no other type seems to have been more interesting to men and even to philosophers—perhaps it is time to become just a little indifferent here, to learn caution, or, better still, to look away, *to go away.*—Yet in the background of the most recent philosophy, that of Schopenhauer, we find almost as the problem in itself, this terrible note of interrogation of the religious crisis and awakening. How is the negation of will *possible?* how is the saint possible?—that seems to have been the very question with which Schopenhauer made a start and became a philosopher. And thus it was a genuine Schopenhauerian consequence, that his most convinced adherent (perhaps also his last, as far as Germany is concerned), namely, Richard Wagner, should bring his own life-work to an end just here, and should finally put that terrible and eternal type upon the stage as Kundry, *type vécu,*[44] and as it loved and lived, at the very time that the mad-doctors in almost all European countries had an opportunity to study the type close at hand, wherever the religious neurosis—or as I call it, "the religious mood"—made its latest epidemical outbreak and display as the "Salvation Army."—If it be a question, however, as to what has been so extremely interesting to men of all sorts in all ages, and even to philosophers, in the whole phenomenon of the saint, it is undoubtedly the appearance of the miraculous therein—namely, the immediate *succession of opposites,* of states of the soul regarded as morally antithetical: it was believed here to be self-evident that a "bad man" was all at once turned into a "saint," a good man. The hitherto existing psychology was wrecked at this point; is it not possible it may have happened principally because psychology had placed itself under the dominion of morals, because it *believed* in oppositions of moral values, and saw, read, and *interpreted* these oppositions into the text and

---

[44] "A type that has lived"

facts of the case? What? "Miracle" only an error of interpretation? A lack of philology?

48.

It seems that the Latin races are far more deeply attached to their Catholicism than we Northerners are to Christianity generally, and that consequently unbelief in Catholic countries means something quite different from what it does among Protestants—namely, a sort of revolt against the spirit of the race, while with us it is rather a return to the spirit (or non-spirit) of the race. We Northerners undoubtedly derive our origin from barbarous races, even as regards our talents for religion—we have *poor* talents for it. One may make an exception in the case of the Celts, who have therefore furnished also the best soil for the Christian infection in the north: the Christian ideal blossomed forth in France as much as ever the pale sun of the north would allow it. How strangely pious for our taste are still these later French sceptics, whenever there is any Celtic blood in their origin! How Catholic, how un-German does Auguste Comte's Sociology seem to us, with the Roman logic of its instincts! How Jesuitical, that amiable and shrewd cicerone of Port-Royal, Sainte-Beuve, in spite of all his hostility to Jesuits! And even Ernest Renan: how inaccessible to us Northerners does the language of such a Renan appear, in whom every instant the merest touch of religious thrill throws his refinedly voluptuous and comfortably couching soul off its balance! Let us repeat after him these fine sentences—and what wickedness and haughtiness is immediately aroused by way of answer in our probably less beautiful but harder souls, that is to say, in our more German souls !—"*Disons donc hardiment que la religion est un produit de l'homme normal, que l'homme est le plus dans le vrai quand il est le plus religieux et le plus assuré d'une destinée infinie. … C'est quand il est bon qu'il veut que la virtu corresponde à un order eternel, cest quand il contemple les choses d'une manière désintéressée qu'il trouve la mort révoltante et absurde. Comment ne pas supposer que c'est dans ces moments-là, que l'homme voit le mieux?"* [45] ... These sentences are so extremely *antipodal* to my ears and habits of thought, that in my first impulse of rage on finding them, I wrote on the margin, *"la niaiserie religieuse par excellence!"* [46] —until in my later rage I even took a fancy to them, these sentences with their truth absolutely inverted! It is so nice and such a distinction to have one's own antipodes!

49.

That which is so astonishing in the religious life of the ancient Greeks is the irrestrainable stream of *gratitude* which it pours forth—it is a very superior kind of man who takes *such* an attitude towards nature and life.—Later on, when the populace got the upper hand in Greece, *fear* became rampant also in religion; and Christianity was preparing itself.

50.

The passion for God: there are churlish, honest-hearted, and importunate kinds of it, like that of Luther—the whole of Protestantism lacks the southern *delicatezza.* There is an Oriental exaltation of the mind in it, like that of an undeservedly favoured or elevated slave, as in the case of St. Augustine, for instance, who lacks in an offensive manner, all nobility in bearing and desires. There is a feminine tenderness and sensuality in it, which modestly and unconsciously longs for a *unio mystica et physica,* as in the case of Madame de Guyon. In many cases it appears, curiously enough, as the disguise of a girl's or youth's puberty; here and there even as the hysteria of an old maid, also as her last ambition. The Church has frequently canonised the woman in such a case.

---

[45] "So let us boldly say that religion is a product of the normal man, that man is closest to the truth when he is most religious and most certain of an infinite destiny. ... It is when he is good that he wants virtue to correspond to an eternal order; it is when he contemplates things in a disinterested manner that he finds death revolting and absurd. How can we but suppose that it is in moments like this that man sees best?"

[46] "the religious stupidity par excellence!"

51.

The mightiest men have hitherto always bowed reverently before the saint, as the enigma of self-subjugation and utter voluntary privation—why did they thus bow? They divined in him—and as it were behind the questionableness of his frail and wretched appearance—the superior force which wished to test itself by such a subjugation; the strength of will, in which they recognised their own strength and love of power, and knew how to honour it: they honoured something in themselves when they honoured the saint. In addition to this, the contemplation of the saint suggested to them a suspicion: such an enormity of self-negation and anti-naturalness will not have been coveted for nothing—they have said, inquiringly. There is perhaps a reason for it, some very great danger, about which the ascetic might wish to be more accurately informed through his secret interlocutors and visitors? In a word, the mighty ones of the world learned to have a new fear before him, they divined a new power, a strange, still unconquered enemy:—it was the "Will to Power" which obliged them to halt before the saint. They had to question him.

52.

In the Jewish "Old Testament," the book of divine justice, there are men, things, and sayings on such an immense scale, that Greek and Indian literature has nothing to compare with it. One stands with fear and reverence before those stupendous remains of what man was formerly, and one has sad thoughts about old Asia and its little out-pushed peninsula Europe, which would like, by all means, to figure before Asia as the "Progress of Mankind." To be sure, he who is himself only a slender, tame house-animal, and knows only the wants of a house-animal (like our cultured people of today, including the Christians of "cultured" Christianity), need neither be amazed nor even sad amid those ruins—the taste for the Old Testament is a touchstone with respect to "great" and "small": perhaps he will find that the New Testament, the book of grace, still appeals more to his heart (there is much of the odour of the genuine, tender, stupid beadsman and petty soul in it). To have bound up this New Testament (a kind of *rococo* of taste in every respect) along with the Old Testament into one book, as the "Bible," as "The Book in Itself," is perhaps the greatest audacity and "sin against the Spirit" which literary Europe has upon its conscience.

53.

Why Atheism nowadays? "The father" in God is thoroughly refuted; equally so "the judge," "the rewarder." Also his "free will": he does not hear—and even if he did, he would not know how to help. The worst is that he seems incapable of communicating himself clearly; is he uncertain?—This is what I have made out (by questioning, and listening at a variety of conversations) to be the cause of the decline of European theism; it appears to me that though the religious instinct is in vigorous growth,—it rejects the theistic satisfaction with profound distrust.

54.

What does all modern philosophy mainly do? Since Descartes— and indeed more in defiance of him than on the basis of his procedure—an *attentat*[47] has been made on the part of all philosophers on the old conception of the soul, under the guise of a criticism of the subject and predicate conception—that is to say, an *attentat* on the fundamental presupposition of Christian doctrine. Modern philosophy, as epistemological scepticism, is secretly or openly *anti-Christian*, although (for keener ears, be it said) by no means anti-religious. Formerly, in effect, one believed in "the soul" as one believed in grammar and the grammatical subject: one said, "I" is the condition, "think" is the predicate and is conditioned—to think is an activity for which one *must* suppose a subject as cause. The attempt was then made, with marvellous tenacity and subtlety, to see if one could not get out of this net,—to see if the opposite was not perhaps true: "think" the condition, and "I" the conditioned; "I," therefore, only a synthesis which has been *made* by thinking itself. *Kant* really wished to prove that, starting from the subject, the subject could not be proved—nor the object either: the possibility of an *apparent existence* of the subject, and therefore of "the soul," may not always have been

---

[47] An attempted attack or assassination, usually unsuccessful

strange to him,—the thought which once had an immense power on earth as the Vedanta philosophy.

55.

There is a great ladder of religious cruelty, with many rounds; but three of these are the most important. Once on a time men sacrificed human beings to their God, and perhaps just those they loved the best —to this category belong the firstling sacrifices of all primitive religions, and also the sacrifice of the Emperor Tiberius in the Mithra-Grotto on the Island of Capri, that most terrible of all Roman anachronisms. Then, during the moral epoch of mankind, they sacrificed to their God the strongest instincts they possessed, their "nature"; *this* festal joy shines in the cruel glances of ascetics and "anti-natural" fanatics. Finally, what still remained to be sacrificed? Was it not necessary in the end for men to sacrifice everything comforting, holy, healing, all hope, all faith in hidden harmonies, in future blessedness and justice? Was it not necessary to sacrifice God himself, and out of cruelty to themselves to worship stone, stupidity, gravity, fate, nothingness? To sacrifice God for nothingness—this paradoxical mystery of the ultimate cruelty has been reserved for the rising generation; we all know something thereof already.

56.

Whoever, like myself, prompted by some enigmatical desire, has long endeavoured to go to the bottom of the question of pessimism and free it from the half-Christian, half-German narrowness and stupidity in which it has finally presented itself to this century, namely, in the form of Schopenhauer's philosophy; whoever, with an Asiatic and super-Asiatic eye, has actually looked inside, and into the most world-renouncing of all possible modes of thought—beyond good and evil, and no longer like Buddha and Schopenhauer, under the dominion and delusion of morality,— whoever has done this, has perhaps just thereby, without really desiring it, opened his eyes to behold the opposite ideal: the ideal of the most world-approving, exuberant and vivacious man, who has not only learnt to compromise and arrange with that which was and is, but wishes to have it again *as it was and is*, for all eternity, insatiably calling out *da capo*, not only to himself, but to the whole piece and play; and not only to the play, but actually to him who requires the play—and makes it necessary: because he always requires himself anew—and makes himself necessary.——What? And this would not be—*circulus vitiosus deus?*

57.

The distance, and as it were the space around man, grows with the strength of his intellectual vision and insight: his world becomes profounder; new stars, new enigmas, and notions are ever coming into view. Perhaps everything on which the intellectual eye has exercised its acuteness and profundity has just been an occasion for its exercise, something of a game, something for children and childish minds. Perhaps the most solemn conceptions that have caused the most fighting and suffering, the conceptions "God" and "sin," will one day seem to us of no more importance than a child's plaything or a child's pain seems to an old man;—and perhaps another plaything and another pain will then be necessary once more for "the old man"— always childish enough, an eternal child!

58.

Has it been observed to what extent outward idleness, or semi-idleness, is necessary to a real religious life (alike for its favourite microscopic labour of self-examination, and for its soft placidity called "prayer," the state of perpetual readiness for the "coming of God"), I mean the idleness with a good conscience, the idleness of olden times and of blood, to which the aristocratic sentiment that work is *dishonouring*—that it vulgarises body and soul—is not quite unfamiliar? And that consequently the modern, noisy, time-engrossing, conceited, foolishly proud laboriousness educates and prepares for "unbelief" more than anything else? Amongst these, for instance, who are at present living apart from religion in Germany, I find "freethinkers" of diversified species and origin, but above all a majority of those in whom laboriousness from generation to generation has dissolved the religious instincts; so that they no longer know what purpose religions serve, and only note their existence in the world with a kind of dull astonishment. They feel themselves already fully occupied, these good people, be it by their business or by their pleasures, not to mention the

"Fatherland," and the newspapers, and their "family duties"; it seems that they have no time whatever left for religion; and above all, it is not obvious to them whether it is a question of a new business or a new pleasure—for it is impossible, they say to themselves, that people should go to church merely to spoil their tempers. They are by no means enemies of religious customs; should certain circumstances, State affairs perhaps, require their participation in such customs, they do what is required, as so many things are done—with a patient and unassuming seriousness, and without much curiosity or discomfort;— they live too much apart and outside to feel even the necessity for a *for* or *against* in such matters. Among those indifferent persons may be reckoned nowadays the majority of German Protestants of the middle classes, especially in the great laborious centres of trade and commerce; also the majority of laborious scholars, and the entire University personnel (with the exception of the theologians, whose existence and possibility there always gives psychologists new and more subtle puzzles to solve). On the part of pious, or merely church-going people, there is seldom any idea of *how much* goodwill, one might say arbitrary will, is now necessary for a German scholar to take the problem of religion seriously; his whole profession (and as I have said, his whole workmanlike laboriousness, to which he is compelled by his modern conscience) inclines him to a lofty and almost charitable serenity as regards religion, with which is occasionally mingled a slight disdain for the "uncleanliness" of spirit which he takes for granted wherever any one still professes to belong to the Church. It is only with the help of history (*not* through his own personal experience, therefore) that the scholar succeeds in bringing himself to a respectful seriousness, and to a certain timid deference in presence of religions; but even when his sentiments have reached the stage of gratitude towards them, he has not personally advanced one step nearer to that which still maintains itself as Church or as piety; perhaps even the contrary. The practical indifference to religious matters in the midst of which he has been born and brought up, usually sublimates itself in his case into circumspection and cleanliness, which shuns contact with religious men and things; and it may be just the depth of his tolerance and humanity which prompts him to avoid the delicate trouble which tolerance itself brings with it. —Every age has its own divine type of naïveté, for the discovery of which other ages may envy it: and how much naïveté—adorable, childlike, and boundlessly foolish naïveté—is involved in this belief of the scholar in his superiority, in the good conscience of his tolerance, in the unsuspecting, simple certainty with which his instinct treats the religious man as a lower and less valuable type, beyond, before, and *above* which he himself has developed—he, the little arrogant dwarf and mob-man, the sedulously alert, head-and-hand drudge of "ideas," of "modern ideas"!

59.

Whoever has seen deeply into the world has doubtless divined what wisdom there is in the fact that men are superficial. It is their preservative instinct which teaches them to be flighty, lightsome, and false. Here and there one finds a passionate and exaggerated adoration of "pure forms" in philosophers as well as in artists: it is not to be doubted that whoever has *need* of the cult of the superficial to that extent, has at one time or another made an unlucky dive *beneath* it. Perhaps there is even an order of rank with respect to those burnt children, the born artists who find the enjoyment of life only in trying to *falsify* its image (as if taking wearisome revenge on it); one might guess to what degree life has disgusted them, by the extent to which they wish to see its image falsified, attenuated, ultrified, and deified;— one might reckon the *homines religiosi* amongst the artists, as their *highest* rank. It is the profound, suspicious fear of an incurable pessimism which compels whole centuries to fasten their teeth into a religious interpretation of existence: the fear of the instinct which divines that truth might be attained *too soon*, before man has become strong enough, hard enough, artist enough. ... Piety, the "Life in God," regarded in this light, would appear as the most elaborate and ultimate product of the *fear* of truth, as artist-adoration and artist-intoxication in presence of the most logical of all falsifications, as the will to the inversion of truth, to untruth at any price. Perhaps there has hitherto been no more effective means of beautifying man than piety; by means of it man can become so artful, so superficial, so iridescent, and so good, that his appearance no longer offends.

60.

To love mankind *for God's sake*—this has so far been the noblest and remotest sentiment to which mankind has attained. That love to mankind, without any redeeming intention in the background, is only an *additional* folly and brutishness, that the inclination to this love has first to get its proportion, its delicacy, its grain of salt and sprinkling of ambergris from a higher inclination:—whoever first perceived and "experienced" this, however his tongue may have stammered as it attempted to express such a delicate matter, let him for all time be holy and respected, as the man who has so far flown highest and gone astray in the finest fashion!

61.

The philosopher, as *we* free spirits understand him—as the man of the greatest responsibility, who has the conscience for the general development of mankind,—will use religion for his disciplining and educating work, just as he will use the contemporary political and economic conditions. The selecting and disciplining influence—destructive, as well as creative and fashioning—which can be exercised by means of religion is manifold and varied, according to the sort of people placed under its spell and protection. For those who are strong and independent, destined and trained to command, in whom the judgment and skill of a ruling race is incorporated, religion is an additional means for overcoming resistance in the exercise of authority—as a bond which binds rulers and subjects in common, betraying and surrendering to the former the conscience of the latter, their inmost heart, which would fain escape obedience. And in the case of the unique natures of noble origin, if by virtue of superior spirituality they should incline to a more retired and contemplative life, reserving to themselves only the more refined forms of government (over chosen disciples or members of an order), religion itself may be used as a means for obtaining peace from the noise and trouble of managing *grosser* affairs, and for securing immunity from the *unavoidable* filth of all political agitation. The Brahmins, for instance, understood this fact. With the help of a religious organisation, they secured to themselves the power of nominating kings for the people, while their sentiments prompted them to keep apart and outside, as men with a higher and super-regal mission. At the same time religion gives inducement and opportunity to some of the subjects to qualify themselves for future ruling and commanding: the slowly ascending ranks and classes, in which, through fortunate marriage customs, volitional power and delight in self-control are on the increase. To them religion offers sufficient incentives and temptations to aspire to higher intellectuality, and to experience the sentiments of authoritative self-control, of silence, and of solitude. Asceticism and Puritanism are almost indispensable means of educating and ennobling a race which seeks to rise above its hereditary baseness and work itself upward to future supremacy. And finally, to ordinary men, to the majority of the people, who exist for service and general utility, and are only so far entitled to exist, religion gives invaluable contentedness with their lot and condition, peace of heart, ennoblement of obedience, additional social happiness and sympathy, with something of transfiguration and embellishment, something of justification of all the commonplaceness, all the meanness, all the semi-animal poverty of their souls. Religion, together with the religious significance of life, sheds sunshine over such perpetually harassed men, and makes even their own aspect endurable to them; it operates upon them as the Epicurean philosophy usually operates upon sufferers of a higher order, in a refreshing and refining manner, almost *turning* suffering *to account*, and in the end even hallowing and vindicating it. There is perhaps nothing so admirable in Christianity and Buddhism as their art of teaching even the lowest to elevate themselves by piety to a seemingly higher order of things, and thereby to retain their satisfaction with the actual world in which they find it difficult enough to live—this very difficulty being necessary.

62.

To be sure—to make also the bad counter-reckoning against such religions, and to bring to light their secret dangers—the cost is always excessive and terrible when religions do *not* operate as an educational and disciplinary medium in the hands of the philosopher, but rule voluntarily and *paramountly*, when they wish to be the final end, and not a means along with other means. Among men, as among all other animals, there is a surplus of defective, diseased, degenerating, infirm, and necessarily suffering individuals; the successful cases, among men also, are always the exception; and in view of the fact that man is *the animal not yet properly adapted to his environment*, the rare exception. But worse still. The higher the type a man represents, the greater is the improbability that he will *succeed;* the accidental, the law of irrationality in the general constitution of mankind, manifests itself most terribly in its destructive effect on the higher orders of men, the conditions of whose lives are delicate, diverse, and difficult to determine. What, then, is the attitude of the two greatest religions above-mentioned to the *surplus* of failures in life? They endeavour to preserve and keep alive whatever can be preserved ; in fact, as the religions *for sufferers*, they take the part of these upon principle; they are always in favour of those who suffer from life as from a disease, and they would fain treat every other experience of life as false and impossible. However highly we may esteem this indulgent and preservative care (inasmuch as in applying to others, it has applied, and applies also to the highest and usually the most suffering type of man), the hitherto *paramount* religions—to give a general appreciation of them—are among the principal causes which have kept the type of "man" upon a lower level—they have preserved too much *that which should have perished.* One has to thank them for invaluable services; and who is sufficiently rich in gratitude not to feel poor at the contemplation of all that the "spiritual men" of Christianity have done for Europe hitherto! But when they had given comfort to the sufferers, courage to the oppressed and despairing, a staff and support to the helpless, and when they had allured from society into convents and spiritual penitentiaries the broken-hearted and distracted: what else had they to do in order to work systematically in that fashion, and with a good conscience, for the preservation of all the sick and suffering, which means, in deed and in truth, to work for *the deterioration of the European race?* To *reverse* all estimates of value—*that* is what they had to do! And to shatter the strong, to spoil great hopes, to cast suspicion on the delight in beauty, to break down everything autonomous, manly, conquering, and imperious—all instincts which are natural to the highest and most successful type of "man"—into uncertainty, distress of conscience, and self-destruction; forsooth, to invert all love of the earthly and of supremacy over the earth, into hatred of the earth and earthly things—*that* is the task the Church imposed on itself, and was obliged to impose, until, according to its standard of value, "unworldiness," "unsensuousness," and "higher man" fused into one sentiment. If one could observe the strangely painful, equally coarse and refined comedy of European Christianity with the derisive and impartial eye of an Epicurean god, I should think one would never cease marvelling and laughing; does it not actually seem that some single will has ruled over Europe for eighteen centuries in order to make a *sublime abortion* of man? He, however who, with opposite requirements (no longer Epicurean) and with some divine hammer in his hand, could approach this almost voluntary degeneration and stunting of mankind, as exemplified in the European Christian (Pascal, for instance), would he not have to cry aloud with rage, pity, and horror: "Oh, you bunglers, presumptuous pitiful bunglers, what have you done! Was that a work for your hands? How you have hacked and botched my finest stone! What have *you* presumed to do!"—I should say that Christianity has hitherto been the most portentous of presumptions. Men, not great enough, nor hard enough, to be entitled as artists to take part in fashioning *man;* men, not sufficiently strong and far-sighted to *allow,* with sublime self-constraint, the obvious law of the thousandfold failures and perishings to prevail; men, not sufficiently noble to see the radically different grades of rank and intervals of rank that separate man from man:— *such* men, with their "equality before God," have hitherto swayed the destiny of Europe; until at last a dwarfed, almost ludicrous species has been produced, a gregarious animal, something obliging, sickly, mediocre, the European of the present day.

*   *   *   *   *

104.

Not their love of humanity, but the impotence of their love, prevents the Christians of today—burning us.

168.

Christianity gave Eros poison to drink; he did not die of it, certainly, but degenerated to Vice.

191.

The old theological problem of "Faith" and "Knowledge," or more plainly, of instinct and reason—the question whether, in respect to the valuation of things, instinct deserves more authority than rationality, which wants to appreciate and act according to motives, according to a "Why," that is to say, in conformity to purpose and utility—it is always the old moral problem that first appeared in the person of Socrates, and had divided men's minds long before Christianity. Socrates himself, following, of course, the taste of his talent—that of a surpassing dialectician—took first the side of reason; and, in fact, what did he do all his life but laugh at the awkward incapacity of the noble Athenians, who were men of instinct, like all noble men, and could never give satisfactory answers concerning the motives of their actions? In the end, however, though silently and secretly, he laughed also at himself: with his finer conscience and introspection, he found in himself the same difficulty and incapacity. "But why"—he said to himself—"should one on that account separate oneself from the instincts! One must set them right, and the reason *also*—one must follow the instincts, but at the same time persuade the reason to support them with good arguments." This was the real *falseness* of that great and mysterious ironist; he brought his conscience up to the point that he was satisfied with a kind of self-outwitting: in fact, he perceived the irrationality in the moral judgment.

Plato, more innocent in such matters, and without the craftiness of the plebeian, wished to prove to himself, at the expenditure of all his strength—the greatest strength a philosopher had ever expended —that reason and instinct lead spontaneously to one goal, to the good, to "God"; and since Plato, all theologians and philosophers have followed the same path—which means that in matters of morality, instinct (or as Christians call it, "Faith," or as I call it, "the herd") has hitherto triumphed. Unless one should make an exception in the case of Descartes, the father of rationalism (and consequently the grandfather of the Revolution), who recognized only the authority of reason: but reason is only a tool, and Descartes was superficial.

202.

Let us at once say again what we have already said a hundred times, for people's ears nowadays are unwilling to hear such truths—

our truths. We know well enough how offensive it sounds when any one plainly, and without metaphor, counts man among the animals, but it will be accounted to us almost a *crime*, that it is precisely in respect to men of "modern ideas" that we have constantly applied the terms "herd," "herd-instincts," and such like expressions. What avail is it? We cannot do otherwise, for it is precisely here that our new insight is. We have found that in all the principal moral judgments, Europe has become unanimous, including likewise the countries where European influence prevails in Europe people evidently *know* what Socrates thought he did not know, and what the famous serpent of old once promised to teach—they "know" today what is good and evil. It must then sound hard and be distasteful to the ear, when we always insist that that which here thinks it knows, that which here glorifies itself with praise and blame, and calls itself good, is the instinct of the herding human animal, the instinct which has come and is ever coming more and more to the front, to preponderance and supremacy over other instincts, according to the increasing physiological approximation and resemblance of which it is the symptom. *Morality in Europe at present is herding-animal morality,* and therefore, as we understand the matter, only one kind of human morality, beside which, before which, and after which many other moralities, and above all *higher* moralities, are or should be possible. Against such a "possibility," against such a "should be," however, this morality defends itself with all its strength, it says obstinately and inexorably "I am morality itself and nothing else is morality!" Indeed, with the help of a religion which has humoured and flattered the sublimest desires of the herding-animal, things have reached such a point that we always find a more visible expression of this morality even in political and social arrangements: the *democractic* movement is the inheritance of the Christian movement. That its *tempo*, however, is much too slow and sleepy for the more impatient ones, for those who are sick and distracted by the herding-instinct, is indicated by the increasingly furious howling, and always less disguised teeth-gnashing of the anarchist dogs, who are now roving through the highways of European culture. Apparently in opposition to the peacefully industrious democrats and Revolution-ideologues, and still more so to the awkward philosophasters and fraternity-visionaries who call themselves Socialists and want a "free society," those are really at one with them all in their thorough and instinctive hostility to every form of society other than that of the *autonomous* herd (to the extent even of repudiating the notions "master" and "servant"—*ni dieu ni maitre*,[48] says a socialist formula); at one in their tenacious opposition to every special claim, every special right and privilege (this means ultimately opposition to *every* right, for when all are equal, no one needs "rights" any longer); at one in their distrust of punitive justice (as though it were a violation of the weak, unfair to the *necessary* consequences of all former society); but equally at one in their religion of sympathy, in their compassion for all that feels, lives, and suffers (down to the very animals, up even to "God"—the extravagance of "sympathy for God" belongs to a democratic age); altogether at one in the cry and impatience of their sympathy, in their deadly hatred of suffering generally, in their almost feminine incapacity for witnessing it or *allowing* it; at one in their involuntary beglooming and heart-softening, under the spell of which Europe seems to be threatened with a new Buddhism; at one in their belief in the morality of *mutual* sympathy, as though it were morality in itself, the climax, the *attained* climax of mankind, the sole hope of the future, the consolation of the present, the great discharge from all the obligations of the past; altogether at one in their belief in the community as the *deliverer*, in the herd, and therefore in "themselves."

222.

Wherever sympathy (fellow-suffering) is preached nowadays— and, if I gather rightly, no other religion is any longer preached—let the psychologist have his ears open through all the vanity, through all the noise which is natural to these preachers (as to all preachers), he will hear a hoarse, groaning, genuine note of *self-contempt*. It belongs to the overshadowing and uglifying of Europe, which has been on the increase for a century (the first symptoms of which are already specified documentarily in a thoughtful letter of Galiani to Madame d'Epinay)—*if it is not really the cause thereof!* The man of "modern ideas," the conceited ape, is excessively dissatisfied with himself—this is perfectly certain. He suffers, and his vanity wants him only "to suffer with his fellows."

---

[48] neither God nor master

229.

In these later ages, which may be proud of their humanity, there still remains so much fear, so much *superstition* of the fear, of the "cruel wild beast," the mastering of which constitutes the very pride of these humaner ages—that even obvious truths, as if by the agreement of centuries, have long remained unuttered, because they have the appearance of helping the finally slain wild beast back to life again. I perhaps risk something when I allow such a truth to escape; let others capture it again and give it so much "milk of pious sentiment"[49] to drink, that it will lie down quiet and forgotten, in its old corner.

One ought to learn anew about cruelty, and open one's eyes; one ought at last to learn impatience, in order that such immodest gross errors—as, for instance, have been fostered by ancient and modern philosophers with regard to tragedy—may no longer wander about virtuously and boldly. Almost everything that we call "higher culture" is based upon the spiritualising and intensifying of *cruelty*—this is my thesis; the "wild beast" has not been slain at all, it lives, it flourishes, it has only been—transfigured. That which constitutes the painful delight of tragedy is cruelty; that which operates agreeably in so-called tragic sympathy, and at the basis even of everything sublime, up to the highest and most delicate thrills of metaphysics, obtains its sweetness solely from the intermingled ingredient of cruelty. What the Roman enjoys in the arena, the Christian in the ecstasies of the cross, the Spaniard at the sight of the faggot and stake, or of the bull-fight, the present-day Japanese who presses his way to the tragedy, the workman of the Parisian suburbs who has a homesickness for bloody revolutions, the Wagnerienne who, with unhinged will, "undergoes" the performance of *Tristan and Isolde*—what all these enjoy, and strive with mysterious ardour to drink in, is the philtre of the great Circe "cruelty."

Here, to be sure, we must put aside entirely the blundering psychology of former times, which could only teach with regard to cruelty that it originated at the sight of the suffering of *others*: there is an abundant, super-abundant enjoyment even in one's own suffering, in causing one's own suffering—and wherever man has allowed himself to be persuaded to self-denial in the *religious* sense, or to self-

---

[49] An expression from Schiller's William Tell, Act IV, Scene 3.

mutilation, as among the Phoenicians and ascetics, or in general, to desensualisation, decarnalisation, and contrition, to Puritanical repentance-spasms, to vivisection of conscience and to Pascal-like *sacrifizia dell' intelleto,*[50] he is secretly allured and impelled forwards by his cruelty, by the dangerous thrill of cruelty *towards himself.*

Finally, let us consider that even the seeker of knowledge operates as an artist and glorifier of cruelty, in that he compels his spirit to perceive *against* its own inclination, and often enough against the wishes of his heart:—he forces it to say Nay, where he would like to affirm, love, and adore; indeed, every instance of taking a thing profoundly and fundamentally, is a violation, an intentional injuring of the fundamental will of the spirit, which instinctively aims at appearance and superficiality,—even in every desire for knowledge there is a drop of cruelty.

263.

There is an *instinct for rank,* which more than anything else is already the sign of a *high* rank; there is a *delight* in the *nuances* of reverence which leads one to infer noble origin and habits. The refinement, goodness, and loftiness of a soul are put to a perilous test when something passes by that is of the highest rank, but is not yet protected by the awe of authority from obtrusive touches and incivilities: something that goes its way like a living touchstone, undistinguished, undiscovered, and tentative, perhaps voluntarily veiled and disguised. He whose task and practice it is to investigate souls, will avail himself of many varieties of this very art to determine the ultimate value of a soul, the unalterable, innate order of rank to which it belongs: he will test it by its *instinct for reverence. Difference engendre haine:* the vulgarity of many a nature spurts up suddenly like dirty water, when any holy vessel, any jewel from closed shrines, any book bearing the marks of great destiny, is brought before it; while on the other hand, there is an involuntary silence, a hesitation of the eye, a cessation of all gestures, by which it is indicated that a soul *feels* the nearness of what is worthiest of respect. The way in which, on the whole, the reverence for the *Bible* has hitherto been maintained in Europe, is perhaps the best example of discipline and refinement of

---

[50] sacrifice of the intellect

manners which Europe owes to Christianity: books of such profoundness and supreme significance require for their protection an external tyranny of authority, in order to acquire the *period* of thousands of years which is necessary to exhaust and unriddle them Much has been achieved when the sentiment has been at last instilled into the masses (the shallow-pates and the boobies of every kind) tha: they are not allowed to touch everything, that there are holy experiences before which they must take off their shoes and keep away the unclean hand—it is almost their highest advance towards humanity. On the contrary. in the so-called cultured classes, the believers in "modern ideas," nothing is perhaps so repulsive as their lack of shame, the easy insolence of eye and hand with which they touch, taste, and finger everything; and it is possible that even yet there is more *relative* nobility of taste, and more tact for reverence among the people, among the lower classes of the people, especially among peasants, than among the newspaper-reading *demimonde* of intellect, the cultured class.

from ON THE GENEALOGY OF MORALS

Preface

3.

Owing to a scrupulosity peculiar to myself, which I confess reluctantly,—it concerns indeed *morality*,—a scrupulosity, which manifests itself in my life at such an early period, with so much spontaneity, with so chronic a persistence and so keen an opposition to environment, epoch, precedent, and ancestry that I should have been almost entitled to style it my "*â priori*"—my curiosity and my suspicion felt themselves betimes bound to halt at the question, of what in point of actual fact was the *origin* of our "Good" and of our "Evil." Indeed, at the boyish age of thirteen the problem of the origin of Evil already haunted me: at an age "when games and God divide one's heart," I devoted to that problem my first childish attempt at the literary game, my first philosophic essay—and as regards my infantile solution of the problem, well, I gave quite properly the honour to God, and made him the *father* of evil. Did my own "*â priori*" demand that precise solution from me? that new, immoral, or at least "amoral" "*â priori*" and that "categorical imperative" which was its voice (but oh! how hostile to the Kantian article, and how pregnant with problems!), to which since then I have given more and more attention, and indeed what is more than attention. Fortunately I soon learned to separate theological from moral prejudices, and I gave up looking for a *supernatural* origin of evil. A certain amount of historical and philological education, to say nothing of an innate faculty of psychological discrimination *par excellence* succeeded in transforming almost immediately my original problem into the following one:— Under what conditions did Man invent for himself those judgments of values, "Good" and "Evil"? *And what intrinsic value do they possess in themselves?* Have they up to the present hindered or advanced human well-being? Are they a symptom of the distress, impoverishment, and degeneration of Human Life? Or, conversely, is it in them that is manifested the fulness, the strength, and the will of Life, its courage, its self-confidence, its future? On this point I found and hazarded in my mind the most diverse answers, I established distinctions in periods, peoples, and castes, I became a specialist in my problem, and from my answers grew new questions, new investigations, new conjectures, new probabilities; until at last I had a land of my own and a soil of my own, a whole secret world growing and flowering, like hidden gardens of whose existence no one could have an inkling —oh, how happy are we, we finders of knowledge, provided that we know how to keep silent sufficiently long.

5.

In reality I had set my heart at that time on something much more important than the nature of the theories of myself or others concerning the origin of morality (or, more precisely, the real function from my view of these theories was to point an end to which they were one among many means). The issue for me was the value of morality, and on that subject I had to place myself in a state of abstraction, in which I was almost alone with my great teacher Schopenhauer, to whom that book, with all its passion and inherent contradiction (for that book also was a polemic), turned for present help as though he were still alive. The issue was, strangely enough, the value of the "un-egoistic" instincts, the instincts of pity, self-denial, and self-sacrifice which Schopenhauer had so persistently painted in golden colours, deified and etherealised, that eventually they appeared to him, as it were, high and dry, as "intrinsic values in themselves," on the strength of which he uttered both to Life and to himself his own negation. But against *these very* instincts there voiced itself in my soul a more and more fundamental mistrust, a scepticism that dug ever deeper and deeper: and in this very instinct I saw the *great* danger of mankind, its most sublime temptation and seduction—seduction to what? to nothingness?—in these very instincts I saw the beginning of the end, stability, the exhaustion that gazes backwards, the will turning *against* Life, the last illness announcing itself with its own mincing melancholy: I realised that the morality of pity which spread wider and wider, and whose grip infected even philosophers with its disease, was the most sinister symptom of our modern European civilisation; I realised that it was the route along which that civilisation slid on its way to—a new Buddhism?—a European Buddhism?—*Nihilism?* This exaggerated estimation in which modern philosophers have held pity, is quite a new phenomenon: up to that time philosophers were

135

absolutely unanimous as to the *worthlessness* of pity. I need only mention Plato, Spinoza, La Rochefoucauld, and Kant—four minds as mutually different as is possible, but united on one point; their contempt of pity.

6.

This problem of the value of pity and of the pity-morality (I am an opponent of the modern infamous emasculation of our emotions) seems at the first blush a mere isolated problem, a note of interrogation for itself; he, however, who once halts at this problem, and learns how to put questions, will experience what I experienced: —a new and immense vista unfolds itself before him, a sense of potentiality seizes him like a vertigo, every species of doubt, mistrust, and fear springs up, the belief in morality, nay, in all morality, totters, —finally a new demand voices itself. Let us speak out this *new demand*: we need a *critique* of moral values, *the value of these values* is for the first time to be called into question—and for this purpose a knowledge is necessary of the conditions and circumstances out of which these values grew, and under which they experienced their evolution and their distortion (morality as a result, as a symptom, as a mask, as Tartuffism, as disease, as a misunderstanding; but also morality as a cause, as a remedy, as a stimulant, as a fetter, as a drug), especially as such a knowledge has neither existed up to the present time nor is even now generally desired. The value of these "values" was taken for granted as an indisputable fact, which was beyond all question. No one has, up to the present, exhibited the faintest doubt or hesitation in judging the "good man" to be of a higher value than the "evil man," of a higher value with regard specifically to human progress, utility, and prosperity generally, not forgetting the future. What? Suppose the converse were the truth! What? Suppose there lurked in the "good man" a symptom of retrogression, such as a danger, a temptation, a poison, a *narcotic*, by means of which the present *battened on the future*! More comfortable and less risky perhaps than its opposite, but also pettier, meaner! So that morality would really be saddled with the guilt, if the *maximum potentiality of the power and splendour* of the human species were never to be attained? So that really morality would be the danger of dangers?

FIRST ESSAY.
"GOOD AND EVIL," "GOOD AND BAD."

1.

Those English psychologists, who up to the present are the only philosophers who are to be thanked for any endeavour to get as far as a history of the origin of morality—these men, I say, offer us in their own personalities no paltry problem;—they even have, if I am to be quite frank about it, in their capacity of living riddles, an advantage over their books—*they themselves are interesting!* These English psychologists—what do they really mean? We always find them voluntarily or involuntarily at the same task of pushing to the front the *partie honteuse*[51] of our inner world, and looking for the efficient, governing, and decisive principle in that precise quarter where the intellectual self-respect of the race would be the most reluctant to find it (for example, in the *vis inertiæ* of habit, or in forgetfulness, or in a blind and fortuitous mechanism and association of ideas, or in some factor that is purely passive, reflex, molecular, or fundamentally stupid)—what is the real motive power which always impels these psychologists in precisely *this* direction? Is it an instinct for human disparagement somewhat sinister, vulgar, and malignant, or perhaps incomprehensible even to itself? or perhaps a touch of pessimistic jealousy, the mistrust of disillusioned idealists who have become gloomy, poisoned, and bitter? or a petty subconscious enmity and rancour against Christianity (and Plato), that has conceivably never crossed the threshold of consciousness? or just a vicious taste for those elements of life which are bizarre, painfully paradoxical, mystical, and illogical? or, as a final alternative, a dash of each of these motives—a little vulgarity, a little gloominess, a little anti-Christianity, a little craving for the necessary piquancy?

But I am told that it is simply a case of old frigid and tedious frogs crawling and hopping around men and inside men, as if they were as thoroughly at home there, as they would be in a *swamp*.

I am opposed to this statement, nay, I do not believe it; and if, in the impossibility of knowledge, one is permitted to wish, so do I wish

---

[51] shameful part

from my heart that just the converse metaphor should apply, and that these analysts with their psychological microscopes should be, at bottom, brave, proud, and magnanimous animals who know how to bridle both their hearts and their smarts, and have specifically trained themselves to sacrifice what is desirable to what is true, *any* truth in fact, even the simple, bitter, ugly, repulsive, unchristian, and immoral truths—for there are truths of that description.

2.

All honour, then, to the noble spirits who would fain dominate these historians of morality. But it is certainly a pity that they lack the *historical sense* itself, that they themselves are quite deserted by all the beneficent spirits of history. The whole train of their thought runs, as was always the way of old-fashioned philosophers, on *thoroughly* unhistorical lines: there is no doubt on this point. The crass ineptitude of their genealogy of morals is immediately apparent when the question arises of ascertaining the origin of the idea and judgment of "good." "Man had originally," so speaks their decree, "praised and called 'good' altruistic acts from the standpoint of those on whom they were conferred, that is, those to whom they were *useful*; subsequently the origin of this praise was *forgotten*, and altruistic acts, simply because, as a sheer matter of habit, they were praised as good, came also to be felt as good—as though they contained in themselves some intrinsic goodness." The thing is obvious:—this initial derivation contains already all the typical and idiosyncratic traits of the English psychologists—we have "utility," "forgetting," "habit," and finally "error," the whole assemblage forming the basis of a system of values, on which the higher man has up to the present prided himself as though it were a kind of privilege of man in general. This pride *must* be brought low, this system of values *must* lose its values: is that attained?

Now the first argument that comes ready to my hand is that the real homestead of the concept "good" is sought and located in the wrong place: the judgment "good" did *not* originate among those to whom goodness was shown. Much rather has it been the good themselves, that is, the aristocratic, the powerful, the high-stationed, the high-minded, who have felt that they themselves were good, and that their actions were good, that is to say of the first order, in contradistinction to all the low, the low-minded, the vulgar, and the plebeian. It was out of this pathos of distance that they first arrogated the right to create values for their own profit, and to coin the names of such values: what had they to do with utility? The standpoint of utility is as alien and as inapplicable as it could possibly be, when we have to deal with so volcanic an effervescence of supreme values, creating and demarcating as they do a hierarchy within themselves: it is at this juncture that one arrives at an appreciation of the contrast to that tepid temperature, which is the presupposition on which every combination of worldly wisdom and every calculation of practical expediency is always based—and not for one occasional, not for one exceptional instance, but chronically. The pathos of nobility and distance, as I have said, the chronic and despotic *esprit de corps* and fundamental instinct of a higher dominant race coming into association with a meaner race, an "under race," this is the origin of the antithesis of good and bad.

(The masters' right of giving names goes so far that it is permissible to look upon language itself as the expression of the power of the masters: they say "this *is* that, and that," they seal finally every object and every event with a sound, and thereby at the same time take possession of it.) It is because of this origin that the word "good" is far from having any necessary connection with altruistic acts, in accordance with the superstitious belief of these moral philosophers. On the contrary, it is on the occasion of the *decay* of aristocratic values, that the antitheses between "egoistic" and "altruistic" presses more and more heavily on the human conscience —it is, to use my own language, the *herd instinct* which finds in this antithesis an expression in many ways. And even then it takes a considerable time for this instinct to become sufficiently dominant, for the valuation to be inextricably dependent on this antithesis (as is the case in contemporary Europe); for today that prejudice is predominant, which, acting even now with all the intensity of an obsession and brain disease, holds that "moral," "altruistic," and "*désintéressé*" are concepts of equal value.

3.

In the second place, quite apart from the fact that this hypothesis as to the genesis of the value "good" cannot be historically upheld, it suffers from an inherent psychological contradiction. The utility of altruistic conduct has presumably been the origin of its being praised, and this origin has become *forgotten*:—But in what conceivable way is this forgetting *possible*! Has perchance the utility of such conduct ceased at some given moment? The contrary is the case. This utility has rather been experienced every day at all times, and is consequently a feature that obtains a new and regular emphasis with every fresh day; it follows that, so far from vanishing from the consciousness, so far indeed from being forgotten, it must necessarily become impressed on the consciousness with ever-increasing distinctness. How much more logical is that contrary theory (it is not the truer for that) which is represented, for instance, by Herbert Spencer, who places the concept "good" as essentially similar to the concept "useful," "purposive," so that in the judgments "good" and "bad" mankind is simply summarising and investing with a sanction its *unforgotten* and *unforgettable* experiences concerning the "useful-purposive" and the "mischievous-non-purposive." According to this theory, "good" is the attribute of that which has previously shown itself useful; and so is able to claim to be considered "valuable in the highest degree," "valuable in itself." This method of explanation is also, as I have said, wrong, but at any rate the explanation itself is coherent, and psychologically tenable.

4.

The guide-post which first put me on the *right* track was this question—what is the true etymological significance of the various symbols for the idea "good" which have been coined in the various languages? I then found that they all led back to *the same evolution of the same idea*—that everywhere "aristocrat," "noble" (in the social sense), is the root idea, out of which have necessarily developed "good" in the sense of "with aristocratic soul," "noble," in the sense of "with a soul of high calibre," "with a privileged soul"—a development which invariably runs parallel with that other evolution by which "vulgar," "plebeian," "low," are made to change finally into "bad." The most eloquent proof of this last contention is the German word "*schlecht*" [bad] itself: this word is identical with "*schlicht*" [plain]—compare "*schlechtweg*" [plainly] and "*schlechterdings*" [simply]—which, originally and as yet without any sinister innuendo, simply denoted the plebeian man in contrast to the aristocratic man. It is at the sufficiently late period of the Thirty Years' War that this sense becomes changed to the sense now current. From the standpoint of the genealogy of morals this discovery seems to be substantial: the lateness of it is to be attributed to the retarding influence exercised in the modern world by democratic prejudice in the sphere of all questions of origin. This extends, as will shortly be shown, even to the province of natural science and physiology, which, *prima facie* is the most objective. The extent of the mischief which is caused by this prejudice (once it is free of all trammels except those of its own malice), particularly to Ethics and History, is shown by the notorious case of Buckle:[52] it was in Buckle that that *plebeianism* of the modern spirit, which is of English origin, broke out once again from its malignant soil with all the violence of a slimy volcano, and with that salted, rampant, and vulgar eloquence with which up to the present time all volcanoes have spoken.

5.

With regard to *our* problem, which can justly be called an *intimate* problem, and which elects to appeal to only a limited number of ears: it is of no small interest to ascertain that in those words and roots which denote "good" we catch glimpses of that arch-trait, on the strength of which the aristocrats feel themselves to be beings of a higher order than their fellows. Indeed, they call themselves in perhaps the most frequent instances simply after their superiority in power (*e.g.* "the powerful," "the lords," "the commanders"), or after the most obvious sign of their superiority, as for example "the rich," "the possessors" (that is the meaning of *arya*; and the Iranian and Slav languages correspond). But they also call themselves after some *characteristic idiosyncrasy*; and this is the case which now concerns us. They name themselves, for instance, "the truthful": this is first done by the Greek nobility whose mouthpiece is found in Theognis, the Megarian poet. The word ἐσθλός [good, brave], which is coined for the purpose, signifies etymologically "one who *is*," who has reality, who is real, who is true; and then with a subjective twist, the "true," as the "truthful": at this stage in the evolution of the idea, it becomes the

---

[52] Henry Thomas Buckle

motto and party cry of the nobility, and quite completes the transition to the meaning "noble," so as to place outside the pale the lying, vulgar man, as Theognis conceives and portrays him—till finally the word after the decay of the nobility is left to delineate psychological *noblesse*, and becomes as it were ripe and mellow.

In the word κακός [bad, ugly] as in δειλός [cowardly, worthless] (the plebeian in contrast to the ἀγαθός [good]) the cowardice is emphasised. This affords perhaps an inkling on what lines the etymological origin of the very ambiguous ἀγαθός is to be investigated. In the Latin *malus* [bad] (which I place side by side with μέλας [dark]) the vulgar man can be distinguished as the dark-coloured, and above all as the black-haired ("*hic niger est*"), as the pre-Aryan inhabitants of the Italian soil, whose complexion formed the clearest feature of distinction from the dominant blondes, namely, the Aryan conquering race:—at any rate Gaelic has afforded me the exact analogue—*Fin* (for instance, in the name *Fin-Gal*), the distinctive word of the nobility, finally—good, noble, clean, but originally the blonde-haired man in contrast to the dark black-haired aboriginals.

The Celts, if I may make a parenthetic statement, were throughout a blonde race; and it is wrong to connect, as Virchow[53] still connects, those traces of an essentially dark-haired population which are to be seen on the more elaborate ethnographical maps of Germany with any Celtic ancestry or with any admixture of Celtic blood: in this context it is rather the *pre-Aryan* population of Germany which surges up to these districts. (The same is true substantially of the whole of Europe: in point of fact, the subject race has finally again obtained the upper hand, in complexion and the shortness of the skull, and perhaps in the intellectual and social qualities. Who can guarantee that modern democracy, still more modern anarchy, and indeed that tendency to the "Commune," the most primitive form of society, which is now common to all the Socialists in Europe, does not in its real essence signify a monstrous reversion—and that the conquering and *master* race—the Aryan race, is not also becoming inferior physiologically?) I believe that I can explain the Latin *bonus* as the "warrior": my hypothesis is that I am right in deriving *bonus* [good] from an older *duonus* (compare *bellum* = *duellum* = *duen-lum*, in

---

[53] Rudolf Virchow

which the word *duonus* appears to me to be contained). *Bonus* accordingly as the man of discord, of variance, "entzweiung" [division] (*duo*), as the warrior: one sees what in ancient Rome "the good" meant for a man. Must not our actual German word *gut* mean "*the godlike, the* man of godlike race"? and be identical with the national name (originally the nobles' name) of the *Goths*? The grounds for this supposition do not appertain to this work.

6.

Above all, there is no exception (though there are opportunities for exceptions) to this rule, that the idea of political superiority always resolves itself into the idea of psychological superiority, in those cases where the highest caste is at the same time the *priestly* caste, and in accordance with its general characteristics confers on itself the privilege of a title which alludes specifically to its priestly function. It is in these cases, for instance, that "clean" and "unclean" confront each other for the first time as badges of class distinction; here again there develops a "good" and a "bad," in a sense which has ceased to be merely social. Moreover, care should be taken not to take these ideas of "clean" and "unclean" too seriously, too broadly, or too symbolically: all the ideas of ancient man have, on the contrary, got to be understood in their initial stages, in a sense which is, to an almost inconceivable extent, crude, coarse, physical, and narrow, and above all essentially *unsymbolical*. The "clean man" is originally only a man who washes himself, who abstains from certain foods which are conducive to skin diseases, who does not sleep with the unclean women of the lower classes, who has a horror of blood—not more, not much more! On the other hand, the very nature of a priestly aristocracy shows the reasons why just at such an early juncture there should ensue a really dangerous sharpening and intensification of opposed values: it is, in fact, through these opposed values that gulfs are cleft in the social plane, which a veritable Achilles of free thought would shudder to cross. There is from the outset a certain *diseased taint* in such sacerdotal aristocracies, and in the habits which prevail in such societies—habits which, *averse* as they are to action, constitute a compound of introspection and explosive emotionalism, as a result of which there appears that introspective morbidity and neurasthenia, which adheres almost inevitably to all priests at all times: with regard, however, to the remedy which they themselves have invented for this disease—the philosopher has no option but to state, that it has proved itself in its effects a hundred times more dangerous than the disease, from which it should have been the deliverer.

Humanity itself is still diseased from the effects of the naïvetés of this priestly cure. Take, for instance, certain kinds of diet (abstention from flesh), fasts, sexual continence, flight into the wilderness (a kind of Weir-Mitchell isolation, though of course without that system of excessive feeding and fattening which is the most efficient antidote to all the hysteria of the ascetic ideal); consider too the whole metaphysic of the priests, with its war on the senses, its enervation, its hair-splitting; consider its self-hypnotism on the fakir and Brahman principles (it uses Brahman as a glass disc and obsession), and that climax which we can understand only too well of an unusual satiety with its panacea of *nothingness* (or God:—the demand for a *unio mystica* with God is the demand of the Buddhist for nothingness, Nirvana—and nothing else!). In sacerdotal societies *every* element is on a more dangerous scale, not merely cures and remedies, but also pride, revenge, cunning, exaltation, love, ambition, virtue, morbidity:—further, it can fairly be stated that it is on the soil of this *essentially dangerous* form of human society, the sacerdotal form, that man really becomes for the first time an *interesting animal,* that it is in this form that the soul of man has in a higher sense attained *depths* and become *evil* —and those are the two fundamental forms of the superiority which up to the present man has exhibited over every other animal.

7.

The reader will have already surmised with what ease the priestly mode of valuation can branch off from the knightly aristocratic mode, and then develop into the very antithesis of the latter: special impetus is given to this opposition, by every occasion when the castes of the priests and warriors confront each other with mutual jealousy and cannot agree over the prize. The knightly-aristocratic "values" are based on a careful cult of the physical, on a flowering, rich, and even effervescing healthiness, that goes considerably beyond what is necessary for maintaining life, on war, adventure, the chase, the dance, the tourney—on everything, in fact, which is contained in strong, free, and joyous action. The priestly-aristocratic mode of valuation is—we have seen—based on other hypotheses: it is bad enough for this class when it is a question of war! Yet the priests are, as is notorious, *the worst enemies*—why? Because they are the weakest. Their weakness causes their hate to expand into a monstrous and sinister shape, a shape which is most crafty and most poisonous. The really great haters in the history of the world have always been priests, who are also the cleverest haters—in comparison with the cleverness of priestly revenge, every other piece of cleverness is practically negligible.

Human history would be too fatuous for anything were it not for the cleverness imported into it by the weak—take at once the most important instance. All the world's efforts against the "aristocrats," the "mighty," the "masters," the "holders of power," are negligible by comparison with what has been accomplished against those classes by *the Jews*—the Jews, that priestly nation which eventually realised that the one method of effecting satisfaction on its enemies and tyrants was by means of a radical transvaluation of values, which was at the same time an act of the *cleverest revenge*. Yet the method was only appropriate to a nation of priests, to a nation of the most jealously nursed priestly revengefulness. It was the Jews who, in opposition to the aristocratic equation (good = aristocratic = beautiful = happy = loved by the gods), dared with a terrifying logic to suggest the contrary equation, and indeed to maintain with the teeth of the most profound hatred (the hatred of weakness) this contrary equation, namely, "the wretched are alone the good; the poor, the weak, the lowly, are alone the good; the suffering, the needy, the sick, the loathsome, are the only ones who are pious, the only ones who are blessed, for them alone is salvation—but you, on the other hand, you aristocrats, you men of power, you are to all eternity the evil, the horrible, the covetous, the insatiate, the godless; eternally also shall you be the unblessed, the cursed, the damned!" We know who it was who reaped the heritage of this Jewish transvaluation. In the context of the monstrous and inordinately fateful initiative which the Jews have exhibited in connection with this most fundamental of all declarations of war, I remember the passage which came to my pen on another occasion

145

(*Beyond Good and Evil*, Aph. 195)[54]—that it was, in fact, with the Jews that the *revolt of the slaves* begins in the sphere *of morals*; that revolt which has behind it a history of two millennia, and which at the present day has only moved out of our sight, because it—has achieved victory.

8.

But you understand this not? You have no eyes for a force which has taken two thousand years to achieve victory?—There is nothing wonderful in this: all *lengthy* processes are hard to see and to realise. But *this* is what took place: from the trunk of that tree of revenge and hate, Jewish hate,—that most profound and sublime hate, which creates ideals and changes old values to new creations, the like of which has never been on earth,—there grew a phenomenon which was equally incomparable, *a new love*, the most profound and sublime of all kinds of love;—and from what other trunk could it have grown? But beware of supposing that this love has soared on its upward growth, as in any way a real negation of that thirst for revenge, as an antithesis to the Jewish hate! No, the contrary is the truth! This love grew out of that hate, as its crown, as its triumphant crown, circling wider and wider amid the clarity and fulness of the sun, and pursuing in the very kingdom of light and height its goal of hatred, its victory, its spoil, its strategy, with the same intensity with which the roots of that tree of hate sank into everything which was deep and evil with increasing stability and increasing desire. This Jesus of Nazareth, the incarnate gospel of love, this "Redeemer" bringing salvation and victory to the poor, the sick, the sinful—was he not really temptation in its most sinister and irresistible form, temptation to take the tortuous path to those very *Jewish* values and those very Jewish ideals? Has not Israel really obtained the final goal of its sublime revenge, by

---

[54] "The Jews—a people 'born for slavery,' as Tacitus and the whole ancient world say of them; 'the chosen people among the nations,' as they themselves say and believe— the Jews performed the miracle of the inversion of valuations, by means of which life on earth obtained a new and dangerous charm for a couple of millenniums. Their prophets fused into one the expressions 'rich,' 'godless,' 'wicked,' 'violent,' 'sensual,' and for the first time coined the word 'world' as a term of reproach. In this inversion of valuations (in which is also included the use of the word 'poor' as synonymous with 'saint' and 'friend') the significance of the Jewish people is to be found; it is with *them* that the *slave-insurrection in morals* commences."

the tortuous paths of this "Redeemer," for all that he might pose as Israel's adversary and Israel's destroyer? Is it not due to the black magic of a really *great* policy of revenge, of a far-seeing, burrowing revenge, both acting and calculating with slowness, that Israel himself must repudiate before all the world the actual instrument of his own revenge and nail it to the cross, so that all the world—that is, all the enemies of Israel—could nibble without suspicion at this very bait? Could, moreover, any human mind with all its elaborate ingenuity invent a bait that was more truly *dangerous*? Anything that was even equivalent in the power of its seductive, intoxicating, defiling, and corrupting influence to that symbol of the holy cross, to that awful paradox of a "god on the cross," to that mystery of the unthinkable, supreme, and utter horror of the self-crucifixion of a god for the *salvation of man*? It is at least certain that *sub hoc signo*[55] Israel, with its revenge and transvaluation of all values, has up to the present always triumphed again over all other ideals, over all more aristocratic ideals.

9.

"But why do you talk of nobler ideals? Let us submit to the facts; that the people have triumphed—or the slaves, or the populace, or the herd, or whatever name you care to give them—if this has happened through the Jews, so be it! In that case no nation ever had a greater mission in the world's history. The 'masters' have been done away with; the morality of the vulgar man has triumphed. This triumph may also be called a blood-poisoning (it has mutually fused the races) —I do not dispute it; but there is no doubt but that this intoxication has succeeded. The 'redemption' of the human race (that is, from the masters) is progressing swimmingly; everything is obviously becoming Judaised, or Christianised, or vulgarised (what is there in the words?). It seems impossible to stop the course of this poisoning through the whole body politic of mankind—but its *tempo* and pace may from the present time be slower, more delicate, quieter, more discreet—there is time enough. In view of this context has the Church nowadays any necessary purpose? has it, in fact, a right to live? Or could man get on

---

[55] under this sign

without it? *Quæritur*.[56] It seems that it fetters and retards this tendency, instead of accelerating it. Well, even that might be its utility. The Church certainly is a crude and boorish institution, that is repugnant to an intelligence with any pretence at delicacy, to a really modern taste. Should it not at any rate learn to be somewhat more subtle? It alienates nowadays, more than it allures. Which of us would, forsooth, be a freethinker if there were no Church? It is the Church which repels us, not its poison—apart from the Church we like the poison." This is the epilogue of a freethinker to my discourse, of an honourable animal (as he has given abundant proof), and a democrat to boot; he had up to that time listened to me, and could not endure my silence, but for me, indeed, with regard to this topic there is much on which to be silent.

10.

The revolt of the slaves in morals begins in the very principle of *ressentiment* becoming creative and giving birth to values—a *ressentiment* experienced by creatures who, deprived as they are of the proper outlet of action, are forced to find their compensation in an imaginary revenge. While every aristocratic morality springs from a triumphant affirmation of its own demands, the slave morality says "no" from the very outset to what is "outside itself," "different from itself," and "not itself": and this "no" is its creative deed. This volte-face of the valuing standpoint—this *inevitable* gravitation to the objective instead of back to the subjective—is typical of *ressentiment*: the slave-morality requires as the condition of its existence an external and objective world, to employ physiological terminology, it requires objective stimuli to be capable of action at all—its action is fundamentally a reaction. The contrary is the case when we come to the aristocrat's system of values: it acts and grows spontaneously, it merely seeks its antithesis in order to pronounce a more grateful and exultant "yes" to its own self;—its negative conception, "low," "vulgar," "bad," is merely a pale late-born foil in comparison with its positive and fundamental conception (saturated as it is with life and passion), of "we aristocrats, we good ones, we beautiful ones, we happy ones."

---

[56] the question under consideration

When the aristocratic morality goes astray and commits sacrilege on reality, this is limited to that particular sphere with which it is *not* sufficiently acquainted—a sphere, in fact, from the real knowledge of which it disdainfully defends itself. It misjudges, in some cases, the sphere which it despises, the sphere of the common vulgar man and the low people: on the other hand, due weight should be given to the consideration that in any case the mood of contempt, of disdain, of superciliousness, even on the supposition that it *falsely* portrays the object of its contempt, will always be far removed from that degree of falsity which will always characterise the attacks—in effigy, of course —of the vindictive hatred and revengefulness of the weak in onslaughts on their enemies. In point of fact, there is in contempt too strong an admixture of nonchalance, of casualness, of boredom, of impatience, even of personal exultation, for it to be capable of distorting its victim into a real caricature or a real monstrosity. Attention again should be paid to the almost benevolent *nuances* which, for instance, the Greek nobility imports into all the words by which it distinguishes the common people from itself; note how continuously a kind of pity, care, and consideration imparts its honeyed *flavour*, until at last almost all the words which are applied to the vulgar man survive finally as expressions for "unhappy," "worthy of pity" (compare δειλο, δείλαιος, πονηρός, μοχθηρός; the latter two names really denoting the vulgar man as labour-slave and beast of burden)—and how, conversely, "bad," "low," "unhappy" have never ceased to ring in the Greek ear with a tone in which "unhappy" is the predominant note: this is a heritage of the old noble aristocratic morality, which remains true to itself even in contempt (let philologists remember the sense in which ὀιζυρός, ἄνολβος, τλήμων, δυστυχεῖν, ξυμφορά used to be employed).[57]

The "well-born" simply *felt* themselves the "happy"; they did not have to manufacture their happiness artificially through looking at their enemies, or in cases to talk and *lie themselves* into happiness (as is the custom with all resentful men); and similarly, complete men as they were, exuberant with strength, and consequently *necessarily* energetic, they were too wise to dissociate happiness from action— activity becomes in their minds necessarily counted as happiness (that

---

[57] All words meaning variations of "miserable," "unlucky," "wretched."

is the etymology of εὖ πράττειν[58])—all in sharp contrast to the "happiness" of the weak and the oppressed, with their festering venom and malignity, among whom happiness appears essentially as a narcotic, a deadening, a quietude, a peace, a "Sabbath," an enervation of the mind and relaxation of the limbs,—in short, a purely *passive* phenomenon.[59] While the aristocratic man lived in confidence and openness with himself (γενναῖος, "nobly-born," emphasises the nuance "sincere," and perhaps also "naïve"), the resentful man, on the other hand, is neither sincere nor naïve, nor honest and candid with himself. His soul *squints*; his mind loves hidden crannies, tortuous paths and back-doors, everything secret appeals to him as *his* world, *his* safety, *his* balm; he is past master in silence, in not forgetting, in waiting, in provisional self-depreciation and self-abasement.

A race of such *resentful* men will of necessity eventually prove more *prudent* than any aristocratic race, it will honour prudence on quite a distinct scale, as, in fact, a paramount condition of existence, while prudence among aristocratic men is apt to be tinged with a delicate flavour of luxury and refinement; so among them it plays nothing like so integral a part as that complete certainty of function of the governing *unconscious* instincts, or as indeed a certain lack of prudence, such as a vehement and valiant charge, whether against danger or the enemy, or as those ecstatic bursts of rage, love, reverence, gratitude, by which at all times noble souls have recognised each other. When the resentment of the aristocratic man manifests itself, it fulfils and exhausts itself in an immediate reaction, and consequently instills no *venom*: on the other hand, it never manifests itself at all in countless instances, when in the case of the feeble and weak it would be inevitable. An inability to take seriously for any length of time their enemies, their disasters, their *misdeeds*—that is the sign of the full strong natures who possess a superfluity of moulding plastic force, that heals completely and produces forgetfulness: a good example of this in the modern world is Mirabeau, who had no memory for any insults and meannesses which were practised on him, and who was only incapable of forgiving because he forgot. Such a

---

[58] to do well

[59] See *The Will to Power* sec. 231

man indeed shakes off with a shrug many a worm which would have buried itself in another; it is only in characters like these that we see the possibility (supposing, of course, that there is such a possibility in the world) of the real "*love* of one's enemies." What respect for his enemies is found, forsooth, in an aristocratic man—and such a reverence is already a bridge to love! He insists on having his enemy to himself as his distinction. He tolerates no other enemy but a man in whose character there is nothing to despise and much to honour! On the other hand, imagine the "enemy" as the resentful man conceives him—and it is here exactly that we see his work, his creativeness; he has conceived "the evil enemy," the "evil one," and indeed that is the root idea from which he now evolves as a contrasting and corresponding figure a "good one," himself—his very self!

11.

The method of this man is quite contrary to that of the aristocratic man, who conceives the root idea "good" spontaneously and straight away, that is to say, out of himself, and from that material then creates for himself a concept of "bad"! This "bad" of aristocratic origin and that "evil" out of the cauldron of unsatisfied hatred—the former an imitation, an "extra," an additional nuance; the latter, on the other hand, the original, the beginning, the essential act in the conception of a slave-morality—these two words "bad" and "evil," how great a difference do they mark, in spite of the fact that they have an identical contrary in the idea "good." But the idea "good" is not the same: much rather let the question be asked, "Who is really evil according to the meaning of the morality of *ressentiment?*" In all sternness let it be answered thus:—*just* the good man of the other morality, just the aristocrat, the powerful one, the one who rules, but who is distorted by the venomous eye of resentfulness, into a new colour, a new signification, a new appearance.

This particular point we would be the last to deny: the man who learnt to know those "good" ones only as enemies, learnt at the same time not to know them only as "*evil enemies*" and the same men who *inter pares* were kept so rigorously in bounds through convention, respect, custom, and gratitude, though much more through mutual vigilance and jealousy *inter pares*, these men who in their relations with each other find so many new ways of manifesting consideration, self-control, delicacy, loyalty, pride, and friendship, these men are in reference to what is outside their circle (where the foreign element, a *foreign* country, begins), not much better than beasts of prey, which have been let loose. They enjoy there freedom from all social control, they feel that in the wilderness they can give vent with impunity to that tension which is produced by enclosure and imprisonment in the peace of society, they *revert* to the innocence of the beast-of-prey conscience, like jubilant monsters, who perhaps come from a ghastly bout of murder, arson, rape, and torture, with bravado and a moral equanimity, as though merely some wild student's prank had been played, perfectly convinced that the poets have now an ample theme to sing and celebrate. It is impossible not to recognise at the core of all these aristocratic races the beast of prey; the magnificent *blonde brute*, avidly rampant for spoil and victory; this hidden core needed an outlet from time to time, the beast must get loose again, must return into the wilderness—the Roman, Arabic, German, and Japanese nobility, the Homeric heroes, the Scandinavian Vikings, are all alike in this need.

It is the aristocratic races who have left the idea "Barbarian" on all the tracks in which they have marched; nay, a consciousness of this very barbarianism, and even a pride in it, manifests itself even in their highest civilisation (for example, when Pericles says to his Athenians in that celebrated funeral oration, "Our audacity has forced a way over every land and sea, rearing everywhere imperishable memorials of itself for *good* and for *evil*"). This audacity of aristocratic races, mad, absurd, and spasmodic as may be its expression; the incalculable and fantastic nature of their enterprises, Pericles sets in special relief and glory the 'ραθυμία[60] of the Athenians, their nonchalance and contempt for safety, body, life, and comfort, their awful joy and intense delight in all destruction, in all the ecstasies of victory and cruelty,—all these features become crystallised, for those who suffered thereby in the picture of the "barbarian," of the "evil enemy," perhaps of the "Goth" and of the "Vandal." The profound, icy mistrust which the German provokes, as soon as he arrives at power,—even at the present time,—is always still an aftermath of that inextinguishable horror with which for whole centuries Europe has regarded the wrath of the

---

[60] calmness of mind

blonde Teuton beast (although between the old Germans and ourselves there exists scarcely a psychological, let alone a physical, relationship).

I have once called attention to the embarrassment of Hesiod, when he conceived the series of social ages, and endeavoured to express them in gold, silver, and bronze. He could only dispose of the contradiction, with which he was confronted, by the Homeric world, an age magnificent indeed, but at the same time so awful and so violent, by making two ages out of one, which he henceforth placed one behind each other—first, the age of the heroes and demigods, as that world had remained in the memories of the aristocratic families, who found therein their own ancestors; secondly, the bronze age, as that corresponding age appeared to the descendants of the oppressed, spoiled, ill-treated, exiled, enslaved; namely, as an age of bronze, as I have said, hard, cold, terrible, without feelings and without conscience, crushing everything, and bespattering everything with blood.

Granted the truth of the theory now believed to be true: that the very *essence of all civilisation* is to *train* out of man, the beast of prey, a tame and civilised animal, a domesticated animal—it follows indubitably that we must regard as the real *tools of civilisation* all those instincts of reaction and resentment, by the help of which the aristocratic races, together with their ideals, were finally degraded and overpowered; though that has not yet come to be synonymous with saying that the bearers of those tools also *represented* the civilisation. It is rather the contrary that is not only probable—nay, it is *palpable* today; these bearers of vindictive instincts that have to be bottled up, these descendants of all European and non-European slavery, especially of the pre-Aryan population—these people, I say, represent the *decline* of humanity! These "tools of civilisation" are a disgrace to humanity, and constitute in reality more of an argument against civilisation, more of a reason why civilisation should be suspected.

One may be perfectly justified in being always afraid of the blonde beast that lies at the core of all aristocratic races, and in being on one's guard: but who would not a hundred times prefer to be afraid, when one at the same time admires, than to be immune from fear, at the cost of being perpetually obsessed with the loathsome spectacle of the distorted, the dwarfed, the stunted, the envenomed?

And is that not our fate? What produces today our repulsion towards "man"?—for we *suffer* from "man," there is no doubt about it. It is not fear; it is rather that we have nothing more to fear from men; it is that the worm "man" is in the foreground and pullulates; it is that the "tame man," the wretched mediocre and unedifying creature, has learnt to consider himself a goal and a pinnacle, an inner meaning, an historic principle, a "higher man"; yes, it is that he has a certain right so to consider himself, in so far as he feels that in contrast to that excess of deformity, disease, exhaustion, and effeteness whose odour is beginning to pollute present-day Europe, he at any rate has achieved a relative success, he at any rate still says "yes" to life.

12.

I cannot refrain at this juncture from uttering a sigh and one last hope. What is it precisely which I find intolerable? That which I alone cannot get rid of, which makes me choke and faint? Bad air! bad air! That something misbegotten comes near me; that I must inhale the odour of the entrails of a misbegotten soul!—That excepted, what can one not endure in the way of need, privation, bad weather, sickness, toil, solitude? In point of fact, one manages to get over everything, born as one is to a burrowing and battling existence; one always returns once again to the light, one always lives again one's golden hour of victory—and then one stands as one was born, unbreakable, tense, ready for something more difficult, for something more distant, like a bow stretched but the tauter by every strain. But, from time to time, grant me—assuming that "beyond good and evil" there are goddesses who can grant—one glimpse, grant me but one glimpse only, of something perfect, fully realised, happy, mighty, triumphant, of something that still gives cause for fear! A glimpse of a man that justifies the existence of man, a glimpse of an incarnate human happiness that realises and redeems, for the sake of which one may hold fast to *the belief in man*! For the position is this: in the dwarfing and levelling of the European man lurks *our* greatest peril, for it is this outlook which fatigues—we see today nothing which wishes to be greater, we surmise that the process is always still backwards, still backwards towards something more attenuated, more inoffensive, more cunning, more comfortable, more mediocre, more indifferent, more Chinese, more Christian—man, there is no doubt about it, grows always "better" —the destiny of Europe lies even in this—that in losing the fear of man, we have also lost the hope in man, yea, the will to be man. The sight of man now fatigues.—What is present-day Nihilism if it is not *that*?—We are tired of *man*.

13.

But let us come back to it; the problem of *another* origin of the *good* —of the good, as the resentful man has thought it out—demands its solution. It is not surprising that the lambs should bear a grudge against the great birds of prey, but that is no reason for blaming the great birds of prey for taking the little lambs. And when the lambs say among themselves, "These birds of prey are evil, and he who is as far removed from being a bird of prey, who is rather its opposite, a lamb, —is he not good?" then there is nothing to cavil at in the setting up of this ideal, though it may also be that the birds of prey will regard it a little sneeringly, and perchance say to themselves, "*We* bear no grudge against them, these good lambs, we even like them: nothing is tastier than a tender lamb." To require of strength that it should *not* express itself as strength, that it should not be a wish to overpower, a wish to overthrow, a wish to become master, a thirst for enemies and antagonisms and triumphs, is just as absurd as to require of weakness that it should express itself as strength.

A quantum of force is just such a quantum of movement, will, action—rather it is nothing else than just those very phenomena of moving, willing, acting, and can only appear otherwise in the misleading errors of language (and the fundamental fallacies of reason which have become petrified therein), which understands, and understands wrongly, all working as conditioned by a worker, by a "subject." And just exactly as the people separate the lightning from its flash, and interpret the latter as a thing done, as the working of a subject which is called lightning, so also does the popular morality separate strength from the expression of strength, as though behind the strong man there existed some indifferent neutral *substratum*, which enjoyed a *caprice and option* as to whether or not it should express strength. But there is no such *substratum*, there is no "being" behind doing, working, becoming; "the doer" is a mere appanage to the action. The action is everything.

In point of fact, the people duplicate the doing, when they make the lightning lighten, that is a "doing-doing": they make the same phenomenon first a cause, and then, secondly, the effect of that cause. The scientists fail to improve matters when they say, "Force moves, force causes," and so on. Our whole science is still, in spite of all its coldness, of all its freedom from passion, a dupe of the tricks of language, and has never succeeded in getting rid of that superstitious changeling "the subject" (the atom, to give another instance, is such a changeling, just as the Kantian "Thing-in-itself").

What wonder, if the suppressed and stealthily simmering passions of revenge and hatred exploit for their own advantage this belief, and indeed hold no belief with a more steadfast enthusiasm than this —"that the strong has the *option* of being weak, and the bird of prey of being a lamb." Thereby do they win for themselves the right of attributing to the birds of prey the *responsibility* for being birds of prey: when the oppressed, down-trodden, and overpowered say to themselves with the vindictive guile of weakness, "Let us be otherwise than the evil, namely, good! and good is every one who does not oppress, who hurts no one, who does not attack, who does not pay back, who hands over revenge to God, who holds himself, as we do, in hiding; who goes out of the way of evil, and demands, in short, little from life; like ourselves the patient, the meek, the just,"—yet all this, in its cold and unprejudiced interpretation, means nothing more than "once for all, the weak are weak; it is good to do *nothing for which we are not strong enough.*"

But this dismal state of affairs, this prudence of the lowest order, which even insects possess (which in a great danger are fain to sham death so as to avoid doing "too much"), has, thanks to the counterfeiting and self-deception of weakness, come to masquerade in the pomp of an ascetic, mute, and expectant virtue, just as though the *very* weakness of the weak—that is, forsooth, its *being*, its working, its whole unique inevitable inseparable reality—were a voluntary result, something wished, chosen, a deed, an act of *merit*. This kind of man finds the belief in a neutral, free-choosing "subject" *necessary* from an instinct of self-preservation, of self-assertion, in which every lie is fain to sanctify itself. The subject (or, to use popular language, the *soul*) has perhaps proved itself the best dogma in the world simply because it rendered possible to the horde of mortal, weak, and oppressed individuals of every kind, that most sublime specimen of self-deception, the interpretation of weakness as freedom, of being this, or being that, as *merit*.

14.

Will any one look a little into—right into—the mystery of how *ideals* are *manufactured* in this world? Who has the courage to do it? Come!

Here we have a vista opened into these grimy workshops. Wait just a moment, dear Mr. Inquisitive and Foolhardy; your eye must first grow accustomed to this false changing light—Yes! Enough! Now speak! What is happening below down yonder? Speak out that what you see, man of the most dangerous curiosity—for now *I* am the listener.

"I see nothing, I hear the more. It is a cautious, spiteful, gentle whispering and muttering together in all the corners and crannies. It seems to me that they are lying; a sugary softness adheres to every sound. Weakness is turned to *merit*, there is no doubt about it—it is just as you say."

Further!

"And the impotence which requites not, is turned to 'goodness,' craven baseness to meekness, submission to those whom one hates, to obedience (namely, obedience to one of whom they say that he ordered this submission—they call him God). The inoffensive character of the weak, the very cowardice in which he is rich, his standing at the door, his forced necessity of waiting, gain here fine names, such as 'patience,' which is also called 'virtue'; not being able to avenge one's self, is called not wishing to avenge one's self, perhaps even forgiveness (for *they* know not what they do—we alone know what *they* do). They also talk of the 'love of their enemies' and sweat thereby."

Further!

"They are miserable, there is no doubt about it, all these whisperers and counterfeiters in the corners, although they try to get warm by crouching close to each other, but they tell me that their misery is a favour and distinction given to them by God, just as one beats the dogs one likes best; that perhaps this misery is also a preparation, a probation, a training; that perhaps it is still more something which will one day be compensated and paid back with a tremendous interest in gold, nay in happiness. This they call 'Blessedness.'"

Further!

"They are now giving me to understand, that not only are they better men than the mighty, the lords of the earth, whose spittle they have got to lick (*not* out of fear, not at all out of fear! But because God ordains that one should honour all authority)—not only are they better men, but that they also have a 'better time,' at any rate, will one day have a 'better time.' But enough! Enough! I can endure it no longer. Bad air! Bad air! These workshops *where ideals are manufactured*— verily they reek with the crassest lies."

Nay. Just one minute! You are saying nothing about the masterpieces of these virtuosos of black magic, who can produce whiteness, milk, and innocence out of any black you like: have you not noticed what a pitch of refinement is attained by their *chef d'œuvre*, their most audacious, subtle, ingenious, and lying artist-trick? Take care! These cellar-beasts, full of revenge and hate—what do they make, forsooth, out of their revenge and hate? Do you hear these words? Would you suspect, if you trusted only their words, that you are among men of *ressentiment* and nothing else?

"I understand, I prick my ears up again (ah! ah! ah! and I hold my nose). Now do I hear for the first time that which they have said so often: 'We good, *we are the righteous*'—what they demand they call not revenge but 'the triumph of *righteousness*'; what they hate is not their enemy, no, they hate 'unrighteousness,' 'godlessness'; what they believe in and hope is not the hope of revenge, the intoxication of sweet revenge (—"sweeter than honey," did Homer call it?), but the victory of God, of the *righteous God* over the 'godless'; what is left for them to love in this world is not their brothers in hate, but their 'brothers in love,' as they say, all the good and righteous on the earth."

And how do they name that which serves them as a solace against all the troubles of life—their phantasmagoria of their anticipated future blessedness?

"How? Do I hear right? They call it 'the last judgment,' the advent of *their* kingdom, 'the kingdom of God'—but *in the meanwhile* they live 'in faith,' 'in love,' 'in hope.'"

Enough! Enough

15.

In the faith in what? In the love for what? In the hope of what? These weaklings!—they also, forsooth, wish to be the strong some time; there is no doubt about it, some time *their* kingdom also must come—"the kingdom of God" is their name for it, as has been mentioned: they are so meek in everything! Yet in order to experience *that* kingdom it is necessary to live long, to live beyond death,—yes, *eternal* life is necessary so that one can make up forever for that earthly life "in faith," "in love," "in hope." Make up for what? Make up by what? Dante, as it seems to me, made a crass mistake when with awe-inspiring ingenuity he placed that inscription over the gate of his hell, "I too was made by eternal love": at any rate the following inscription would have a much better right to stand over the gate of the Christian Paradise and its "eternal blessedness"—"I too was made by eternal hate"—granted of course that a truth may rightly stand over the gate to a lie! For what is the blessedness of that Paradise? Possibly we could quickly surmise it; but it is better that it should be explicitly attested by an authority who in such matters is not to be disparaged, Thomas of Aquinas, the great teacher and saint. *"Beati in regno celesti"* says he, as gently as a lamb, *"videsunt pœnas damnatorum, ut beatitudo illis magis complaceat."*[61]

Or if we wish to hear a stronger tone, a word from the mouth of a triumphant father of the Church, who warned his disciples against the cruel ecstasies of the public spectacles—But why? Faith offers us much more,—says he, *De Spectaculis*, c. 29 ss.,—something much stronger; thanks to the redemption, joys of quite another kind stand at our disposal; instead of athletes we have our martyrs; we wish for blood, well, we have the blood of Christ—but what then awaits us on the day of his return, of his triumph. And then does he proceed, does this enraptured visionary: *"at enim supersunt alia spectacula, ille ultimas et*

---

[61] "The blessed in the kingdom of heaven will see the punishments of the damned in order that their bliss be more delightful for them."

perpetuus judicii dies, ille nationibus insperatus, ille derisus, cum tanta sæculi vetustas et tot ejus nativitates uno igne haurientur. Quæ tunc spectaculi latitudo! Quid admirer! quid rideam! Ubi gaudeam! Ubi exultem, spectans tot et tantos reges, qui in cælum recepti nuntiabantur, cum ipso Jove et ipsis suis testibus in imis tenebris congemescentes! Item præsides" (the provincial governors) "*persecutores dominici nominis sævioribus quam ipsi flammis sævierunt insultantibus contra Christianos liquescentes! Quos præterea sapientes illos philosophos coram discipulis suis una conflagrantibus erubescentes, quibus nihil ad deum pertinere suadebant, quibus animas aut nullas aut non in pristina corpora redituras affirmabant! Etiam poetas non ad Rhadamanti nec ad Minois, sed ad inopinati Christi tribunal palpitantes! Tunc magis tragœdi audiendi, magis scilicet vocales*" (with louder tones and more violent shrieks) "*in sua propria calamitate; tunc histriones cognoscendi, solutiores multo per ignem; tunc spectandus auriga in flammea rota totus rubens, tunc xystici contemplandi non in gymnasiis, sed in igne jaculati, nisi quod ne tunc quidem illos velim vivos, ut qui malim ad eos potius conspectum insatiabilem conferre, qui in dominum scevierunt. Hic est ille, dicam fabri aut quæstuariæ filius*" (as is shown by the whole of the following, and in particular by this well-known description of the mother of Jesus from the Talmud, Tertullian is henceforth referring to the Jews), "*sabbati destructor, Samarites et dæmonium habens. Hic est quem a Juda redemistis, hic est ille arundine et colaphis diverberatus, sputamentis de decoratus, felle et aceto potatus. Hic est, quem clam discentes subripuerunt, ut resurrexisse dicatur vel hortulanus detraxit, ne lactucæ suæ frequentia commeantium laderentur. Ut talia species, ut talibus exultes, quis tibi prætor aut consul aut sacerdos de sua liberalitate prastabit? Et tamen hæc jam habemus quodammodo per fidem spiritu imaginante repræsentata. Ceterum qualia illa sunt, quæ nec oculus vidit nec auris audivit nec in cor hominis ascenderunt?*" (I Cor. ii. 9.) "*Credo circo et utraque cavea*" (first and fourth row, or, according to others, the comic and the tragic stage) "*et omni studio gratiora.*" *Per fidem*: so stands it written.[62]

16.

Let us come to a conclusion. The two *opposing values*, "good and bad," "good and evil," have fought a dreadful, thousand-year fight in the world, and though indubitably the second value has been for a long time in the preponderance, there are not wanting places where the fortune of the fight is still undecisive. It can almost be said that in the meanwhile the fight reaches a higher and higher level, and that in the meanwhile it has become more and more intense, and always

---

[62] "Yes, and there are other sights: that last day of judgment, with its everlasting issues; that day unlooked for by the nations, the theme of their derision, when the world hoary with age, and all its many products, shall be consumed in one great flame! How vast a spectacle then bursts upon the eye! What there excites my admiration? what my derision? Which sight gives me joy? which rouses me to exultation?—as I see so many illustrious monarchs, whose reception into the heavens was publicly announced, groaning now in the lowest darkness with great Jove himself, and those, too, who bore witness of their exultation; governors of provinces, too, who persecuted the Christian name, in fires more fierce than those with which in the days of their pride they raged against the followers of Christ. What world's wise men besides, the very philosophers, in fact, who taught their followers that God had no concern in ought that is sublunary, and were wont to assure them that either they had no souls, or that they would never return to the bodies which at death they had left, now covered with shame before the poor deluded ones, as one fire consumes them! Poets also, trembling not before the judgment-seat of Rhadamanthus or Minos, but of the unexpected Christ! I shall have a better opportunity then of hearing the tragedians, louder-voiced in their own calamity; of viewing the play-actors, much more "dissolute" in the dissolving flame; of looking upon the charioteer, all glowing in his chariot of fire; of beholding the wrestlers, not in their gymnasia, but tossing in the fiery billows; unless even then I shall not care to attend to such ministers of sin, in my eager wish rather to fix a gaze insatiable on those whose fury vented itself against the Lord. "This," I shall say, "this is that carpenter's or hireling's son, that Sabbath-breaker, that Samaritan and devil-possessed! This is He whom you purchased from Judas! This is He whom you struck with reed and fist, whom you contemptuously spat upon, to whom you gave gall and vinegar to drink! This is He whom His disciples secretly stole away, that it might be said He had risen again, or the gardener abstracted, that his lettuces might come to no harm from the crowds of visitants!" What quæstor or priest in his munificence will bestow on you the favour of seeing and exulting in such things as these? And yet even now we in a measure have them by faith in the picturings of imagination. But what are the things which eye has not seen, ear has not heard, and which have not so much as dimly dawned upon the human heart? Whatever they are, they are nobler, I believe, than circus, and both theatres,[3] and every race-course." (Thelwall translation)

more and more psychological; so that nowadays there is perhaps no more decisive mark of the *higher nature*, of the more psychological nature, than to be in that sense self-contradictory, and to be actually still a battleground for those two opposites.

The symbol of this fight, written in a writing which has remained worthy of perusal throughout the course of history up to the present time, is called "Rome against Judæa, Judæa against Rome." Hitherto there has been no greater event than *that* fight, the putting of *that* question, *that* deadly antagonism. Rome found in the Jew the incarnation of the unnatural, as though it were its diametrically opposed monstrosity, and in Rome the Jew was held to be *convicted of hatred* of the whole human race: and rightly so, in so far as it is right to link the well-being and the future of the human race to the unconditional mastery of the aristocratic values, of the Roman values.

What, conversely, did the Jews feel against Rome? One can surmise it from a thousand symptoms, but it is sufficient to carry one's mind back to the Johannian Apocalypse, that most obscene of all the written outbursts, which has revenge on its conscience. (One should also appraise at its full value the profound logic of the Christian instinct, when over this very book of hate it wrote the name of the Disciple of Love, that self-same disciple to whom it attributed that impassioned and ecstatic Gospel—therein lurks a portion of truth, however much literary forging may have been necessary for this purpose.) The Romans were the strong and aristocratic; a nation stronger and more aristocratic has never existed in the world, has never even been dreamed of; every relic of them, every inscription enraptures, granted that one can divine *what* it is that writes the inscription. The Jews, conversely, were that priestly nation of resentment *par excellence*, possessed by a unique genius for popular morals: just compare with the Jews the nations with analogous gifts, such as the Chinese or the Germans, so as to realise afterwards what is first rate, and what is fifth rate.

Which of them has been provisionally victorious, Rome or Judæa? but there is not a shadow of doubt; just consider to whom in Rome itself nowadays you bow down, as though before the quintessence of all the highest values—and not only in Rome, but almost over half the world, everywhere where man has been tamed or is about to be tamed —to *three Jews*, as we know, and *one Jewess* (to Jesus of Nazareth, to

Peter the fisher, to Paul the tent-maker, and to the mother of the aforesaid Jesus, named Mary). This is very remarkable: Rome is undoubtedly defeated. At any rate there took place in the Renaissance a brilliantly sinister revival of the classical ideal, of the aristocratic valuation of all things: Rome herself, like a man waking up from a trance, stirred beneath the burden of the new Judaised Rome that had been built over her, which presented the appearance of an œcumenical synagogue and was called the "Church": but immediately Judæa triumphed again, thanks to that fundamentally popular (German and English) movement of revenge, which is called the Reformation, and taking also into account its inevitable corollary, the restoration of the Church—the restoration also of the ancient graveyard peace of classical Rome.

Judæa proved yet once more victorious over the classical ideal in the French Revolution, and in a sense which was even more crucial and even more profound: the last political aristocracy that existed in Europe, that of the *French* seventeenth and eighteenth centuries, broke into pieces beneath the instincts of a resentful populace—never had the world heard a greater jubilation, a more uproarious enthusiasm: indeed, there took place in the midst of it the most monstrous and unexpected phenomenon; the ancient ideal *itself* swept before the eyes and conscience of humanity with all its life and with unheard-of splendour, and in opposition to resentment's lying war-cry of *the prerogative of the most*, in opposition to the will to lowliness, abasement, and equalisation, the will to a retrogression and twilight of humanity, there rang out once again, stronger, simpler, more penetrating than ever, the terrible and enchanting counter-warcry of *the prerogative of the few*! Like a final signpost to other ways, there appeared Napoleon, the most unique and violent anachronism that ever existed, and in him the incarnate problem *of the aristocratic ideal in itself*—consider well what a problem it is:—Napoleon, that synthesis of Monster and Superman.

17.

Was it therewith over? Was that greatest of all antitheses of ideals thereby relegated *ad acta*[63] for all time? Or only postponed, postponed for a long time? May there not take place at some time or other a

---

[63] "to the records"

much more awful, much more carefully prepared flaring up of the old conflagration? Further! Should not one wish *that* consummation with all one's strength?—will it one's self? demand it one's self? He who at this juncture begins, like my readers, to reflect, to think further, will have difficulty in coming quickly to a conclusion,—ground enough for me to come myself to a conclusion, taking it for granted that for some time past what I mean has been sufficiently clear, what I exactly *mean* by that dangerous motto which is inscribed on the body of my last book: *Beyond Good and Evil*—at any rate that is not the same as "Beyond Good and Bad." ...

from THE CASE OF WAGNER

Epilogue

... I shall now give my notion of what is *modern*. According to the measure of energy of every age, there is also a standard that determines which virtues shall be allowed and which forbidden. The age either has the virtues of *ascending* life, in which case it resists the virtues of degeneration with all its deepest instincts. Or it is in itself an age of degeneration, in which case it requires the virtues of declining life,—in which case it hates everything that justifies itself, solely as being the outcome of a plenitude, or a superabundance of strength. Aesthetic is inextricably bound up with these biological principles: there is decadent aesthetic, and *classical* aesthetic,—"beauty in itself" is just as much a chimera as any other kind of idealism.—

Within the narrow sphere of the so-called moral values, no greater antithesis could be found than that of *master-morality* and the morality of *Christian* valuations: the latter having grown out of a thoroughly morbid soil, (—the gospels present us with the same physiological types, as do the novels of Dostoyevsky); the master-morality ("Roman," "pagan," "classical," "Renaissance"), on the other hand, being the symbolic speech of well-constitutedness, of *ascending* life, and of the Will to Power as a vital principle. Master-morality *affirms* just as instinctively as Christian morality *denies* ("God," "Beyond," "self-denial,"—all of them negations). The first reflects its plenitude upon things,—it transfigures, it embellishes, it *rationalises* the world,—the latter impoverishes, bleaches, mars the value of things; it *suppresses* the world. "World" is a Christian term of abuse.

These antithetical forms in the optics of values, are *both* necessary: they are different points of view which cannot be circumvented either with arguments or counter-arguments. One cannot refute Christianity: it is impossible to refute a diseased eyesight. That people should have combated pessimism as if it had been a philosophy, was the very acme of learned stupidity. The concepts "true" and "untrue" do not seem to me to have any sense in optics.—That, alone, which has to be guarded against is the falsity, the instinctive duplicity which *would fain* regard this antithesis as no antithesis at all: just as Wagner did,—and his mastery in this kind of falseness was of no mean order. To cast side-long glances at master-morality, at *noble* morality (— Icelandic saga is perhaps the greatest documentary evidence of these values), and at the same time to have the opposite teaching, the "gospel of the lowly," the doctrine of the *need* of salvation, on one's lips!...

Incidentally, I admire the modesty of Christians who go to Bayreuth. As for myself, I could *not* endure to hear the sound of certain words on Wagner's lips. There are some concepts which are too good for Bayreuth ... What? Christianity adjusted for female Wagnerites, perhaps *by* female Wagnerites—for, in his latter days Wagner was thoroughly *feminini generis*[64]—? Again I say, the Christians of today are too modest for me.... If Wagner were a Christian, then Liszt was perhaps a Father of the Church!—The need of *salvation*, the quintessence of all Christian needs, has nothing in common with such clowns; it is the most straightforward expression of decadence, it is the most convincing and most painful affirmation of decadence, in sublime symbols and practices. The Christian wishes *to be rid* of himself. *Le moi est toujours haissable.*[65]

Noble morality, master-morality, on the other hand, is rooted in a triumphant saying of yea to *one's self*,—it is the self-affirmation and self-glorification of life; it also requires sublime symbols and practices; but only "because its heart is too full." The whole of beautiful art and of great art belongs here; their common essence is gratitude. But we must allow it a certain instinctive repugnance *to décadents*, and a scorn and horror of the latter's symbolism: such things almost prove it. The noble Romans considered Christianity as a *fœda superstitio*:[66] let me call to your minds the feelings which the last German of noble taste— Goethe—had in regard to the cross. It is idle to look for more valuable, more *necessary* contrasts.

But the kind of falsity which is characteristic of the Bayreuthians is not exceptional today. We all know the hybrid concept of the

---

[64] "of the feminine gender"

[65] "The self is always hateful."

[66] "disgusting superstition"

Christian gentleman. This *innocence* in contradiction, this "clean conscience" in falsehood, is rather modern *par excellence*, with it modernity is almost defined. Biologically, modern man represents a *contradiction of values*, he sits between two stools, he says yea and nay in one breath. No wonder that it is precisely in our age that falseness itself became flesh and blood, and even genius! No wonder *Wagner* dwelt amongst us! It was not without reason that I called Wagner the Cagliostro of modernity.... But all of us, though we do not know it, involuntarily have values, words, formulae, and morals in our bodies, which are quite *antagonistic* in their origin—regarded from a physiological standpoint, we are *false*.... How would a *diagnosis of the modern soul* begin? With a determined incision into this agglomeration of contradictory instincts, with the total suppression of its antagonistic values, with vivisection applied to its most *instructive* case. ...

from THE WILL TO POWER

1. (1885-1886)

... The downfall of Christianity,—through its morality (which is insuperable), which finally turns against the Christian God Himself (the sense of truth, highly developed through Christianity, ultimately revolts against the falsehood and fictitiousness of all Christian interpretations of the world and its history. The recoil-stroke of "God is Truth" in the fanatical Belief, is: "All is false." Buddhism of *action....*).

4. (June 1887)

What *advantages* did the Christian hypothesis of morality offer?

(1) It bestowed an intrinsic value upon men, which contrasted with their apparent insignificance and subordination to chance in the eternal flux of becoming and perishing.

(2) It served the purpose of God's advocates, inasmuch as it granted the world a certain *perfection* despite its sorrow and evil—it also granted the world that proverbial "freedom": evil seemed full of *meaning.*

(3) It assumed that man could have a *knowledge* of absolute values, and thus granted him *adequate perception* for the most important things.

(4) It prevented man from despising himself as man, from turning against life, and from being driven to despair by knowledge: it was a self-preservative measure.

In short: Morality was the great *antidote* against practical and theoretical Nihilism.

87. (Spring-Fall 1887)

The Decline of *Protestantism*: theoretically and historically understood as a half-measure. Undeniable predominance of Catholicism to-day: Protestant feeling is so dead that the strongest *anti-Protestant* movements (Wagner's *Parsifal*, for instance) are no longer regarded as such. The whole of the more elevated intellectuality in

France is *Catholic* in instinct; Bismarck recognised that there was no longer any such thing as Protestantism.

88. (Spring-Fall 1887)

Protestantism, that spiritually unclean and tiresome form of decadence, in which Christianity has known how to survive in the mediocre North, is something incomplete and complexly valuable for knowledge, in so far as it was able to bring experiences of different kinds and origins into the same heads.

89. (March-June 1888)

What has the German spirit not made out of Christianity! And, to refer to Protestantism again, how much beer is there not still in Protestant Christianity! Can a crasser, more indolent, and more lounging form of Christian belief be imagined, than that of the average German Protestant?... It is indeed a very humble Christianity. I call it the Homœopathy of Christianity! I am reminded that, to-day, there also exists a less humble sort of Protestantism; it is taught by royal chaplains and anti-Semitic speculators: but nobody has ever maintained that any "spirit" "hovers" over these waters. It is merely a less respectable form of Christian faith, not by any means a more comprehensible one.

94. (1884)

Chivalry—the position won by power: its gradual break-up (and partial transference to broader and more bourgeois spheres). In the case of Larochefoucauld we find a knowledge of the actual impulses of a noble temperament—together with the gloomy Christian estimate of these impulses.

The *protraction of Christianity* through the *French Revolution.* The seducer is Rousseau; he once again liberates woman, who thenceforward is always represented as ever more interesting—*suffering.* Then come the slaves and Mrs. Beecher-Stowe. Then the poor and the workmen. Then the vicious and the sick—all this is drawn into the foreground (even for the purpose of disposing people in favour of the genius, it has been customary for five hundred years to press him forward as the great sufferer!). Then comes the cursing of all voluptuousness (Baudelaire and Schopenhauer), the most decided conviction that the lust of power is the greatest vice; absolute certainty that morality and disinterestedness are identical things; that the "happiness of all" is a goal worth striving after (*i.e.,* Christ's Kingdom of Heaven). We are on the best road to it: the Kingdom of Heaven of the poor in spirit has begun.—Intermediate stages: the bourgeois (as a result of the *nouveau riche*) and the workman (as a result of the machine).

Greek and French culture of the time of Louis XIV. compared. A decided belief in oneself. A leisure-class which makes things hard for itself and exercises a great deal of self-control. The power of form, the will to form *oneself.* "Happiness" acknowledged as a purpose. Much strength and energy *behind* all formality of manners. Pleasure at the sight of a life that is *seemingly so easy.* The *Greeks* seemed like *children* to the French.

BOOK TWO
I.
CRITICISM OF RELIGION.

All the beauty and sublimity with which we have invested real and imagined things, I will show to be the property and product of man, and this should be his most beautiful apology. Man as a poet, as a thinker, as a god, as love, as power. Oh, the regal liberality with which he has lavished gifts upon things in order *to impoverish* himself and make himself feel wretched! Hitherto, this has been his greatest disinterestedness, that he admired and worshipped, and knew how to conceal from himself that *he* it was who had created what he admired.

1. CONCERNING THE ORIGIN OF RELIGIONS.

135. (March-June 1888)

The origin of religion.—Just as the illiterate man of today believes that his wrath is the cause of his being angry, that his mind is the cause of his thinking, that his soul is the cause of his feeling, in short, just as a mass of psychological entities are still unthinkingly postulated as causes; so, in a still more primitive age, the same phenomena were interpreted by man by means of personal entities. Those conditions of his soul which seemed strange, overwhelming, and rapturous, he regarded as obsessions and bewitching influences emanating from the power of some personality. (Thus the Christian, the most puerile and backward man of this age, traces hope, peace, and the feeling of deliverance to a psychological inspiration on the part of God: being by nature a sufferer and a creature in need of repose, states of happiness, peace, and resignation, perforce seem strange to him, and seem to need some explanation.) Among intelligent, strong, and vigorous races, the epileptic is mostly the cause of a belief in the existence of some *foreign power*; but all such examples of apparent subjection—as, for instance, the bearing of the exalted man, of the poet, of the great criminal, or the passions, love and revenge—lead to the invention of supernatural powers. A condition is made concrete by being identified with a personality, and when this condition overtakes anybody, it is ascribed to that personality. In other words: in the psychological concept of God, a certain state of the soul is personified as a cause in order to appear as an effect.

The psychological logic is as follows: when the *feeling of power* suddenly seizes and overwhelms a man,—and this takes place in the case of all the great passions,—a doubt arises in him concerning his own person: he dare not think himself the cause of this astonishing sensation—and thus he posits a *stronger* person, a Godhead as its cause. In short, the origin of religion lies in the extreme feelings of power, which, being *strange*, take men by surprise: and just as the sick man, who feels one of his limbs unaccountably heavy, concludes that another man must be sitting on it, so the ingenuous *homo religiosus*, divides himself up into *several people*. Religion is an example of the "*altération de la personalité*." A sort of *fear* and *sensation of terror* in one's own presence…. But also a feeling of inordinate *rapture* and *exaltation*. Among sick people, the *sensation of health* suffices to awaken a belief in the proximity of God.

136. (March-June 1888)

Rudimentary psychology of the religious man:—All changes are effects; all effects are effects of will (the notion of "Nature" and of "natural law," is lacking); all effects presuppose an agent. Rudimentary psychology: one is only a cause oneself, when one knows that one has willed something.

Result: States of power impute to man the feeling that he is *not* the cause of them, that he is not *responsible* for them: they come without being willed to do so—consequently we cannot be their originators: will that is not free (that is to say, the knowledge of a change in our condition which we have not helped to bring about) requires a *strong* will.

Consequence of this rudimentary psychology: Man has never dared to credit *himself* with his strong and startling moods, he has always conceived them as "passive," as "imposed upon him from outside": Religion is the offshoot of a *doubt* concerning the entity of the person, an *altération* of the personality: in so far as everything great and strong in man was considered *superhuman* and *foreign*, man belittled himself,— he laid the two sides, the very pitiable and weak side, and the very strong and startling side apart, in two spheres, and called the one "Man" and the other "God."

And he has continued to act on these lines; during the period of the *moral idiosyncrasy* he did not interpret his lofty and sublime moral states as "proceeding from his own will" or as the "work" of the person. Even the Christian himself divides his personality into two parts, the one a mean and weak fiction which he calls man, and the other which he calls God (Deliverer and Saviour).

Religion has lowered the concept "man"; its ultimate conclusion is that all goodness, greatness, and truth are superhuman, and are only obtainable by the grace of God.

137. (March-June 1888)

One way of raising man out of his self-abasement, which brought about the decline of the point of view that classed all lofty and strong states of the soul, as strange, was the theory of relationship. These lofty and strong states of the soul could at least be interpreted as the influence of our *forebears*; we belonged to each other, we were irrevocably joined; we grew in our own esteem, by acting according to the example of a model known to us all.

There is an attempt on the part of noble families to associate religion with their own feelings of self-respect. Poets and seers do the same thing; they feel proud that they have been worthy,—that they have been *selected* for such association,—they esteem it an honour, not to be considered at all as individuals, but as mere mouthpieces (Homer).

Man gradually takes possession of the highest and proudest states of his soul, as also of his acts and his works. Formerly it was believed that one paid oneself the greatest honour by denying one's own responsibility for the highest deeds one accomplished, and by ascribing them to—God. The will which was not free, appeared to be that which imparted a higher value to a deed: in those days a god was postulated as the author of the deed.

138. (1883-1888)

Priests are the actors of something which is supernatural, either in the way of ideals, gods, or saviours, and they have to make people believe in them; in this they find their calling, this is the purpose of their instincts; in order to make it as credible as possible, they have to exert themselves to the utmost extent in the art of posing; their actor's sagacity must, above all, aim at giving them *a clean conscience*, by means of which, alone, it is possible to persuade effectively.

139. (March-June 1888)

The priest wishes to make it an understood thing, that he is the *highest type* of man, that he rules,—even over those who wield the power,—that he is indispensable and unassailable,—that he is the *strongest power* in the community, not by any means to be replaced or undervalued.

Means thereto: he alone is cultured; he alone is the *man of virtue*; he alone has *sovereign power over himself*: he alone is, in a certain sense, God, and ultimately goes back to the Godhead; he alone is the middleman between God and *others*; the Godhead administers punishment to every one who puts the priest at a disadvantage, or who thinks in opposition to him.

Means thereto: Truth exists. There is only one way of attaining to it, and that is to become a priest. Everything good, which relates either to order, nature, or tradition, is to be traced to the wisdom of the priests. The Holy Book is their work. The whole of nature is only a fulfilment of the maxims which it contains. No other *source of goodness* exists than the priests. Every other kind of perfection, even the *warrior's,* is different in rank from that of the priests.

Consequence: If the priest is to be the *highest* type, then the *degrees* which lead to his *virtues* must be the degrees of value among men. *Study, emancipation from material things, inactivity, impassibility, absence of passion, solemnity*;—the opposite of all this is found in the *lowest* type of man.

The priest has taught a kind of morality which conduced to his being considered the *highest type* of man. He conceives a *type* which is the *reverse* of his own: the Chandala.[67] By making *these* as contemptible as possible, some strength is lent to the *order of castes.* The priest's excessive fear of *sensuality* also implies that the latter is the most serious threat to the *order of castes* (that is to say, *order* in general).... Every "free tendency" *in puncto puncti* overthrows the laws of marriage.

140. (March-June 1888)

The *philosopher* considered as the development of the *priestly* type: —He has the heritage of the priest in his blood; even as a rival he is compelled to fight with the same weapons as the priest of his time;— he aspires to the *highest authority.*

What is it that bestows *authority* upon men who have no physical power to wield (no army, no arms at all ...)? How do such men gain authority *over* those who are in possession of material power, and who represent authority? (Philosophers enter the lists against princes, victorious conquerors, and wise statesmen.)

They can do it only by establishing the belief that they are in possession of a power which is higher and stronger—*God.* Nothing is strong enough: every one is in *need* of the mediation and the services

---

[67] The lowest caste in Hinduism

of priests. They establish themselves as indispensable *intercessors*. The conditions of their existence are: (1) That people believe in the absolute superiority of their god, in fact believe in *their god*; (2) that there is no other access, no direct access to god, save through them The *second* condition alone gives rise to the concept "heterodoxy"; the *first* to the concept "disbelievers" (that is to say, he who believes in another god).

141. (January-Fall 1888)

A Criticism of the Holy Lie.—That a lie is allowed in pursuit of holy ends is a principle which belongs to the theory of all priestcraft, and the object of this inquiry is to discover to what extent it belongs to its practice.

But philosophers, too, whenever they intend taking over the leadership of mankind, with the ulterior motives of priests in their minds, have never failed to arrogate to themselves the right to lie: Plato above all. But the most elaborate of lies is the double lie, developed by the typically Aryan philosophers of the Vedanta: two systems, contradicting each other in all their main points, but interchangeable, complementary, and mutually expletory, when educational ends were in question. The lie of the one has to create a condition in which the truth of the other can alone become *intelligible*.

. . .

How *far* does the holy lie of priests and philosophers go?—The question here is, what hypotheses do they advance in regard to education, and what are the dogmas they are compelled to *invent* in order to do justice to these hypotheses?

First: they must have power, authority, and absolute credibility on their side.

Secondly: they must have the direction of the whole of Nature, so that everything affecting the individual seems to be determined by their law.

Thirdly: their domain of power must be very extensive, in order that its control may escape the notice of those they subject: they must know the penal code of the life beyond—of the life "after death,"—and, of course, the means whereby the road to blessedness may be discovered. They have to put the notion of a natural course of things

175

out of sight, but as they are intelligent and thoughtful people, they are able to *promise* a host of effects, which they naturally say are conditioned by prayer or by the strict observance of their law. They can, moreover, *prescribe* a large number of things which are exceedingly reasonable—only they must not point to experience or empiricism as the source of this wisdom, but to revelation or to the fruits of the "most severe exercises of penance."

The *holy lie*, therefore, applies principally to the *purpose* of an action (the natural purpose, reason, is made to vanish: a moral purpose, the observance of some law, a service to God, seems to be the purpose): to the *consequence* of an action (the natural consequence is interpreted as something supernatural, and, in order to be on surer ground, other incontrollable and supernatural consequences are foretold).

In this way the concepts *good* and *evil* are created, and seem quite divorced from the natural concepts: "useful," "harmful," "life-promoting," "life-retarding,"—indeed, inasmuch as *another* life is imagined, the former concepts may even be *antagonistic* to Nature's concepts of good and evil. In this way, the proverbial concept "conscience" is created: an inner voice, which, though it makes itself heard in regard to every action, does not measure the worth of that action according to its results, but according to its conformity or non-conformity to the "law."

The holy lie therefore invented: (1) a *god* who *punishes* and *rewards*, who recognises and carefully observes the law-book of the priests, and who is particular about sending them into the world as his mouthpieces and plenipotentiaries; (2) an *After Life*, in which, alone, the great penal machine is supposed to be active—to this end the *immortality of the soul* was invented; (3) a *conscience in man*, understood as the knowledge that good and evil are permanent values—that God himself speaks through it, whenever its counsels are in conformity with priestly precepts; (4) *Morality* as the denial of all natural processes, as the subjection of all phenomena to a moral order, as the interpretation of all phenomena as the effects of a moral order of things (that is to say, the concept of punishment and reward), as the only power and only creator of all transformations; (5) *Truths* given, revealed, and identical with the teaching of the priests: as the condition to all salvation and happiness in this and the next world.

176

In short: what is the price paid for the *improvement* supposed to be due to morality?—The unhinging of *reason*, the reduction of all motives to fear and hope (punishment and reward); *dependence* upon the tutelage of priests, and upon a formulary exactitude which is supposed to express a divine will; the implantation of a "conscience" which establishes a false science in the place of experience and experiment: as though all one had to do or had not to do were predetermined—a kind of contraction of the seeking and striving spirit;—*in short*: the worst *mutilation* of man that can be imagined, and it is pretended that "the good man" is the result.

Practically speaking, all reason, the whole heritage of intelligence, subtlety, and caution, the first condition of the priestly canon, is arbitrarily reduced, when it is too late, to a simple *mechanical* process: conformity with the law becomes a purpose in itself, it is the highest purpose; *Life no longer contains any problems*;—the whole conception of the world is polluted by the notion of *punishment*;—Life itself, owing to the fact that the *priest's life* is upheld as the *non plus ultra* of perfection, is transformed into a denial and pollution of life;—the concept "God" represents an aversion to Life, and even a criticism and a contemning of it. Truth is transformed in the mind, into *priestly* prevarication; the striving after truth, into the *study of the Scriptures*, into the way to *become a theologian*.

142. (January-Fall 1888)

A criticism of the Law-Book of Manu.—The whole book is founded upon the holy lie. Was it the well-being of humanity that inspired the whole of this system? Was this kind of man, who believes in the *interested* nature of every action, interested or not interested in the success of this system? The desire to improve mankind—whence comes the inspiration to this feeling? Whence is the concept improvement taken?

We find a class of men, *the sacerdotal class*, who consider themselves the standard pattern, the highest example and most perfect expression of the type man. The notion of "improving" mankind, to this class of men, means to make mankind like themselves. They believe in their own superiority, they *will* be superior in practice: the cause of the holy lie is the *will to power*....

Establishment of the dominion: to this end, ideas which place a *non plus ultra* of power with the priesthood are made to prevail. Power acquired by lying was the result of the recognition of the fact that it was not already possessed physically, in a military form.... Lying as a supplement to power—this is a new concept of "truth."

It is a mistake to presuppose *unconscious* and *innocent* development in this quarter—a sort of self-deception. Fanatics are not the discoverers of such exhaustive systems of oppression.... Cold-blooded reflection must have been at work here; the same sort of reflection which Plato showed when he worked out his "State"—"One must desire the means when one desires the end." Concerning this political maxim, all legislators have always been quite clear.

We possess the classical model, and it is specifically Aryan: we can therefore hold the most gifted and most reflective type of man responsible for the most systematic lie that has ever been told.... Everywhere almost the lie was copied, and thus *Aryan influence* corrupted the world....

143. (March-June 1888)

Much is said today about the *Semitic* spirit of the *New Testament*: but the thing referred to is merely priestcraft,—and in the purest example of an Aryan law-book, in Manu, this kind of "Semitic spirit"—that is to say, *Sacerdotalism*, is worse than anywhere else.

The development of the Jewish hierarchy is *not* original: they learnt the scheme in Babylon—it is Aryan. When, later on, the same thing became dominant in Europe, under the preponderance of Germanic blood, this was in conformity to the spirit of the *ruling race*: a striking case of atavism. The Germanic middle ages aimed at a revival of the *Aryan order of castes*.

Mohammedanism in its turn learned from Christianity the use of a "Beyond" as an instrument of punishment.

The scheme of a *permanent community*, with priests at its head—this oldest product of Asia's great culture in the domain of organisation—*naturally* provoked reflection and imitation in every way.—Plato is an example of this, but above all, the Egyptians.

144. (1885)

Moralities and *religions* are the principal means by which one can modify men into whatever one likes; provided one is possessed of an overflow of creative power, and can cause one's will to prevail over long periods of time.

145. (1884-1888)

If one wishes to see an *affirmative* Aryan religion which is the product of a *ruling* class, one should read the law-book of Manu. (The deification of the feeling of power in the Brahmin: it is interesting to note that it originated in the warrior-caste, and was later transferred to the priests.)

If one wishes to see an *affirmative* religion of the Semitic order, which is the product of the *ruling* class, one should read the Koran or the earlier portions of the Old Testament. (*Mohammedanism*, as a religion for men, has profound contempt for the sentimentality and prevarication of Christianity. ... which, according to Mohammedans, is a woman's religion.)

If one wishes to see a *negative* religion of the Semitic order, which is the product of the *oppressed* class, one should read the New Testament (which, according to Indian and Aryan points of view, is a religion for the Chandala).

If one wishes to see a *negative* Aryan religion, which is the product of the *ruling* classes, one should study Buddhism.

It is quite in the nature of things that we have no Aryan religion which is the product of the *oppressed* classes; for that would have been a contradiction: a race of masters is either paramount or else it goes to the dogs.

146. (1885-1886)

Religion, *per se*, has nothing to do with morality; yet both offshoots of the Jewish religion are *essentially* moral religions—which prescribe the rules of living, and procure obedience to their principles by means of rewards and punishment.

147. (Spring-Fall 1887)

Paganism—Christianity.—Paganism is that which says yea to all that is natural, it is innocence in being natural, "naturalness." *Christianity* is that which says no to all that is natural, it is a certain lack of dignity in being natural; hostility to Nature.

"Innocent":—Petronius is innocent, for instance. Beside this happy man a Christian is absolutely devoid of innocence. But since even the *Christian* status is ultimately only a natural condition, the term "Christian" soon begins to mean the *counterfeiting of the psychological interpretation.*

148. (1883-1886)

The Christian priest is from the root a mortal enemy of sensuality: one cannot imagine a greater contrast to his attitude than the guileless, slightly awed, and solemn attitude, which the religious rites of the most honourable women in Athens maintained in the presence of the symbol of sex. In all non-ascetic religions the procreative act is *the* secret *per se*: a sort of symbol of perfection and of the designs of the future: re-birth, immortality.

149. (1880-1881)

Our belief in ourselves is the greatest fetter, the most telling spur, and the *strongest pinion.* Christianity ought to have elevated the innocence of man to the position of an article of belief—men would then have become gods: in those days believing was still possible.

150. (Spring-Fall 1887)

The egregious *lie* of history: as if it were the *corruption* of Paganism that opened the road to Christianity. As a matter of fact, it was the enfeeblement and *moralisation* of the man of antiquity. The new interpretation of natural functions, which made them appear like *vices,* had already gone before!

DIONYSUS VERSUS THE CRUCIFIED

151. (1885-1886)

Religions are ultimately wrecked by the belief in morality. The idea of the Christian moral God becomes untenable,—hence "Atheism,"—as though there could be no other god.

Culture is likewise wrecked by the belief in morality. For when the necessary and only possible conditions of its growth are revealed, nobody *will* any longer countenance it (Buddhism).

152. (March-June 1888)

The physiology of Nihilistic religions.—All in all, the *Nihilistic* religions are *systematised histories of sickness* described in religious and moral terminology.

In pagan cultures it is around the interpretation of the great annual cycles that the religious cult turns; in Christianity it is around a cycle of *paralytic phenomena.*

153. (November 1887-March 1888)

This *Nihilistic* religion gathers together all the *decadent elements* and things of like order which it can find in antiquity, viz.:—

(a) The *weak* and the *botched* (the refuse of the ancient world, and that of which it rid itself with most violence).

(b) Those who are *morally obsessed* and *anti-pagan.*

(c) Those who are *weary of politics* and indifferent (the *blasé* Romans), the *denationalised,* who know not what they are.

(d) Those who are tired of themselves—who are happy to be party to a subterranean conspiracy.

154. (March-June 1888)

Buddha versus *Christ.*—Among the Nihilistic religions, Christianity and *Buddhism* may always be sharply distinguished. *Buddhism* is the expression of a *fine evening,* perfectly sweet and mild—it is a sort of gratitude towards all that lies hidden, including that which it entirely lacks, viz., bitterness, disillusionment, and resentment. Finally it possesses lofty intellectual love; it has got over all the subtlety of philosophical contradictions, and is even resting after it, though it is precisely from that source that it derives its intellectual glory and its glow as of a sunset (it originated in the higher classes).

Christianity is a degenerative movement, consisting of all kinds of decaying and excremental elements: it is *not* the expression of the downfall of a race; it is, from the root, an agglomeration of all the morbid elements which are mutually attractive and which gravitate to one another.... It is therefore *not* a national religion, *not* determined by race: it appeals to the disinherited everywhere; it consists of a foundation of resentment against all that is successful and dominant: it is in need of a symbol which represents the damnation of everything successful and dominant. It is opposed to every form of *intellectual* movement, to all philosophy: it takes up the cudgels for idiots, and utters a curse upon all intellect. Resentment against those who are gifted, learned, intellectually independent: in all these it suspects the element of success and domination.

155. (Spring-Fall 1887)

In Buddhism this thought prevails: "All passions, everything which creates emotions and leads to blood, is a call to action"—to this extent alone are its believers *warned* against evil. For action has no sense, it merely binds one to existence. All existence, however, has no sense. Evil is interpreted as that which leads to irrationalism: to the affirmation of means whose end is denied. A road to nonentity is the desideratum, *hence all* emotional impulses are regarded with horror. For instance: "On no account seek after revenge! Be the enemy of no one!"—The Hedonism of the weary finds its highest expression here. Nothing is more utterly foreign to Buddhism than the Jewish fanaticism of St. Paul: nothing could be more contrary to its instinct than the tension, fire, and unrest of the religious man, and, above all, that form of sensuality which sanctifies Christianity with the name "Love." Moreover, it is the cultured and very intellectual classes who find blessedness in Buddhism: a race wearied and besotted by centuries of philosophical quarrels, but not *beneath all culture* as those classes were from which Christianity sprang.... In the Buddhistic ideal, there is essentially an emancipation from good and evil: a very subtle suggestion of a Beyond to all morality is thought out in its teaching, and this Beyond is supposed to be compatible with perfection,—the condition being, that even good actions are only needed *pro tem.*,[68] merely as a means,—that is to say, in order to be free from *all* action.

156. (November 1887-March 1888)

How very curious it is to see a *Nihilistic* religion such as Christianity, sprung from, and in keeping with, a decrepit and worn-out people, who have outlived all strong instincts, being transferred step by step to another environment—that is to say, to a land of young people, *who have not yet lived at all.* The joy of the final chapter, of the fold and of the evening, preached to barbarians and Germans! How thoroughly all of it must first have been barbarised, Germanised! To those who had dreamed of a *Walhalla:* who found happiness only in war!—A *super*national religion preached in the midst of chaos, where *no nations yet existed even.*

157. (January-Fall 1888)

The only way to refute priests and religions is this: to show that their errors are no longer *beneficent*—that they are rather harmful; in short, that their own "proof of power" no longer holds good....

---

2. CONCERNING THE HISTORY OF CHRISTIANITY.

158. (1888)

Christianity as an *historical reality* should not be confounded with that one root which its name recalls. The *other* roots, from which it has sprung, are by far the more important. It is an unprecedented abuse of names to identify such manifestations of decay and such abortions as the "Christian Church," "Christian belief," and "Christian life," with that Holy Name. What did Christ *deny?*—Everything which today is called Christian.

---

[68] "for the time being"

159. (November 1887-March 1888)

The whole of the Christian *creed*—all Christian "truth," is idle falsehood and deception, and is precisely the reverse of that which was at the bottom of the first Christian movement.

All that which in the *ecclesiastical* sense is Christian, is just exactly what is most radically *anti-Christian*: crowds of things and people appear instead of symbols, history takes the place of eternal facts, it is all forms, rites, and dogmas instead of a "practice" of life. To be really Christian would mean to be absolutely indifferent to dogmas, cults, priests, church, and theology.

The practice of Christianity is no more an impossible phantasy than the practice of Buddhism is: it is merely a means to happiness.

160. (November 1887-March 1888)

Jesus goes straight to the point, the "Kingdom of Heaven" in the heart, and He does *not* find the means in duty to the Jewish Church; He even regards the reality of Judaism (its need to maintain itself) as nothing; He is concerned purely with the *inner* man.

Neither does He make anything of all the coarse forms relating to man's intercourse with God: He is opposed to the whole of the teaching of repentance and atonement; He points out how man ought to live in order to feel himself "deified," and how futile it is on his part to hope to live properly by showing repentance and contrition for his sins. "Sin is of no account" is practically his chief standpoint.

Sin, repentance, forgiveness,—all this does not belong to Christianity ... it is Judaism or Paganism which has become mixed up with Christ's teaching.

161. (November 1887-March 1888)

The *Kingdom of Heaven* is a state of the heart (of children it is written, "for theirs is the Kingdom of Heaven"): it has nothing to do with superterrestrial things. The Kingdom of God "cometh," not chronologically or historically, not on a certain day in the calendar; it is not something which one day appears and was not previously there; it is a "change of feeling in the individual," it is something which may come at any time and which may be absent at any time....

162. (November 1887-March 1888)

The thief on the cross;—When the criminal himself, who endures a painful death, declares: "the way this Jesus suffers and dies, without a murmur of revolt or enmity, graciously and resignedly, is the only right way," he assents to the gospel; and by this very fact *he is in Paradise*....

163. (November 1887-March 1888)

Jesus bids us:—not to resist, either by deeds or in our heart, him who ill-treats us;

He bids us admit of no grounds for separating ourselves from our wives;

He bids us make no distinction between foreigners and fellow-countrymen, strangers and familiars;

He bids us show anger to no one, and treat no one with contempt;—give alms secretly; not to desire to become rich;—not to swear;—not to stand in judgment;—become reconciled with our enemies and forgive offences;—not to worship in public.

"Blessedness" is nothing promised: it is here, with us, if we only wish to live and act in a particular way.

164. (November 1887-March 1888)

Subsequent Additions;—The whole of the prophet- and thaumaturgist-attitudes and the bad temper; while the conjuring-up of a supreme tribunal of justice is an abominable corruption (see Mark vi. 11: "And whosoever shall not receive you.... Verily I say unto you, It shall be more tolerable for Sodom and Gomorrah," etc.). The "fig tree" (Matt. xxi. 18, 19): "Now in the morning as he returned into the city, he hungered. And when he saw a fig tree in the way, he came to it, and found nothing thereon, but leaves only, and said unto it, Let no fruit grow on thee henceforward for ever. And presently the fig tree withered away."

165. (November 1887-March 1888)

The teaching of rewards and punishments has become mixed up with Christianity in a way which is quite absurd; everything is thereby spoilt. In the same way, the practice of the first *ecclesia militans*,[69] of the Apostle Paul and his attitude, is put forward as if it had been *commanded* or predetermined.

The subsequent glorification of the actual *life* and *teaching* of the first Christians: as if everything had been *prescribed beforehand* and had been only a matter of *following* directions——And as for the *fulfilment of scriptural prophecies*: how much of all that is more than forgery and cooking?

166. (November 1887-March 1888)

Jesus opposed a real life, a life in truth, to ordinary life: nothing could have been more foreign to His mind than the somewhat heavy nonsense of an "eternal Peter,"—of the eternal duration of a single person. Precisely what He combats is the exaggerated importance of the "person": how can He wish to immortalise it?

He likewise combats the hierarchy within the community; He never promises a certain proportion of reward for a certain proportion of deserts: how can He have meant to teach the doctrine of punishment and reward in a Beyond?

167. (November 1887-March 1888)

Christianity is an ingenuous attempt at bringing about a *Buddhistic movement in favour of peace,* sprung from the very heart of the resenting masses ... but transformed by *Paul* into a mysterious pagan cult, which was ultimately able to accord with the whole of *State organisation* ... and which carries on war, condemns, tortures, conjures, and hates.

Paul bases his teaching upon the need of mystery felt by the great masses capable of religious emotions: he seeks a *victim,* a bloody phantasmagoria, which may be equal to a contest with the images of a secret cult: God on the cross, the drinking of blood, the *unio mystica* with the "victim."

---

[69] "church militant"

He seeks the prolongation of life after death (the blessed and atoned after-life of the individual soul) which he puts in causal relation with the *victim* already referred to (according to the type of Dionysos, Mithras, Osiris).

He feels the necessity of bringing notions of *guilt* and *sin* into the foreground, *not* a new practice of life (as Jesus Himself demonstrated and taught), but a new cult, a new belief, a belief in a miraculous metamorphosis ("Salvation" through belief).

He understood the *great needs of the pagan worlds* and he gave quite an absolutely arbitrary picture of those two plain facts, Christ's life and death. He gave the whole a new accent, altering the equilibrium everywhere … he was one of the most active destroyers of primitive Christianity.

The attempt made on the life of *priests and theologians* culminated, thanks to Paul, in a new priesthood and theology—a *ruling* caste and a *Church*.

The attempt made to suppress the fussy importance of the "person," culminated in the belief in the eternal "personality" (and in the anxiety concerning "eternal salvation" …), and in the most paradoxical exaggeration of individual egoism.

This is the humorous side of the question—tragic humour: Paul again set up on a large scale precisely what Jesus had overthrown by His life. At last, when the Church edifice was complete, it even sanctioned the *existence* of the *State*.

168. (November 1887-March 1888)

The Church is precisely that against which Jesus inveighed—and against which He taught His disciples to fight.

169. (November 1887-March 1888)

A God who died for our sins, salvation through faith, resurrection after death—all these things are the counterfeit coins of real Christianity, for which that pernicious blockhead Paul must be held responsible.

The *life which must serve as an example* consists in love and humility; in the abundance of hearty emotion which does not even exclude the lowliest; in the formal renunciation of all desire of making its rights felt; in conquest, in the sense of triumph over oneself; in the belief in salvation in this world, despite all sorrow, opposition, and death; in forgiveness and the absence of anger and contempt; in the absence of a desire to be rewarded; in the refusal to be bound to anybody; abandonment to all that is most spiritual and intellectual;—in fact, a very proud life controlled by the will of a servile and poor life.

Once the Church had allowed itself to take over *all the Christian practice*, and had formally sanctioned the State,—that kind of life which Jesus combats and condemns,—it was obliged to lay the sense of Christianity in other things than early Christian ideals—that is to say, in the *faith* in incredible things, in the ceremonial of prayers, worship, feasts, etc. etc. The notions "sin," "forgiveness," "punishment," "reward"—everything, in fact, which had nothing in common with, and was quite *absent* from, primitive Christianity, now comes into the foreground.

An appalling stew of Greek philosophy and Judaism; asceticism; continual judgments and condemnations; the order of rank, etc.

170. (November 1887-March 1888)

Christianity has, from the first, always transformed the symbolical into crude realities:

(1) The antitheses "true life" and "false life" were misunderstood and changed into "life here" and "life beyond."

(2) The notion "eternal life," as opposed to the personal life which is ephemeral, is translated into "personal immortality";

(3) The process of fraternising by means of sharing the same food and drink, after the Hebrew-Arabian manner, is interpreted as the "miracle of transubstantiation."

(4) "Resurrection" which was intended to mean the entrance to the "true life," in the sense of being intellectually "born again," becomes an historical contingency, supposed to take place at some moment after death;

(5) The teaching of the Son of man as the "Son of God,"—that is to say, the life-relationship between man and God,—becomes the

"second person of the Trinity," and thus the filial relationship of every man—even the lowest—to God, is *done away with*;

(6) Salvation through faith (that is to say, that there is no other way to this filial relationship to God, save through the *practice of life* taught by Christ) becomes transformed into the belief that there is a miraculous way of *atoning* for all *sin*; though not through our own endeavours, but by means of Christ:

For all these purposes, "Christ on the Cross" had to be interpreted afresh. The *death* itself would certainly not be the principal feature of the event ... it was only another sign pointing to the way in which one should behave towards the authorities and the laws of the world—*that one was not to defend oneself—this was the exemplary life.*

171. (March-June 1888)

Concerning the psychology of *Paul*.[70]—The important fact is Christ's death. This remains to be *explained* .... That there may be truth or error in an explanation never entered these people's heads: one day a sublime possibility strikes them, "His death *might* mean so and so"—and it forthwith *becomes* so and so. An hypothesis is proved by the sublime *ardour* it lends to its discoverer....

"The proof of strength": *i.e.,* a thought is demonstrated by its *effects* ("by their fruits," as the Bible ingenuously says); that which fires enthusiasm must be *true*,—what one loses one's blood for must be *true*
—

In every department of this world of thought, the sudden feeling of power which an idea imparts to him who is responsible for it, is placed to the *credit* of that idea:—and as there seems no other way of honouring an idea than by calling it true, the first epithet it is honoured with is the word *true*.... How could it have any effect otherwise? It was imagined by some power: if that power were not real, it could not be the cause of anything.... The thought is then understood as *inspired*: the effect it causes has something of the violent nature of a demoniacal influence—

A thought which a decadent like Paul could not resist and to which he completely yields, is thus "proved" *true*!!!

---

[70] See also *The Dawn* sec. 68 and *The Antichrist* sec. 42, 44, 47.

Friedrich Nietzsche

All these holy epileptics and visionaries did not possess a thousandth part of the honesty in self-criticism with which a philologist, nowadays, reads a text, or tests the truth of an historical event.... Beside us, such people were moral cretins.

172. (Spring-Fall 1887)

It matters little *whether a thing be true*, provided it be *effective*: total *absence of intellectual uprightness*. Everything is good, whether it be lying, slander, or shameless "cooking," provided it serve to heighten the degree of heat to the point at which people "believe."

We are face to face with an actual school for the teaching of *the means wherewith* men are *seduced* to a belief: we see systematic *contempt* for those spheres whence contradiction might come (that is to say, for reason, philosophy, wisdom, doubt, and caution); a shameless praising and glorification of the teaching, with continual references to the fact that it was God who presented us with it—that the apostle signifies nothing—that no criticism is brooked, but only faith, acceptance; that it is the greatest blessing and favour to receive such a doctrine of salvation; that the state in which one should receive it, ought to be one of the profoundest thankfulness and humility....

The resentment which the lowly feel against all those in high places, is continually turned to account: the fact that this teaching is revealed to them as the reverse of the wisdom of the world, against the power of the world, seduces them to it. This teaching convinces the outcasts and the botched of all sorts and conditions; it promises blessedness, advantages, and privileges to the most insignificant and most humble men; it fanaticises the poor, the small, and the foolish, and fills them with insane vanity, as though *they* were the meaning and salt of the earth.

Again, I say, all this cannot be sufficiently contemned, we spare ourselves a criticism of the teaching; it is sufficient to take note of the means it uses in order to be aware of the nature of the phenomenon one is examining. It identified itself with *virtue*, it appropriated the whole of the *fascinating power of virtue*, shamelessly, for its own purposes ... it availed itself of the power of paradox, and of the need, manifested by old civilisation, for pepper and absurdity; it amazed and revolted at the same time; it provoked persecutions and ill-treatment.

It is the same kind of *well-thought-out meanness* with which the Jewish priesthood established their power and built up their Church....

One must be able to discern: (1) that warmth of passion "love" (resting on a base of ardent sensuality); (2) the thoroughly *ignoble character* of Christianity:—the continual exaggeration and verbosity;—the lack of cool intellectuality and irony;—the unmilitary character of all its instincts;—the priestly prejudices against manly pride, sensuality, the sciences, the arts.

173. (Summer-Fall 1888)

Paul: seeks power *against* ruling Judaism,—his attempt is too weak.... Transvaluation of the notion "Jew": the "race" is put aside: but that means denying the very basis of the whole structure. The "martyr," the "fanatic," the value of all *strong* belief. Christianity is the *form of decay* of the old world, after the latter's collapse, and it is characterised by the fact that it brings all the most sickly and unhealthy elements and needs to the top.

Consequently other instincts had to step into the foreground, in order to *constitute* an entity, a power able to stand alone—in short, a condition of tense sorrow was necessary, like that out of which the Jews had derived their *instinct of self-preservation*....

The persecution of Christians was invaluable for this purpose.

Unity in the face of danger; the conversion of the masses becomes the only means of putting an end to the persecution of the individual. (The notion "conversion" is therefore made as elastic as possible.)

174. (Spring-Fall 1887; revised Spring-Fall 1888)

The *Christian Judaic* life: here resentment did not prevail. The great persecutions alone could have driven out the passions to that extent—as also the *ardour of love* and *hate*.

When the creatures a man most loves are sacrificed before his eyes for the sake of his faith, that man becomes *aggressive*; the triumph of Christianity is due to its persecutors.

Asceticism is not specifically Christian: this is what Schopenhauer misunderstood. It only shoots up in Christianity, wherever it would have existed without that religion.

Melancholy Christianity, the torture and torment of the conscience, also only a peculiarity of a particular soil, where Christian values have taken root: it is not Christianity properly speaking. Christianity has absorbed all the different kinds of diseases which grow from morbid soil: one could refute it at one blow by showing that it did not know how to resist any contagion. But *that* precisely is the essential feature of it. Christianity is a type of decadence.

175. (Spring-Fall 1887; revised Spring-Fall 1888)

The reality on which Christianity was able to build up its power consisted of the small dispersed *Jewish families*, with their warmth, tenderness, and peculiar readiness to help, which, to the whole of the Roman Empire, was perhaps the most incomprehensible and least familiar of their characteristics; they were also united by their pride at being a "chosen people," concealed beneath a cloak of humility, and by their secret denial of all that was uppermost and that possessed power and splendour, although there was no shade of envy in their denial. *To have recognised this as a power,* to have regarded this *blessed* state as communicable, seductive, and infectious even where pagans were concerned—this constituted Paul's genius: to use up the treasure of latent energy and cautious happiness for the purposes of "a Jewish Church of free confession," and to avail himself of all the Jewish experience, their propaganda, and their expertness in *the preservation of a community* under a foreign power—this is what he conceived to be his duty. He it was who discovered that absolutely unpolitical and isolated body of *paltry people*, and their art of asserting themselves and pushing themselves to the front, by means of a host of acquired virtues which are made to represent the only forms of virtue ("the self-preservative measure and weapon of success of a certain class of man").

The principle of *love* comes from the small community of Jewish people: a *very passionate* soul glows here, beneath the ashes of humility and wretchedness: it is neither Greek, Indian, nor German. The song in praise of love which Paul wrote is not Christian; it is the Jewish flare of that eternal flame which is Semitic. If Christianity has done anything essentially new in a psychological sense, it is this, that it has *increased the temperature of the soul* among those cooler and more noble races who were at one time at the head of affairs; it discovered that the most wretched life could be made rich and invaluable, by means of an elevation of the temperature of the soul....

It is easily understood that a transfer of this sort could *not* take place among the ruling classes: the Jews and Christians were at a disadvantage owing to their bad manners—spiritual strength and passion, when accompanied by bad manners, only provoke loathing (I become aware of these bad manners while reading the New Testament). It was necessary to be related both in baseness and sorrow with this type of lower manhood in order to feel anything attractive in him.... The attitude a man maintains towards the New Testament is a test of the amount of taste he may have for the classics (see Tacitus`; he who is not revolted by it, he who does not feel honestly and deeply that he is in the presence of a sort of *foeda superstitio*[71] when reading it, and who does not draw his hand back so as not to soil his fingers— such a man does not know what is classical. A man must feel about "the cross" as Goethe did.[72]

176. (March-June 1888)

The reaction of paltry people:—Love provides the feeling of highest power. It should be understood to what extent, not man in general, but only a certain kind of man is speaking here.

---

[71] "ugly superstition"

[72] Vieles kann ich ertragen. Die meisten beschwerlichen Dinge
Duld' ich mit ruhigem Mut, wie es ein Gott mir gebeut.
Wenige sind mir jedoch wie Gift und Schlange zuwider;
Viere: Rauch des Tabaks, Warzen, und Knoblauch und

Goethe's *Venetian Epigrams* No. 67.

Much can I bear. Things the most irksome
I endure with such patience as comes from a god.
Four things, however, repulse me like venom:—Tobacco
smoke, garlic, bugs, and the cross.

"We are godly in love, we shall be 'the children of God'; God loves us and wants nothing from us save love"; that is to say: all morality, obedience, and action, do not produce the same feeling of power and freedom as love does;—a man does nothing wicked from sheer love, but he does much more than if he were prompted by obedience and virtue alone.

Here is the happiness of the herd, the communal feeling in big things as in small, the living sentiment of unity felt as the *sum of the feeling of life.* Helping, caring for, and being useful, constantly kindle the feeling of power; visible success, the expression of pleasure, emphasise the feeling of power; pride is not lacking either, it is felt in the form of the community, the House of God, and the "chosen people."

As a matter of fact, man has once more experienced an *"altération" of his personality*: this time he called his feeling of love— God. The awakening of such a feeling must be pictured; it is a sort of ecstasy, a strange language, a "Gospel"—it was this newness which did not allow man to attribute love to himself—he thought it was God leading him on and taking shape in his heart. "God descends among men," one's neighbour is transfigured and becomes a God (in so far as he provokes the sentiment of love), *Jesus is the neighbour,* the moment He is transfigured in thought into a God, and into a cause *provoking the feeling of power.*

177. (January-Fall 1888)

Believers are aware that they owe an infinite amount to Christianity, and therefore conclude that its Founder must have been a man of the first rank.... This conclusion is false, but it is typical of the reverents. Regarded objectively, it is, *in the first place,* just possible that they are mistaken concerning the extent of their debt to Christianity: a man's convictions prove nothing concerning the thing he is convinced about, and in religions they are more likely to give rise to suspicions.... Secondly, it is possible that the debt owing to Christianity is not due to its Founder at all, but to the whole structure, the whole thing—to the Church, etc. The notion "Founder" is so very equivocal, that it may stand even for the accidental cause of a movement: the person of the Founder has been inflated in proportion as the Church has grown: but even this process of veneration allows of the conclusion that, at one time or other, this Founder was something exceedingly insecure and doubtful—in the beginning… Let any one think of the *free and easy way* in which Paul treats the problem of the personality of Jesus, how he almost juggles with it some one who died, who was seen after His death,—some one whom the Jews delivered up to death—all this was only the theme—*Paul* wrote the music to it.

178. (1884)

The founder of a religion *may* be quite insignificant—a match and *no more*!

179. (November 1887-March 1888)

Concerning the psychological problem of Christianity.—*The driving forces are*: *ressentiment*, popular insurrection, the revolt of the bungled and the botched. (In Buddhism it is different: it is not *born* of *ressentiment*. It rather combats *ressentiment* because the latter leads to *action*!)

This party, which stands for freedom, understands that the *abandonment of antagonism in thought and deed* is a condition of distinction and preservation. Here lies the psychological difficulty which has stood in the way of Christianity being understood: the force which created it, urges to a struggle against itself.

Only as a party standing *for peace* and *innocence* can this insurrectionary movement hope to be successful: it must conquer by means of excessive mildness, sweetness, softness, and its instincts are aware of this. The *feat* was to deny and condemn the force, of which man is the expression, and to press the reverse of that force continually to the fore, by word and deed.

180. (November 1887-March 1888)

The pretence of youthfulness.—It is a mistake to imagine that, with Christianity, an ingenuous and youthful people rose against an old culture; the story goes that it was out of the lowest levels of society, where Christianity flourished and shot its roots, that the more profound source of life gushed forth afresh: but nothing can be understood of the psychology of Christianity, if it be supposed that it was the expression of revived youth among a people, or of the resuscitated strength of a race. It is rather a typical form of decadence, of moral-softening and of hysteria, amid a general hotch-potch of races and people that had lost all aims and had grown weary and sick. The wonderful company which gathered round this master-seducer of the populace, would not be at all out of place in a Russian novel: all the diseases of the nerves seem to give one another a rendezvous in this crowd—the absence of a known duty, the feeling that everything is nearing its end, that nothing is any longer worth while, and that contentment lies in *dolce far niente*.[73]

The power and certainty of the future in the Jew's instinct, its monstrous will for life and for power, lies in its ruling classes; the people who upheld primitive Christianity are best distinguished by this *exhausted condition* of their instincts. On the one hand, they are sick of everything; on the other, they are content with each other, with themselves and for themselves.

181. (Spring-Fall 1887)

Christianity regarded as *emancipated Judaism* (just as a nobility which is both racial and indigenous ultimately emancipates itself from these conditions, and *goes in search of* kindred elements....).

(1) As a Church (community) on the territory of the State, as an unpolitical institution.

(2) As life, breeding, practice, art of living.

(3) As a *religion of sin* (sin committed against *God, being the only recognised kind,* and the only cause of all suffering), with a universal cure for it. There is no sin save against God; what is done against men, man shall not sit in judgment upon, nor call to account, except in the name of God. At the same time, all commandments (love): everything is associated with God, and all acts are performed according to God's will. Beneath this arrangement there lies exceptional intelligence (a very narrow life, such as that led by the Eskimo, can only be endured by most peaceful and indulgent people: the Judeo-Christian dogma turns against sin in favour of the "sinner").

---

[73] "sweet doing nothing"

182. (Spring-Fall 1887)

The Jewish priesthood understood how to present everything it claimed to be right as a *divine precept*, as an act of obedience to God, and also to introduce all those things which conduced to *preserve Israel* and were the *conditions* of its existence (for instance: the large number of "*works*": circumcision and the cult of sacrifices, as the very pivot of the national conscience), not as Nature, but as God.

This process continued; within the very heart of Judaism, where the need of these "works" was not felt (that is to say, as a means of keeping a race distinct), a priestly sort of man was pictured, whose bearing towards the aristocracy was like that of "noble nature"; a sacerdotalism of the soul, which now, in order to throw its opposite into strong relief, attaches value, not to the "dutiful acts" themselves, but to the sentiment....

At bottom, the problem was once again, how to make a certain kind of soul *prevail*: it was also *a popular insurrection in the midst of a priestly people*—a pietistic movement coming from below (sinners, publicans, women, and children). Jesus of Nazareth was the symbol of their sect. And again, in order to believe in themselves, they were in need of a *theological transfiguration*: they require nothing less than "the Son of God" in order to create a belief for themselves. And just as the priesthood had falsified the whole history of Israel, another attempt was made, here, to *alter and falsify* the whole history of mankind in such a way as to make Christianity seem like the most important event it contained. This movement could have originated only upon the soil of Judaism, the main feature of which was the confounding of *guilt with sorrow* and the reduction of all *sin* to *sin against God*. Of all this, Christianity is the *second degree of power.*

183. (November 1887-March 1888)

The symbolism of Christianity is based upon that of *Judaism*, which had already transfigured all reality (history, Nature) into a holy and artificial unreality—which refused to recognise real history, and which showed no more interest in a natural course of things.

184. (March-June 1888)

The Jews made the attempt to prevail, after two of their castes—the warrior and the agricultural castes, had disappeared from their midst.

In this sense they are the "castrated people": they have their priests and then—their Chandala....

How easily a disturbance occurs among them—an insurrection of their Chandala. This was the origin of *Christianity.*

Owing to the fact that they had no knowledge of warriors except as their masters, they introduced enmity towards the nobles, the men of honour, pride, and power, and the *ruling* classes, into their religion: they are pessimists from *indignation....*

Thus they created a very important and novel position: the priests in the van of the Chandala—against the *noble classes....*

Christianity was the logical conclusion of this movement: even in the Jewish priesthood, it still scented the existence of the caste, of the privileged and noble minority—*it therefore did away with priests.*

Christ is the unit of the Chandala who removes the priest ... the Chandala who redeems himself....

That is why the *French* Revolution is the lineal descendant and the continuator of *Christianity*— it is characterised by an instinct of hate towards castes, nobles, and the last privileges.

185. (Spring-Fall 1887)

The "*Christian Ideal*" put on the stage with Jewish astuteness—these are the fundamental *psychological forces* of its "nature":—

Revolt against the ruling spiritual powers;

The attempt to make those virtues which facilitate the *happiness of the lowly,* a standard of all values—in fact, to call *God* that which is no more than the self-preservative instinct of that class of man possessed of least vitality;

Obedience and absolute *abstention* from war and resistance, justified by this ideal;

The love of one another as a result of the love of God.

The trick: The *denial* of all *natural mobilia*, and their transference to the spiritual world beyond ... the exploitation of *virtue* and its *veneration* for wholly interested motives, gradual *denial* of virtue in everything that is not Christian.

186. (Spring-Fall 1887)

The *profound contempt* with which the Christian was treated by the noble people of antiquity, is of the same order as the present instinctive aversion to Jews: it is the hatred which free and self-respecting classes feel towards those *who wish to creep in secretly*, and who combine an awkward bearing with foolish self-sufficiency.

The New Testament is the gospel of a completely *ignoble* species of man; its pretensions to highest values—*yea, to all* values, is, as a matter of fact, revolting—even nowadays.

187. (Spring-Fall 1887)

How little the subject matters! It is the spirit which gives the thing life! What a quantity of stuffy and sick-room air there is in all that chatter about "redemption," "love," "blessedness," "faith," "truth," "eternal life"! Let any one look into a really pagan book and compare the two; for instance, in Petronius, nothing at all is done, said, desired, and valued, which, according to a bigoted Christian estimate, is not sin, or even deadly sin. And yet how happy one feels with the purer air, the superior intellectuality, the quicker pace, and the free overflowing strength which is certain of the future! In the whole of the New Testament there is not one *bouffonnerie*:[74] but that fact alone would suffice to refute any book....

188. (Spring-Fall 1887)

The *profound lack of dignity* with which all life, which is not Christian, is condemned: it does not suffice them to think meanly of their actual opponents, they cannot do with less than a general slander of everything that is not *themselves*.... An abject and crafty soul is in the

---

[74] "buffoonery," incidence of clownishness

most perfect harmony with the arrogance of piety, as witness the early Christians.

The *future*: they see that *they are heavily paid for it.... Theirs is the muddiest kind of spirit that exists.* The whole of Christ's life is so arranged as to confirm the prophecies of the Scriptures: He behaves in such wise *in order that* they may be right....

189. (Spring-Fall 1887)

The deceptive interpretation of the words, the doings, and the condition of *dying people*; the natural fear of death, for instance, is systematically confounded with the supposed fear of what is to happen "after death." ...

190. (Spring-Fall 1887)

The *Christians* have done exactly what the Jews did before them. They introduced what they conceived to be an innovation and a thing necessary to self-preservation into their Master's teaching, and wove His life into it. They likewise credited Him with all the wisdom of a maker of proverbs—*in short,* they represented their everyday life and activity as an act of obedience, and thus sanctified their propaganda.

What it all depends upon, may be gathered from Paul: it is *not much.* What remains is the development of a type of saint, out of the values which these people regarded as saintly.

The whole of the "doctrine of miracles," including the resurrection, is the result of self-glorification on the part of the community, which ascribed to its Master those qualities it ascribed to itself, but in a higher degree (or, better still, it derived its strength from Him....)

191. (November 1887-March 1888)

The Christians have never led the life which Jesus commanded them to lead, and the impudent fable of the "justification by faith," and its unique and transcendental significance, is only the result of the Church's lack of courage and will in acknowledging those *"works"* which Jesus commanded.

The Buddhist behaves differently from the non-Buddhist; but *the Christian behaves as all the rest of the world does,* and possesses a Christianity of ceremonies and *states of the soul.*

The profound and contemptible falsehood of Christianity in Europe makes us deserve the contempt of the Arabs, Hindus, and Chinese.... Let any one listen to the words of the first German statesman, concerning that which has preoccupied Europe for the last forty years.

192. (Spring-Fall 1887; revised Spring-Fall 1888)

"Faith" or *"works"*?[75]—But that the "works," the habit of particular works may engender a certain *set of values or thoughts,* is just as natural as it would be unnatural for "works" to proceed from mere valuations. Man must practise, *not* how to strengthen feelings of value, but how to strengthen action: first of all, one must be able *to do something....* Luther's Christian Dilettantism. Faith is an asses' bridge. The background consists of a profound conviction on the part of Luther and his peers, that they are enabled to accomplish Christian "works," a personal fact, disguised under an extreme doubt as to whether *all* action is not sin and devil's work, so that the worth of life depends upon isolated and highly-strained conditions of *inactivity* (prayer, effusion, etc.).—Ultimately, Luther would be right: the instincts which are expressed by the whole bearing of the reformers are the most brutal that exist. Only in *turning absolutely away* from themselves, and in becoming absorbed in the *opposite* of themselves, only by means of an *illusion* ("faith") was existence endurable to them.

193. (November 1887-March 1888)

"What was to be done in order to believe?"—an absurd question. That which is wrong with Christianity is, that it does none of the things that Christ *commanded.*

It is a mean life, but *seen* through the eye of contempt.

---

[75] See also *The Dawn* section 22.

194. (November 1887-March 1888)

The entrance into the *real* life—*a man saves his own life by living the life of the multitude.*

195. (November 1887-March 1888)

Christianity has become something fundamentally different from what its Founder wished it to be. It is the great *anti-pagan movement* of antiquity, formulated with the use of the life, teaching, and "words" of the Founder of Christianity, but interpreted quite *arbitrarily*, according to a scheme embodying *profoundly different needs*: translated into the language of all the *subterranean religions* then existing.

It is the rise of Pessimism (whereas Jesus wished to bring the peace and the happiness of the lambs): and moreover the Pessimism of the weak, of the inferior, of the suffering, and of the oppressed.

Its mortal enemies are (1) *Power*, whether in the form of character, intellect, or taste, and "worldliness"; (2) the "good cheer" of classical times, the noble levity and scepticism, hard pride, eccentric dissipation, and cold frugality of the sage, Greek refinement in manners, words, and form. Its mortal enemy is as much the *Roman* as the *Greek*.

The attempt on the part of *anti-paganism* to establish itself on a philosophical basis, and to make its tenets possible: it shows a taste for the ambiguous figures of antique culture, and above all for Plato, who was, more than any other, an anti-Hellene and Semite in instinct…. It also shows a taste for Stoicism, which is essentially the work of Semites ("dignity" is regarded as severity, law; virtue is held to be greatness, self-responsibility, authority, greatest sovereignty over oneself—this is Semitic.) The Stoic is an Arabian sheik wrapped in Greek togas and notions.

196. (November 1887-March 1888)

Christianity only resumes the fight which had already been begun against the *classical* ideal and *noble* religion.

As a matter of fact, the whole process of *transformation* is only an adaptation to the needs and to the level of intelligence of *religious* masses then existing:—those masses which believed in Isis, Mithras,

Dionysos, and the "great mother," and which demanded the following things of a religion: (1) hopes of a beyond, (2) the bloody phantasmagoria of animal sacrifice (the mystery), (3) holy legend and the redeeming *deed*, (4) asceticism, denial of the world, superstitious "purification," (5) a hierarchy as a part of the community. In short, Christianity everywhere fitted the already prevailing and increasing *anti-pagan tendency*—those cults which Epicurus combated,—or more exactly, those *religions proper to the lower herd, women, slaves, and ignoble classes.*

The misunderstandings are therefore the following:—

(1) The immortality of the individual;

(2) The assumed existence of *another* world;[76]

(3) The absurd notion of punishment and expiation in the heart of the interpretation of existence;

(4) The profanation of the divine nature of man, instead of its accentuation, and the construction of a very profound chasm, which can only be crossed by the help of a miracle or by means of the most thorough self-contempt;

(5) The whole world of corrupted imagination and morbid passion, instead of a simple and loving life of action, instead of Buddhistic happiness attainable on earth;

(6) An ecclesiastical order with a priesthood, theology, cults, and sacraments; in short, everything that Jesus of Nazareth *combated*;

(7) The *miraculous* in everything and everybody, superstition too: while precisely the trait which distinguished Judaism and primitive Christianity was their *repugnance to* miracles and their relative *rationalism.*

197. (Spring-Fall 1887)

The psychological pre-requisites:—Ignorance and *lack of culture,*—the sort of ignorance which has unlearned every kind of shame: let any one imagine those impudent saints in the heart of Athens;

---

[76] See *Twilight of the Idols* "How The 'True World' Ultimately Became A Fable"

The *Jewish instinct of a chosen people*: they appropriate *all the virtues*, without further ado, as their own, and regard the rest of the world as their opposite; this is a profound sign of *spiritual depravity*;

The total lack of real aims and real *duties*, for which other virtues are required than those of the bigot—*the State undertook this work for them*: and the impudent people still behaved as though they had no need of the State. "Except ye become as little children" —oh, how far we are from this psychological ingenuousness!

198. (November 1887-March 1888)

The Founder of Christianity had to pay dearly for having directed His teaching at the lowest classes of Jewish society and intelligence. They understood Him only according to the limitations of their own spirit.... It was a disgrace to concoct a history of salvation, a personal God, a personal Saviour, a personal immortality, and to have retained all the meanness of the "person," and of the "history" of a doctrine which denies the reality of all that is personal and historical.

The legend of salvation takes the place of the symbolic "now" and "all time," of the symbolic "here" and "everywhere"; and miracles appear instead of the psychological symbol.

199. (Spring-Fall 1887)

Nothing is less innocent than the New Testament. The soil from which it sprang is known. These people, possessed of an inflexible will to assert themselves, and who, once they had lost all natural hold on life, and had long existed without any right to existence, still knew how to prevail by means of hypotheses which were as unnatural as they were imaginary (calling themselves the chosen people, the community of saints, the people of the promised land, and the "Church"): these people made use of their *pia fraus*[77] with such skill, and with such "clean consciences," that one cannot be too cautious when they preach morality. When Jews step forward as the personification of innocence, the danger must be great. While reading the New

---

[77] "holy lie"

Testament a man should have his small fund of intelligence, mistrust, and wickedness constantly at hand.

People of the lowest origin, partly mob, outcasts not only from good society, but also from respectable society; grown away from the *atmosphere* of culture, and free from discipline; ignorant, without even a suspicion of the fact that conscience can also rule in spiritual matters in a word—the Jews: an instinctively crafty people, able to create an advantage, a means of *seduction* out of every conceivable hypothesis of superstition, even out of ignorance itself.

200. (Spring-Fall 1887; revised 1888)

I regard Christianity as the most fatal and seductive lie that has ever yet existed—as the greatest and most *impious lie*: I can discern the last sprouts and branches of its ideal beneath every form of disguise, I decline to enter into any compromise or false position in reference to it—I urge people to declare open war with it.

The *morality of paltry people* as the measure of all things: this is the most repugnant kind of degeneracy that civilisation has ever yet brought into existence. And this *kind of ideal* is hanging still, under the name of "God," over men's heads!!

201. (Spring-Fall 1887)

However modest one's demands may be concerning intellectual cleanliness, when one touches the New Testament one cannot help experiencing a sort of inexpressible feeling of discomfort; for the unbounded cheek with which the least qualified people will have their say in its pages, in regard to the greatest problems of existence, and claim to sit in judgment on such matters, exceeds all limits. The impudent levity with which the most unwieldy problems are spoken of here (life, the world, God, the purpose of life), as if they were not problems at all, but the most simple things which these little bigots *know all about*!!!

202. (Spring-Fall 1887; revised Spring-Fall 1888)

This was the most fatal form of insanity that has ever yet existed on earth:—when these little lying abortions of bigotry begin laying claim to the words "God," "last judgment," "truth," "love," "wisdom," "Holy Spirit," and thereby distinguishing themselves from the rest of the world; when such men begin to transvalue values to suit themselves, as though they were the sense, the salt, the standard, and the measure of all things; then all that one should do is this: build lunatic asylums for their incarceration. To *persecute* them was an egregious act of antique folly: this was taking them too seriously; it was making them serious.

The whole fatality was made possible by the fact that a similar form of megalomania was already *in existence,* the *Jewish* form (once the gulf separating the Jews from the Christian-Jews was bridged, the Christian-Jews *were compelled* to employ those self-preservative measures afresh which were discovered by the Jewish instinct, for their own self-preservation, after having accentuated them); and again through the fact that Greek moral philosophy had done everything that could be done to prepare the way for moral-fanaticism, even among Greeks and Romans, and to render it palatable.... Plato, the great importer of corruption, who was the first who refused to see Nature in morality, and who had already deprived the Greek gods of all their worth by his notion *"good"* was already tainted with *Jewish bigotry* (in Egypt?).

203. (Spring-Fall 1887; revised Spring-Fall 1888)

These small virtues of gregarious animals do not by any means lead to "eternal life": to put them on the stage in such a way, and to use them for one's own purpose is perhaps very smart; but to him who keeps his eyes open, even here, it remains, in spite of all, the most ludicrous performance. A man by no means deserves privileges, either on earth or in heaven, because he happens to have attained to perfection in the art of behaving like a good-natured little sheep; at best, he only remains a dear, absurd little ram with horns—provided, of course, he does not burst with vanity or excite indignation by assuming the airs of a supreme judge.

What a terrible glow of false colouring here floods the meanest virtues—as though they were the reflection of divine qualities!

The *natural* purpose and utility of every virtue is systematically *hushed up*; it can only be valuable in the light of a *divine* command or model, or in the light of the good which belongs to a beyond or a spiritual world. (This is magnificent!—As if it were a question of the *salvation of the soul*: but it was a means of making things bearable here with as many beautiful sentiments as possible.)

204. (Spring-Fall 1887; revised Spring-Fall 1888)

The *law*, which is the fundamentally realistic formula of certain self-preservative measures of a community, forbids certain actions that have a definite tendency to jeopardise the welfare of that community: it does *not* forbid the attitude of mind which gives rise to these actions —for in the pursuit of other ends the community requires these forbidden actions, namely, when it is a matter of opposing its *enemies*. The moral idealist now steps forward and says: "God sees into men's hearts: the action itself counts for nothing; the reprehensible attitude of mind from which it proceeds must be extirpated ..." In normal conditions men laugh at such things; it is only in exceptional cases, when a community lives *quite* beyond the need of waging war in order to maintain itself, that an ear is lent to such things. Any attitude of mind is abandoned, the utility of which cannot be conceived.

This was the case, for example, when Buddha appeared among a people that was both peaceable and afflicted with great intellectual weariness.

This was also the case in regard to the first Christian community (as also the Jewish), the primary condition of which was the absolutely *unpolitical* Jewish society. Christianity could grow only upon the soil of Judaism—that is to say, among a people that had already renounced the political life, and which led a sort of parasitic existence within the Roman sphere of government, Christianity goes a step *farther*: it allows men to "emasculate" themselves even more; the circumstances actually favour their doing so.—*Nature* is *expelled* from morality when it is said, "Love ye your enemies": for *Nature's* injunction, "Ye shall *love* your neighbour and *hate* your enemy," has now become senseless in the law (in instinct); now, even *the love a man feels for his neighbour* must first be based upon something (*a sort of love of God*). *God* is introduced everywhere, and *utility* is withdrawn; the natural *origin* of morality is denied everywhere: the *veneration of Nature*, which lies in *acknowledging a natural morality*, is *destroyed* to the roots....

Whence comes the *seductive charm* of this emasculate ideal of man? Why are we not *disgusted* by it, just as we are disgusted at the thought of a eunuch?... The answer is obvious: it is not the voice of the eunuch that revolts us, despite the cruel mutilation of which it is the result; for, as a matter of fact, it has grown sweeter.... And owing to the very fact that the "male organ" has been amputated from virtue, its voice now has a feminine ring, which, formerly, was not to be discerned.

On the other hand, we have only to think of the terrible hardness, dangers, and accidents to which a life of manly virtues leads—the life of a Corsican, even at the present day, or that of a heathen Arab (which resembles the Corsican's life even to the smallest detail: the Arab's songs might have been written by Corsicans)—in order to perceive how the most robust type of man was fascinated and moved by the voluptuous ring of this "goodness" and "purity." ... A pastoral melody ... an idyll ... the "good man": such things have most effect in ages when tragedy is abroad.

***

With this, we have realised to what extent the "idealist" (the ideal eunuch) also proceeds from a definite reality and is not merely a visionary.... He has perceived precisely that, for his kind of reality, a brutal injunction of the sort which prohibits certain actions has no sense (because the instinct which would urge him to these actions is *weakened,* thanks to a long need of practice, and of compulsion to practise). The castrator formulates a host of new self-preservative measures for a perfectly definite species of men: in this sense he is a realist. The *means* to which he has recourse for establishing his legislation, are the same as those of ancient legislators: he appeals to all authorities, to "God," and he exploits the notions "guilt and punishment"—that is to say, he avails himself of the whole of the older ideal, but interprets it differently; for instance: punishment is given a place in the inner self (it is called the pang of conscience).

In practice this kind of man *meets with his end* the moment the exceptional conditions favouring his existence cease to prevail—a sort of insular happiness, like that of Tahiti, and of the little Jews in the Roman provinces. Their only *natural* foe is the soil from which they spring: they must wage war against that, and once more give their *offensive* and *defensive* passions rope in order to be equal to it: their opponents are the adherents of the old ideal (this kind of hostility is shown on a grand scale by Paul in relation to Judaism, and by Luther in relation to the priestly ascetic ideal). The mildest form of this antagonism is certainly that of the first Buddhists; perhaps nothing has given rise to so much work, as the enfeeblement and discouragement of the feeling of *antagonism.* The struggle against resentment almost seems the Buddhist's first duty; thus only is his *peace* of soul secured. To isolate oneself without bitterness, this presupposes the existence of a surprisingly mild and sweet order of men,— saints....

***

The *Astuteness of moral castration.*—How is war waged against the virile passions and valuations? No violent physical means are available; the war must therefore be one of ruses, spells, and lies—in short, a "spiritual war."

First recipe: One appropriates virtue in general, and makes it the main feature of one's ideal; the older ideal is denied and declared to be *the reverse of all ideals.* Slander has to be carried to a fine art for this purpose.

Second recipe: A type of man is set up as a general *standard*; and this is projected into all things, behind all things, and behind the destiny of all things—as God.

Third recipe: The opponents of one's ideal are declared to be the opponents of God; one arrogates to oneself a *right* to great pathos, to power, and a right to curse and to bless.

Fourth recipe: All suffering, all gruesome, terrible, and fatal things are declared to be the results of opposition to *one's* ideal—all suffering is *punishment* even in the case of one's adherents (except it be a trial, etc.).

Fifth recipe: One goes so far as to regard Nature as the reverse of one's ideal, and the lengthy sojourn amid natural conditions is considered a great trial of patience—a sort of martyrdom; one studies contempt, both in one's attitudes and one's looks towards all "natural things."

Sixth recipe: The triumph of anti-naturalism and ideal castration, the triumph of the world of the pure, good, sinless, and blessed, is projected into the future as the consummation, the finale, the great hope, and the "Coming of the Kingdom of God."

I hope that one may still be allowed to *laugh* at this artificial hoisting up of a small species of man to the position of an absolute standard of all things?

205. (Spring-Fall 1887)

What I do not at all like in Jesus of Nazareth and His Apostle Paul, is that they *stuffed so much into the heads of paltry people,* as if their modest virtues were worth so much ado. We have had to pay dearly for it all; for they brought the most valuable qualities of both virtue and man into ill repute; they set the guilty conscience and the self-respect of noble souls at loggerheads, and they led the *braver, more magnanimous, more daring, and more excessive* tendencies of strong souls astray—even to self-destruction.

206. (Spring-Fall 1887)

In the New Testament, and especially in the Gospels, I discern absolutely no sign of a *"Divine"* voice: but rather an *indirect form* of the most subterranean fury, both in slander and destructiveness—one of the most dishonest forms of hatred. It lacks *all* knowledge of the qualities of a *higher nature.* It makes an impudent abuse of all kinds of plausibilities, and the whole stock of proverbs is used up and foisted upon one in its pages. Was it necessary to make a *God* come in order to appeal to those publicans and to say to them, etc. etc.?

Nothing could be more vulgar than this struggle with the *Pharisees,* carried on with a host of absurd and unpractical moral pretences; the mob, of course, has always been entertained by such feats. Fancy the reproach of "hypocrisy!" coming from those lips! Nothing could be more vulgar than this treatment of one's opponents—a most insidious sign of nobility or its *reverse....*

207. (November 1887-March 1888)

Primitive Christianity is the *abolition* of the *State*: it prohibits oaths, military service, courts of justice, self-defence or the defence of a community, and denies the difference between fellow-countrymen and strangers, as also the *order of castes*.

Christs example; He does not withstand those who ill-treat Him; He does not defend Himself; He does more, He "offers the left cheek" (to the demand: "Tell us whether thou be the Christ?" He replies: "Hereafter shall ye see the Son of man sitting on the right hand of power, and coming in the clouds of heaven"). He forbids His disciples to defend Him; He calls attention to the fact that He could get help if He wished to, but *will* not.

Christianity also means the *abolition of society*, it prizes everything that society despises, its very growth takes place among the outcasts, the condemned, and the leprous of all kinds, as also among "publicans," "sinners," prostitutes, and the most foolish of men (the "fisher folk"); it despises the rich, the scholarly, the noble, the virtuous, and the "punctilious." ...

208. (November 1887-March 1888)

The war against the noble and the powerful, as it is waged in the New Testament, is reminiscent of Reynard the Fox[78] and his methods: but *plus* the Christian unction and the more absolute refusal to recognise one's own craftiness.

209. (November 1887-March 1888)

The Gospel is the announcement that the road to happiness lies open for the lowly and the poor—that all one has to do is to emancipate one's self from all institutions, traditions, and the tutelage of the higher classes. Thus Christianity is no more than the *typical teaching of Socialists*.

Property, acquisitions, mother-country, status and rank, tribunals, the police, the State, the Church, Education, Art, militarism: all these are so many obstacles in the way of happiness, so many mistakes, snares, and devil's artifices, on which the Gospel passes sentence—all this is typical of socialistic doctrines.

---

[78] A trickster character in a series of medieval fables written by multiple authors.

Behind all this there is the outburst, the explosion, of a concentrated loathing of the "masters,"—the instinct which discerns the happiness of freedom after such long oppression.... (Mostly a symptom of the fact that the inferior classes have been treated too humanely, that their tongues already taste a joy which is forbidden them.... It is not hunger that provokes revolutions, but the fact that the mob have contracted an appetite *en mangeant* [79]....)

210. (Spring-Fall 1887)

Let the *New Testament only be read as a book of seduction*: in it virtue is appropriated, with the idea that public opinion is best won with it,— and as a matter of fact it is a very modest kind of *virtue*, which recognises only the ideal gregarious animal and nothing more (including, of course, the herdsmen): a puny, soft, benevolent, helpful, and gushingly-satisfied kind of virtue which to the outside world is quite devoid of pretensions,—and which separates the "world" entirely from itself. The *crassest arrogance* which fancies that the destiny of man turns around it, and it alone, and that on the one side the community of believers represents what is right, and on the other the world represents what is false and eternally to be reproved and rejected. The most *imbecile hatred* of all things in power, which, however, never goes so far as to touch these things. A kind of *inner detachment* which, outwardly, leaves everything as it was (servitude and slavery; and knowing how to convert *everything* into a means of serving God and virtue).

211. (Spring-Fall 1887; revised Spring-Fall 1888)

Christianity is possible as the *most private* form of life; it presupposes the existence of a narrow, isolated, and absolutely unpolitical society—it belongs to the conventicle. On the other hand, a "Christian *State*," "Christian politics," are pieces of downright impudence; they are lies, like, for instance, a Christian leadership of an army, which in the end regards "the God of hosts" as chief of the staff. Even the Papacy has never been able to carry on politics in a Christian way...; and when Reformers indulge in politics, as Luther

---

[79] "through eating"

did, it is well known that they are just as ardent followers of Machiavelli as any other immoralists or tyrants.

212. (November 1887-March 1888)

Christianity is still possible at any moment. It is not bound to any one of the impudent dogmas that have adorned themselves with its name: it needs neither the teaching of the *personal God*, nor of *sin*, nor of *immortality*, nor of *redemption*, nor of *faith*; it has absolutely no need whatever of metaphysics, and it needs asceticism and Christian "natural science" still less. Christianity is a *method of life*, not a system of belief. It tells us how we should behave, not what we should believe.

He who says today: "I refuse to be a soldier," "I care not for tribunals," "I lay no claim to the services of the police," "I will not do anything that disturbs the peace within me: and if I must suffer on that account, nothing can so well maintain my inward peace as suffering"—such a man would be a Christian.

213. (November 1887-March 1888)

Concerning the history of Christianity.—Continual change of environment: Christian teaching is thus continually changing its *centre of gravity*. The favouring of *low* and *paltry* people…. The development of *Caritas* [80]…. The type "Christian" gradually adopts everything that it originally rejected (*and in the rejection of which it asserted its right to exist*). The Christian becomes a citizen, a soldier, a judge, a workman, a merchant, a scholar, a theologian, a priest, a philosopher, a farmer, an artist, a patriot, a politician, a prince … he re-enters all those *departments of active life* which he had forsworn (he defends himself, he establishes tribunals, he punishes, he swears, he differentiates between people and people, he contemns, and he shows anger). The whole life of the Christian is ultimately exactly that life *from which Christ preached deliverance*…. The Church is just as much a factor in the *triumph* of the Antichrist, as the modern State and modern Nationalism…. The Church is the barbarisation of Christianity.

---

[80] "charity"

214. (November 1887-March 1888)

Among the powers that have mastered Christianity are: Judaism (Paul); Platonism (Augustine); The cult of mystery (the teaching of salvation, the emblem of the "cross"); Asceticism (hostility towards "Nature," "Reason," the "senses,"—the Orient ...).

215. (Spring-Fall 1887)

Christianity is a denaturalisation of gregarious morality: under the power of the most complete misapprehensions and self-deceptions. Democracy is a more natural form of it, and less sown with falsehood. It is a fact that the oppressed, the low, and whole mob of slaves and half-castes, *will prevail.*

First step: they make themselves free—they detach themselves, at first in fancy only; they recognise each other; they make themselves paramount.

Second step: they enter the lists, they demand acknowledgment, equal rights, "Justice."

Third step: they demand privileges (they draw the representatives of power over to their side).

Fourth step: they *alone* want all power, and they *have* it.

There are *three elements* in Christianity which must be distinguished: *(a)* the oppressed of all kinds, *(b)* the mediocre of all kinds, *(c)* the dissatisfied and diseased of all kinds. The *first* struggle against the politically noble and their ideal; the second contend with the exceptions and those who are in any way privileged (mentally or physically); the third oppose the *natural instinct* of the happy and the sound.

Whenever a triumph is achieved, the second element steps to the fore; for then Christianity has won over the sound and happy to its side (as warriors in its cause), likewise the powerful (interested to this extent in the conquest of the crowd)—and now it is the *gregarious instinct,* that *mediocre nature* which is valuable in every respect, that now gets its highest sanction through Christianity. This mediocre nature ultimately becomes so conscious of itself (gains such courage in regard to its own opinions), that it arrogates to itself even *political power....*

Democracy is Christianity *made natural*: a sort of "return to Nature," once Christianity, owing to extreme anti-naturalness, might have been overcome by the opposite valuation. Result: the aristocratic ideal begins to *lose its natural character* ("the higher man," "noble," "artist," "passion," "knowledge"; Romanticism as the cult of the exceptional, genius, etc. etc.).

216. (Spring-Fall 1887; revised Spring-Fall 1888)

When the "masters" may also become Christians.—It is of the nature of a *community* (race, family, herd, tribe) to regard all those conditions and aspirations which favour its survival, as in themselves *valuable*; for instance: obedience, mutual assistance, respect, moderation, pity—as also, to *suppress* everything that happens to stand in the way of the above.

It is likewise of the nature of the *rulers* (whether they are individuals or classes) to patronise and applaud those virtues which make their subjects *amenable* and *submissive*—conditions and passions which may be utterly different from their own.

The *gregarious instinct* and the *instinct of the rulers* sometimes *agree* in approving of a certain number of qualities and conditions,—but for different reasons: the first do so out of direct egoism, the second out of indirect egoism.

The submission to Christianity on the part of master races is essentially the result of the conviction that Christianity is a *religion for the herd*, that it teaches obedience: in short, that Christians are more easily ruled than non-Christians. With a hint of this nature, the Pope, even nowadays, recommends Christian propaganda to the ruling Sovereign of China.

It should also be added that the seductive power of the Christian ideal works most strongly upon natures that love danger, adventure, and contrasts; that love everything *that entails a risk*, and wherewith a *non plus ultra* of powerful feeling may be attained. In this respect, one has only to think of Saint Theresa, surrounded by the heroic instincts of her brothers:—Christianity appears in those circumstances as a dissipation of the will, as strength of will, as a will that is Quixotic.

3. CHRISTIAN IDEALS.

217. (Spring-Fall 1887)

War against the *Christian ideal,* against the doctrine of "blessedness" and "salvation" as the aims of life, against the supremacy of the fools, of the pure in heart, of the suffering and of the botched!

When and where has any man, *of any note at all,* resembled the Christian ideal?—at least in the eyes of those who are psychologists and triers of the heart and reins. Look at all Plutarch's heroes!

218. (November 1887-March 1888)

Our claim to superiority: we live in an age of *comparisons;* we are able to calculate as men have never yet calculated; in every way we are history become self-conscious. We enjoy things in a different way; we suffer in a different way: our instinctive activity is the comparison of an enormous variety of things. We understand everything; we experience everything, we no longer have a hostile feeling left within us. However disastrous the results may be to ourselves, our plunging and almost lustful inquisitiveness, attacks, unabashed, the most dangerous of subjects....

"Everything is good"—it gives us pain to say "nay" to anything. We suffer when we feel that we are sufficiently foolish to make a definite stand against anything.... At bottom, it is we scholars who today are fulfilling Christ's teaching most thoroughly.

219. (1885-1886)

We cannot suppress a certain irony when we contemplate those who think they have overcome Christianity by means of modern natural science. Christian values are by no means overcome by such people.[81] "Christ on the cross" is still the most sublime symbol—even now....

---

[81] See *Human, All-Too Human* section 131

220. (November 1887-March 1888)

The two great Nihilistic movements are: *(a)* Buddhism, *(b)* Christianity. The latter has only just about reached a state of culture in which it can fulfil its original object,—it has found its *level*,—and now it can manifest itself *without disguise*.....

221. (November 1887-March 1888)

We have *re-established* the Christian ideal, it now only remains *to determine* its value.

(1) Which values does it *deny*? What does *the ideal that opposes it* stand for?—Pride, pathos of distance, great responsibility, exuberant spirits, splendid animalism, the instincts of war and of conquest; the deification of passion, revenge, cunning, anger, voluptuousness, adventure, knowledge—the *noble ideal* is denied: the beauty, wisdom, power, pomp, and awfulness of the type man: the man who postulates aims, the "future" man (here Christianity presents itself as the *logical result* of *Judaism*).

(2) *Can it be realised?*—Yes, of course, when the climatic conditions are favourable—as in the case of the Indian ideal. Both neglect the factor *work*.—It separates a creature from a people, a state, a civilised community, and jurisdiction; it rejects education, wisdom, the cultivation of good manners, acquisition and commerce; it cuts adrift everything which is of use and value to men—by means of an idiosyncrasy of sentiment it *isolates* a man. It is non-political, anti-national, neither aggressive nor defensive,—and only possible within a strictly-ordered State or state of society, which allows these *holy parasites* to flourish at the cost of their neighbours.....

(3) It has now become the will to be *happy*—and nothing else! "Blessedness" stands for something self-evident, that no longer requires any justification—everything else (the way to live and let live) is only a means to an end....

But what follows is the result of a *low order of thought*, the fear of pain, of defilement, of corruption, is great enough to provide ample grounds for allowing everything to go to the dogs.... This is a *poor way* of thinking, and is the sign of an exhausted race; we *must* not allow ourselves to be deceived. ("Become as little children." Natures *of the same order*: Francis of Assisi, neurotic, epileptic, visionary, like Jesus.)

222. (November 1887-March 1888)

The *higher* man distinguishes himself from the *lower* by his fearlessness and his readiness to challenge misfortune: it is a sign of *degeneration* when eudaemonistic values begin to prevail (physiological fatigue and enfeeblement of will-power). Christianity, with its prospect of "blessedness," is the typical attitude of mind of a suffering and impoverished species of man. Abundant strength will be active, will suffer, and will go under: to it the bigotry of Christian salvation is bad music and hieratic posing and vexation.

223. (1885-1886)

Poverty, humility, and chastity are dangerous and slanderous ideals; but like poisons, which are useful cures in the case of certain diseases, they were also necessary in the time of the Roman Empire.

All ideals are dangerous: because they lower and brand realities; they are all poisons, but occasionally indispensable as cures.

224. (November 1887-March 1888)

God created man, happy, idle, innocent, and immortal: our actual life is a false, decadent, and sinful existence, a punishment.... Suffering, struggle, work, and death are raised as objections against life, they make life questionable, unnatural—something that must cease, and for which one not only requires but also *has*—remedies!

Since the time of Adam, man has been in an abnormal state: God Himself delivered up His Son for Adam's sin, in order to put an end to the abnormal condition of things: the natural character of life is a *curse*; to those who believe in Him, Christ restores normal life: He makes them happy, idle, and innocent. But the world did not become fruitful without labour; women do not bear children without pain; illness has not ceased: believers are served just as badly as unbelievers in this respect. All that has happened is, that man is delivered from *death* and *sin*—two assertions which allow of no verification, and which are therefore emphasised by the Church with more than usual heartiness. "He is free from sin,"—not owing to his own efforts, nor owing to a vigorous struggle on his part, but *redeemed by the death of the Saviour,*—consequently, perfectly innocent and paradisaical.

Actual life is nothing more than an illusion (that is to say, a deception, an insanity). The whole of struggling, fighting, and real existence—so full of light and shade, is only bad and false: everybody's duty is to be *delivered* from it.

"Man, innocent, idle, immortal, and happy"—this concept, which is the object of the "most supreme desires," must be criticised before anything else. Why should guilt, work, death, and pain (*and,* from the Christian point of view, also *knowledge* ...) be *contrary* to all supreme desires?—The lazy Christian notions: "blessedness," "innocence," "immortality."

225. (November 1887-March 1888)

The eccentric concept "holiness" does not exist—"God" and "man" have not been divorced from each other. "Miracles" do not exist—such spheres do not exist: the only one to be considered is the "intellectual" (that is to say, the symbolically-psychological). As decadence: a counterpart to "Epicureanism." ... Paradise according to Greek notions was only "Epicurus' Garden."

A life of this sort lacks a purpose: it *strives after* nothing;—a form of the "Epicurean gods"—there is no longer any reason to aim at anything,—not even at having children:—everything has been done.

226. (March-June 1888)

They despised the body: they did not reckon with it: nay, more—they treated it as an enemy. It was their delirium to think that a man could carry a "beautiful soul" about in a body that was a cadaverous abortion.... In order to inoculate others with this insanity they had to present the concept "beautiful soul" in a different way, and to transvalue the natural value, until, at last, a pale, sickly, idiotically exalted creature, something angelic, some extreme perfection and transfiguration was declared to be the higher man.

227. (January-Fall 1888)

Ignorance in matters psychological.—The Christian has no nervous system;—contempt for, and deliberate and wilful turning away from, the demands of the body, and the *naked* body; it is assumed that all this is in keeping with man's nature, and *must perforce work the ultimate good of the soul*;—all functions of the body are systematically reduced to moral values; illness itself is regarded as determined by morality, it is held to be the result of sin, or it is a trial or a state of salvation, through which man becomes more perfect than he could become in a state of health (Pascal's idea); under certain circumstances, there are wilful attempts at inducing illness.

228. (1883-1888)

What in sooth is this struggle "against Nature" on the part of the Christian? We shall not, of course, let ourselves be deceived by his words and explanations. It is Nature against something which is also Nature. With many, it is fear; with others, it is loathing; with yet others, it is the sign of a certain intellectuality, the love of a bloodless and passionless ideal; and in the case of the most superior men, it is love of an abstract Nature—these try to live up to their ideal. It is easily understood that humiliation in the place of self-esteem, anxious cautiousness towards the passions, emancipation from the usual duties (whereby, a higher notion of rank is created), the incitement to constant war on behalf of enormous issues, habituation to effusiveness of feelings—all this goes to constitute a type: in such a type the *hypersensitiveness* of a perishing body preponderates; but the nervousness and the inspirations it engenders are *interpreted* differently. The *taste* of this kind of creature tends either (1) to subtilise, (2) to indulge in bombastic eloquence, or (3) to go in for extreme feelings. The natural inclinations *do* get satisfied, but they are interpreted in a new way; for instance, as "justification before God," "the feeling of redemption through grace," every undeniable *feeling of pleasure* becomes (interpreted in this way!) pride, voluptuousness, etc. General problem: what will become of the man who slanders and practically denies and belittles what is natural? As a matter of fact, the Christian is an example of exaggerated self-control: in order to tame his passions, he seems to find it necessary to extirpate or crucify them.

229. (March-June 1888)

Man did not know himself physiologically throughout the ages his history covers; he does not even know himself now. The knowledge, for instance, that man has a nervous system (but no "soul") is still the privilege of the most educated people. But man is not satisfied, in this respect, to say he does not know. A man must be very superior to be able to say: "I do not know this,"—that is to say, to be able to admit his ignorance.

Suppose he is in pain or in a good mood, he never questions that he can find the reason of either condition if only he seeks.... In truth, he cannot find the reason; for he does not even suspect where it lies.... What happens?... He takes the *result* of his condition for its *cause*; for instance, if he should undertake some work (really undertaken because his good mood gave him the courage to do so) and carry it through successfully: behold, the work itself is the *reason* of his good mood.... As a matter of fact, his success was determined by the same cause as that which brought about his good mood—that is to say, the happy co-ordination of physiological powers and functions.

He feels bad: *consequently* he cannot overcome a care, a scruple, or an attitude of self-criticism.... He really fancies that his disagreeable condition is the result of his scruple, of his "sin," or of his "self-criticism."

But after profound exhaustion and prostration, a state of recovery sets in. "How is it possible that I can feel so free, so happy? It is a miracle; only a God could have effected this change."—Conclusion: "He has forgiven my sin." ...

From this follow certain practices: in order to provoke feelings of sinfulness and to prepare the way for crushed spirits it is necessary to induce a condition of morbidity and nervousness in the body. The methods of doing this are well known. Of course, nobody suspects the causal logic of the fact: the *maceration* of the *flesh* is interpreted religiously, it seems like an end in itself, whereas it is no more than a *means* of bringing about that morbid state of indigestion which is known as repentance (the "fixed idea" of sin, the hypnotising of the hen by means of the chalk-line "sin").

The mishandling of the body prepares the ground for the required range of "guilty feelings"—that is to say, for that general state of pain which *demands an explanation*....

On the other hand, the *method* of "salvation" may also develop from the above: every dissipation of the feelings, whether prayers, movements, attitudes, or oaths, has been provoked, and exhaustion follows; very often it is acute, or it appears in the form of epilepsy. And behind this condition of deep somnolence there come signs of recovery—or, in religious parlance, "Salvation."

230. (January-Fall 1888)

Formerly, the conditions and results of *physiological exhaustion* were considered more important than healthy conditions and their results, and this was owing to the suddenness, fearfulness, and mysteriousness of the former. Men were terrified by themselves, and postulated the existence of a *higher* world. People have ascribed the origin of the idea of two worlds—one this side of the grave and the other beyond it—to sleep and dreams, to shadows, to night, and to the fear of Nature: but the symptoms of physiological exhaustion should, above all, have been considered.[82]

Ancient religions have quite special methods of disciplining the pious into states of exhaustion, in which they *must* experience such things.... The idea was, that one entered into a new order of things, where everything ceases to be known.—The *semblance* of a higher power....

231. (March-June 1888)

Sleep is the result of every kind of exhaustion; exhaustion follows upon all excessive excitement....

In all pessimistic religions and philosophies there is a yearning for sleep; the very notion "sleep" is deified and worshipped.[83]

---

[82] See *The Dawn* sec. 33 and *Twilight of the Idols* "How the 'True World' Ultimately Became A Fable"

[83] See *On The Genealogy of Morals* Book 1 sec. 10

In this case the exhaustion is racial; sleep regarded psychologically is only a symbol of a much deeper and longer *compulsion to rest....* *In praxi* it is death which rules here in the seductive image of its brother sleep....

232. (March-June 1888)

The whole of the Christian training in repentance and redemption may be regarded as a *folie circulaire*[84] arbitrarily produced; though, of course, it can be produced only in people who are predisposed to it—that is to say, who have morbid tendencies in their constitutions.

233. (March-June 1888)

Against remorse and its purely psychical treatment.—To be unable to have done with an experience is already a sign of decadence.[85] This reopening of old wounds, this wallowing in self-contempt and depression, is an additional form of disease; no "salvation of the soul" ever results from it, but only a new kind of spiritual illness....

These "conditions of salvation" of which the Christian is conscious are merely variations of the same diseased state—the interpretation of an attack of epilepsy by means of a particular formula which is provided, *not* by science, but by religious mania.

When a man is ill his very *goodness* is sickly.... By far the greatest portion of the psychical apparatus which Christianity has used, is now classed among the various forms of hysteria and epilepsy.

The whole process of spiritual healing must be remodelled on a physiological basis: the "sting of conscience" as such is an obstacle in the way of recovery—as soon as possible the attempt must be made to counterbalance everything by means of new actions, so that there may be an escape from the morbidness of *self-torture*.... The purely psychical practices of the Church and of the various sects should be

---

[84] "circular madness," manic-depressive psychosis

[85] This is a key component of Nietzsche's concept of *ressentiment*—to be unable to get over some past experience and thus to re-experience (re-sense) it again and again, a kind of psychic indigestion. See *On The Genealogy of Morals* Book 1 sec. 10 [Ed.]

decried as dangerous to the health. No invalid is ever cured by prayers or by the exorcising of evil spirits: the states of "repose" which follow upon such methods of treatment, by no means inspire confidence, in the psychological sense....

A man is *healthy* when he can laugh at the seriousness and ardour with which he has allowed himself to be *hypnotised* to any extent by any detail in his life—when his remorse seems to him like the action of a dog biting a stone—when he is ashamed of his repentance.

The purely psychological and religious practices, which have existed hitherto, only led to an *alteration in the symptoms*: according to them a man had recovered when he bowed before the cross, and swore that in future he would be a good man.... But a criminal, who, with a certain gloomy seriousness cleaves to his fate and refuses to malign his deed once it is done, has more *spiritual health*.... The criminals with whom Dostoyevsky associated in prison, were all, without exception, unbroken natures,—are they not a hundred times more valuable than a "broken-spirited" Christian?

(For the treatment of pangs of conscience I recommend Mitchell's Treatment.)[86]

234. (1883-1888)

A *pang of conscience* in a man is a sign that his character is not yet equal to his *deed*. There is such a thing as a pang of conscience after *good deeds*: in this case it is their unfamiliarity, their incompatibility with an old environment.

235. (Spring-Fall 1887; revised Spring-Fall 1888)

Against remorse.—I do not like this form of cowardice in regard to one's own actions, one must not leave one's self in the lurch under the pressure of sudden shame or distress. Extreme pride is much more fitting here. What is the good of it all in the end! No deed gets undone because it is regretted, no more than because it is "forgiven" or "expiated." A man must be a theologian in order to believe in a power

---

[86] A method of treating cases of neurasthenia and hysteria ... by removal from home, rest in bed, massage twice a day, electrical excitation of the muscles, and excessive feeding, at first with milk.

that erases faults: we immoralists prefer to disbelieve in "faults." We believe that all deeds, of what kind soever, are identically the same at root; just as deeds which turn *against* us may be useful from an economical point of view, and even *generally desirable*. In certain individual cases, we admit that we might well have been *spared* a given action; the circumstances alone predisposed us in its favour. Which of us, if *favoured* by circumstances, would not already have committed every possible crime?… That is why one should never say: "Thou shouldst never have done such and such a thing," but only: "How strange it is that I have not done such and such a thing hundreds of times already!"

As a matter of fact, only a very small number of acts are *typical* acts and real epitomes of a personality, and seeing what a small number of people really are personalities, a single act very rarely *characterises* a man. Acts are mostly dictated by circumstances; they are superficial or merely reflex movements performed in response to a stimulus, long before the depths of our beings are affected or consulted in the matter. A fit of temper, a gesture, a blow with a knife: how little of the individual resides in these acts!—A deed very often brings a sort of stupor or feeling of constraint in its wake: so that the agent feels almost spellbound at its recollection, or as though he *belonged to it*, and were not an independent creature. This mental disorder, which is a form of hypnotism, must be resisted at all costs: surely a single deed, whatever it be, when it is compared with all one has done, is *nothing*, and may be deducted from the sum without making the account wrong. The unfair interest which society manifests in controlling the whole of our lives in one direction, as though the very purpose of its existence were to cultivate a certain individual act, should not infect the man of action: but unfortunately this happens almost continually. The reason of this is, that every deed, if followed by unexpected consequences, leads to a certain mental disturbance, no matter whether the consequences be good or bad. Behold a lover who has been given a promise, or a poet while he is receiving applause from an audience: as far as *intellectual torpor* is concerned, these men are in no way different from the anarchist who is suddenly confronted by a detective bearing a search warrant.

There are some acts which are *unworthy* of us: acts which, if they were regarded as typical, would set us down as belonging to a lower class of man. The one fault that has to be avoided here, is to regard them as typical. There is another kind of act of which *we* are unworthy: exceptional acts, born of a particular abundance of happiness and health; they are the highest waves of our spring tides, driven to an unusual height by a storm—an accident: such acts and "deeds" are also not typical. An artist should never be judged according to the measure of his works.

236. (January-Fall 1888)

A. In proportion as Christianity seems necessary today, man is still wild and fatal....

B. In another sense, it is not necessary, but extremely dangerous, though it is captivating and seductive, because it corresponds with the *morbid* character of whole classes and types of modern humanity, ... they simply follow their inclinations when they aspire to Christianity —they are decadents of all kinds.

A and B must be kept very sharply apart. In the *case of A,* Christianity is a cure, or at least a taming process (under certain circumstances it serves the purpose of making people ill: and this is sometimes useful as a means of subduing savage and brutal natures). In the *case of B,* it is a symptom of illness itself, it renders the state of decadence *more acute*; in this case it stands opposed to a *corroborating* system of treatment, it is the invalid's instinct standing *against* that which would be most salutary to him.

237. (January-Fall 1888)

On one side there are the *serious,* the *dignified,* and *reflective* people: and on the other the barbarous, the unclean, and the irresponsible beasts: it is merely a question of *taming animals*—and in this case the tamer must be hard, terrible, and awe-inspiring, at least to his beasts.

All essential requirements must be imposed upon the unruly creatures with almost brutal distinctness—that is to say, magnified a thousand times.

Even the fulfilment of the requirement must be presented in the coarsest way possible, so that it may command respect, as in the case of the spiritualisation of the Brahmins.

*

The struggle with the rabble and the herd. If any degree of tameness and order has been reached. the chasm separating these *purified* and *regenerated* people from the terrible *remainder* must have been bridged....

This chasm is a means of increasing self-respect in higher castes, and of confirming their belief in *that* which they represent—hence the *Chandala*. Contempt and its excess are perfectly correct psychologically —that is to say, magnified a hundred times, so that it may at least be felt.

238. (January-Fall 1888)

The struggle against *brutal* instincts is quite different from the struggle against *morbid* instincts; it may even be a means of overcoming brutality by making the brutes *ill*. The psychical treatment practised by Christianity is often nothing more than the process of converting a brute into a sick and *therefore* tame animal.

The struggle against raw and savage natures must be a struggle with weapons which are able to affect such natures: *superstitions* and such means are therefore indispensable and essential.

239. (November 1887-March 1888)

Our age, in a certain sense, is *mature* (that is to say, decadent), just as Buddha's was.... That is why a sort of Christianity is possible without all the absurd dogmas (the most repulsive offshoots of ancient hybridism).

240. (1885-1886)

Supposing it were impossible to disprove Christianity, Pascal thinks, in view of the *terrible* possibility that it may be true, that it is in the highest degree prudent to be a Christian. As a proof of how much Christianity has lost of its terrible nature, today we find that other attempt to justify it. which consists in asserting, that even if it were a mistake, it nevertheless provides the greatest advantages and pleasures for its adherents throughout their lives:—it therefore seems that this belief should be upheld owing to the peace and quiet it ensures—not owing to the terror of a threatening possibility, but rather out of fear of a life that has lost its charm. This hedonistic turn of thought, which uses happiness as a proof, is a symptom of decline: it takes the place of the proof resulting from power or from that which to the Christian mind is most terrible—namely, *fear.* With this new interpretation, Christianity is, as a matter of fact, nearing its stage of exhaustion. People are satisfied with a Christianity which is an *opiate,* because they no longer have the strength to seek, to struggle, to dare, to stand alone, nor to take up Pascal's position and to share that gloomily brooding self-contempt, that belief in human unworthiness, and that anxiety which believes that it "may be damned." But a Christianity the chief object of which is to soothe diseased nerves, does *not require* the terrible solution consisting of a "God on the cross"; that is why Buddhism is secretly gaining ground all over Europe.

241. (November 1887-March 1888)

The humour of European culture: people regard one thing as true, but do *the other.* For instance, what is the use of all the art of reading and criticising, if the ecclesiastical interpretation of the Bible, whether according to Catholics or Protestants, is still upheld!

242. (November 1887-March 1888)

No one is sufficiently aware of the barbarity of the notions among which we Europeans still live. To think that men have been able to believe that the "Salvation of the soul" depended upon a book!... And I am told that this is still believed.

What is the good of all scientific education, all criticism and all hermeneutics, if such nonsense as the Church's interpretation of the Bible has not yet turned the colours of our bodies permanently into the red of shame?

243. (Spring-Fall 1887; revised Spring-Fall 1888)

Subject for reflection: To what extent does the fatal belief in "Divine Providence"—the most *paralysing* belief for both the hand and the understanding that has ever existed—continue to prevail; to what extent have the Christian hypothesis and interpretation of Life continued their lives under the cover of terms like "Nature,"

"Progress," "perfectionment," "Darwinism," or beneath the superstition that there is a certain relation between happiness and virtue, unhappiness and sin? That absurd *belief* in the course of things in "Life" and in the "instinct of Life"; that foolish *resignation* which arises from the notion that if only every one did his duty *all* would go well—all this sort of thing can only have a meaning if one assumes that there is a direction of things *sub specie boni*.[87] Even *fatalism*, our present form of philosophical sensibility, is the result of a *long* belief in Divine Providence, an unconscious result: as though it were nothing to do with us how everything goes! (As though we *might* let things take their own course; the individual being only a *modus* of the absolute reality.)

244. (November 1887-March 1888)

It is the height of psychological falsity on the part of man to imagine a being according to his own petty standard, who is a beginning, a "thing-in-itself," and who appears to him good, wise, mighty, and precious; for thus he suppresses in thoughts *all the causality* by means of which every kind of goodness, wisdom, and power comes into existence and has value. In short, elements of the most recent and most conditional origin were regarded not as evolved, but as spontaneously generated and "things-in-themselves," and perhaps as the cause of all things…. Experience teaches us that, in every case in which a man has elevated himself to any great extent above the average of his fellows, every high degree of *power* always involves a corresponding degree of *freedom* from Good and Evil as also from "true" and "false," and cannot take into account what goodness dictates: the same holds good of a high degree of wisdom—in this case goodness is just as much suppressed as truthfulness, justice, virtue, and other popular whims in valuations. In fact, is it not obvious that every high degree of goodness itself presupposes a certain intellectual myopia and obtuseness? as also an inability to distinguish at a great distance between true and false, useful and harmful?—not to mention the fact that a high degree of power in the hands of the highest

---

[87] "under the auspices of the good"

goodness might lead to the most baleful consequences ("the suppression of evil").

In sooth it is enough to perceive with what aspirations the "God of Love" inspires His believers: they ruin mankind for the benefit of "good men." In practice, this same God has shown Himself to be a God of the most *acute myopia, devilry*, and *impotence*, in the face of the actual arrangement of the universe, and from this the value of His conception may be estimated. Knowledge and wisdom can have no value in themselves, any more than goodness can: the goal they are striving after must be known first, for then only can their value or worthlessness be judged—*a goal might be* imagined which would make excessive wisdom a great disadvantage (if, for instance, complete deception were a prerequisite to the enhancement of life; likewise, if goodness were able to paralyse and depress the main springs of the great passions)....

Taking our human life as it is, it cannot be denied that all "truth," "goodness," "holiness," and "Godliness" in the Christian sense, have hitherto shown themselves to be great dangers—even now mankind is in danger of perishing owing to an ideal which is hostile to life.

245. (Spring-Fall 1887)

Let any one think of the *loss* which all human institutions suffer, when a divine and transcendental, *higher sphere* is postulated which must first sanction these institutions! By recognising their worth in this sanction alone (as in the case of marriage, for instance) *their natural dignity is reduced*, and under certain circumstances *denied*.... Nature is spitefully misjudged in the same ratio as the anti-natural notion of a God is held in honour. "Nature" then comes to mean no more than "contemptible," "bad." ...

The fatal nature of a belief in God as the *reality of the highest moral qualities*: through it, all real values were denied and systematically regarded as *valueless*. Thus *Anti-Nature* ascended the throne. With relentless logic the last step was reached, and this was the absolute demand to *deny Nature*.

246. (January-Fall 1888)

By pressing the doctrine of disinterestedness and love into the foreground, Christianity by no means elevated the interests of the species above those of the individual. Its real *historical* effect, its fatal effect, remains precisely the *increase of egotism*, of individual egotism, to excess (to the extreme which consists in the belief in individual immortality). The individual was made so important and so absolute, by means of Christian values, that he could no longer be *sacrificed*, despite the fact that the species can only be maintained by human sacrifices. All "souls" became *equal* before God: but this is the most pernicious of all valuations! If one regards individuals as equals, the demands of the species are ignored, and a process is initiated which ultimately leads to its ruin. Christianity is the *reverse of the* principle of *selection.* If the degenerate and sick man ("the Christian") is to be of the same value as the healthy man ("the pagan"), or if he is even to be valued higher than the latter, as Pascal's view of health and sickness would have us value him, the natural course of evolution is thwarted and the *unnatural* becomes law.

In practice this general love of mankind is nothing more than deliberately favouring all the suffering, the botched, and the degenerate: it is this love that has reduced and weakened the power, responsibility, and lofty duty of sacrificing men. According to the scheme of Christian values, all that remained was the alternative of self-sacrifice, but this *vestige* of human sacrifice, which Christianity conceded and even recommended, has no meaning when regarded in the light of rearing a whole species. The prosperity of the species is by no means affected by the sacrifice of one individual (whether in the monastic and ascetic manner, or by means of crosses, stakes, and scaffolds, as the "martyrs" of error). What the species requires is the suppression of the physiologically botched, the weak and the degenerate: but it was precisely to these people that Christianity appealed as a *preservative* force, it simply strengthened that natural and very strong instinct of all the weak which bids them protect, maintain, and mutually support each other. What is Christian "virtue" and "love of men," if not precisely this mutual assistance with a view to survival, this solidarity of the weak, this thwarting of selection? What is Christian altruism, if it is not the mob-egotism of the weak which divines that, if everybody looks after everybody else, every individual will be preserved for a longer period of time?... He who does not consider this attitude of mind as *immoral,* as a crime against life, himself belongs to the sickly crowd, and also shares their instincts.... Genuine love of mankind exacts sacrifice for the good of the species —it is hard, full of self-control, because it needs human sacrifices. And this pseudo-humanity which is called Christianity, would fain establish the rule that nobody should be sacrificed.

247. (March-June 1888)

Nothing could be more useful and deserves more promotion than systematic *Nihilism in action.*—As I understand the phenomena of Christianity and pessimism, this is what they say: "We are ripe for nonentity, for us it is reasonable not to be." This hint from "reason" in this case, is simply the voice of *selective Nature.*

On the other hand, what deserves the most rigorous condemnation, is the ambiguous and cowardly infirmity of purpose of a religion like *Christianity,*—or rather like the *Church,*—which, instead of recommending death and self-destruction, actually protects all the botched and bungled, and encourages them to propagate their kind.

Problem: with what kind of means could one lead up to a severe form of really contagious Nihilism—a Nihilism which would teach and practise voluntary death with scientific conscientiousness (and not the feeble continuation of a vegetative sort of life with false hopes of a life after death)?

Christianity cannot be sufficiently condemned for having depreciated the *value* of a great *cleansing* Nihilistic movement (like the one which was probably in the process of formation), by its teaching of the immortality of the private individual, as also by the hopes of resurrection which it held out: that is to say, by dissuading people from performing the *deed of Nihilism* which is suicide.... In the latter's place it puts lingering suicide, and gradually a puny, meagre, but durable life; gradually a perfectly ordinary, bourgeois, mediocre life, etc.

248. (March-June 1888)

Christian moral quackery.—Pity and contempt succeed each other at short intervals, and at the sight of them I feel as indignant as if I were in the presence of the most despicable crime. Here error is made a duty—a virtue, misapprehension has become a knack, the destructive instinct is systematised under the name of "redemption"; here every operation becomes a wound, an amputation of those very organs whose energy would be the prerequisite to a return of health. And in the best of cases no cure is effected; all that is done is to exchange one set of evil symptoms for another set.... And this pernicious nonsense, this systematised profanation and castration of life, passes for holy and sacred; to be in its service, to be an instrument of this art of healing— that is to say, to be a priest, is to be rendered distinguished, reverent, holy, and sacred. God alone could have been the Author of this supreme art of healing; redemption is only possible as a revelation, as an act of grace, as an unearned gift, made by the Creator Himself.

Proposition I. : Spiritual healthiness is regarded as morbid, and creates suspicion....

Proposition II. : The prerequisites of a strong, exuberant life— strong desires and passions—are reckoned as objections against strong and exuberant life.

Proposition III. : Everything which threatens danger to man, and which can overcome and ruin him, is evil—and should be torn root and branch from his soul.

Proposition IV. : Man converted into a weak creature, inoffensive to himself and others, crushed by humility and modesty, and conscious of his weakness,—in fact, the "sinner,"—this is the desirable type, and one which one can *produce* by means of a little spiritual surgery....

249. (Spring-Fall 1887)

What is it I protest against? That people should regard this paltry and peaceful mediocrity, this spiritual equilibrium which knows nothing of the fine impulses of great accumulations of strength, as something high, or possibly as the standard of all things.

Bacon of Verulam says: *Infimarum virtutum apud vulgus laus est, mediarum admiratio, supremarum sensus nullus.*[88] Christianity as a religion, however, belongs to the *vulgus*: it has no feeling for the highest kind of *virtus*.

250. (Spring-Fall 1887)

Let us see what the "genuine Christian" does of all the things which his instincts forbid him to do:—he covers beauty, pride, riches, self-reliance, brilliancy, knowledge, and power with suspicion and *mud* —in short, *all culture*: his object is to deprive the latter of its *clean conscience.*

251. (January-Fall 1888)

The attacks made upon Christianity, hitherto, have been not only timid but false. So long as Christian morality was not felt to be a *capital crime against Life*, its apologists had a good time. The question concerning the mere "truth" of Christianity—whether in regard to the existence of its God, or to the legendary history of its origin, not to speak of its astronomy and natural science—is quite beside the point so long as no inquiry is made into the value of Christian *morality.* Are Christian morals *worth anything*, or are they a profanation and an outrage, despite all the arts of holiness and seduction with which they are enforced? The question concerning the truth of the religion may be met by all sorts of subterfuges; and the most fervent believers can, in the end, avail themselves of the logic used by their opponents, in order to create a right for their side to assert that certain things are irrefutable—that is to say, they *transcend* the means employed to refute them (nowadays this trick of dialectics is called "Kantian Criticism").

252. (November 1887-March 1888)

Christianity should never be forgiven for having ruined such men as Pascal. This is precisely what should be combated in Christianity, namely, that it has the will to break the spirit of the strongest and noblest natures. One should take no rest until this thing is utterly

---

[88] "The common man praises the lowest virtues, admires the mediocre, and for the superior has no sense at all."

destroyed:—the ideal of mankind which Christianity advances, the demands it makes upon men, and its "Nay" and "Yea" relative to humanity. The whole of the remaining absurdities, that is to say, Christian fable, Christian cobweb-spinning in ideas and principles, and Christian theology, do not concern us; they might be a thousand times more absurd and we should not raise a finger to destroy them. But what we do stand up against, is that ideal which, thanks to its morbid beauty and feminine seductiveness, thanks to its insidious and slanderous eloquence, appeals to all the cowardices and vanities of wearied souls,—and the strongest have their moments of fatigue,—as though all that which seems most useful and desirable at such moments—that is to say, confidence, artlessness, modesty, patience, love of one's like, resignation, submission to God, and a sort of self-surrender—were useful and desirable *per se*; as though the puny, modest abortion which in these creatures takes the place of a soul, this virtuous, mediocre animal and sheep of the flock—which deigns to call itself man, were not only to take precedence of the stronger, more evil, more passionate, more defiant, and more prodigal type of man, who by virtue of these very qualities is exposed to a hundred times more dangers than the former, but were actually to stand as an ideal for man in general, as a goal, a measure—the highest desideratum. The creation of *this* ideal was the most appalling temptation that had ever been put in the way of mankind; for, with it, the stronger and more successful exceptions, the lucky cases among men, in which the will to power and to growth leads the whole species "man" one step farther forward, this type was threatened with disaster. By means of the values of this ideal, the growth of such higher men would be checked at the root. For these men, owing to their superior demands and duties, readily accept a more dangerous life (speaking economically, it is a case of an increase in the costs of the undertaking coinciding with a greater chance of failure).

What is it we combat in Christianity? That it aims at destroying the strong, at breaking their spirit, at exploiting their moments of weariness and debility, at converting their proud assurance into anxiety and conscience-trouble; that it knows how to poison the noblest instincts and to infect them with disease, until their strength, their will to power, turns inwards, against themselves—until the strong perish through their excessive self-contempt and self-immolation: that gruesome way of perishing, of which *Pascal* is the most famous example.

---

340. (Spring-Fall 1887)

The more concealed forms of the cult of Christian, moral ideals.—The *insipid and cowardly notion "Nature"* invented by Nature-enthusiasts (without any knowledge whatsoever of the terrible, the implacable, and the cynical element in even "the most beautiful" aspects), is only a sort of attempt at *reading* the moral and Christian notion of "humanity" into Nature;—Rousseau's concept of Nature, for instance, which took for granted that "Nature" meant freedom, goodness, innocence, equity, justice, and *Idylls,* was nothing more at bottom than the cult of Christian morality. We should collect passages from the poets in order to see *what* they admired, in lofty mountains, for instance. What Goethe had to do with them—why he admired Spinoza. Absolute *ignorance* concerning the reasons of this *cult....*

The *insipid and cowardly concept "Man"* à la Comte and Stuart Mill, is at times the subject of a cult.... This is only the Christian moral ideal again under another name.... Refer also to the freethinkers— Guyau for example.

The *insipid and cowardly concept "Art"* which is held to mean sympathy with all suffering and with everything botched and bungled (the same thing happens to *history,* cf. Thierry): again it is the cult of the Christian moral ideal.

And now, as to the whole *socialistic ideal:* it is nothing but a blockheaded misunderstanding of the Christian moral ideal.

373. (March-June 1888)

The origin of moral values.—Selfishness has as much value as the physiological value of him who possesses it. Each individual represents the whole course of Evolution, and he is not, as morals teach, something that begins at his birth. If he represent the *ascent* of the line of mankind, his value is, in fact, very great; and the concern about his maintenance and the promoting of his growth may even be extreme. (It is the concern about the promise of the future in him which gives the well-constituted individual such an extraordinary right to egoism.) If he represent *descending* development, decay, chronic sickening, he has little worth: and the greatest fairness would have him take as little room, strength, and sunshine as possible from the well-constituted. In this case society's duty is to *suppress egoism* (for the latter may sometimes manifest itself in an absurd, morbid, and seditious manner): whether it be a question of the decline and pining away of single individuals or of whole classes of mankind. A morality and a religion of "love," the *curbing* of the self-affirming spirit, and a doctrine encouraging patience, resignation, helpfulness, and co-operation in word and deed may be of the highest value within the confines of such classes, even in the eyes of their rulers: for it restrains the feelings of rivalry, of resentment, and of envy,—feelings which are only too natural in the bungled and the botched,—and it even deifies them under the ideal of humility, of obedience, of slave-life, of being ruled, of poverty, of illness, and of lowliness. This explains why the ruling classes (or races) and individuals of all ages have always upheld the cult of unselfishness, the gospel of the lowly and of "God on the Cross."

The preponderance of an altruistic way of valuing is the result of a consciousness of the fact that one is botched and bungled. Upon examination, this point of view turns out to be: "I am not worth much," simply a psychological valuation; more plainly still: it is the feeling of impotence, of the lack of the great self-asserting impulses of power (in muscles, nerves, and ganglia). This valuation gets translated, according to the particular culture of these classes, into a moral or religious principle (the pre-eminence of religious or moral precepts is always a sign of low culture): it tries to justify itself in spheres whence, as far as it is concerned, the notion "value" hails. The interpretation by means of which the Christian sinner tries to understand himself, is an attempt at justifying his lack of power and of self-confidence: he prefers to feel himself a sinner rather than feel bad for nothing: it is in itself a symptom of decay when interpretations of this sort are used at all. In some cases the bungled and the botched do not look for the reason of their unfortunate condition in their own guilt (as the Christian does), but in society: when, however, the Socialist, the Anarchist, and the Nihilist are conscious that their existence is something for which someone must be *guilty*, they are very closely related to the Christian, who also believes that he can more easily endure his ill ease and his wretched constitution when he has found some one whom he can hold *responsible* for it. The instinct of *revenge* and *resentment* appears in both cases here as a means of enduring life, as a self-preservative measure, as is also the favour shown to *altruistic* theory and practice. The *hatred of egoism*, whether it be one's own (as in the case of the Christian), or another's (as in the case of the Socialists), thus appears as a valuation reached under the predominance of revenge; and also as an act of prudence on the part of the preservative instinct of the suffering, in the form of an increase in their feelings of co-operation and unity.... At bottom, as I have already suggested, the discharge of resentment which takes place in the act of judging, rejecting, and punishing egoism (one's own or that of others) is still a self-preservative measure on the part of the bungled and the botched. In short: the cult of altruism is merely a particular form of egoism, which regularly appears under certain definite physiological circumstances.

When the Socialist, with righteous indignation, cries for "justice," "rights," "equal rights," it only shows that he is oppressed by his inadequate culture, and is unable to understand why he suffers: he also finds pleasure in crying;—if he were more at ease he would take jolly good care not to cry in that way: in that case he would seek his pleasure elsewhere. The same holds good of the Christian: he curses, condemns, and slanders the "world"—and does not even except himself. But that is no reason for taking him seriously. In both cases we are in the presence of invalids who feel better for crying, and who find relief in slander.

438. (Spring 1888)

The war against the "old faith," as Epicurus waged it, was, strictly speaking, a struggle against *pre-existing* Christianity—the struggle against a world then already gloomy, moralised, acidified throughout with feelings of guilt, and grown old and sick.

Not the "moral corruption" of antiquity, but precisely its *moral infectedness* was the prerequisite which enabled Christianity to become its master. Moral fanaticism (in short: Plato) destroyed paganism by transvaluing its values and poisoning its innocence. We ought at last to understand that what was then destroyed was *higher* than what prevailed! Christianity grew on the soil of psychological corruption, and could only take root in rotten ground.

572. (1883-1888)

An artist cannot endure reality; he turns away or back from it: his earnest opinion is that the worth of a thing consists in that nebulous residue of it which one derives from colour, form, sound, and thought; he believes that the more subtle, attenuated, and volatile, a thing or a man becomes, *the more valuable he becomes: the less real,* the greater the worth. This is Platonism but Plato was guilty of yet further audacity in the matter of turning tables—he measured the degree of reality according to the degree of value, and said: The more there is of "idea" the more there is of Being. He twisted the concept "reality" round and said: "What ye regard as real is an error, and the nearer we get to the 'idea' the nearer we are to 'truth.'"—Is this understood? It was the *greatest of all rech-istenings:* and because Christianity adopted it, we are blind to its astounding features. At bottom, Plato, like the artist he was, *placed appearance before* Being! and therefore lies and fiction before truth! unreality before actuality!—He was, however, so convinced of the value of appearance, that he granted it the attributes of "Being," "causality," "goodness," and "truth," and, in short, all those things which are associated with value.

The concept value itself regarded as a cause: first standpoint.

The ideal granted all attributes, conferring honour: second standpoint.

765. (January-Fall 1888)

"The Atonement of all Sin."

People speak of the profound injustice of the social arrangement, as if the fact that one man is born in favourable circumstances and that another is born in unfavourable ones—or that one should possess gifts the other has not, were on the face of it an injustice. Among the more honest of these opponents of society this is what is said: "We, with all the bad, morbid, criminal qualities which we acknowledge we possess, are only the inevitable result of the oppression for ages of the weak by the strong"; thus they insinuate their evil natures into the consciences of the ruling classes. They threaten and storm and curse. They become virtuous from sheer indignation—they don't want to have become bad men and *canaille* for nothing.

The name for this attitude, which is an invention of the last century, is, if I am not mistaken, pessimism; and even that pessimism which is the outcome of indignation. It is in this attitude of mind that history is judged, that it is deprived of its inevitable fatality, and that responsibility and even guilt is discovered in it. For the great desideratum is to find guilty people in it. The botched and the bungled, the decadents of all kinds, are revolted at themselves, and require sacrifices in order that they may not slake their thirst for destruction upon themselves (which might, indeed, be the most reasonable procedure). But for this purpose they at least require a semblance of justification, *i.e.* a theory according to which the fact of their existence, and of their character, may be expiated by a scapegoat. This scapegoat may be God,—in Russia such resentful atheists are not wanting,—or the order of society, or education and upbringing, or the Jews, or the nobles, or, finally, the well-constituted of every kind. "It is a sin for a man to have been born in decent circumstances, for by so doing he disinherits the others, he pushes them aside, he imposes upon them the curse of vice and of work.... How can I be made answerable for my misery; surely some one must be responsible for it, or I could not bear to live."...In short, resentful pessimism discovers responsible parties in order to create a pleasurable sensation for itself—revenge.... "Sweeter than honey"— thus does even old Homer speak of revenge.

***

The fact that such a theory no longer meets with understanding— or rather, let us say, contempt is accounted for by that particle of Christianity which still circulates in the blood of every one of us; it makes us tolerant towards things simply because we scent a Christian savour about them.... The Socialists appeal to the Christian instincts; this is their really refined piece of cleverness.... Thanks to Christianity, we have now grown accustomed to the superstitious concept of a soul—of an immortal soul, of soul monads, which, as a matter of fact, hails from somewhere else, and which has only become inherent in certain cases—that is to say, become incarnate in them—

by accident: but the nature of these cases is not altered, let alone determined by it. The circumstances of society, of relationship, and of history are only accidents for the soul, perhaps misadventures: in any case, the world is not their work. By means of the idea of soul the individual is made transcendental; thanks to it, a ridiculous amount of importance can be attributed to him.

As a matter of fact, it was Christianity which first induced the individual to take up this position of judge of all things. It made megalomania almost his duty: it has made everything temporary and limited subordinate to eternal rights! What is the State, what is society, what are historical laws, what is physiology to me? Thus speaks something from beyond Becoming, an immutable entity throughout history: thus speaks something immortal, something divine—it is the soul!

Another Christian, but no less insane, concept has percolated even deeper into the tissues of modern ideas: the concept of the equality of all souls before God. In this concept the prototype of all theories concerning equal rights is to be found. Man was first taught to stammer this proposition religiously: later, it was converted into a moral; no wonder he has ultimately begun to take it seriously, to take it *practically*!—that is to say, politically, socialistically, resento-pessimistically.

Wherever responsible circumstances or people have been looked for, it was the *instinct of revenge* that sought them. This instinct of revenge obtained such an ascendancy over man in the course of centuries that the whole of metaphysics, psychology, ideas of society, and, above all, morality, are tainted with it. Man has nourished this idea of responsibility to such an extent that he has introduced the bacillus of vengeance into everything. By means of it he has made God Himself ill, and killed innocence in the universe, by tracing every condition of things to acts of will, to intentions, to responsible agents. The whole teaching of will, this most fatal fraud that has ever existed in psychology hitherto, was invented essentially for the purpose of punishment. It was the social utility of punishment that lent this concept its dignity, its power, and its truth. The originator of that psychology, that we shall call volitional psychology, must be sought in those classes which had the right of punishment in their hands; above all, therefore, among the priests who stood on the very pinnacle of ancient social systems: these people wanted to create for themselves the right to wreak revenge—they wanted to supply God with the privilege of vengeance. For this purpose; man was declared "free": to this end every action had to be regarded as voluntary, and the origin of every deed had to be considered as lying in consciousness. But by such propositions as these ancient psychology is refuted.

Today, when Europe seems to have taken the contrary direction; when we halcyonians would fain withdraw, dissipate, and banish the concept of guilt and punishment with all our might from the world; when our most serious endeavours are concentrated upon purifying psychology, morality, history, nature, social institutions and privileges, and even God Himself, from this filth; in whom must we recognise our most mortal enemies? Precisely in those apostles of revenge and resentment, in those who are *par excellence* pessimists from indignation, who make it their mission to sanctify their filth with the name of "righteous indignation."... We others, whose one desire is to reclaim innocence on behalf of Becoming, would fain be the missionaries of a purer thought, namely, that no one is responsible for man's qualities; neither God, nor society, nor his parents, nor his ancestors, nor himself—in fact, that no one is to blame for him ... The being who might be made responsible for a man's existence, for the fact that he is constituted in a particular way, or for his birth in certain circumstances and in a certain environment, is absolutely lacking.— *And it is a great blessing that such a being is non-existent ....* We are *not* the result of an eternal design, of a will, of a desire: there is no attempt being made with us to attain to an "ideal of perfection," to an "ideal of happiness," to an "ideal of virtue,"—and we are just as little the result of a mistake on God's part in the presence of which He ought to feel uneasy (a thought which is known to be at the very root of the Old Testament). There is not a place nor a purpose nor a sense to which we can attribute our existence or our kind of existence. In the first place, no one is in a position to do this: it is quite impossible to judge, to measure, or to compare, or even to deny the whole universe! And why?—For five reasons, all accessible to the man of average intelligence: for instance, *because there is no existence outside the universe* ... and let us say it again, this is a great blessing, for therein lies the whole innocence of our lives.

822. (1888)

If I have sufficiently initated my readers into the doctrine that even "goodness," in the whole comedy of existence, represents a form of exhaustion, they will now credit Christianity with consistency for having conceived the good to be the ugly. In this respect Christianity was right.

It is absolutely unworthy of a philosopher to say that "the good and the beautiful are one"; if he should add "and also the true," he deserves to be thrashed. Truth is ugly.

Art is with us in order that we may not perish through truth.

845. (1885-1886)

Is art the result of dissatisfaction with reality? or is it the expression of gratitude for happiness experienced? In the first case, it is romanticism; in the second, it is glorification and dithyramb (in short, apotheosis art): even Raphael belongs to this, except for the fact that he was guilty of the duplicity of having defied the appearance of the Christian view of the world. He was thankful for life precisely where it was not exactly Christian.

With a moral interpretation the world is insufferable; Christianity was the attempt to overcome the world with morality: *i.e.* to deny it. *In praxi* such a mad experiment—an imbecile elevation of man above the world—could only end in the beglooming, the dwarfing, and the impoverishment of mankind: the only kind of man who gained anything by it, who was promoted by it, was the most mediocre, the most harmless and gregarious type.

Homer as an apotheosis artist; Rubens also. Music has not yet had such an artist.

The idealisation of the great criminal (the feeling for his greatness) is Greek; the depreciation, the slander, the contempt of the sinner, is Judæo-Christian.[89]

---

[89] See *The Birth of Tragedy* sec. 9 where Nietzsche contrasts the myth of Prometheus to that of Adam and Eve.

1052. (March-June 1888)

The two types; Dionysus and Christ on the Cross. We should ascertain whether the typically *religious* man is a decadent phenomenon (the great innovators are one and all morbid and epileptic); but do not let us forget to include that type of the religious man who is *pagan.* Is the pagan cult not a form of gratitude for, and affirmation of, Life? Ought not its most representative type to be an apology and deification of Life? The type of a well-constituted and ecstatically overflowing spirit! The type of a spirit which absorbs the contradictions and problems of existence, and which *solves* them!

At this point I set up the *Dionysus* of the Greeks: the religious affirmation of Life, of the whole of Life, not of denied and partial Life (it is typical that in this cult the sexual act awakens ideas of depth, mystery, and reverence). Dionysus *versus* "Christ"; here you have the contrast. It is *not* a difference in regard to the martyrdom,—but the latter has a different meaning. Life itself—Life's eternal fruitfulness and recurrence caused anguish, destruction, and the will to annihilation. In the other case, the suffering of the "Christ as the Innocent One" stands as an objection against Life, it is the formula of Life's condemnation.

Readers will guess that the problem concerns the meaning of suffering; whether a Christian or a tragic meaning be given to it. In the first case it is the road to a holy mode of existence; in the second case *existence itself is regarded as sufficiently holy* to justify an enormous amount of suffering. The tragic man says yea even to the most excruciating suffering: he is sufficiently strong, rich, and capable of deifying, to be able to do this; the Christian denies even the happy lots on earth: he is weak, poor, and disinherited enough to suffer from life in any form. God on the Cross is a curse upon Life, a signpost directing people to deliver themselves from it;—Dionysus cut into pieces is a *promise* of Life: it will be for ever born anew, and rise afresh from destruction.

from TWILIGHT OF THE IDOLS

"REASON" IN PHILOSOPHY

4.

The other idiosyncrasy of philosophers is no less dangerous; it consists in confusing the last and the first things. They place that which makes its appearance last—unfortunately! for it ought not to appear at all!—the "highest concept," that is to say, the most general, the emptiest, the last cloudy streak of evaporating reality, at the beginning as the beginning. This again is only their manner of expressing their veneration: the highest thing must not have grown out of the lowest, it must not have grown at all…. Moral: everything of the first rank must be *causa sui*. To have been derived from something else, is as good as an objection, it sets the value of a thing in question. All superior values are of the first rank, all the highest concepts—that of Being, of the Absolute, of Goodness, of Truth, and of Perfection; all these things cannot have been evolved, they must therefore be *causa sui*. All these things cannot however be unlike one another, they cannot be opposed to one another. Thus they attain to their stupendous concept "God." The last, most attenuated and emptiest thing is postulated as the first thing, as the absolute cause, as *ens realissimum*. Fancy humanity having to take the brain diseases of morbid cobweb-spinners seriously!—And it has paid dearly for having done so.

5.

Against this let us set the different manner in which we (—you observe that I am courteous enough to say "we") conceive the problem of the error and deceptiveness of things. Formerly people regarded change and evolution in general as the proof of appearance, as a sign of the fact that something must be there that leads us astray. Today, on the other hand, we realise that precisely as far as the rational bias forces us to postulate unity, identity, permanence, substance, cause, materiality and being, we are in a measure involved in error, driven necessarily to error; however certain we may feel, as the result of a strict examination of the matter, that the error lies here. It is just the same here as with the motion of the sun: In its case it was our eyes that were wrong; in the matter of the concepts above mentioned it is our language itself that pleads most constantly in their favour. In its origin language belongs to an age of the most rudimentary forms of psychology: if we try to conceive of the first conditions of the metaphysics of language, *i.e.* in plain English, of reason, we immediately find ourselves in the midst of a system of fetichism. For here, the doer and his deed are seen in all circumstances, will is believed in as a cause in general; the ego is taken for granted, the ego as Being, and as substance, and the faith in the ego as substance is projected into all things—in this way, alone, the concept "thing" is created. Being is thought into and insinuated into everything as cause; from the concept "ego," alone, can the concept "Being" proceed. At the beginning stands the tremendously fatal error of supposing the will to be something that actuates,—a faculty. Now we know that it is only a word.[1] Very much later, in a world a thousand times more enlightened, the assurance, the subjective certitude, in the handling of the categories of reason came into the minds of philosophers as a surprise. They concluded that these categories could not be derived from experience,—on the contrary, the whole of experience rather contradicts them. *Whence do they come therefore?* In India, as in Greece, the same mistake was made: "we must already once have lived in a higher world (—instead of in a much lower one, which would have been the truth!), we must have been divine, for we possess reason!" ... Nothing indeed has exercised a more simple power of persuasion hitherto than the error of Being, as it was formulated by the Eleatics for instance: in its favour are every word and every sentence that we utter!—Even the opponents of the Eleatics succumbed to the seductive powers of their concept of Being. Among others there was Democritus in his discovery of the atom. "Reason" in language!—oh what a deceptive old witch it has been! I fear we shall never be rid of God, so long as we still believe in grammar.

246

6.

People will feel grateful to me if I condense a point of view, which is at once so important and so new, into four theses: by this means I shall facilitate comprehension, and shall likewise challenge contradiction.

Proposition One. The reasons upon which the apparent nature of "this" world have been based, rather tend to prove its reality,—any other kind of reality defies demonstration.

Proposition Two. The characteristics with which man has endowed the "true Being" of things, are the characteristics of non-Being, of *nonentity.* The "true world" has been erected upon a contradiction of the real world; and it is indeed an apparent world, seeing that it is merely a *moralo-optical* delusion.

Proposition Three. There is no sense in spinning yarns about another world, provided, of course, that we do not possess a mighty instinct which urges us to slander, belittle, and cast suspicion upon this life: in this case we should be avenging ourselves on this life with the phantasmagoria of "another," of a "better" life.

Proposition Four. To divide the world into a "true" and an "apparent" world, whether after the manner of Christianity or of Kant (after all a Christian in disguise), is only a sign of decadence,—a symptom of *degenerating* life. The fact that the artist esteems the appearance of a thing higher than reality, is no objection to this statement. For "appearance" signifies once more reality here, but in a selected, strengthened and corrected form. The tragic artist is no pessimist,—he says *Yea* to everything questionable and terrible, he is Dionysian.

How The "True World" Ultimately Became A Fable [90]
The History of an Error

1. The true world, attainable to the sage, the pious man and the man of virtue,—he lives in it, *he is it.*

(The most ancient form of the idea was relatively clever, simple, convincing. It was a paraphrase of the proposition "I, Plato, am the truth.")

2. The true world which is unattainable for the moment, is promised to the sage, to the pious man and to the man of virtue ("to the sinner who repents").

(Progress of the idea: it becomes more subtle, more insidious, more evasive,—It *becomes a woman,* it becomes Christian.)

3. The true world is unattainable, it cannot be proved, it cannot promise anything; but even as a thought, alone, it is a comfort, an obligation, a command.

(At bottom this is still the old sun; but seen through mist and scepticism: the idea has become sublime, pale, northern, Königsbergian.[91])

4. The true world—is it unattainable? At all events it is unattained. And as unattained it is also *unknown.* Consequently it no longer comforts, nor saves, nor constrains: what could something unknown constrain us to?

(The grey of dawn. Reason stretches itself and yawns for the first time. The cock-crow of positivism.)

5. The "true world"—an idea that no longer serves any purpose, that no longer constrains one to anything,—a useless idea that has become quite superfluous, consequently an exploded idea: let us abolish it!

(Bright daylight; breakfast; the return of common sense and of cheerfulness; Plato blushes for shame and all free-spirits kick up a shindy.)

---

[90] See also *The Dawn* sec. 33, *The Gay Science* sec. 151, *The Will to Power* sec. 230

[91] A referent to Kant

6. We have suppressed the true world: what world survives? the apparent world perhaps?... Certainly not! *In abolishing the true world we have also abolished the world of appearance!*

(Noon; the moment of the shortest shadows; the end of the longest error; mankind's zenith; *Incipit Zarathustra.*)

MORALITY AS THE ENEMY OF NATURE

1.

There is a time when all passions are simply fatal in their action, when they wreck their victims with the weight of their folly,—and there is a later period, a very much later period, when they marry with the spirit, when they "spiritualise" themselves. Formerly, owing to the stupidity inherent in passion, men waged war against passion itself: men pledged themselves to annihilate it,—all ancient moral-mongers were unanimous on this point, *"il faut tuer les passions."* The most famous formula for this stands in the New Testament, in that Sermon on the Mount, where, let it be said incidentally, things are by no means regarded *from a height*. It is said there, for instance, with an application to sexuality: "if thy eye offend thee, pluck it out": fortunately no Christian acts in obedience to this precept. To annihilate the passions and desires, simply on account of their stupidity, and to obviate the unpleasant consequences of their stupidity, seems to us to-day merely an aggravated form of stupidity. We no longer admire those dentists who extract teeth simply in order that they may not ache again. On the other hand, it will be admitted with some reason, that on the soil from which Christianity grew, the idea of the "spiritualisation of passion" could not possibly have been conceived. The early Church, as everyone knows, certainly did wage war against the "intelligent," in favour of the "poor in spirit" In these circumstances how could the passions be combated intelligently? The Church combats passion by means of excision of all kinds: its practice, its "remedy," is *castration*. It never inquires "how can a desire be spiritualised, beautified, deified?"—In all ages it has laid the weight of discipline in the process of extirpation (the extirpation of

249

sensuality, pride, lust of dominion, lust of property, and revenge).—
But to attack the passions at their roots, means attacking life itself at
its source: the method of the Church is hostile to life.

4.

I will formulate a principle. All naturalism in morality—that is to
say, every sound morality is ruled by a life instinct,—any one of the
laws of life is fulfilled by the definite canon "thou shalt," "thou shalt
not," and any sort of obstacle or hostile element in the road of life is
thus cleared away. Conversely, the morality which is antagonistic to
nature—that is to say, almost every morality that has been taught,
honoured and preached hitherto, is directed precisely against the life-
instincts,—it is a condemnation, now secret, now blatant and
impudent, of these very instincts. Inasmuch as it says "God sees into
the heart of man," it says Nay to the profoundest and most superior
desires of life and takes God as the enemy of life. The saint in whom
God is well pleased, is the ideal eunuch. Life terminates where the
"Kingdom of God" begins.

THE FOUR GREAT ERRORS

6.

*The whole Domain of Morality and Religion may be classified under the
Rubric "Imaginary Causes."* The "explanation" of general unpleasant
sensations. These sensations are dependent upon certain creatures
who are hostile to us (evil spirits: the most famous example of this—
the mistaking of hysterical women for witches). These sensations are
dependent upon actions which are reprehensible (the feeling of "sin,"
"sinfulness" is a manner of accounting for a certain physiological
disorder—people always find reasons for being dissatisfied with
themselves). These sensations depend upon punishment, upon
compensation for something which we ought not to have done, which
we ought not to have been (this idea was generalised in a more
impudent form by Schopenhauer, into that principle in which

morality appears in its real colours,—that is to say, as a veritable poisoner and slanderer of life: "all great suffering, whether mental or physical, reveals what we deserve: for it could not visit us if we did not deserve it," "The World as Will and Idea," vol. 2, p. 666). These sensations are the outcome of ill-considered actions, having evil consequences, (—the passions, the senses, postulated as causes, as guilty. By means of other calamities distressing physiological conditions are interpreted as "merited").—The "explanation" of pleasant sensations. These sensations are dependent upon a trust in God. They may depend upon our consciousness of having done one or two good actions (a so-called "good conscience" is a physiological condition, which may be the outcome of good digestion). They may depend upon the happy issue of certain undertakings (—an ingenuous mistake: the happy issue of an undertaking certainly does not give a hypochondriac or a Pascal any general sensation of pleasure). They may depend upon faith, love and hope,—the Christian virtues. As a matter of fact all these pretended explanations are but the results of certain states, and as it were translations of feelings of pleasure and pain into a false dialect: a man is in a condition of hopefulness because the dominant physiological sensation of his being is again one of strength and wealth; he trusts in God because the feeling of abundance and power gives him a peaceful state of mind. Morality and religion are completely and utterly parts of the psychology of error: in every particular case cause and effect are confounded; as truth is confounded with the effect of that which is believed to be true; or a certain state of consciousness is confounded with the chain of causes which brought it about.

7.

The Error of Free-Will. At present we no longer have any mercy upon the concept "free-will": we know only too well what it is—the most egregious theological trick that has ever existed for the purpose of making mankind "responsible" in a theological manner,—that is to say, to make mankind dependent upon theologians. I will now explain to you only the psychology of the whole process of inculcating the sense of responsibility. Wherever men try to trace responsibility home to anyone, it is the instinct of punishment and of the desire to judge which is active. Becoming is robbed of its innocence when any particular condition of things is traced to a will, to intentions and to responsible actions. The doctrine of the will was invented principally for the purpose of punishment,—that is to say, with the intention of tracing guilt. The whole of ancient psychology, or the psychology of the will, is the outcome of the fact that its originators, who were the priests at the head of ancient communities, wanted to create for themselves a right to administer punishments—or the right for God to do so. Men were thought of as "free" in order that they might be judged and punished—in order that they might be held guilty: consequently every action had to be regarded as voluntary, and the origin of every action had to be imagined as lying in consciousness(— in this way the most fundamentally fraudulent character of psychology was established as the very principle of psychology itself). Now that we have entered upon the opposite movement, now that we immoralists are trying with all our power to eliminate the concepts of guilt and punishment from the world once more, and to cleanse psychology, history, nature and all social institutions and customs of all signs of those two concepts, we recognise no more radical opponents than the theologians, who with their notion of "a moral order of things," still continue to pollute the innocence of Becoming with punishment and guilt Christianity is the metaphysics of the hangman.

THE "IMPROVERS" OF MANKIND

2.

... In all ages there have been people who wished to "improve" mankind: this above all is what was called morality. But the most different tendencies are concealed beneath the same word. Both the taming of the beast man, and the rearing of a particular type of man, have been called "improvement": these zoological *termini*, alone, represent real things—real things of which the typical "improver," the priest, naturally knows nothing, and will know nothing. To call the taming of an animal "improving" it, sounds to our ears almost like a joke. He who knows what goes on in menageries, doubts very much whether an animal is improved in such places. It is certainly weakened, it is made less dangerous, and by means of the depressing influence of fear, pain, wounds, and hunger, it is converted into a sick animal. And the same holds good of the tamed man whom the priest has "improved." In the early years of the Middle Ages, during which the Church was most distinctly and above all a menagerie, the most beautiful examples of the "blond beast" were hunted down in all directions,—the noble Germans, for instance, were "improved." But what did this "improved" German, who had been lured to the monastery look like after the process? He looked like a caricature of man, like an abortion: he had become a "sinner," he was caged up, he had been imprisoned behind a host of apparling notions. He now lay there, sick, wretched, malevolent even toward himself: full of hate for the instincts of life, full of suspicion in regard to all that is still strong and happy. In short a "Christian." In physiological terms: in a fight with an animal, the only way of making it weak may be to make it sick. The Church understood this: it ruined man, it made him weak, —but it laid claim to having "improved" him.

SKIRMISHES IN A WAR WITH THE AGE

5.

G. Eliot.—They are rid of the Christian God and therefore think it all the more incumbent upon them to hold tight to Christian morality: this is an English way of reasoning; but let us not take it ill in moral females *à la* Eliot. In England, every man who indulges in any trifling emancipation from theology, must retrieve his honour in the most terrifying manner by becoming a moral fanatic. That is how they do penance in that country.—As for us, we act differently. When we renounce the Christian faith, we abandon all right to Christian morality. This is not by any means self-evident and in defiance of English shallow-pates the point must be made ever more and more plain. Christianity is a system, a complete outlook upon the world, conceived as a whole. If its leading concept, the belief in God, is wrenched from it, the whole is destroyed; nothing vital remains in our grasp. Christianity presupposes that man does not and cannot know what is good or bad for him: the Christian believes in God who, alone, can know these things. Christian morality is a command, its origin is transcendental. It is beyond all criticism, all right to criticism; it is true only on condition that God is truth,—it stands or falls with the belief in God. If the English really believe that they know intuitively, and of their own accord, what is good and evil; if, therefore, they assert that they no longer need Christianity as a guarantee of morality, this in itself is simply the outcome of the dominion of Christian valuations, and a proof of the strength and profundity of this dominion. It only shows that the origin of English morality has been forgotten, and that its exceedingly relative right to exist is no longer felt. For Englishmen morality is not yet a problem.

34.

The Christian and the Anarchist.—When the anarchist, as the mouthpiece of the decaying strata of society, raises his voice in splendid indignation for "right," "justice," "equal rights," he is only groaning under the burden of his ignorance, which cannot understand *why* he actually suffers,—what his poverty consists of—the poverty of life. An instinct of causality is active in him: someone must be responsible for his being so ill at ease. His "splendid indignation" alone relieves him somewhat, it is a pleasure for all poor devils to grumble—it gives them a little intoxicating sensation of power. The very act of complaining, the mere fact that one bewails one's lot, may lend such a charm to life that on that account alone, one is ready to endure it. There is a small dose of revenge in every lamentation. One casts one's afflictions, and, under certain circumstances, even one's baseness, in the teeth of those who are different, as if their condition were an injustice, an *iniquitous* privilege. "Since I am *a blackguard* you ought to be one too." It is upon such reasoning that revolutions are based.—To bewail one's lot is always despicable: it is always the outcome of weakness. Whether one ascribes one's afflictions to others or to *one's self,* it is all the same. The socialist does the former, the Christian, for instance, does the latter. That which is common to both attitudes, or rather that which is equally ignoble in them both, is the fact that somebody must be to *blame* if one suffers—in short that the sufferer drugs himself with the honey of revenge to allay his anguish. The objects towards which this lust of vengeance, like a lust of pleasure, are directed, are purely accidental causes. In all directions the sufferer finds reasons for cooling his petty passion for revenge. If he is a Christian, I repeat, he finds these reasons in himself. The Christian and the Anarchist—both are decadents. But even when the Christian condemns, slanders, and sullies the world, he is actuated by precisely the same instinct as that which leads the socialistic workman to curse, calumniate and cast dirt at society. The last "Judgment" itself is still the sweetest solace to revenge—revolution, as the socialistic workman expects it, only thought of as a little more remote.... The notion of a "Beyond," as well—why a Beyond, if it be not a means of splashing mud over a "Here," over this world? ...

THE ANTICHRIST

An Attempted Criticism of Christianity [92]

PREFACE

This book belongs to the most rare of men. Perhaps not one of them is yet alive. It is possible that they may be among those who understand my "Zarathustra": how *could* I confound myself with those who are now sprouting ears?—First the day after tomorrow must come for me. Some men are born posthumously.

The conditions under which any one understands me, and *necessarily* understands me—I know them only too well. Even to endure my seriousness, my passion, he must carry intellectual integrity to the verge of hardness. He must be accustomed to living on mountain tops—and to looking upon the wretched gabble of politics and nationalism as *beneath* him. He must have become indifferent; he must never ask of the truth whether it brings profit to him or a fatality to him.... He must have an inclination, born of strength, for questions that no one has the courage for; the courage for the *forbidden*; predestination for the labyrinth. The experience of seven solitudes. New ears for new music. New eyes for what is most distant. A new conscience for truths that have hitherto remained unheard. *And* the will to economize in the grand manner—to hold together his strength, his enthusiasm.... Reverence for self; love of self; absolute freedom of self....

Very well, then! of that sort only are my readers, my true readers, my readers foreordained: of what account are the *rest*?—The rest are merely humanity.—One must make one's self superior to humanity, in power, in *loftiness* of soul,—in contempt.

---

[92]The German title, *Der Antichrist,* can mean both "Antichrist" and "Anti-Christian." While the latter is in some ways a more appropriate title insofar as Nietzsche attacks Christianity but has some words of praise for Jesus, he was never one to shy away from controversy and doubtless intended both meanings.

DIONYSUS VERSUS THE CRUCIFIED

1.

Let us look each other in the face. We are Hyperboreans—we know well enough how remote our place is. "Neither by land nor by water will you find the road to the Hyperboreans": even Pindar,[93] in his day, knew *that* much about us. Beyond the North, beyond the ice, beyond *death*—*our* life, *our* happiness.... We have discovered that happiness; we know the way; we got our knowledge of it from thousands of years in the labyrinth. Who *else* has found it?—The man of today?—"I don't know either the way out or the way in; I am whatever doesn't know either the way out or the way in"—so sighs the man of today.... *This* is the sort of modernity that made us ill,—we sickened on lazy peace, cowardly compromise, the whole virtuous dirtiness of the modern Yea and Nay. This tolerance and *largeur* of the heart that "forgives" everything because it "understands" everything is a sirocco to us. Rather live amid the ice than among modern virtues and other such south-winds!... We were brave enough; we spared neither ourselves nor others; but we were a long time finding out *where* to direct our courage. We grew dismal; they called us fatalists. *Our* fate —it was the fulness, the tension, the *storing up* of powers. We thirsted for the lightnings and great deeds; we kept as far as possible from the happiness of the weakling, from "resignation"... There was thunder in our air; nature, as we embodied it, became overcast—*for we had not yet found the way.* The formula of our happiness: a Yea, a Nay, a straight line, a *goal....*

2.

What is good?—Whatever augments the feeling of power, the will to power, power itself, in man.

What is evil?—Whatever springs from weakness.

What is happiness?—The feeling that power *increases*—that resistance is overcome.

Not contentment, but more power; *not* peace at any price, but war; *not* virtue, but efficiency (virtue in the Renaissance sense, *virtu*, virtue free of moral acid).

---

[93] *Cf.* the tenth Pythian ode. See also the fourth book of Herodotus. The Hyperboreans were a mythical people beyond the Rhipaean mountains, in the far North. They enjoyed unbroken happiness and perpetual youth.

The weak and the botched shall perish: first principle of *our* charity. And one should help them to it.

What is more harmful than any vice?—Practical sympathy for the botched and the weak—Christianity....

3.

The problem that I set here is not what shall replace mankind in the order of living creatures (—man is an end—): but what type of man must be *bred*, must be *willed*, as being the most valuable, the most worthy of life, the most secure guarantee of the future.

This more valuable type has appeared often enough in the past: but always as a happy accident, as an exception, never as deliberately *willed*. Very often it has been precisely the most feared; hitherto it has been almost *the* terror of terrors;—and out of that terror the contrary type has been willed, cultivated and *attained*: the domestic animal, the herd animal, the sick brute-man—the Christian....

4.

Mankind surely does *not* represent an evolution toward a better or stronger or higher level, as progress is now understood. This "progress" is merely a modern idea, which is to say, a false idea. The European of today, in his essential worth, falls far below the European of the Renaissance; the process of evolution does *not* necessarily mean elevation, enhancement, strengthening.

True enough, it succeeds in isolated and individual cases in various parts of the earth and under the most widely different cultures, and in these cases a *higher* type certainly manifests itself; something which, compared to mankind in the mass, appears as a sort of superman. Such happy strokes of high success have always been possible, and will remain possible, perhaps, for all time to come. Even whole races, tribes and nations may occasionally represent such lucky accidents.

5.

We should not deck out and embellish Christianity: it has waged a war to the death against this *higher* type of man, it has put all the deepest instincts of this type under its ban, it has developed its concept of evil, of the Evil One himself, out of these instincts—the strong man as the typical reprobate, the "outcast among men." Christianity has taken the part of all the weak, the low, the botched; it has made an ideal out of *antagonism* to all the self-preservative instincts of sound life; it has corrupted even the faculties of those natures that are intellectually most vigorous, by representing the highest intellectual values as sinful, as misleading, as full of temptation. The most lamentable example: the corruption of Pascal, who believed that his intellect had been destroyed by original sin, whereas it was actually destroyed by Christianity!—

6.

It is a painful and tragic spectacle that rises before me: I have drawn back the curtain from the *rottenness* of man. This word, in my mouth, is at least free from one suspicion: that it involves a moral accusation against humanity. It is used—and I wish to emphasize the fact again—without any moral significance: and this is so far true that the rottenness I speak of is most apparent to me precisely in those quarters where there has been most aspiration, hitherto, toward "virtue" and "godliness." As you probably surmise, I understand rottenness in the sense of *décadence*: my argument is that all the values on which mankind now fixes its highest aspirations are *décadence*-values.

I call an animal, a species, an individual corrupt, when it loses its instincts, when it chooses, when it *prefers*, what is injurious to it. A history of the "higher feelings," the "ideals of humanity"—and it is possible that I'll have to write it—would almost explain why man is so degenerate. Life itself appears to me as an instinct for growth, for survival, for the accumulation of forces, for *power*: whenever the will to power fails there is disaster. My contention is that all the highest values of humanity have been emptied of this will—that the values of *décadence*, of *nihilism*, now prevail under the holiest names.

7.

Christianity is called the religion of *pity*.—Pity stands in opposition to all the tonic passions that augment the energy of the feeling of aliveness: it is a depressant. A man loses power when he pities. Through pity that drain upon strength which suffering works is multiplied a thousandfold. Suffering is made contagious by pity; under certain circumstances it may lead to a total sacrifice of life and living energy—a loss out of all proportion to the magnitude of the cause (— the case of the death of the Nazarene). This is the first view of it; there is, however, a still more important one. If one measures the effects of pity by the gravity of the reactions it sets up, its character as a menace to life appears in a much clearer light. Pity thwarts the whole law of evolution, which is the law of natural selection. It preserves whatever is ripe for destruction; it fights on the side of those disinherited and condemned by life; by maintaining life in so many of the botched of all kinds, it gives life itself a gloomy and dubious aspect.

Mankind has ventured to call pity a virtue (—in every *superior* moral system it appears as a weakness—); going still further, it has been called *the* virtue, the source and foundation of all other virtues— but let us always bear in mind that this was from the standpoint of a philosophy that was nihilistic, and upon whose shield *the denial of life* was inscribed. Schopenhauer was right in this: that by means of pity life is denied, and made *worthy of denial*—pity is the technic of nihilism. Let me repeat: this depressing and contagious instinct stands against all those instincts which work for the preservation and enhancement of life: in the role of *protector* of the miserable, it is a prime agent in the promotion of *décadence*—pity persuades to extinction…. Of course, one doesn't say "extinction": one says "the other world," or "God," or "the *true* life," or Nirvana, salvation, blessedness…. This innocent rhetoric, from the realm of religious-ethical balderdash, appears *a good deal less innocent* when one reflects upon the tendency that it conceals beneath sublime words: the tendency to *destroy life*. Schopenhauer was hostile to life: that is why pity appeared to him as a virtue…. Aristotle, as every one knows, saw in pity a sickly and dangerous state of mind, the remedy for which was an occasional purgative: he regarded tragedy as that purgative. The instinct of life should prompt us to seek some means of puncturing any such pathological and dangerous accumulation of pity as that appearing in Schopenhauer's case (and also, alack, in that of our whole literary *décadence*, from St. Petersburg to Paris, from Tolstoy to Wagner), that it may burst and be discharged…. Nothing is more unhealthy, amid all our unhealthy modernism, than Christian pity. To be the doctors *here*, to be unmerciful *here*, to wield the knife *here*—all this is *our* business, all this is *our* sort of humanity, by this sign we are philosophers, we Hyperboreans!—

8.

It is necessary to say just *whom* we regard as our antagonists: theologians and all who have any theological blood in their veins—this is our whole philosophy…. One must have faced that menace at close hand; better still, one must have had experience of it directly and almost succumbed to it, to realize that it is not to be taken lightly (—the alleged free-thinking of our naturalists and physiologists seems to me to be a joke—they have no passion about such things; they have not suffered—). This poisoning goes a great deal further than most people think: I find the arrogant habit of the theologian among all who regard themselves as "idealists"—among all who, by virtue of a higher point of departure, claim a right to rise above reality, and to look upon it with suspicion…. The idealist, like the ecclesiastic, carries all sorts of lofty concepts in his hand (—and not only in his hand!); he launches them with benevolent contempt against "understanding," "the senses," "honor," "good living," "science"; he sees such things as *beneath* him, as pernicious and seductive forces, on which "the soul" soars as a pure thing-in-itself—as if humility, chastity, poverty, in a word, *holiness*, had not already done much more damage to life than all imaginable horrors and vices…. The pure soul is a pure lie…. So long as the priest, that *professional* denier, calumniator and poisoner of life, is accepted as a *higher* variety of man, there can be no answer to the question, What *is* truth? Truth has already been stood on its head when the obvious attorney of mere emptiness is mistaken for its representative….

9.

Upon this theological instinct I make war: I find the tracks of it everywhere. Whoever has theological blood in his veins is shifty and dishonourable in all things. The pathetic thing that grows out of this condition is called *faith*: in other words, closing one's eyes upon one's self once for all, to avoid suffering the sight of incurable falsehood. People erect a concept of morality, of virtue, of holiness upon this false view of all things; they ground good conscience upon faulty vision; they argue that no *other* sort of vision has value any more, once they have made theirs sacrosanct with the names of "God," "salvation" and "eternity." I unearth this theological instinct in all directions: it is the most widespread and the most *subterranean* form of falsehood to be found on earth. Whatever a theologian regards as true *must* be false: there you have almost a criterion of truth. His profound instinct of self-preservation stands against truth ever coming into honour in any way, or even getting stated. Wherever the influence of theologians is felt there is a transvaluation of values, and the concepts "true" and "false" are forced to change places: whatever is most damaging to life is there called "true," and whatever exalts it, intensifies it, approves it, justifies it and makes it triumphant is there called "false."... When theologians, working through the "consciences" of princes (or of peoples—), stretch out their hands for *power*, there is never any doubt as to the fundamental issue: the will to make an end, the *nihilistic* will exerts that power....

10.

Among Germans I am immediately understood when I say that theological blood is the ruin of philosophy. The Protestant pastor is the grandfather of German philosophy; Protestantism itself is its *peccatum originale*.[94] Definition of Protestantism: hemiplegic paralysis of Christianity—*and* of reason.... One need only utter the words "Tübingen School" to get an understanding of what German philosophy is at bottom—a very artful form of theology.... The Swabians are the best liars in Germany; they lie innocently.... Why all the rejoicing over the appearance of Kant that went through the learned world of Germany, three-fourths of which is made up of the sons of preachers and teachers—why the German conviction, still echoing, that with Kant came a change for the *better*? The theological instinct of German scholars made them see clearly just *what* had become possible again.... A backstairs leading to the old ideal stood open; the concept of the "true world," the concept of morality as the

---

[94] original sin

essence of the world (—the two most vicious errors that ever existed!), were once more, thanks to a subtle and wily scepticism, if not actually demonstrable, then *at least* no longer *refutable*.... *Reason*, the *prerogative* of reason, does not go so far.... Out of reality there had been made "appearance"; an absolutely false world, that of being, had been turned into reality.... The success of Kant is merely a theological success; he was, like Luther and Leibniz, but one more impediment to German integrity, already far from steady.—

11.

A word now against Kant as a moralist. A virtue must be *our* invention; it must spring out of *our* personal need and defence. In every other case it is a source of danger. That which does not belong to our life *menaces* it; a virtue which has its roots in mere respect for the concept of "virtue," as Kant would have it, is pernicious. "Virtue," "duty," "good for its own sake," goodness grounded upon impersonality or a notion of universal validity—these are all chimeras, and in them one finds only an expression of the decay, the last collapse of life, the Chinese spirit of Königsberg. Quite the contrary is demanded by the most profound laws of self-preservation and of growth: to wit, that every man find his *own* virtue, his *own* categorical imperative. A nation goes to pieces when it confounds *its* duty with the general concept of duty. Nothing works a more complete and penetrating disaster than every "impersonal" duty, every sacrifice before the Moloch of abstraction.—To think that no one has thought of Kant's categorical imperative as *dangerous to life*!... The theological instinct alone took it under protection!—An action prompted by the life-instinct proves that it is a *right* action by the amount of pleasure that goes with it: and yet that Nihilist, with his bowels of Christian dogmatism, regarded pleasure as an *objection*.... What destroys a man more quickly than to work, think and feel without inner necessity, without any deep personal desire, without pleasure—as a mere automaton of duty? That is the recipe for *décadence*, and no less for idiocy.... Kant became an idiot.—And such a man was the contemporary of Goethe! This calamitous spinner of cobwebs passed for *the* German philosopher—still passes today!... I forbid myself to say what I think of the Germans.... Didn't Kant see in the French Revolution the transformation of the state from the inorganic form to the *organic*? Didn't he ask himself if there was a single event that could be explained save on the assumption of a moral faculty in man, so that on the basis of it, "the tendency of mankind toward the good" could be *explained*, once and for all time? Kant's answer: "That is revolution." Instinct at fault in everything and anything, instinct as a revolt against nature, German *décadence* as a philosophy—*that is Kant!*—

12.

I put aside a few sceptics, the types of decency in the history of philosophy: the rest haven't the slightest conception of intellectual integrity. They behave like women, all these great enthusiasts and prodigies—they regard "beautiful feelings" as arguments, the "heaving breast" as the bellows of divine inspiration, conviction as the *criterion* of truth. In the end, with "German" innocence, Kant tried to give a scientific flavour to this form of corruption, this dearth of intellectual conscience, by calling it "practical reason." He deliberately invented a variety of reasons for use on occasions when it was desirable not to trouble with reason—that is, when morality, when the sublime command "thou shalt," was heard. When one recalls the fact that, among all peoples, the philosopher is no more than a development from the old type of priest, this inheritance from the priest, this *fraud upon self*, ceases to be remarkable. When a man feels that he has a divine mission, say to lift up, to save or to liberate mankind—when a man feels the divine spark in his heart and believes that he is the mouthpiece of supernatural imperatives—when such a mission inflames him, it is only natural that he should stand beyond all merely reasonable standards of judgment. He feels that he is *himself* sanctified by this mission, that he is himself a type of a higher order!... What has a priest to do with philosophy! He stands far above it!—And hitherto the priest has *ruled!*—He has determined the meaning of "true" and "not true"!...

13.

Let us not underestimate this fact: that *we ourselves*, we free spirits, are already a "transvaluation of all values," a *visualized* declaration of war and victory against all the old concepts of "true" and "not true."

The most valuable intuitions are the last to be attained; the most valuable of all are those which determine *methods*. All the methods, all the principles of the scientific spirit of today, were the targets for thousands of years of the most profound contempt; if a man inclined to them he was excluded from the society of "decent" people—he passed as "an enemy of God," as a scoffer at the truth, as one "possessed." As a man of science, he belonged to the Chandala…. We have had the whole pathetic stupidity of mankind against us—their every notion of what the truth *ought* to be, of what the service of the truth *ought* to be—their every "thou shalt" was launched against us…. Our objectives, our methods, our quiet, cautious, distrustful manner—all appeared to them as absolutely discreditable and contemptible.—Looking back, one may almost ask one's self with reason if it was not actually an *aesthetic* sense that kept men blind so long: what they demanded of the truth was picturesque effectiveness, and of the learned a strong appeal to their senses. It was our *modesty* that stood out longest against their taste…. How well they guessed that, these turkey-cocks of God!

14.

We have unlearned something. We have become more modest in every way. We no longer derive man from the "spirit," from the "godhead"; we have dropped him back among the beasts. We regard him as the strongest of the beasts because he is the craftiest; one of the results thereof is his intellectuality. On the other hand, we guard ourselves against a conceit which would assert itself even here: that man is the great second thought in the process of organic evolution. He is, in truth, anything but the crown of creation: beside him stand many other animals, all at similar stages of development…. And even when we say that we say a bit too much, for man, relatively speaking, is the most botched of all the animals and the sickliest, and he has wandered the most dangerously from his instincts—though for all that, to be sure, he remains the most *interesting*!—As regards the lower animals, it was Descartes who first had the really admirable daring to describe them as *machina*; the whole of our physiology is directed toward proving the truth of this doctrine. Moreover, it is illogical to set man apart, as Descartes did: what we know of man today is limited precisely by the extent to which we have regarded him, too, as a machine. Formerly we accorded to man, as his inheritance from some higher order of beings, what was called "free will"; now we have taken even this will from him, for the term no longer describes anything that we can understand. The old word "will" now connotes only a sort of result, an individual reaction, that follows inevitably upon a series of partly discordant and partly harmonious stimuli—the will no longer "acts," or "moves."... Formerly it was thought that man's consciousness, his "spirit," offered evidence of his high origin, his divinity. That he might be *perfected*, he was advised, tortoise-like, to draw his senses in, to have no traffic with earthly things, to shuffle off his mortal coil—then only the important part of him, the "pure spirit," would remain. Here again we have thought out the thing better: to us consciousness, or "the spirit," appears as a symptom of a relative imperfection of the organism, as an experiment, a groping, a misunderstanding, as an affliction which uses up nervous force unnecessarily—we deny that anything can be done perfectly so long as it is done consciously. The "pure spirit" is a piece of pure stupidity: take away the nervous system and the senses, the so-called "mortal shell," and *the rest is miscalculation*—that is all!...

15.

Under Christianity neither morality nor religion has any point of contact with actuality. It offers purely imaginary *causes* ("God," "soul," "ego," "spirit," "free will"—or even "unfree"), and purely imaginary *effects* ("sin," "salvation," "grace," "punishment," "forgiveness of sins"). Intercourse between imaginary *beings* ("God," "spirits," "souls"); an imaginary *natural history* (anthropocentric; a total denial of the concept of natural causes); an imaginary *psychology* (misunderstandings of self, misinterpretations of agreeable or disagreeable general feelings—for example, of the states of the *nervus sympathicus* with the help of the sign-language of religio-ethical balderdash—, "repentance," "pangs of conscience," "temptation by the devil," "the presence of God"); an imaginary *teleology* (the "kingdom of God," "the last judgment," "eternal life").—This purely *fictitious world*, greatly to its disadvantage, is to be differentiated from the world of dreams; the latter at least reflects reality, whereas the former falsifies it, cheapens it and denies it. Once the concept of "nature" had been opposed to the concept of "God," the word "natural" necessarily took on the meaning of "abominable"—the whole of that fictitious world has its sources in hatred of the natural (—the real!—), and is no more than evidence of a profound uneasiness in the presence of reality…. *This explains everything.* Who alone has any reason for living his way out of reality? The man who suffers under it. But to suffer from reality one must be a *botched* reality…. The preponderance of pains over pleasures is the cause of this fictitious morality and religion: but such a preponderance also supplies the formula for *décadence*….

16.

A criticism of the *Christian concept of God* leads inevitably to the same conclusion.—A nation that still believes in itself holds fast to its own god. In him it does honour to the conditions which enable it to survive, to its virtues—it projects its joy in itself, its feeling of power, into a being to whom one may offer thanks. He who is rich will give of his riches; a proud people need a god to whom they can make *sacrifices*…. Religion, within these limits, is a form of gratitude. A man is grateful for his own existence: to that end he needs a god.—Such a god must be able to work both benefits and injuries; he must be able to play either friend or foe—he is wondered at for the good he does as well as for the evil he does. But the castration, against all nature, of such a god, making him a god of goodness alone, would be contrary to human inclination. Mankind has just as much need for an evil god as for a good god; it doesn't have to thank mere tolerance and humanitarianism for its own existence…. What would be the value of a god who knew nothing of anger, revenge, envy, scorn, cunning, violence? who had perhaps never experienced the rapturous *ardeurs* of victory and of destruction? No one would understand such a god: why should any one want him?—True enough, when a nation is on the downward path, when it feels its belief in its own future, its hope of freedom slipping from it, when it begins to see submission as a first necessity and the virtues of submission as measures of self-preservation, then it *must* overhaul its god. He then becomes a hypocrite, timorous and demure; he counsels "peace of soul," hate-no-more, leniency, "love" of friend and foe. He moralizes endlessly; he creeps into every private virtue; he becomes the god of every man; he becomes a private citizen, a cosmopolitan…. Formerly he represented a people, the strength of a people, everything aggressive and thirsty for power in the soul of a people; now he is simply *the good god*.... The truth is that there is no other alternative for gods: *either* they are the will to power—in which case they are national gods—*or* incapacity for power—in which case they have to be good....

17.

Wherever the will to power begins to decline, in whatever form, there is always an accompanying decline physiologically, a *décadence*. The divinity of this *décadence*, shorn of its masculine virtues and passions, is converted perforce into a god of the physiologically degraded, of the weak. Of course, they do not *call* themselves the weak; they call themselves "the good."... No hint is needed to indicate the moments in history at which the dualistic fiction of a good and an evil god first became possible. The same instinct which prompts the inferior to reduce their own god to "goodness-in-itself" also prompts them to eliminate all good qualities from the god of their superiors; they make revenge on their masters by making a *devil* of the latter's god.

The *good* god, and the devil like him—both are abortions of *décadence*.—How can we be so tolerant of the naïveté of Christian theologians as to join in their doctrine that the evolution of the concept of god from "the god of Israel," the god of a people, to the Christian god, the essence of all goodness, is to be described as *progress*?—But even Renan does this. As if Renan had a right to be naïve! The contrary actually stares one in the face. When everything necessary to *ascending* life; when all that is strong, courageous, masterful and proud has been eliminated from the concept of a god; when he has sunk step by step to the level of a staff for the weary, a sheet-anchor for the drowning; when he becomes the poor man's god, the sinner's god, the invalid's god *par excellence*, and the attribute of "saviour" or "redeemer" remains as the one essential attribute of divinity—just *what* is the significance of such a metamorphosis? what does such a *reduction* of the godhead imply?

To be sure, the "kingdom of God" has thus grown larger. Formerly he had only his own people, his "chosen" people. But since then he has gone wandering, like his people themselves, into foreign parts; he has given up settling down quietly anywhere; finally he has come to feel at home everywhere, and is the great cosmopolitan—until now he has the "great majority" on his side, and half the earth. But this god of the "great majority," this democrat among gods, has not become a proud heathen god: on the contrary, he remains a Jew, he remains a god in a corner, a god of all the dark nooks and crevices, of all the noisesome quarters of the world!... His earthly kingdom, now as always, is a kingdom of the underworld, a *souterrain* kingdom, a ghetto kingdom.... And he himself is so pale, so weak, so *décadent*.... Even the palest of the pale are able to master him—messieurs the metaphysicians, those albinos of the intellect. They spun their webs around him for so long that finally he was hypnotized, and began to spin himself, and became another metaphysician. Thereafter he resumed once more his old business of spinning the world out of his inmost being *sub specie Spinozae*; thereafter he became ever thinner and paler—became the "ideal," became "pure spirit," became "the absolute," became "the thing-in-itself."... *The collapse of a god*: he became a "thing-in-itself."

18.

The Christian concept of a god—the god as the patron of the sick, the god as a spinner of cobwebs, the god as a spirit—is one of the most corrupt concepts that has ever been set up in the world: it probably touches low-water mark in the ebbing evolution of the god-type. God degenerated into the *contradiction of life*. Instead of being its transfiguration and eternal Yea! In him war is declared on life, on nature, on the will to live! God becomes the formula for every slander upon the "here and now," and for every lie about the "beyond"! In him nothingness is deified, and the will to nothingness is made holy!...

19.

The fact that the strong races of northern Europe did not repudiate this Christian god does little credit to their gift for religion—and not much more to their taste. They ought to have been able to make an end of such a moribund and worn-out product of the *décadence*. A curse lies upon them because they were not equal to it; they made illness, decrepitude and contradiction a part of their instincts—and since then they have not managed to *create* any more gods. Two thousand years have come and gone—and not a single new god! Instead, there still exists, and as if by some intrinsic right,—as if he were the *ultimatum* and *maximum* of the power to create gods, of the *creator spiritus* in mankind—this pitiful god of Christian monotono-theism! This hybrid image of decay, conjured up out of emptiness, contradiction and vain imagining, in which all the instincts of *décadence*, all the cowardices and wearinesses of the soul find their sanction!—

20.

In my condemnation of Christianity I surely hope I do no injustice to a related religion with an even larger number of believers: I allude to *Buddhism*. Both are to be reckoned among the nihilistic religions—they are both *décadence* religions—but they are separated from each other in a very remarkable way. For the fact that he is able to *compare* them at all the critic of Christianity is indebted to the scholars of India.—Buddhism is a hundred times more realistic than Christianity—it is part of its living heritage that it is able to face problems objectively and coolly; it is the product of long centuries of philosophical speculation. The concept, "god," was already disposed of before it appeared. Buddhism is the only genuinely *positive* religion to be encountered in history, and this applies even to its epistemology (which is a strict phenomenalism). It does not speak of a "struggle with sin," but, yielding to reality, of the "struggle with suffering." Sharply differentiating itself from Christianity, it puts the self-deception that lies in moral concepts behind it; it is, in my phrase, *beyond* good and evil.

The two physiological facts upon which it grounds itself and upon which it bestows its chief attention are: first, an excessive sensitiveness to sensation, which manifests itself as a refined susceptibility to pain, and *secondly*, an extraordinary spirituality, a too protracted concern with concepts and logical procedures, under the influence of which the instinct of personality has yielded to a notion of the "impersonal." (—Both of these states will be familiar to a few of my readers, the objectivists, by experience, as they are to me). These physiological states produced a *depression*, and Buddha tried to combat it by hygienic measures. Against it he prescribed a life in the open, a life of travel; moderation in eating and a careful selection of foods; caution in the use of intoxicants; the same caution in arousing any of the passions that foster a bilious habit and heat the blood; finally, no *worry*, either on one's own account or on account of others. He encourages ideas that make for either quiet contentment or good cheer—he finds means to combat ideas of other sorts. He understands good, the state of goodness, as something which promotes health. *Prayer* is not included, and neither is *asceticism*. There is no categorical imperative nor any disciplines, even within the walls of a monastery (—it is always possible to leave—). These things would have been simply means of increasing the excessive sensitiveness above mentioned. For the same reason he does not advocate any conflict with unbelievers; his teaching is antagonistic to nothing so much as to revenge, aversion, *ressentiment* (—"enmity never brings an end to enmity": the moving refrain of all Buddhism....) And in all this he was right, for it is precisely these passions which, in view of his main regiminal purpose, are *unhealthful*. The mental fatigue that he observes, already plainly displayed in too much "objectivity" (that is, in the individual's loss of interest in himself, in loss of balance and of "egoism"), he combats by strong efforts to lead even the spiritual interests back to the *ego*. In Buddha's teaching egoism is a duty. The "one thing needful," the question "how can you be delivered from suffering," regulates and determines the whole spiritual diet. (—Perhaps one will here recall that Athenian who also declared war upon pure "scientificality," to wit, Socrates, who also elevated egoism to the estate of a morality).

21.

The things necessary to Buddhism are a very mild climate, customs of great gentleness and liberality, and *no* militarism; moreover, it must get its start among the higher and better educated classes. Cheerfulness, quiet and the absence of desire are the chief desiderata, and they are *attained*. Buddhism is not a religion in which perfection is merely an object of aspiration: perfection is actually normal.

Under Christianity the instincts of the subjugated and the oppressed come to the fore: it is only those who are at the bottom who seek their salvation in it. Here the prevailing pastime, the favourite remedy for boredom is the discussion of sin, self-criticism, the inquisition of conscience; here the emotion produced by *power* (called

"God") is pumped up (by prayer); here the highest good is regarded as unattainable, as a gift, as "grace." Here, too, open dealing is lacking; concealment and the darkened room are Christian. Here body is despised and hygiene is denounced as sensual; the church even ranges itself against cleanliness (—the first Christian order after the banishment of the Moors closed the public baths, of which there were 270 in Cordova alone).

Christian, too, is a certain cruelty toward one's self and toward others; hatred of unbelievers; the will to persecute. Sombre and disquieting ideas are in the foreground; the most esteemed states of mind, bearing the most respectable names, are epileptoid; the diet is so regulated as to engender morbid symptoms and over-stimulate the nerves. Christian, again, is all deadly enmity to the rulers of the earth, to the "aristocratic"—along with a sort of secret rivalry with them (—one resigns one's "body" to them; one wants *only* one's "soul"...). And Christian is all hatred of the intellect, of pride, of courage, of freedom, of intellectual *libertinage*; Christian is all hatred of the senses, of joy in the senses, of joy in general....

22.

When Christianity departed from its native soil, that of the lowest orders, the *underworld* of the ancient world, and began seeking power among barbarian peoples, it no longer had to deal with *exhausted* men, but with men still inwardly savage and capable of self-torture—in brief, strong men, but bungled men. Here, unlike in the case of the Buddhists, the cause of discontent with self, suffering through self, is *not* merely a general sensitiveness and susceptibility to pain, but, on the contrary, an inordinate thirst for inflicting pain on others, a tendency to obtain subjective satisfaction in hostile deeds and ideas. Christianity had to embrace *barbaric* concepts and valuations in order to obtain mastery over barbarians: of such sort, for example, are the sacrifices of the first-born, the drinking of blood as a sacrament, the disdain of the intellect and of culture; torture in all its forms, whether bodily or not; the whole pomp of the cult. Buddhism is a religion for peoples in a further state of development, for races that have become kind, gentle and over-spiritualized (—Europe is not yet ripe for it—): it is a summons that takes them back to peace and cheerfulness, to a careful rationing of the spirit, to a certain hardening of the body.

Christianity aims at mastering *beasts of prey*; its modus operandi is to make them *ill*—to make feeble is the Christian recipe for taming, for "*civilizing*." Buddhism is a religion for the closing, over-wearied stages of civilization. Christianity appears before civilization has so much as begun—under certain circumstances it lays the very foundations thereof.

23.

Buddhism, I repeat, is a hundred times more austere, more honest, more objective. It no longer has to *justify* its pains, its susceptibility to suffering, by interpreting these things in terms of sin —it simply says, as it simply thinks, "I suffer." To the barbarian, however, suffering in itself is scarcely understandable: what he needs, first of all, is an explanation as to *why* he suffers. (His mere instinct prompts him to deny his suffering altogether, or to endure it in silence.) Here the word "devil" was a blessing: man had to have an omnipotent and terrible enemy—there was no need to be ashamed of suffering at the hands of such an enemy.

At the bottom of Christianity there are several subtleties that belong to the Orient. In the first place, it knows that it is of very little consequence whether a thing be true or not, so long as it is *believed* to be true. Truth and *faith*: here we have two wholly distinct worlds of ideas, almost two diametrically *opposite* worlds—the road to the one and the road to the other lie miles apart. To understand that fact thoroughly—this is almost enough, in the Orient, to *make* one a sage. The Brahmins knew it, Plato knew it, every student of the esoteric knows it. When, for example, a man gets any *pleasure* out of the notion that he has been saved from sin, it is *not* necessary for him to be actually sinful, but merely to *feel* sinful. But when *faith* is thus exalted above everything else, it necessarily follows that reason, knowledge and patient inquiry have to be discredited: the road to the truth becomes a forbidden road.—Hope, in its stronger forms, is a great deal more powerful *stimulans* to life than any sort of realized joy can ever be. Man must be sustained in suffering by a hope so high that no conflict with actuality can dash it—so high, indeed, that no fulfilment can *satisfy* it: a hope reaching out beyond this world. (Precisely because of this power that hope has of making the suffering hold out, the

Greeks regarded it as the evil of evils, as the most *malign* of evils; it remained behind at the source of all evil.)

In order that *love* may be possible, God must become a person; in order that the lower instincts may take a hand in the matter God must be young. To satisfy the ardor of the woman a beautiful saint must appear on the scene, and to satisfy that of the men there must be a virgin. These things are necessary if Christianity is to assume lordship over a soil on which some aphrodisiacal or Adonis cult has already established a notion as to what a cult ought to be. To insist upon *chastity* greatly strengthens the vehemence and subjectivity of the religious instinct—it makes the cult warmer, more enthusiastic, more soulful.—Love is the state in which man sees things most decidedly as they are *not*. The force of illusion reaches its highest here, and so does the capacity for sweetening, for *transfiguring*. When a man is in love he endures more than at any other time; he submits to anything. The problem was to devise a religion which would allow one to love: by this means the worst that life has to offer is overcome—it is scarcely even noticed.—So much for the three Christian virtues: faith, hope and charity: I call them the three Christian *ingenuities*.—Buddhism is in too late a stage of development, too full of positivism, to be shrewd in any such way.

24.

Here I barely touch upon the problem of the *origin* of Christianity. The *first* thing necessary to its solution is this: that Christianity is to be understood only by examining the soil from which it sprung—it is *not* a reaction against Jewish instincts; it is their inevitable product; it is simply one more step in the awe-inspiring logic of the Jews. In the words of the Saviour, "salvation is of the Jews."—The *second* thing to remember is this: that the psychological type of the Galilean is still to be recognized, but it was only in its most degenerate form (which is at once maimed and overladen with foreign features) that it could serve in the manner in which it has been used: as a type of the *Saviour* of mankind.

The Jews are the most remarkable people in the history of the world, for when they were confronted with the question, to be or not to be, they chose, with perfectly unearthly deliberation, to be *at any price*: this price involved a radical *falsification* of all nature, of all naturalness, of all reality, of the whole inner world, as well as of the outer. They put themselves *against* all those conditions under which, hitherto, a people had been able to live, or had even been *permitted* to live; out of themselves they evolved an idea which stood in direct opposition to *natural* conditions—one by one they distorted religion, civilization, morality, history and psychology until each became a *contradiction* of its *natural significance*. We meet with the same phenomenon later on, in an incalculably exaggerated form, but only as a copy: the Christian church, put beside the "people of God," shows a complete lack of any claim to originality. Precisely for this reason the Jews are the most *fateful* people in the history of the world: their influence has so falsified the reasoning of mankind in this matter that today the Christian can cherish anti-Semitism without realizing that it is no more than the *final consequence of Judaism*.

In my *Genealogy of Morals* I give the first psychological explanation of the concepts underlying those two antithetical things, a *noble* morality and a *ressentiment* morality, the second of which is a mere product of the denial of the former. The Judaeo-Christian moral system belongs to the second division, and in every detail. In order to be able to say Nay to everything representing an *ascending* evolution of life—that is, to well-being, to power, to beauty, to self-approval—the instincts of *ressentiment*, here become downright genius, had to invent an *other* world in which the *acceptance of life* appeared as the most evil and abominable thing imaginable. Psychologically, the Jews are a people gifted with the very strongest vitality, so much so that when they found themselves facing impossible conditions of life they chose voluntarily, and with a profound talent for self-preservation, the side of all those instincts which make for *décadence*—*not* as if mastered by them, but as if detecting in them a power by which "the world" could be *defied*. The Jews are the very opposite of *décadents*: they have simply been forced into *appearing* in that guise, and with a degree of skill approaching the *non plus ultra* of histrionic genius they have managed to put themselves at the head of all *décadent* movements (—for example, the Christianity of Paul—), and so make of them something stronger than any party frankly saying *Yes* to life. To the sort of men who reach out for power under Judaism and Christianity,—that is to say, to the *priestly* class—*décadence* is no more than a means to an end. Men of this sort have a vital interest in making mankind sick, and in confusing the values of "good" and "bad," "true" and "false" in a manner that is not only dangerous to life, but also slanders it.

25.

The history of Israel is invaluable as a typical history of an attempt to *denaturize* all natural values: I point to five facts which bear this out. Originally, and above all in the time of the monarchy, Israel maintained the *right* attitude of things, which is to say, the natural attitude. Its Yahweh was an expression of its consciousness of power, its joy in itself, its hopes for itself: to him the Jews looked for victory and salvation and through him they expected nature to give them whatever was necessary to their existence—above all, rain. Yahweh is the god of Israel, and *consequently* the god of justice: this is the logic of every race that has power in its hands and a good conscience in the use of it. In the religious ceremonial of the Jews both aspects of this self-approval stand revealed. The nation is grateful for the high destiny that has enabled it to obtain dominion; it is grateful for the benign procession of the seasons, and for the good fortune attending its herds and its crops.—This view of things remained an ideal for a long while, even after it had been robbed of validity by tragic blows: anarchy within and the Assyrian without. But the people still retained, as a projection of their highest yearnings, that vision of a king who was at once a gallant warrior and an upright judge—a vision best visualized in the typical prophet (*i. e.*, critic and satirist of the moment), Isaiah.

But every hope remained unfulfilled. The old god no longer *could* do what he used to do. He ought to have been abandoned. But what actually happened? Simply this: the conception of him was *changed*— the conception of him was *denaturized*; this was the price that had to be paid for keeping him.—Yahweh, the god of "justice"—he is in accord with Israel *no more*, he no longer visualizes the national egoism; he is now a god only conditionally.... The public notion of this god now becomes merely a weapon in the hands of clerical agitators, who interpret all happiness as a reward and all unhappiness as a punishment for obedience or disobedience to him, for "sin": that most fraudulent of all imaginable interpretations, whereby a "moral order of the world" is set up, and the fundamental concepts, "cause" and "effect," are stood on their heads. Once natural causation has been swept out of the world by doctrines of reward and punishment some sort of *un*-natural causation becomes necessary: and all other varieties of the denial of nature follow it. A god who *demands*—in place of a god who helps, who gives counsel, who is at bottom merely a name for every happy inspiration of courage and self-reliance.... *Morality* is no longer a reflection of the conditions which make for the sound life and development of the people; it is no longer the primary life-instinct, instead it has become abstract and in opposition to life—a fundamental perversion of the fancy, an "evil eye" on all things. *What* is Jewish, *what* is Christian morality? Chance robbed of its innocence; unhappiness polluted with the idea of "sin"; well-being represented as a danger, as a "temptation"; a physiological disorder produced by the canker worm of conscience....

26.

The concept of god falsified; the concept of morality falsified;— but even here Jewish priest-craft did not stop. The whole history of Israel ceased to be of any value: out with it!—These priests accomplished that miracle of falsification of which a great part of the Bible is the documentary evidence; with a degree of contempt unparalleled, and in the face of all tradition and all historical reality, they translated the past of their people into *religious* terms, which is to say, they converted it into an idiotic mechanism of salvation, whereby all offences against Yahweh were punished and all devotion to him was rewarded. We would regard this act of historical falsification as something far more shameful if familiarity with the *ecclesiastical* interpretation of history for thousands of years had not blunted our inclinations for uprightness *in historicis*. And the philosophers support the church: the *lie* about a "moral order of the world" runs through the whole of philosophy, even the newest.

What is the meaning of a "moral order of the world"? That there is a thing called the will of God which, once and for all time, determines what man ought to do and what he ought not to do; that the worth of a people, or of an individual thereof, is to be measured by the extent to which they or he obey this will of God; that the destinies of a people or of an individual are *controlled* by this will of God, which rewards or punishes according to the degree of obedience manifested.—In place of all that pitiable lie *reality* has this to say: the *priest*, a parasitical variety of man who can exist only at the cost of every sound view of life, takes the name of God in vain: he calls that state of human society in which he himself determines the value of all things "the kingdom of God"; he calls the means whereby that state of affairs is attained "the will of God"; with cold-blooded cynicism he estimates all peoples, all ages and all individuals by the extent of their subservience or opposition to the power of the priestly order. One observes him at work: under the hand of the Jewish priesthood the *great* age of Israel became an age of decline; the Exile, with its long series of misfortunes, was transformed into a *punishment* for that great age—during which priests had not yet come into existence. Out of the powerful and *wholly free* heroes of Israel's history they fashioned, according to their changing needs, either wretched bigots and hypocrites or men entirely "godless." They reduced every great event to the idiotic formula: "obedient *or* disobedient to God."

They went a step further: the "will of God" (in other words some means necessary for preserving the power of the priests) had to be *determined*—and to this end they had to have a "revelation." In plain English, a gigantic literary fraud had to be perpetrated, and "holy scriptures" had to be concocted—and so, with the utmost hierarchical pomp, and days of penance and much lamentation over the long days of "sin" now ended, they were duly published. The "will of God," it appears, had long stood like a rock; the trouble was that mankind had neglected the "holy scriptures".... But the "will of God" had already been revealed to Moses.... What happened? Simply this: the priest had formulated, once and for all time and with the strictest meticulousness, what tithes were to be paid to him, from the largest to the smallest (—not forgetting the most appetizing cuts of meat, for the priest is a great consumer of beefsteaks); in brief, he let it be known just *what he wanted*, what "the will of God" was....

From this time forward things were so arranged that the priest became *indispensable everywhere*; at all the great natural events of life, at birth, at marriage, in sickness, at death, not to say at the "*sacrifice*" (that is, at meal-times), the holy parasite put in his appearance, and proceeded to *denaturize* it—in his own phrase, to "sanctify" it.... For this should be noted: that every natural habit, every natural institution (the state, the administration of justice, marriage, the care of the sick and of the poor), everything demanded by the life-instinct, in short, everything that has any value *in itself*, is reduced to absolute worthlessness and even made the *reverse* of valuable by the parasitism of priests (or, if you chose, by the "moral order of the world"). The fact requires a sanction—a power to *grant values* becomes necessary, and the only way it can create such values is by denying nature.... The priest depreciates and desecrates nature: it is only at this price that he can exist at all.

Disobedience to God, which actually means to the priest, to "the law," now gets the name of "sin"; the means prescribed for "reconciliation with God" are, of course, precisely the means which bring one most effectively under the thumb of the priest; he alone can "save".... Psychologically considered, "sins" are indispensable to every society organized on an ecclesiastical basis; they are the only reliable weapons of power; the priest *lives* upon sins; it is necessary to him that there be "sinning".... Prime axiom: "God forgiveth him that repenteth"—in plain English, *him that submitteth to the priest.*

27.

Christianity sprang from a soil so corrupt that on it everything natural, every natural value, every *reality* was opposed by the deepest instincts of the ruling class—it grew up as a sort of war to the death upon reality, and as such it has never been surpassed. The "holy people," who had adopted priestly values and priestly names for all things, and who, with a terrible logical consistency, had rejected everything of the earth as "unholy," "worldly," "sinful"—this people put its instinct into a final formula that was logical to the point of self-annihilation: as *Christianity* it actually denied even the last form of reality, the "holy people," the "chosen people," *Jewish* reality itself. The phenomenon is of the first order of importance: the small insurrectionary movement which took the name of Jesus of Nazareth is simply the Jewish instinct *redivivus*[95]—in other words, it is the priestly instinct come to such a pass that it can no longer endure the priest as a fact; it is the discovery of a state of existence even more fantastic than any before it, of a vision of life even more *unreal* than that necessary to an ecclesiastical organization. Christianity actually *denies* the church....

---

[95] reborn

I am unable to determine what was the target of the insurrection said to have been led (whether rightly or *wrongly*) by Jesus, if it was not the Jewish church—"church" being here used in exactly the same sense that the word has today. It was an insurrection against the "good and just," against the "prophets of Israel," against the whole hierarchy of society—*not* against corruption, but against caste, privilege, order, formalism. It was *unbelief* in "superior men," a Nay flung at everything that priests and theologians stood for. But the hierarchy that was called into question, if only for an instant, by this movement was the structure of piles which, above everything, was necessary to the safety of the Jewish people in the midst of the "waters"—it represented their *last* possibility of survival; it was the final *residuum* of their independent political existence; an attack upon it was an attack upon the most profound national instinct, the most powerful national will to live, that has ever appeared on earth. This saintly anarchist, who aroused the people of the abyss, the outcasts and "sinners," the Chandala of Judaism, to rise in revolt against the established order of things—and in language which, if the Gospels are to be credited, would get him sent to Siberia today—this man was certainly a political criminal, at least in so far as it was possible to be one in so *absurdly unpolitical* a community. This is what brought him to the cross: the proof thereof is to be found in the inscription that was put upon the cross. He died for his *own* sins—there is not the slightest ground for believing, no matter how often it is asserted, that he died for the sins of others.

28.

As to whether he himself was conscious of this contradiction—whether, in fact, this was the only contradiction he was cognizant of—that is quite another question. Here, for the first time, I touch upon the problem of the *psychology of the Saviour.*—I confess, to begin with, that there are very few books which offer me harder reading than the Gospels. My difficulties are quite different from those which enabled the learned curiosity of the German mind to achieve one of its most unforgettable triumphs. It is a long while since I, like all other young scholars, enjoyed with all the sapient laboriousness of a fastidious philologist the work of the incomparable Strauss.[96] At that time I was twenty years old: now I am too serious for that sort of thing. What do I care for the contradictions of "tradition"? How can any one call pious legends "traditions"? The histories of saints present the most dubious variety of literature in existence; to examine them by the scientific method, *in the entire absence of corroborative documents*, seems to me to condemn the whole inquiry from the start—it is simply learned idling....

29.

What concerns *me* is the psychological type of the Saviour. This type might be depicted in the Gospels, in however mutilated a form and however much overladen with extraneous characters—that is, in *spite* of the Gospels; just as the figure of Francis of Assisi shows itself in his legends in spite of his legends. It is *not* a question of mere truthful evidence as to what he did, what he said and how he actually died; the question is, whether his type is still conceivable, whether it has been handed down to us.

All the attempts that I know of to read the *history* of a "soul" in the Gospels seem to me to reveal only a lamentable psychological levity. M. Renan, that mountebank *in psychologicus*, has contributed the two most *unseemly* notions to this business of explaining the type of Jesus: the notion of the *genius* and that of the *hero* ("*héros*"). But if there is anything essentially unevangelical, it is surely the concept of the hero. What the Gospels make instinctive is precisely the reverse of all heroic struggle, of all taste for conflict: the very incapacity for resistance is here converted into something moral: ("resist not evil!"—the most profound sentence in the Gospels, perhaps the true key to them), to wit, the blessedness of peace, of gentleness, the *inability* to be an enemy. What is the meaning of "glad tidings"?—The true life, the life eternal has been found—it is not merely promised, it is here, it is in *you*; it is the life that lies in love free from all retreats and exclusions, from all keeping of distances. Every one is the child of God—Jesus claims nothing for himself alone—as the child of God each man is the equal of every other man.... Imagine making Jesus a *hero*!—And

---

[96] David Friedrich Strauss (1808-74), author of *Das Leben Jesu* (1835-6), a very famous work in its day. Nietzsche here refers to it.

what a tremendous misunderstanding appears in the word "genius"! Our whole conception of the "spiritual," the whole conception of our civilization, could have had no meaning in the world that Jesus lived in. In the strict sense of the physiologist, a quite different word ought to be used here.... We all know that there is a morbid sensibility of the tactile nerves which causes those suffering from it to recoil from every touch, and from every effort to grasp a solid object. Brought to its logical conclusion, such a physiological *habitus* becomes an instinctive hatred of all reality, a flight into the "intangible," into the "incomprehensible"; a distaste for all formulae, for all conceptions of time and space, for everything established—customs, institutions, the church—; a feeling of being at home in a world in which no sort of reality survives, a merely "inner" world, a "true" world, an "eternal" world.... "The Kingdom of God is within *you*"....

30.

The instinctive hatred of reality: the consequence of an extreme susceptibility to pain and irritation—so great that merely to be "touched" becomes unendurable, for every sensation is too profound.

The instinctive exclusion of all aversion, all hostility, all bounds and distances in feeling: the consequence of an extreme susceptibility to pain and irritation—so great that it senses all resistance, all compulsion to resistance, as unbearable *anguish* (—that is to say, as *harmful*, as *prohibited* by the instinct of self-preservation), and regards blessedness (joy) as possible only when it is no longer necessary to offer resistance to anybody or anything, however evil or dangerous—love, as the only, as the *ultimate* possibility of life....

These are the two *physiological realities* upon and out of which the doctrine of salvation has sprung. I call them a sublime super-development of hedonism upon a thoroughly unsalubrious soil. What stands most closely related to them, though with a large admixture of Greek vitality and nerve-force, is epicureanism, the theory of salvation of paganism. Epicurus was a *typical décadent*: I was the first to recognize him.—The fear of pain, even of infinitely slight pain—the end of this *can* be nothing save a *religion of love*....

31.

I have already given my answer to the problem. The prerequisite to it is the assumption that the type of the Saviour has reached us only in a greatly distorted form. This distortion is very probable: there are many reasons why a type of that sort should not be handed down in a pure form, complete and free of additions. The milieu in which this strange figure moved must have left marks upon him, and more must have been imprinted by the history, the *destiny*, of the early Christian communities; the latter indeed, must have embellished the type retrospectively with characters which can be understood only as serving the purposes of war and of propaganda. That strange and sickly world into which the Gospels lead us—a world apparently out of a Russian novel, in which the scum of society, nervous maladies and "childish" idiocy keep a tryst—must, in any case, have *coarsened* the type: the first disciples, in particular, must have been forced to translate an existence visible only in symbols and incomprehensibilities into their own crudity, in order to understand it at all—in their sight the type could take on reality only after it had been recast in a familiar mould…. The prophet, the messiah, the future judge, the teacher of morals, the worker of wonders, John the Baptist—all these merely presented chances to misunderstand it…. Finally, let us not underrate the *proprium*[97] of all great, and especially all sectarian veneration: it tends to erase from the venerated objects all its original traits and idiosyncrasies, often so painfully strange—*it does not even see them*. It is greatly to be regretted that no Dostoyevsky lived in the neighbourhood of this most interesting *décadent*—I mean some one who would have felt the poignant charm of such a compound of the sublime, the morbid and the childish.

In the last analysis, the type, as a type of the *décadence*, may actually have been peculiarly complex and contradictory: such a possibility is not to be lost sight of. Nevertheless, the probabilities seem to be against it, for in that case tradition would have been particularly accurate and objective, whereas we have reasons for assuming the contrary. Meanwhile, there is a contradiction between the peaceful preacher of the mount, the sea-shore and the fields, who appears like a new Buddha on a soil very unlike India's, and the aggressive fanatic,

---

[97] property, attribute

the mortal enemy of theologians and ecclesiastics, who stands glorified by Renan's malice as "*le grand maître en ironie*." I myself haven't any doubt that the greater part of this venom (and no less of *esprit*) got itself into the concept of the Master only as a result of the excited nature of Christian propaganda: we all know the unscrupulousness of sectarians when they set out to turn their leader into an *apologia* for themselves. When the early Christians had need of an adroit, contentious, pugnacious and maliciously subtle theologian to tackle other theologians, they *created* a "god" that met that need, just as they put into his mouth without hesitation certain ideas that were necessary to them but that were utterly at odds with the Gospels —"the second coming," "the last judgment," all sorts of expectations and promises, current at the time.

32.

I can only repeat that I set myself against all efforts to intrude the fanatic into the figure of the Saviour: the very word *impérieux*,[98] used by Renan, is alone enough to *annul* the type. What the "glad tidings" tell us is simply that there are no more contradictions; the kingdom of heaven belongs to *children*; the faith that is voiced here is no more an embattled faith—it is at hand, it has been from the beginning, it is a sort of recrudescent childishness of the spirit. The physiologists, at all events, are familiar with such a delayed and incomplete puberty in the living organism, the result of degeneration.

A faith of this sort is not furious, it does not denounce, it does not defend itself: it does not come with "the sword"—it does not realize how it will one day set man against man. It does not manifest itself either by miracles, or by rewards and promises, or by "scriptures": it is itself, first and last, its own miracle, its own reward, its own promise, its own "kingdom of God." This faith does not formulate itself—it simply *lives*, and so guards itself against formulae.

To be sure, the accident of environment, of educational background gives prominence to concepts of a certain sort: in primitive Christianity one finds *only* concepts of a Judaeo-Semitic character (—that of eating and drinking at the last supper belongs to

---

[98] imperious

this category—an idea which, like everything else Jewish, has been badly mauled by the church). But let us be careful not to see in all this anything more than symbolical language, semantics[99] an opportunity to speak in parables. It is only on the theory that no work is to be taken literally that this anti-realist is able to speak at all. Set down among Hindus he would have made use of the concepts of Sankhya, and among Chinese he would have employed those of Lao Tzu[100]— and in neither case would it have made any difference to him.

With a little freedom in the use of words, one might actually call Jesus a "free spirit"—he cares nothing for what is established: the word *killeth*, whatever is established *killeth*. The idea of "life" as an *experience*, as he alone conceives it, stands opposed to his mind to every sort of word, formula, law, belief and dogma. He speaks only of inner things: "life" or "truth" or "light" is his word for the innermost—in his sight everything else, the whole of reality, all nature, even language, has significance only as sign, as allegory.

Here it is of paramount importance to be led into no error by the temptations lying in Christian, or rather *ecclesiastical* prejudices: such a symbolism *par excellence* stands outside all religion, all notions of worship, all history, all natural science, all worldly experience, all knowledge, all politics, all psychology, all books, all art—his "wisdom" is precisely a *pure ignorance*[101] of all such things. He has never heard of *culture*; he doesn't have to make war on it—he doesn't even deny it.... The same thing may be said of the *state*, of the whole bourgeoise social order, of labour, of war—he has no ground for denying "the world," for he knows nothing of the ecclesiastical concept of "the world".... *Denial* is precisely the thing that is impossible to him.

In the same way he lacks argumentative capacity, and has no belief that an article of faith, a "truth," may be established by proofs (—*his* proofs are inner "lights," subjective sensations of happiness and

---

[99] The word *Semiotik* is in the text, but it is probable that *Semantik* is what Nietzsche had in mind.

[100] Indeed, when missionaries translated the Bible into Chinese, they used Lao Tzu's "tao" as the term for *logos*, such that the Gospel of John reads: "In the beginning was the Tao ..."

[101] A reference to the "pure ignorance" (*reine Thorheit*) of Parsifal. See also Buddhist and particularly Zen ideas of "not-knowing."

self-approval, simple "proofs of power"—). Such a doctrine *cannot* contradict: it doesn't know that other doctrines exist, or *can* exist, and is wholly incapable of imagining anything opposed to it.... If anything of the sort is ever encountered, it laments the "blindness" with sincere sympathy—for it alone has "light"—but it does not offer objections....

33.

In the whole psychology of the "Gospels" the concepts of guilt and punishment are lacking, and so is that of reward. "Sin," which means anything that puts a distance between God and man, is abolished—*this is precisely the "glad tidings."* Eternal bliss is not merely promised, nor is it bound up with conditions: it is conceived as the *only* reality—what remains consists merely of signs useful in speaking of it.

The *results* of such a point of view project themselves into a new *way of life*, the special evangelical way of life. It is not a "belief" that marks off the Christian; he is distinguished by a different mode of action; he acts *differently*. He offers no resistance, either by word or in his heart, to those who stand against him. He draws no distinction between strangers and countrymen, Jews and Gentiles ("neighbour," of course, means fellow-believer, Jew). He is angry with no one, and he despises no one. He neither appeals to the courts of justice nor heeds their mandates ("Swear not at all"). He never under any circumstances divorces his wife, even when he has proofs of her infidelity.—And under all of this is one principle; all of it arises from one instinct.

The life of the Saviour was simply a carrying out of this way of life—and so was his death.... He no longer needed any formula or ritual in his relations with God—not even prayer. He had rejected the whole of the Jewish doctrine of repentance and atonement; he *knew* that it was only by a *way* of life that one could feel one's self "divine," "blessed," "evangelical," a "child of God." *Not* by "repentance," *not* by "prayer and forgiveness" is the way to God: *only the Gospel way* leads to God—it is *itself* "God!"—What the Gospels *abolished* was the Judaism in the concepts of "sin," "forgiveness of sin," "faith," "salvation through faith"—the whole *ecclesiastical* dogma of the Jews was denied by the "glad tidings."

The deep instinct which prompts the Christian how to *live* so that he will feel that he is "in heaven" and is "immortal," despite many reasons for feeling that he is *not* "in heaven": this is the only psychological reality in "salvation."—A new way of life, *not* a new faith....

34.

If I understand anything at all about this great symbolist, it is this: that he regarded only *subjective* realities as realities, as "truths"—that he saw everything else, everything natural, temporal, spatial and historical, merely as signs, as materials for parables. The concept of "the Son of God" does not connote a concrete person in history, an isolated and definite individual, but an "eternal" fact, a psychological symbol set free from the concept of time. The same thing is true, and in the highest sense, of the *God* of this typical symbolist, of the "kingdom of God," and of the "sonship of God." Nothing could be more un-Christian than the *crude ecclesiastical* notions of God as a *person*, of a "kingdom of God" that is to come, of a "kingdom of heaven" beyond, and of a "son of God" as the *second person* of the Trinity. All this—if I may be forgiven the phrase—is like thrusting one's fist into the eye (and what an eye!) of the Gospels: a disrespect for symbols amounting to *world-historical cynicism*....

But it is nevertheless obvious enough what is meant by the symbols "Father" and "Son"—not, of course, to every one—: the word "Son" expresses *entrance* into the feeling that there is a general transformation of all things (beatitude), and "Father" expresses *that feeling itself*—the sensation of eternity and of perfection.—I am ashamed to remind you of what the church has made of this symbolism: has it not set an Amphitryon story[102] at the threshold of the Christian "faith"? And a dogma of "immaculate conception" for good measure?... *And thereby it has robbed conception of its immaculateness*—

The "kingdom of heaven" is a state of the heart—not something to come "beyond the world" or "after death." The whole idea of natural death is *absent* from the Gospels: death is not a bridge, not a passing; it is absent because it belongs to a quite different, a merely

---

[102] Amphitryon was the son of Alcaeus, King of Tiryns. His wife was Alcmene. During his absence she was visited by Zeus, and bore Heracles.

apparent world, useful only as a symbol. The "hour of death" is *not* a Christian idea—"hours," time, the physical life and its crises have no existence for the bearer of "glad tidings.".... The "kingdom of God" is not something that men wait for: it had no yesterday and no day after tomorrow, it is not going to come at a "millennium"—it is an experience of the heart, it is everywhere and it is nowhere....

35.

This "bearer of glad tidings" died as he lived and *taught*—not to "save mankind," but to show mankind how to live. It was a *way of life* that he bequeathed to man: his demeanour before the judges, before the officers, before his accusers—his demeanour on the *cross*. He does not resist; he does not defend his rights; he makes no effort to ward off the most extreme penalty—more, *he invites it*.... And he prays, suffers and loves *with* those, *in* those, who do him evil.... *Not* to defend one's self, *not* to show anger, *not* to lay blames.... On the contrary, to submit even to the Evil One—to *love* him....

36.

We free spirits—we are the first to have the necessary prerequisite to understanding what nineteen centuries have misunderstood—that instinct and passion for integrity which makes war upon the "holy lie" even more than upon all other lies.... Mankind was unspeakably far from our benevolent and cautious neutrality, from that discipline of the spirit which alone makes possible the solution of such strange and subtle things: what men always sought, with shameless egoism, was their *own* advantage therein; they created the *church* out of denial of the Gospels....

Whoever sought for signs of an ironical divinity's hand in the great drama of existence would find no small indication thereof in the *stupendous question-mark* that is called Christianity. That mankind should be on its knees before the very antithesis of what was the origin, the meaning and the *law* of the Gospels—that in the concept of the "church" the very things should be pronounced holy that the "bearer of glad tidings" regards as *beneath* him and *behind* him—it would be impossible to surpass this as a grand example of *world-historical irony*—

37.

Our age is proud of its historical sense: how, then, could it delude itself into believing that the *crude fable of the wonder-worker and Saviour* constituted the beginnings of Christianity—and that everything spiritual and symbolical in it only came later? Quite to the contrary the whole history of Christianity—from the death on the cross onward—is the history of a progressively clumsier misunderstanding of an *original* symbolism. With every extension of Christianity among larger and ruder masses, even less capable of grasping the principles that gave birth to it, the need arose to make it more and more *vulgar* and *barbarous*—it absorbed the teachings and rites of all the *subterranean* cults of the *imperium Romanum*, and the absurdities engendered by all sorts of sickly reasoning. It was the fate of Christianity that its faith had to become as sickly, as low and as vulgar as the needs were sickly, low and vulgar to which it had to administer. A *sickly barbarism* finally lifts itself to power as the church—the church, that incarnation of deadly hostility to all honesty, to all loftiness of soul, to all discipline of the spirit, to all spontaneous and kindly humanity.—*Christian* values—*noble* values: it is only we, we *free* spirits, who have re-established this greatest of all antitheses in values!…

38.

I cannot, at this place, avoid a sigh. There are days when I am visited by a feeling blacker than the blackest melancholy—*contempt of man*. Let me leave no doubt as to *what* I despise, *whom* I despise: it is the man of today, the man with whom I am unhappily contemporaneous. The man of today—I am suffocated by his foul breath!… Toward the past, like all who understand, I am full of tolerance, which is to say, *generous* self-control: with gloomy caution I pass through whole millenniums of this madhouse of a world, call it "Christianity," "Christian faith" or the "Christian church," as you will —I take care not to hold mankind responsible for its lunacies.

But my feeling changes and breaks out irresistibly the moment I enter modern times, *our* times. Our age *knows better*…. What was formerly merely sickly now becomes indecent—it is indecent to be a Christian today. *And here my disgust begins.*—I look about me: not a word survives of what was once called "truth"; we can no longer bear to hear a priest pronounce the word. Even a man who makes the most modest pretensions to integrity *must* know that a theologian, a priest, a pope of today not only errs when he speaks, but actually *lies*—and that he no longer escapes blame for his lie through "innocence" or "ignorance." The priest knows, as every one knows, that there is no longer any "God," or any "sinner," or any "Saviour"—that "free will" and the "moral order of the world" are lies—: serious reflection, the profound self-conquest of the spirit, *allow* no man to pretend that he does *not* know it....

All the ideas of the church are now recognized for what they are —as the worst counterfeits in existence, invented to debase nature and all natural values; the priest himself is seen as he actually is—as the most dangerous form of parasite, as the venomous spider of creation.... We know, our *conscience* now knows—just *what* the real value of all those sinister inventions of priest and church has been and *what ends they have served*, with their debasement of humanity to a state of self-pollution, the very sight of which excites loathing,—the concepts "the other world," "the last judgment," "the immortality of the soul," the "soul" itself: they are all merely so many instruments of torture, systems of cruelty, whereby the priest becomes master and remains master....

Everyone knows this, *but nevertheless things remain as before*. What has become of the last trace of decent feeling, of self-respect, when our statesmen, otherwise an unconventional class of men and thoroughly anti-Christian in their acts, now call themselves Christians and go to the communion-table?... A prince at the head of his armies, magnificent as the expression of the egoism and arrogance of his people—and yet acknowledging, *without* any shame, that he is a Christian!... Whom, then, does Christianity deny? *what* does it call "the world"? To be a *soldier*, to be a judge, to be a patriot; to defend one's self; to be careful of one's honour; to desire one's own advantage; to be *proud* ... every act of everyday, every instinct, every valuation that shows itself in a *deed*, is now anti-Christian: what a *monster of falsehood* the modern man must be to call himself nevertheless, and *without* shame, a Christian!

39.

I shall go back a bit, and tell you the *authentic* history of Christianity.—The very word "Christianity" is a misunderstanding—

at bottom there was only one Christian, and he died on the cross. The "Gospels" *died* on the cross. What, from that moment onward, was called the "Gospels" was the very reverse of what *he* had lived: "bad tidings," a *Dysangelium*.[103] It is an error amounting to nonsensicality to see in "faith," and particularly in faith in salvation through Christ, the distinguishing mark of the Christian: only the Christian *way of life*, the life *lived* by him who died on the cross, is Christian…. To this day *such* a life is still possible, and for *certain* men even necessary: genuine, primitive Christianity will remain possible in all ages…. *Not* faith, but acts; above all, an *avoidance* of acts, a different *state of being*….

States of consciousness, faith of a sort, the acceptance, for example, of anything as true—as every psychologist knows, the value of these things is perfectly indifferent and fifth-rate compared to that of the instincts: strictly speaking, the whole concept of intellectual causality is false. To reduce being a Christian, the state of Christianity, to an acceptance of truth, to a mere phenomenon of consciousness, is to formulate the negation of Christianity. *In fact, there are no Christians.* The "Christian"—he who for two thousand years has passed as a Christian—is simply a psychological self-delusion. Closely examined, it appears that, *despite* all his "faith," he has been ruled *only* by his instincts—and *what instincts*!

In all ages—for example, in the case of Luther—"faith" has been no more than a cloak, a pretense, a *curtain* behind which the instincts have played their game—a shrewd *blindness* to the domination of *certain* of the instincts…. I have already called "faith" the specially Christian form of *shrewdness*—people always *talk* of their "faith" and *act* according to their instincts…. In the world of ideas of the Christian there is nothing that so much as touches reality: on the contrary, one recognizes an instinctive *hatred* of reality as the motive power, the only motive power at the bottom of Christianity. What follows therefrom? That even here, in *psychologicis*, there is a radical error, which is to say one conditioning fundamentals, which is to say, one in *substance*. Take away one idea and put a genuine reality in its place—and the whole of Christianity crumbles to nothingness!

---

[103] So in the text. One of Nietzsche's numerous coinages, obviously suggested by *Evangelium*, the German for *gospel*.

Viewed calmly, this strangest of all phenomena, a religion not only depending on errors, but inventive and ingenious *only* in devising injurious errors, poisonous to life and to the heart—this remains a *spectacle for the gods*—for those gods who are also philosophers, and whom I have encountered, for example, in the celebrated dialogues at Naxos. At the moment when their *disgust* leaves them (—and us!) they will be thankful for the spectacle afforded by the Christians: perhaps because of *this* curious exhibition alone the wretched little planet called the earth deserves a glance from omnipotence, a show of divine interest.... Therefore, let us not underestimate the Christians: the Christian, false *to the point of innocence,* is far above the ape—in its application to the Christians a well-known theory of descent becomes a mere piece of politeness....

40.

The fate of the Gospels was decided by death—it hung on the "cross."... It was only death, that unexpected and shameful death; it was only the cross, which was usually reserved for the *canaille*[104] only— it was only this appalling paradox which brought the disciples face to face with the real riddle: "*Who was it? what was it?*"

The feeling of dismay, of profound affront and injury; the suspicion that such a death might involve a *refutation* of their cause; the terrible question, "Why just in this way?"—this state of mind is only too easy to understand. Here everything *must* be accounted for as necessary; everything must have a meaning, a reason, the highest sort of reason; the love of a disciple excludes all chance. Only then did the chasm of doubt yawn: "*Who* put him to death? who was his natural enemy?"—this question flashed like a lightning-stroke. Answer: dominant Judaism, its ruling class. From that moment, one found one's self in revolt *against* the established order, and began to understand Jesus as *in revolt against the established order.* Until then this militant, this nay-saying, nay-doing element in his character had been lacking; what is more, he had appeared to present its opposite.

Obviously, the little community had *not* understood what was precisely the most important thing of all: the example offered by this

---

[104] the masses, common people

way of dying, the freedom from and superiority to every feeling of *ressentiment*—a plain indication of how little he was understood at all! All that Jesus could hope to accomplish by his death, in itself, was to offer the strongest possible proof, or *example*, of his teachings in the most public manner…. But his disciples were very far from *forgiving* his death—though to have done so would have accorded with the Gospels in the highest degree; and neither were they prepared to *offer* themselves, with gentle and serene calmness of heart, for a similar death…. On the contrary, it was precisely the most unevangelical of feelings, *revenge*, that now possessed them. It seemed impossible that the cause should perish with his death: "recompense" and "judgment" became necessary (—yet what could be less evangelical than "recompense," "punishment," and "sitting in judgment"!). Once more the popular belief in the coming of a messiah appeared in the foreground; attention was rivetted upon an historical moment: the "kingdom of God" is to come, with judgment upon his enemies….

But in all this there was a wholesale misunderstanding: imagine the "kingdom of God" as a last act, as a mere promise! The Gospels had been, in fact, the incarnation, the fulfilment, the *realization* of this "kingdom of God." It was only now that all the familiar contempt for and bitterness against Pharisees and theologians began to appear in the character of the Master—he was thereby *turned* into a Pharisee and theologian himself! On the other hand, the savage veneration of these completely unbalanced souls could no longer endure the Gospel doctrine, taught by Jesus, of the equal right of all men to be children of God: their revenge took the form of *elevating* Jesus in an extravagant fashion, and thus separating him from themselves: just as, in earlier times, the Jews, to revenge themselves upon their enemies, separated themselves from their God, and placed him on a great height. The One God and the Only Son of God: both were products of *ressentiment*….

41.

And from that time onward an absurd problem offered itself: "how *could* God allow it!" To which the deranged reason of the little community formulated an answer that was terrifying in its absurdity: God gave his son as a *sacrifice* for the forgiveness of sins. At once there was an end of the gospels! Sacrifice for sin, and in its most obnoxious and barbarous form: sacrifice of the *innocent* for the sins of the guilty! What appalling paganism!—Jesus himself had done away with the very concept of "guilt," he denied that there was any gulf fixed between God and man; he *lived* this unity between God and man, and that was precisely *his* "glad tidings".... And *not* as a mere privilege!

From this time forward the type of the Saviour was corrupted, bit by bit, by the doctrine of judgment and of the second coming, the doctrine of death as a sacrifice, the doctrine of the *resurrection*, by means of which the entire concept of "blessedness," the whole and only reality of the gospels, is juggled away—in favour of a state of existence *after* death!... St. Paul, with that rabbinical impudence which shows itself in all his doings, gave a logical quality to that conception, that *indecent* conception, in this way: "*If* Christ did not rise from the dead, then all our faith is in vain!"—And at once there sprang from the Gospels the most contemptible of all unfulfillable promises, the *shameless* doctrine of personal immortality.... Paul even preached it as a *reward*....

42.

One now begins to see just *what* it was that came to an end with the death on the cross: a new and thoroughly original effort to found a Buddhistic peace movement, and so establish *happiness on earth*—real, *not* merely promised. For this remains—as I have already pointed out —the essential difference between the two religions of *décadence*: Buddhism promises nothing, but actually fulfils; Christianity promises everything, but *fulfils nothing*.

Hard upon the heels of the "glad tidings" came the worst imaginable: those of Paul. In Paul is incarnated the very opposite of the "bearer of glad tidings"; he represents the genius for hatred, the vision of hatred, the relentless logic of hatred. *What*, indeed, has not this dysangelist sacrificed to hatred! Above all, the Saviour: he nailed him to *his own* cross. The life, the example, the teaching, the death of Christ, the meaning and the law of the whole gospels—nothing was left of all this after that counterfeiter in hatred had reduced it to his uses. Surely *not* reality; surely *not* historical truth!

Once more the priestly instinct of the Jew perpetrated the same old master crime against history—he simply struck out the yesterday and the day before yesterday of Christianity, and *invented his own history of Christian beginnings*. Going further, he treated the history of Israel to another falsification, so that it became a mere prologue to *his* achievement: all the prophets, it now appeared, had referred to *his* "Saviour."...[105] Later on the church even falsified the history of man in order to make it a prologue to Christianity.

The figure of the Saviour, his teaching, his way of life, his death, the meaning of his death, even the consequences of his death—nothing remained untouched, nothing remained in even remote contact with reality. Paul simply shifted the centre of gravity of that whole life to a place *behind* this existence—in the *lie* of the "risen" Jesus. At bottom, he had no use for the life of the Saviour—what he needed was the death on the cross, *and* something more. To see anything honest in such a man as Paul, whose home was at the centre of the Stoical enlightenment, when he converts an hallucination into a *proof* of the resurrection of the Saviour, or even to believe his tale that he suffered from this hallucination himself—this would be a genuine *niaiserie*[106] in a psychologist. Paul willed the end; *therefore* he also willed the means.... What he himself didn't believe was swallowed readily enough by the idiots among whom he spread *his* teaching.—What *he* wanted was power; in Paul the priest once more reached out for power—he had use only for such concepts, teachings and symbols as served the purpose of tyrannizing over the masses and organizing mobs. *What* was the only part of Christianity that Mohammed borrowed later on? Paul's invention, his device for establishing priestly tyranny and organizing the mob: the belief in the immortality of the soul—*that is to say, the doctrine of "judgment"*....

43.

When the centre of gravity of life is placed, *not* in life itself, but in "the beyond"—in *nothingness*—then one has taken away its centre of gravity altogether. The vast lie of personal immortality destroys all reason, all natural instinct—henceforth, everything in the instincts that is beneficial, that fosters life and that safeguards the future is a

---

[105] See *The Dawn* section 84.

[106] foolishness

cause of suspicion. So to live that life no longer has any meaning: *this* is now the "meaning" of life…. Why be public-spirited? Why take any pride in descent and forefathers? Why labour together, trust one another, or concern one's self about the common welfare, and try to serve it?… Merely so many "temptations," so many strayings from the "straight path."—"*One* thing only is necessary"…. That every man, because he has an "immortal soul," is as good as every other man; that in an infinite universe of things the "salvation" of *every* individual may lay claim to eternal importance; that insignificant bigots and the three-fourths insane may assume that the laws of nature are constantly *suspended* in their behalf—it is impossible to lavish too much contempt upon such a magnification of every sort of selfishness to infinity, to *insolence*. And yet Christianity has to thank precisely *this* miserable flattery of personal vanity for its *triumph*—it was thus that it lured all the botched, the dissatisfied, the fallen upon evil days, the whole refuse and off-scouring of humanity to its side. The "salvation of the soul"—in plain English: "the world revolves around *me*."

The poisonous doctrine, "*equal* rights for all," has been propagated as a Christian principle: out of the secret nooks and crannies of bad instinct Christianity has waged a deadly war upon all feelings of reverence and distance between man and man, which is to say, upon the first *prerequisite* to every step upward, to every development of civilization—out of the *ressentiment* of the masses it has forged its chief weapons against *us*, against everything noble, joyous and high-spirited on earth, against our happiness on earth…. To allow "immortality" to every Peter and Paul was the greatest, the most vicious outrage upon *noble* humanity ever perpetrated.

And let us not underestimate the fatal influence that Christianity has had, even upon politics! Nowadays no one has courage any more for special rights, for the right of dominion, for feelings of honourable pride in himself and his equals—for the *pathos of distance*…. Our politics is sick with this lack of courage!—The aristocratic attitude of mind has been undermined by the lie of the equality of souls; and if belief in the "privileges of the majority" makes and *will continue to make* revolutions—it is Christianity, let us not doubt, and *Christian* valuations, which convert every revolution into a carnival of blood and crime! Christianity is a revolt of all creatures that creep on the

ground against everything that is *lofty*: the gospel of the "lowly"
lowers....

44.

The gospels are invaluable as evidence of the corruption that was
already persistent *within* the primitive community. That which Paul,
with the cynical logic of a rabbi, later developed to a conclusion was
at bottom merely a process of decay that had begun with the death of
the Saviour.—These gospels cannot be read too carefully; difficulties
lurk behind every word. I confess—I hope it will not be held against
me—that it is precisely for this reason that they offer first-rate joy to a
psychologist—as the *opposite* of all merely naïve corruption, as
refinement *par excellence*, as an artistic triumph in psychological
corruption. The gospels, in fact, stand alone. The Bible as a whole is
not to be compared to them. Here we are among Jews: this is the *first*
thing to be borne in mind if we are not to lose the thread of the
matter. This positive genius for conjuring up a delusion of personal
"holiness" unmatched anywhere else, either in books or by men; this
elevation of fraud in word and attitude to the level of an *art*—all this
is not an accident due to the chance talents of an individual, or to any
violation of nature.

The thing responsible is *race*. The whole of Judaism appears in
Christianity as the art of concocting holy lies, and there, after many
centuries of earnest Jewish training and hard practice of Jewish
technic, the business comes to the stage of mastery. The Christian,
that *ultima ratio*[107] of lying, is the Jew all over again—he is *threefold* the
Jew.... The underlying will to make use only of such concepts,
symbols and attitudes as fit into priestly practice, the instinctive
repudiation of every *other* mode of thought, and every other method
of estimating values and utilities—this is not only tradition, it is
inheritance: only as an inheritance is it able to operate with the force of
nature. The whole of mankind, even the best minds of the best ages
(with one exception, perhaps hardly human—), have permitted
themselves to be deceived. The gospels have been read as a *book of
innocence* ... surely no small indication of the high skill with which the
trick has been done.—Of course, if we could actually *see* these

---

[107] last resort

astounding bigots and bogus saints, even if only for an instant, the farce would come to an end,—and it is precisely because *I* cannot read a word of theirs without seeing their attitudinizing that *I have made an end of them*.... I simply cannot endure the way they have of rolling up their eyes.

For the majority, happily enough, books are mere *literature.*—Let us not be led astray: they say "judge not," and yet they condemn to hell whoever stands in their way. In letting God sit in judgment they judge themselves; in glorifying God they glorify themselves; in *demanding* that every one show the virtues which they themselves happen to be capable of—still more, which they *must* have in order to remain on top—they assume the grand air of men struggling for virtue, of men engaging in a war that virtue may prevail. "We live, we die, we sacrifice ourselves *for the good*" (—"the truth," "the light," "the kingdom of God"): in point of fact, they simply do what they cannot help doing. Forced, like hypocrites, to be sneaky, to hide in corners, to slink along in the shadows, they convert their necessity into a *duty*: it is on grounds of duty that they account for their lives of humility, and that humility becomes merely one more proof of their piety.... Ah, that humble, chaste, charitable brand of fraud! "Virtue itself shall bear witness for us."...

One may read the gospels as books of *moral* seduction: these petty folks fasten themselves to morality—they know the uses of morality! Morality is the best of all devices for leading mankind *by the nose!*— The fact is that the conscious conceit of the chosen here disguises itself as modesty: it is in this way that *they*, the "community," the "good and just," range themselves, once and for always, on one side, the side of "the truth"—and the rest of mankind, "the world," on the other.... In *that* we observe the most fatal sort of megalomania that the earth has ever seen: little abortions of bigots and liars began to claim exclusive rights in the concepts of "God," "the truth," "the light," "the spirit," "love," "wisdom" and "life," as if these things were synonyms of themselves and thereby they sought to fence themselves off from the "world"; little super-Jews, ripe for some sort of madhouse, turned values upside down in order to meet *their* notions, just as if the Christian were the meaning, the salt, the standard and even the *last judgment* of all the rest.... The whole disaster was only made possible by the fact that there already existed in the world a similar megalomania, allied to this one in race, to wit, the *Jewish*: once a chasm began to yawn between Jews and Judaeo-Christians, the latter had no choice but to employ the self-preservative measures that the Jewish instinct had devised, even *against* the Jews themselves, whereas the Jews had employed them only against non-Jews. The Christian is simply a Jew of the "reformed" confession.

45.

I offer a few examples of the sort of thing these petty people have got into their heads—what they have *put into the mouth* of the Master: the unalloyed creed of "beautiful souls."—

"And whosoever shall not receive you, nor hear you, when ye depart thence, shake off the dust under your feet for a testimony against them. Verily I say unto you, it shall be more tolerable for Sodom and Gomorrah in the day of judgment, than for that city" (Mark vi, 11)—How *evangelical!*...

"And whosoever shall offend one of *these* little ones that believe in me, it is better for him that a millstone were hanged about his neck, and he were cast into the sea" (Mark ix, 42).—How *evangelical!*...

"And if thine eye offend thee, pluck it out: it is better for thee to enter into the kingdom of God with one eye, than having two eyes to be cast into hell fire; Where the worm dieth not, and the fire is not quenched." (Mark ix, 47-48.)—It is not exactly the eye that is meant....

"Verily I say unto you, That there be some of them that stand here, which shall not taste of death, till they have seen the kingdom of God come with power." (Mark ix, 1.)—Well *lied*, lion![108]....

"Whosoever will come after me, let him deny himself, and take up his cross, and follow me. *For...*" (*Note of a psychologist.* Christian morality is refuted by its *fors*: its reasons are against it,—this makes it Christian.) Mark viii, 34.—

---

[108] A paraphrase of Demetrius' "Well roar'd, Lion!" in act v, scene 1 of "A Midsummer Night's Dream." The lion, of course, is the familiar Christian symbol for Mark. [Tr.]

"Judge not, that ye be not judged. With what measure ye mete, it shall be measured to you again." (Matthew vii, 1-2.)—What a notion of justice, of a "just" judge!…

"For if ye love them which love you, what reward have ye? do not even the publicans the same? And if ye salute your brethren only, what do ye more *than others*? do not even the publicans so?" (Matthew v, 46-7.)—Principle of "Christian love": it insists upon being well *paid* in the end….

"But if ye forgive not men their trespasses, neither will your Father forgive your trespasses." (Matthew vi, 15.)—Very compromising for the said "father."…

"But seek ye first the kingdom of God, and his righteousness; and all these things shall be added unto you." (Matthew vi, 33.)—All these things: namely, food, clothing, all the necessities of life. An *error*, to put it mildly…. A bit before this God appears as a tailor, at least in certain cases….

"Rejoice ye in that day, and leap for joy: for, behold, your reward *is* great in heaven: for in the like manner did their fathers unto the prophets." (Luke vi, 23.)—*Impudent* rabble! It compares itself to the prophets….

"Know ye not that ye are the temple of God, and *that* the spirit of God dwelleth in you? If any man defile the temple of God, *him shall God destroy*; for the temple of God is holy, *which temple ye are*." (Paul, 1 Corinthians iii, 16-7.)—For that sort of thing one cannot have enough contempt….

"Do ye not know that the saints shall judge the world? and if the world shall be judged by you, are ye unworthy to judge the smallest matters?" (Paul, 1 Corinthians vi, 2.)—Unfortunately, not merely the speech of a lunatic…. This *frightful impostor* then proceeds: "Know ye not that we shall judge angels? how much more things that pertain to this life?"…

"Hath not God made foolish the wisdom of this world? For after that in the wisdom of God the world by wisdom knew not God, it pleased God by the foolishness of preaching to save them that believe…. Not many wise men after the flesh, not men mighty, not many noble *are called*: But God hath chosen the foolish things of the world to confound the wise; and God hath chosen the weak things of the world to confound the things which are mighty; And base things of the world, and things which are despised, hath God chosen, *yea*, and things which are not, to bring to nought things that are: That no flesh should glory in his presence." (Paul, 1 Corinthians i, 20ff.)—In order to *understand* this passage, a first-rate example of the psychology underlying every Chandala-morality, one should read the first part of my *Genealogy of Morals*: there, for the first time, the antagonism between a *noble* morality and a morality born of *ressentiment* and impotent vengefulness is exhibited. Paul was the greatest of all apostles of revenge....

46.

What follows, then? That one had better put on gloves before reading the New Testament. The presence of so much filth makes it very advisable. One would as little choose "early Christians" for companions as Polish Jews: not that one need seek out an objection to them.... Neither has a pleasant smell.

I have searched the New Testament in vain for a single sympathetic touch; nothing is there that is free, kindly, open-hearted or upright. In it humanity does not even make the first step upward—the instinct for *cleanliness* is lacking.... Only *evil* instincts are there, and there is not even the courage of these evil instincts. It is all cowardice; it is all a shutting of the eyes, a self-deception. Every other book becomes clean, once one has read the New Testament: for example, immediately after reading Paul I took up with delight that most charming and wanton of scoffers, Petronius, of whom one may say what Domenico Boccaccio wrote of Caesar Borgia to the Duke of Parma: "*è tutto festo*"—immortally healthy, immortally cheerful and sound.... These petty bigots make a capital miscalculation. They attack, but everything they attack is thereby *distinguished*. Whoever is attacked by an "early Christian" is surely *not* befouled.... On the contrary, it is an honour to have an "early Christian" as an opponent. One cannot read the New Testament without acquired admiration for whatever it abuses—not to speak of the "wisdom of this world," which an impudent wind-bag tries to dispose of "by the foolishness of preaching."... Even the scribes and pharisees are benefitted by such opposition: they must certainly have been worth something to have been hated in such an indecent manner. Hypocrisy—as if this were a charge that the "early Christians" *dared* to make!—After all, they were the *privileged*, and that was enough: the hatred of the Chandala needed no other excuse.

The "early Christian"—and also, I fear, the "last Christian," *whom I may perhaps live to see*—is a rebel against all privilege by profound instinct—he lives and makes war for ever for "equal rights.".... Strictly speaking, he has no alternative. When a man proposes to represent, in his own person, the "chosen of God"—or to be a "temple of God," or a "judge of the angels"—then every *other* criterion, whether based upon honesty, upon intellect, upon manliness and pride, or upon beauty and freedom of the heart, becomes simply "worldly"—*evil in itself*.... Moral: every word that comes from the lips of an "early Christian" is a lie, and his every act is instinctively dishonest—all his values, all his aims are noxious, but *whoever* he hates, *whatever* he hates, has real *value*.... The Christian, and particularly the Christian priest, is thus a *criterion of values*.

Must I add that, in the whole New Testament, there appears but a *solitary* figure worthy of honour? Pilate, the Roman viceroy. To regard a Jewish imbroglio *seriously*—that was quite beyond him. One Jew more or less—what did it matter?... The noble scorn of a Roman, before whom the word "truth" was shamelessly mishandled, enriched the New Testament with the only saying *that has any value*—and that is at once its criticism and its *destruction*: "What is truth?...."

47.

The thing that sets us apart is not that we are unable to find God, either in history, or in nature, or behind nature—but that we regard what has been honoured as God, not as "divine," but as pitiable, as absurd, as injurious; not as a mere error, but as a *crime against life*.... We deny that God is God.... If any one were to *show* us this Christian God, we'd be still less inclined to believe in him.—In a formula: *deus, qualem Paulus creavit, dei negatio*.[109]

Such a religion as Christianity, which does not touch reality at a single point and which goes to pieces the moment reality asserts its rights at any point, must be inevitably the deadly enemy of the

---

[109] "God, as created by Paul, is the negation of God."

"wisdom of this world," which is to say, of *science*—and it will give the name of good to whatever means serve to poison, calumniate and *cry down* all intellectual discipline, all lucidity and strictness in matters of intellectual conscience, and all noble coolness and freedom of the mind. "Faith," as an imperative, vetoes science—*in praxi*, lying at any price…. Paul *well knew* that lying—that "faith"—was necessary; later on the church borrowed the fact from Paul.—The God that Paul invented for himself, a God who "reduced to absurdity" "the wisdom of this world" (especially the two great enemies of superstition, philology and medicine), is in truth only an indication of Paul's resolute *determination* to accomplish that very thing himself: to give one's own will the name of God, *torah*—that is essentially Jewish. Paul *wants* to dispose of the "wisdom of this world": his enemies are the *good* philologians and physicians of the Alexandrine school—on them he makes his war. As a matter of fact no man can be a *philologian* or a physician without being also *Antichrist*. That is to say, as a philologian a man sees *behind* the "holy books," and as a physician he sees *behind* the physiological degeneration of the typical Christian. The physician says "incurable"; the philologian says "fraud."…

48.

Has any one ever clearly understood the celebrated story at the beginning of the Bible—of God's mortal terror of *science*?… No one, in fact, has understood it. This priest-book *par excellence* opens, as is fitting, with the great inner difficulty of the priest: *he* faces only one great danger; *ergo*, "God" faces only one great danger.

The old God, wholly "spirit," wholly the high-priest, wholly perfect, is promenading his garden: he is bored and trying to kill time. Against boredom even gods struggle in vain.[110] What does he do? He creates man—man is entertaining…. But then he notices that man is also bored. God's pity for the only form of distress that invades all paradises knows no bounds: so he forthwith creates other animals. God's first mistake: to man these other animals were not entertaining —he sought dominion over them; he did not want to be an "animal" himself.—So God created woman. In the act he brought boredom to an end—and also many other things! Woman was the *second* mistake

---

110 A paraphrase of Schiller's "Against stupidity even gods struggle in vain." [Tr.]

of God.—"Woman, at bottom, is a serpent, *Heva*"—every priest knows that; "from woman comes every evil in the world"—every priest knows that, too. *Ergo*, she is also to blame for *science*.... It was through woman that man learned to taste of the tree of knowledge.— What happened? The old God was seized by mortal terror. Man himself had been his *greatest* blunder; he had created a rival to himself; science makes men *godlike*—it is all up with priests and gods when man becomes scientific!—*Moral*: science is the forbidden *per se*; it alone is forbidden. Science is the *first* of sins, the germ of all sins, the *original* sin. *This is all there is of morality.*—"Thou shall *not* know":—the rest follows from that.

God's mortal terror, however, did not hinder him from being shrewd. How is one to *protect* one's self against science? For a long while this was the capital problem. Answer: Out of paradise with man! Happiness, leisure, foster thought—and all thoughts are bad thoughts!—Man *must* not think.—And so the priest invents distress, death, the mortal dangers of childbirth, all sorts of misery, old age, decrepitude, above all, *sickness*—nothing but devices for making war on science! The troubles of man don't *allow* him to think.... Nevertheless—how terrible!—, the edifice of knowledge begins to tower aloft, invading heaven, shadowing the gods—what is to be done?—The old God invents *war*; he separates the peoples; he makes men destroy one another (—the priests have always had need of war....). War—among other things, a great disturber of science!— Incredible! Knowledge, *deliverance from the priests*, prospers in spite of war.—So the old God comes to his final resolution: "Man has become scientific—*there is no help for it: he must be drowned!*"...

49.

I have been understood. At the opening of the Bible there is the *whole* psychology of the priest.—The priest knows of only one great danger: that is science—the sound comprehension of cause and effect. But science flourishes, on the whole, only under favourable conditions —a man must have time, he must have an *overflowing* intellect, in order to "know."... "*Therefore*, man must be made unhappy,"—this has been, in all ages, the logic of the priest.

It is easy to see just *what*, by this logic, was the first thing to come into the world:—"*sin*."... The concept of guilt and punishment, the whole "moral order of the world," was set up *against* science—*against* the deliverance of man from priests.... Man must *not* look outward; he must look inward. He must *not* look at things shrewdly and cautiously, to learn about them; he must not look at all; he must *suffer*.... And he must suffer so much that he is always in need of the priest.—Away with physicians! *What is needed is a Saviour.*—The concept of guilt and punishment, including the doctrines of "grace," of "salvation," of "forgiveness"—*lies* through and through, and absolutely without psychological reality—were devised to destroy man's *sense of causality*: they are an attack upon the concept of cause and effect!—And *not* an attack with the fist, with the knife, with honesty in hate and love! On the contrary, one inspired by the most cowardly, the most crafty, the most ignoble of instincts! An attack of *priests*! An attack of *parasites*! The vampirism of pale, subterranean leeches!... When the natural consequences of an act are no longer "natural," but are regarded as produced by the ghostly creations of superstition—by "God," by "spirits," by "souls"—and reckoned as merely "moral" consequences, as rewards, as punishments, as hints, as lessons, then the whole ground-work of knowledge is destroyed—*then the greatest of crimes against humanity has been perpetrated.*—I repeat that sin, man's self-desecration *par excellence*, was invented in order to make science, culture, and every elevation and ennobling of man impossible; the priest *rules* through the invention of sin.—

50.

In this place I can't permit myself to omit a psychology of "belief," of the "believer," for the special benefit of "believers." If there remain any today who do not yet know how *indecent* it is to be "believing"—*or* how much a sign of *décadence*, of a broken will to live—then they will know it well enough tomorrow. My voice reaches even the deaf.

It appears, unless I have been incorrectly informed, that there prevails among Christians a sort of criterion of truth that is called "proof by power." "Faith makes blessed: *therefore* it is true."—It might be objected right here that blessedness is not demonstrated, it is merely *promised*: it hangs upon "faith" as a condition—one *shall* be blessed *because* one believes.... But what of the thing that the priest promises to the believer, the wholly transcendental "beyond"—how is

305

that to be demonstrated?—The "proof by power," thus assumed, is actually no more at bottom than a belief that the effects which faith promises will not fail to appear. In a formula: "I believe that faith makes for blessedness—*therefore*, it is true.".... But this is as far as we may go. This "therefore" would be *absurdum* itself as a criterion of truth.

But let us admit, for the sake of politeness, that blessedness by faith may be demonstrated (—*not* merely hoped for, and *not* merely promised by the suspicious lips of a priest): even so, *could* blessedness —in a technical term, *pleasure*—ever be a proof of truth? So little is this true that it is almost a proof against truth when sensations of pleasure influence the answer to the question "What is true?" or, at all events, it is enough to make that "truth" highly suspicious. The proof by "pleasure" is a proof *of* "pleasure"—nothing more; why in the world should it be assumed that *true* judgments give more pleasure than false ones, and that, in conformity to some pre-established harmony, they necessarily bring agreeable feelings in their train?

The experience of all disciplined and profound minds teaches *the contrary*. Man has had to fight for every atom of the truth, and has had to pay for it almost everything that the heart, that human love, that human trust cling to. Greatness of soul is needed for this business: the service of truth is the hardest of all services.—What, then, is the meaning of *integrity* in things intellectual? It means that a man must be severe with his own heart, that he must scorn "beautiful feelings," and that he makes every Yea and Nay a matter of conscience!—Faith makes blessed: *therefore*, it lies....

51.

The fact that faith, under certain circumstances, may work for blessedness, but that this blessedness produced by an *idée fixe* by no means makes the idea itself true, and the fact that faith actually moves no mountains, but instead *raises them up* where there were none before: all this is made sufficiently clear by a walk through a *lunatic asylum*. *Not*, of course, to a priest: for his instincts prompt him to the lie that sickness is not sickness and lunatic asylums not lunatic asylums. Christianity finds sickness *necessary*, just as the Greek spirit had need of a superabundance of health—the actual ulterior purpose of the whole system of salvation of the church is to *make* people ill. And the church

itself—doesn't it set up a Catholic lunatic asylum as the ultimate ideal?
—The whole earth as a madhouse?—The sort of religious man that
the church *wants* is a typical *décadent*; the moment at which a religious
crisis dominates a people is always marked by epidemics of nervous
disorder; the "inner world" of the religious man is so much like the
"inner world" of the overstrung and exhausted that it is difficult to
distinguish between them: the "highest" states of mind, held up before
mankind by Christianity as of supreme worth, are actually epileptoid
in form—the church has granted the name of holy only to lunatics or
to gigantic frauds *in maiorem dei honorem*....[111] Once I ventured to
designate the whole Christian system of *training*[112] in penance and
salvation (now best studied in England) as a method of producing a
folie circulaire [113]upon a soil already prepared for it, which is to say, a
soil thoroughly unhealthy. Not every one may be a Christian: one is
not "converted" to Christianity—one must first be sick enough for
it....

We others, who have the *courage* for health *and* likewise for
contempt,—we may well despise a religion that teaches
misunderstanding of the body! that refuses to rid itself of the
superstition about the soul! that makes a "virtue" of insufficient
nourishment! that combats health as a sort of enemy, devil,
temptation! that persuades itself that it is possible to carry about a
"perfect soul" in a cadaver of a body, and that, to this end, had to
devise for itself a new concept of "perfection," a pale, sickly,
idiotically ecstatic state of existence, so-called "holiness"—a holiness
that is itself merely a series of symptoms of an impoverished,
enervated and incurably disordered body!...

The Christian movement, as a European movement, was from the
start no more than a general uprising of all sorts of outcast and refuse
elements (—who now, under cover of Christianity, aspire to power). It
does *not* represent the decay of a race; it represents, on the contrary, a
conglomeration of *décadence* products from all directions, crowding
together and seeking one another out. It was *not*, as has been thought,

---

[111] "in the greater honor of God"

[112] The word *training* is in English in the text.

[113] "circular madness," manic-depressive psychosis

the corruption of antiquity, of *noble* antiquity, which made Christianity
possible; one cannot too sharply challenge the learned imbecility
which today maintains that theory. At the time when the sick and
rotten Chandala classes in the whole *imperium* were Christianized, the
contrary type, the nobility, reached its finest and ripest development.
The majority became master; democracy, with its Christian instincts,
triumphed.... Christianity was not "national," it was not based on race
—it appealed to all the varieties of men disinherited by life, it had its
allies everywhere. Christianity has the rancour of the sick at its very
core—the instinct against the *healthy*, against *health*. Everything that is
well-constituted, proud, gallant and, above all, beautiful gives offence
to its ears and eyes. Again I remind you of Paul's priceless saying:
"And God hath chosen the *weak* things of the world, the *foolish* things
of the world, the *base* things of the world, and things which are
despised":[114] *this* was the formula; *in hoc signo* the *décadence* triumphed.

God on the cross—is man always to miss the frightful inner
significance of this symbol?—Everything that suffers, everything that
hangs on the cross, is *divine*.... We all hang on the cross, consequently
we are divine.... We alone are divine.... Christianity was thus a
victory: a nobler attitude of mind was destroyed by it—Christianity
remains to this day the greatest misfortune of humanity.—

52.

Christianity also stands in opposition to all *intellectual* well-being,—
sick reasoning is the only sort that it *can* use as Christian reasoning; it
takes the side of everything that is idiotic; it pronounces a curse upon
"intellect," upon the *superbia*[115] of the healthy intellect. Since sickness
is inherent in Christianity, it follows that the typically Christian state
of "faith" *must* be a form of sickness too, and that all straight,
straightforward and scientific paths to knowledge *must* be banned by
the church as *forbidden* ways. Doubt is thus a sin from the start....

The complete lack of psychological cleanliness in the priest—
revealed by a glance at him—is a phenomenon *resulting* from *décadence*,
—one may observe in hysterical women and in rachitic children how

---

[114] 1 Corinthians i, 27, 28.

[115] pride

regularly the falsification of instincts, delight in lying for the mere sake of lying, and incapacity for looking straight and walking straight are symptoms of *décadence*. "Faith" means the will to avoid knowing what is true. The pietist, the priest of either sex, is a fraud *because* he is sick: his instinct *demands* that the truth shall never be allowed its rights on any point. "Whatever makes for illness is *good*; whatever issues from abundance, from superabundance, from power, is *evil*": so argues the believer. The *impulse to lie*—it is by this that I recognize every foreordained theologian.

Another characteristic of the theologian is his *unfitness for philology* What I here mean by philology is, in a general sense, the art of reading with profit—the capacity for absorbing facts *without* interpreting them falsely, and *without* losing caution, patience and subtlety in the effort to understand them. Philology as *ephexis*[116] in interpretation: whether one be dealing with books, with newspaper reports, with the most fateful events or with weather statistics—not to mention the "salvation of the soul."... The way in which a theologian, whether in Berlin or in Rome, is ready to explain, say, a "passage of Scripture," or an experience, or a victory by the national army, by turning upon it the high illumination of the Psalms of David, is always so *daring* that it is enough to make a philologian run up a wall. But what shall he do when pietists and other such cows from Swabia[117] use the "finger of God" to convert their miserably commonplace and huggermugger existence into a miracle of "grace," a "providence" and an "experience of salvation"?

The most modest exercise of the intellect, not to say of decency, should certainly be enough to convince these interpreters of the perfect childishness and unworthiness of such a misuse of the divine digital dexterity. However small our piety, if we ever encountered a god who always cured us of a cold in the head at just the right time, or got us into our carriage at the very instant heavy rain began to fall,

---

[116] That is, to say, scepticism. Among the Greeks scepticism was also occasionally called ephecticism. [Tr.]

[117] A reference to the University of Tübingen and its famous school of Biblical criticism. The leader of this school was F. C. Baur, and one of the men greatly influenced by it was Nietzsche's pet abomination, David F. Strauss, himself a Suabian. *Vide* § 10 and § 28. [Tr.]

he would seem so absurd a god that he'd have to be abolished even if he existed. God as a domestic servant, as a letter carrier, as an almanac-man—at bottom, he is a mere name for the stupidest sort of chance.... "Divine Providence," which every third man in "educated Germany" still believes in, is so strong an argument against God that it would be impossible to think of a stronger. And in any case it is an argument against Germans!...

53.

It is so little true that *martyrs* offer any support to the truth of a cause that I am inclined to deny that any martyr has ever had anything to do with the truth at all. In the very tone in which a martyr flings what he fancies to be true at the head of the world there appears so low a grade of intellectual honesty and such *insensibility* to the problem of "truth," that it is never necessary to refute him. Truth is not something that one man has and another man has not: at best, only peasants, or peasant-apostles like Luther, can think of truth in any such way. One may rest assured that the greater the degree of a man's intellectual conscience the greater will be his modesty, his *discretion*, on this point. To *know* in five cases, and to refuse, with delicacy, to know anything *further*.... "Truth," as the word is understood by every prophet, every sectarian, every free-thinker, every Socialist and every churchman, is simply a complete proof that not even a beginning has been made in the intellectual discipline and self-control that are necessary to the unearthing of even the smallest truth.

The deaths of the martyrs, it may be said in passing, have been misfortunes of history: they have *misled*.... The conclusion that all idiots, women and plebeians come to, that there must be something in a cause for which any one goes to his death (or which, as under primitive Christianity, sets off epidemics of death-seeking)—this conclusion has been an unspeakable drag upon the testing of facts, upon the whole spirit of inquiry and investigation. The martyrs have *damaged* the truth.... Even to this day the crude fact of persecution is enough to give an honourable name to the most empty sort of sectarianism.—But why? Is the worth of a cause altered by the fact that some one had laid down his life for it?—An error that becomes honourable is simply an error that has acquired one seductive charm the more: do you suppose, Messrs. Theologians, that we shall give you the chance to be martyred for your lies?

One best disposes of a cause by respectfully putting it on ice— that is also the best way to dispose of theologians…. This was precisely the world-historical stupidity of all the persecutors: that they gave the appearance of honour to the cause they opposed—that they made it a present of the fascination of martyrdom…. Women are still on their knees before an error because they have been told that someone died on the cross for it. *Is the cross, then, an argument?*—But about all these things there is one, and one only, who has said what has been needed for thousands of years—*Zarathustra.*

They made signs in blood along the way that they went, and their folly taught them that the truth is proved by blood.

But blood is the worst of all testimonies to the truth; blood poisoneth even the purest teaching and turneth it into madness and hatred in the heart.

And when one goeth through fire for his teaching—what doth that prove? Verily, it is more when one's teaching cometh out of one's own burning![118]

54.

Do not let yourself be deceived: great intellects are sceptical. Zarathustra is a sceptic. The strength, the *freedom* which proceed from intellectual power, from a superabundance of intellectual power, *manifest* themselves as scepticism. Men of fixed convictions do not count when it comes to determining what is fundamental in values and lack of values. Men of convictions are prisoners. They do not see far enough, they do not see what is *below* them: whereas a man who would talk to any purpose about value and non-value must be able to see five hundred convictions *beneath* him—and *behind* him…. A mind that aspires to great things, and that wills the means thereto, is necessarily sceptical. Freedom from any sort of conviction *belongs* to strength, and to an independent point of view…. That grand passion which is at once the foundation and the power of a sceptic's existence, and is both more enlightened and more despotic than he is himself,

---

[118] The quotations are from *Thus Spoke Zarathustra*, ii, 24: "Of Priests."

drafts the whole of his intellect into its service; it makes him unscrupulous; it gives him courage to employ unholy means; under certain circumstances it does not *begrudge* him even convictions. Conviction as a means: one may achieve a good deal by means of a conviction. A grand passion makes use of and uses up convictions; it does not yield to them—it knows itself to be sovereign.

On the contrary, the need of faith, of something unconditioned by yea or nay, of Carlylism, if I may be allowed the word, is a need of *weakness*. The man of faith, the "believer" of any sort, is necessarily a dependent man—such a man cannot posit *himself* as a goal, nor can he find goals within himself. The "believer" does not belong to himself; he can only be a means to an end; he must be *used up*; he needs some one to use him up. His instinct gives the highest honours to an ethic of self-effacement; he is prompted to embrace it by everything: his prudence, his experience, his vanity. Every sort of faith is in itself an evidence of self-effacement, of self-estrangement....

When one reflects how necessary it is to the great majority that there be regulations to restrain them from without and hold them fast, and to what extent control, or, in a higher sense, *slavery*, is the one and only condition which makes for the well-being of the weak-willed man, and especially woman, then one at once understands conviction and "faith." To the man with convictions they are his backbone. To *avoid* seeing many things, to be impartial about nothing, to be a party man through and through, to estimate all values strictly and infallibly—these are conditions necessary to the existence of such a man. But by the same token they are *antagonists* of the truthful man—of the truth....

The believer is not free to answer the question, "true" or "not true," according to the dictates of his own conscience: integrity on *this* point would work his instant downfall. The pathological limitations of his vision turn the man of convictions into a fanatic—Savonarola, Luther, Rousseau, Robespierre, Saint-Simon—these types stand in opposition to the strong, *emancipated* spirit. But the grandiose attitudes of these *sick* intellects, these intellectual epileptics, are of influence upon the great masses—fanatics are picturesque, and mankind prefers observing poses to listening to *reasons*....

55.

One step further in the psychology of conviction, of "faith." It is now a good while since I first proposed for consideration the question whether convictions are not even more dangerous enemies to truth than lies. (*Human, All-Too-Human,* I, aphorism 483.)[119] This time I desire to put the question definitely: is there any actual difference between a lie and a conviction?—All the world believes that there is; but what is not believed by all the world!—Every conviction has its history, its primitive forms, its stage of tentativeness and error: it *becomes* a conviction only after having been, for a long time, *not* one, and then, for an even longer time, *hardly* one. What if falsehood be also one of these embryonic forms of conviction?—Sometimes all that is needed is a change in persons: what was a lie in the father becomes a conviction in the son.—I call it lying to refuse to see what one sees, or to refuse to see it *as* it is: whether the lie be uttered before witnesses or not before witnesses is of no consequence. The most common sort of lie is that by which a man deceives himself: the deception of others is a relatively rare offence.

Now, this will *not* to see what one sees, this will *not* to see it as it is, is almost the first requisite for all who belong to a party of whatever sort: the party man becomes inevitably a liar. For example, the German historians are convinced that Rome was synonymous with despotism and that the Germanic peoples brought the spirit of liberty into the world: what is the difference between this conviction and a lie? Is it to be wondered at that all partisans, including the German historians, instinctively roll the fine phrases of morality upon their tongues—that morality almost owes its very *survival* to the fact that the party man of every sort has need of it every moment?—"This is *our* conviction: we publish it to the whole world; we live and die for it—let us respect all who have convictions!"—I have actually heard such sentiments from the mouths of anti-Semites. On the contrary, gentlemen! An anti-Semite surely does not become more respectable because he lies on principle.. . The priests, who have more finesse in such matters, and who well understand the objection that lies against the notion of a conviction, which is to say, of a falsehood that

---

[119] The aphorism, which is headed "The Enemies of Truth," makes the direct statement: "Convictions are more dangerous enemies of truth than lies." [Tr.]

becomes a matter of principle *because* it serves a purpose, have borrowed from the Jews the shrewd device of sneaking in the concepts, "God," "the will of God" and "the revelation of God" at this place.

Kant, too, with his categorical imperative, was on the same road: this was his *practical* reason. There are questions regarding the truth or untruth of which it is *not* for man to decide; all the capital questions, all the capital problems of valuation, are beyond human reason.... To know the limits of reason—*that* alone is genuine philosophy.... Why did God make a revelation to man? Would God have done anything superfluous? Man *could* not find out for himself what was good and what was evil, so God taught him His will.... Moral: the priest does *not* lie—the question, "true" or "untrue," has nothing to do with such things as the priest discusses; it is impossible to lie about these things. In order to lie here it would be necessary to know *what* is true. But this is more than man *can* know; therefore, the priest is simply the mouthpiece of God.

Such a priestly syllogism is by no means merely Jewish and Christian; the right to lie and the *shrewd dodge* of "revelation" belong to the general priestly type—to the priest of the *décadence* as well as to the priest of pagan times (—Pagans are all those who say yes to life, and to whom "God" is a word signifying acquiescence in all things).[120]— The "law," the "will of God," the "holy book," and "inspiration"—all these things are merely words for the conditions *under* which the priest comes to power and *with* which he maintains his power,—these concepts are to be found at the bottom of all priestly organizations, and of all priestly or priestly-philosophical schemes of governments. The "holy lie"—common alike to Confucius, to the Code of Manu, to Mohammed and to the Christian church—is not even wanting in Plato. "Truth is here": this means, no matter where it is heard, *the priest lies....*

56.

In the last analysis it comes to this: what is the *end* of lying? The fact that, in Christianity, "holy" ends are not visible is *my* objection to

---

[120] See *The Will to Power* sec. 147

the means it employs. Only *bad* ends appear: the poisoning, the calumniation, the denial of life, the despising of the body, the degradation and self-contamination of man by the concept of sin—*therefore*, its means are also bad

I have a contrary feeling when I read the Code of Manu, an incomparably more intellectual and superior work, which it would be a sin against the *intelligence* to so much as *name* in the same breath with the Bible. It is easy to see why: there is a genuine philosophy behind it, *in* it, not merely an evil-smelling mess of Jewish rabbinism and superstition,—it gives even the most fastidious psychologist something to sink his teeth into. And, *not* to forget what is most important, it differs fundamentally from every kind of Bible: by means of it the *nobles*, the philosophers and the warriors keep the whip-hand over the majority; it is full of noble valuations, it shows a feeling of perfection, an acceptance of life, and triumphant feeling toward self and life—the *sun* shines upon the whole book.—All the things on which Christianity vents its fathomless vulgarity—for example, procreation, women and marriage—are here handled earnestly, with reverence and with love and confidence. How can any one really put into the hands of children and ladies a book which contains such vile things as this: "to avoid fornication, let every man have his own wife, and let every woman have her own husband; ... it is better to marry than to burn"?[121] And is it *possible* to be a Christian so long as the origin of man is Christianized, which is to say, *befouled*, by the doctrine of the *immaculata conceptio*?... I know of no book in which so many delicate and kindly things are said of women as in the Code of Manu; these old grey-beards and saints have a way of being gallant to women that it would be impossible, perhaps, to surpass. "The mouth of a woman," it says in one place, "the breasts of a maiden, the prayer of a child and the smoke of sacrifice are always pure." In another place: "there is nothing purer than the light of the sun, the shadow cast by a cow, air, water, fire and the breath of a maiden." Finally, in still another place—perhaps this is also a holy lie—: "all the orifices of the body above the navel are pure, and all below are impure. Only in the maiden is the whole body pure."

---

[121] 1 Corinthians vii, 2, 9.

57.

One catches the *unholiness* of Christian means *in flagranti* by the simple process of putting the ends sought by Christianity beside the ends sought by the Code of Manu—by putting these enormously antithetical ends under a strong light. The critic of Christianity cannot evade the necessity of making Christianity *contemptible*.

A book of laws such as the Code of Manu has the same origin as every other good law-book: it epitomizes the experience, the sagacity and the ethical experimentation of long centuries; it brings things to a conclusion; it no longer creates. The prerequisite to a codification of this sort is recognition of the fact that the means which establish the authority of a slowly and painfully attained *truth* are fundamentally different from those which one would make use of to prove it. A law-book never recites the utility, the grounds, the casuistical antecedents of a law: for if it did so it would lose the imperative tone, the "thou shall," on which obedience is based. The problem lies exactly here.

At a certain point in the evolution of a people, the class within it of the greatest insight, which is to say, the greatest hindsight and foresight, declares that the series of experiences determining how all shall live—or *can* live—has come to an end. The object now is to reap as rich and as complete a harvest as possible from the days of experiment and *hard* experience. In consequence, the thing that is to be avoided above everything is further experimentation—the continuation of the state in which values are fluent, and are tested, chosen and criticized *ad infinitum*. Against this a double wall is set up: on the one hand, *revelation*, which is the assumption that the reasons lying behind the laws are *not* of human origin, that they were *not* sought out and found by a slow process and after many errors, but that they are of divine ancestry, and came into being complete, perfect, without a history, as a free gift, a miracle...; and on the other hand, *tradition*, which is the assumption that the law has stood unchanged from time immemorial, and that it is impious and a crime against one's forefathers to bring it into question. The authority of the law is thus grounded on the thesis: God gave it, and the fathers *lived* it.

The higher motive of such procedure lies in the design to distract consciousness, step by step, from its concern with notions of right living (that is to say, those that have been *proved* to be right by wide and carefully considered experience), so that instinct attains to a perfect automatism—a primary necessity to every sort of mastery, to every sort of perfection in the art of life. To draw up such a law-book as Manu's means to lay before a people the possibility of future mastery, of attainable perfection—it permits them to aspire to the highest reaches of the art of life. *To that end the thing must be made unconscious:* that is the aim of every holy lie.

The *order of castes*, the highest, the dominating law, is merely the ratification of an *order of nature*, of a natural law of the first rank, over which no arbitrary fiat, no "modern idea," can exert any influence. In every healthy society there are three physiological types, gravitating toward differentiation but mutually conditioning one another, and each of these has its own hygiene, its own sphere of work, its own special mastery and feeling of perfection. It is *not* Manu but nature that sets off in one class those who are chiefly intellectual, in another those who are marked by muscular strength and temperament, and in a third those who are distinguished in neither one way or the other, but show only mediocrity—the last-named represents the great majority, and the first two the select.

The superior caste—I call it the *fewest*—has, as the most perfect, the privileges of the few: it stands for happiness, for beauty, for everything good upon earth. Only the most intellectual of men have any right to beauty, to the beautiful; only in them can goodness escape being weakness. *Pulchrum est paucorum hominum:*[122] goodness is a privilege. Nothing could be more unbecoming to them than uncouth manners or a pessimistic look, or an eye that sees *ugliness*—or indignation against the general aspect of things. Indignation is the privilege of the Chandala; so is pessimism. *"The world is perfect"*—so prompts the instinct of the intellectual, the instinct of the man who says yes to life. "Imperfection, whatever is *inferior* to us, distance, the pathos of distance, even the Chandala themselves are parts of this perfection." The most intelligent men, like the *strongest*, find their happiness where others would find only disaster: in the labyrinth, in being hard with themselves and with others, in effort; their delight is in self-mastery; in them asceticism becomes second nature, a necessity, an instinct. They regard a difficult task as a privilege; it is to them a *recreation* to play with burdens that would crush all others....

---

[122] "Few men are noble"

Knowledge—a form of asceticism.—They are the most honourable kind of men: but that does not prevent them being the most cheerful and most amiable. They rule, not because they want to, but because they *are*; they are not at liberty to play second.

The *second caste*: to this belong the guardians of the law, the keepers of order and security, the more noble warriors, above all, the king as the highest form of warrior, judge and preserver of the law. The second in rank constitute the executive arm of the intellectuals, the nearest to them in rank, taking from them all that is *rough* in the business of ruling—their followers, their right hand, their most apt disciples.—In all this, I repeat, there is nothing arbitrary, nothing "made up"; whatever is to the *contrary* is made up—by it nature is brought to shame.... The order of castes, the *order of rank*, simply formulates the supreme law of life itself; the separation of the three types is necessary to the maintenance of society, and to the evolution of higher types, and the highest types—the *inequality* of rights is essential to the existence of any rights at all.

A right is a privilege. Every one enjoys the privileges that accord with his state of existence. Let us not underestimate the privileges of the *mediocre*. Life is always harder as one mounts the *heights*—the cold increases, responsibility increases. A high civilization is a pyramid: it can stand only on a broad base; its primary prerequisite is a strong and soundly consolidated mediocrity. The handicrafts, commerce, agriculture, *science*, the greater part of art, in brief, the whole range of *occupational* activities, are compatible only with mediocre ability and aspiration; such callings would be out of place for exceptional men; the instincts which belong to them stand as much opposed to aristocracy as to anarchism. The fact that a man is publicly useful, that he is a wheel, a function, is evidence of a natural predisposition; it is not *society*, but the only sort of happiness that the majority are capable of, that makes them intelligent machines. To the mediocre mediocrity is a form of happiness; they have a natural instinct for mastering one thing, for specialization. It would be altogether unworthy of a profound intellect to see anything objectionable in mediocrity in itself. It is, in fact, the *first* prerequisite to the appearance of the exceptional: it is a necessary condition to a high degree of civilization. When the exceptional man handles the mediocre man with more delicate fingers than he applies to himself or to his equals, this is not merely kindness of heart—it is simply his *duty*....

Whom do I hate most heartily among the rabbles of today? The rabble of Socialists, the apostles to the Chandala, who undermine the workingman's instincts, his pleasure, his feeling of contentment with his petty existence—who make him envious and teach him revenge.... Wrong never lies in unequal rights; it lies in the assertion of "equal" rights.... What is *bad*? But I have already answered: all that proceeds from weakness, from envy, from *revenge*.—The anarchist and the Christian have the same ancestry....

58.

In point of fact, the end for which one lies makes a great difference: whether one preserves thereby or destroys. There is a perfect likeness between Christian and anarchist: their object, their instinct, points only toward destruction. One need only turn to history for a proof of this: there it appears with appalling distinctness. We have just studied a code of religious legislation whose object it was to convert the conditions which cause life to *flourish* into an "eternal" social organization,—Christianity found its mission in putting an end to such an organization, *because life flourished under it*. There the benefits that reason had produced during long ages of experiment and insecurity were applied to the most remote uses, and an effort was made to bring in a harvest that should be as large, as rich and as complete as possible; here, on the contrary, the harvest is *blighted* overnight.... That which stood there *aere perennis*, the *imperium Romanum*, the most magnificent form of organization under difficult conditions that has ever been achieved, and compared to which everything before it and after it appears as patchwork, bungling, *dilletantism*—those holy anarchists made it a matter of "piety" to destroy "the world," *which is to say*, the *imperium Romanum*, so that in the end not a stone stood upon another—and even Germans and other such louts were able to become its masters....

The Christian and the anarchist: both are *décadents*; both are incapable of any act that is not disintegrating, poisonous, degenerating, *blood-sucking*; both have an instinct of *mortal hatred* of everything that stands up, and is great, and has durability, and promises life a future.... Christianity was the vampire of the *imperium*

Romanum,—overnight it destroyed the vast achievement of the Romans: the conquest of the soil for a great culture *that could await its time*. Can it be that this fact is not yet understood?

The *imperium Romanum* that we know, and that the history of the Roman provinces teaches us to know better and better,—this most admirable of all works of art in the grand manner was merely the beginning, and the structure to follow was not to *prove* its worth for thousands of years. To this day, nothing on a like scale *sub specie aeterni* has been brought into being, or even dreamed of!—This organization was strong enough to withstand bad emperors: the accident of personality has nothing to do with such things—the *first* principle of all genuinely great architecture. But it was not strong enough to stand up against the *corruptest* of all forms of corruption—against Christians.... These stealthy worms, which under the cover of night, mist and duplicity, crept upon every individual, sucking him dry of all earnest interest in *real* things, of all instinct for *reality*—this cowardly, effeminate and sugar-coated gang gradually alienated all "souls," step by step, from that colossal edifice, turning against it all the meritorious, manly and noble natures that had found in the cause of Rome their own cause, their own serious purpose, their own *pride*. The sneakishness of hypocrisy, the secrecy of the conventicle, concepts as black as hell, such as the sacrifice of the innocent, the *unio mystica* in the drinking of blood, above all, the slowly rekindled fire of revenge, of Chandala revenge—all *that* sort of thing became master of Rome: the same kind of religion which, in a pre-existent form, Epicurus had combatted. One has but to read Lucretius to know *what* Epicurus made war upon—*not* paganism, but "Christianity," which is to say, the corruption of souls by means of the concepts of guilt, punishment and immortality.—He combatted the *subterranean* cults, the whole of latent Christianity—to deny immortality was already a form of genuine *salvation*.

Epicurus had triumphed, and every respectable intellect in Rome was Epicurean—*when Paul appeared* ... Paul, the Chandala hatred of Rome, of "the world," in the flesh and inspired by genius—the Jew, the *eternal* Jew *par excellence*.... What he saw was how, with the aid of the small sectarian Christian movement that stood apart from Judaism, a "world conflagration" might be kindled; how, with the symbol of "God on the cross," all secret seditions, all the fruits of anarchistic intrigues in the empire, might be amalgamated into one immense power. "Salvation is of the Jews."—Christianity is the formula for exceeding *and* summing up the subterranean cults of all varieties, that of Osiris, that of the Great Mother, that of Mithras, for instance: in his discernment of this fact the genius of Paul showed itself. His instinct was here so sure that, with reckless violence to the truth, he put the ideas which lent fascination to every sort of Chandala religion into the mouth of the "Saviour" as his own inventions, and not only into the mouth—he *made* out of him something that even a priest of Mithras could understand.... This was his revelation at Damascus: he grasped the fact that he *needed* the belief in immortality in order to rob "the world" of its value, that the concept of "hell" would master Rome—that the notion of a "beyond" is the *death of life*.... Nihilist and Christian: they rhyme in German, and they do more than rhyme....

59.

The whole labour of the ancient world gone for *naught*: I have no word to describe the feelings that such an enormity arouses in me.— And, considering the fact that its labour was merely preparatory, that with adamantine self-consciousness it laid only the foundations for a work to go on for thousands of years, the whole *meaning* of antiquity disappears!... To what end the Greeks? to what end the Romans?— All the prerequisites to a learned culture, all the *methods* of science, were already there; man had already perfected the great and incomparable art of reading profitably—that first necessity to the tradition of culture, the unity of the sciences; the natural sciences, in alliance with mathematics and mechanics, were on the right road,— *the sense of fact*, the last and more valuable of all the senses, had its schools, and its traditions were already centuries old! Is all this properly understood? Every *essential* to the beginning of the work was ready:—and the *most* essential, it cannot be said too often, are methods, and also the most difficult to develop, and the longest opposed by habit and laziness. What we have today reconquered, with unspeakable self-discipline, for ourselves—for certain bad instincts, certain Christian instincts, still lurk in our bodies—that is to say, the keen eye for reality, the cautious hand, patience and seriousness in the smallest things, the whole *integrity* of knowledge—all these things were already there, and had been there for two thousand years! *More*, there was also a refined and excellent tact and taste! *Not* as mere brain-drilling! *Not* as "German" culture, with its loutish manners! But as body, as bearing, as instinct—in short, as reality.... *All gone for naught!* Overnight it became merely a memory!

The Greeks! The Romans! Instinctive nobility, taste, methodical inquiry, genius for organization and administration, faith in and the *will* to secure the future of man, a great yes to everything entering into the *imperium Romanum* and palpable to all the senses, a grand style that was beyond mere art, but had become reality, truth, *life*....—All overwhelmed in a night, but not by a convulsion of nature! Not trampled to death by Teutons and others of heavy hoof! But brought to shame by crafty, sneaking, invisible, anæmic vampires! Not conquered,—only sucked dry!... Hidden vengefulness, petty envy, became *master*! Everything wretched, intrinsically ailing, and invaded by bad feelings, the whole *ghetto-world* of the soul, was at once *on top*!

One needs but read any of the Christian agitators, for example, St. Augustine, in order to realize, in order to smell, what filthy fellows came to the top. It would be an error, however, to assume that there was any lack of understanding in the leaders of the Christian movement:—ah, but they were clever, clever to the point of holiness, these fathers of the church! What they lacked was something quite different. Nature neglected—perhaps forgot—to give them even the most modest endowment of respectable, of upright, of *cleanly* instincts.... Between ourselves, they are not even men.... If Islam despises Christianity, it has a thousandfold right to do so: Islam at least assumes that it is dealing with *men*....

60.

Christianity destroyed for us the whole harvest of ancient civilization, and later it also destroyed for us the whole harvest of *Mohammedan* civilization. The wonderful culture of the Moors in Spain, which was fundamentally nearer to *us* and appealed more to our senses and tastes than that of Rome and Greece, was *trampled down* (—I do not say by what sort of feet—) Why? Because it had to thank noble and manly instincts for its origin—because it said yes to life, even to the rare and refined luxuriousness of Moorish life!... The crusaders later made war on something before which it would have been more fitting for them to have grovelled in the dust—a civilization beside which even that of our nineteenth century seems very poor and very "senile."

What they wanted, of course, was booty: the orient was rich.... Let us put aside our prejudices! The crusades were a higher form of piracy, nothing more! The German nobility, which is fundamentally a Viking nobility, was in its element there: the church knew only too well how the German nobility was to be *won*.... The German noble, always the "Swiss guard" of the church, always in the service of every bad instinct of the church—*but well paid*.... Consider the fact that it is precisely the aid of German swords and German blood and valour that has enabled the church to carry through its war to the death upon everything noble on earth! At this point a host of painful questions suggest themselves. The German nobility stands *outside* the history of the higher civilization: the reason is obvious.... Christianity, alcohol—the two *great* means of corruption.... Intrinsically there should be no more choice between Islam and Christianity than there is between an Arab and a Jew. The decision is already reached; nobody remains at liberty to choose here. Either a man is a Chandala or he is not.... "War to the knife with Rome! Peace and friendship with Islam!": this was the feeling, this was the *act*, of that great free spirit, that genius among German emperors, Frederick II. What! must a German first be a genius, a free spirit, before he can feel *decently*? I can't make out how a German could ever feel *Christian*....

61.

Here it becomes necessary to call up a memory that must be a hundred times more painful to Germans. The Germans have destroyed for Europe the last great harvest of civilization that Europe was ever to reap—the *Renaissance*. Is it understood at last, *will* it ever be understood, *what* the Renaissance was? *The transvaluation of Christian values*,—an attempt with all available means, all instincts and all the resources of genius to bring about a triumph of the *opposite* values, the more *noble* values.... This has been the one great war of the past; there has never been a more critical question than that of the Renaissance—it is *my* question too—; there has never been a form of *attack* more fundamental, more direct, or more violently delivered by a whole front upon the center of the enemy! To attack at the critical place, at the very seat of Christianity, and there enthrone the more noble values—that is to say, to *insinuate* them into the instincts, into the most fundamental needs and appetites of those sitting there.... I see before me the *possibility* of a perfectly heavenly enchantment and spectacle:—it seems to me to scintillate with all the vibrations of a fine and delicate beauty, and within it there is an art so divine, so infernally divine, that one might search in vain for thousands of years for another such possibility; I see a spectacle so rich in significance and at the same time so wonderfully full of paradox that it should arouse all the gods on Olympus to immortal laughter—*Caesar Borgia as pope!*... Am I understood?... Well then, *that* would have been the sort of triumph that *I* alone am longing for today—: by it Christianity would have been *swept away*!

What happened? A German monk, Luther, came to Rome. This monk, with all the vengeful instincts of an unsuccessful priest in him, raised a rebellion *against* the Renaissance in Rome.... Instead of grasping, with profound thanksgiving, the miracle that had taken place: the conquest of Christianity at its *capital*—instead of this, his hatred was stimulated by the spectacle. A religious man thinks only of himself.—Luther saw only the *depravity* of the papacy at the very moment when the opposite was becoming apparent: the old corruption, the *peccatum originale*,[123] Christianity itself, no longer occupied the papal chair! Instead there was life! Instead there was the triumph of life! Instead there was a great yea to all lofty, beautiful and daring things!... And Luther *restored the church*: he attacked it.... The Renaissance—an event without meaning, a great futility!

Ah, these Germans, what they have not cost us! *Futility*—that has always been the work of the Germans.—The Reformation; Leibniz; Kant and so-called German philosophy; the war of "liberation"; the empire—every time a futile substitute for something that once existed, for something *irrecoverable*.... These Germans, I confess, are my enemies: I despise all their uncleanliness in concept and valuation, their cowardice before every honest yea and nay. For nearly a thousand years they have tangled and confused everything their fingers have touched; they have on their conscience all the half-way measures, all the three-eighths-way measures, that Europe is sick of,—

---

[123] original sin

they also have on their conscience the uncleanest variety of Christianity that exists, and the most incurable and indestructible—Protestantism.... If mankind never manages to get rid of Christianity the *Germans* will be to blame.. .

62.

With this I come to a conclusion and pronounce my judgment. I *condemn* Christianity; I bring against the Christian church the most terrible of all the accusations that an accuser has ever had in his mouth. It is, to me, the greatest of all imaginable corruptions; it seeks to work the ultimate corruption, the worst possible corruption. The Christian church has left nothing untouched by its depravity; it has turned every value into worthlessness, and every truth into a lie, and every integrity into baseness of soul. Let any one dare to speak to me of its "humanitarian" blessings! Its deepest necessities range it against any effort to abolish distress; it lives by distress; it *creates* distress to make *itself* immortal.... For example, the worm of sin: it was the church that first enriched mankind with this misery!—The "equality of souls before God"—this fraud, this *pretext* for the *rancunes* of all the base-minded—this explosive concept, ending in revolution, the modern idea, and the notion of overthrowing the whole social order —this is *Christian* dynamite.... The "humanitarian" blessings of Christianity forsooth! To breed out of *humanitas* a self-contradiction, an art of self-pollution, a will to lie at any price, an aversion and contempt for all good and honest instincts! All this, to me, is the "humanitarianism" of Christianity!—Parasitism as the *only* practice of the church; with its anæmic and "holy" ideals, sucking all the blood, all the love, all the hope out of life; the beyond as the will to deny all reality; the cross as the distinguishing mark of the most subterranean conspiracy ever heard of,—against health, beauty, well-being, intellect, *kindness* of soul—*against life itself*....

This eternal accusation against Christianity I shall write upon all walls, wherever walls are to be found—I have letters that even the blind will be able to see.... I call Christianity the one great curse, the one great intrinsic depravity, the one great instinct of revenge, for which no means are venomous enough, or secret, subterranean and *small* enough,—I call it the one immortal blemish upon the human race....

FRIEDRICH NIETZSCHE

And mankind reckons *time* from the *dies nefastus* when this fatality befell—from the *first* day of Christianity!—*Why not rather from its last?*—*From today?*—The transvaluation of all values!...

from ECCE HOMO

6.

But I have chosen the title of Immoralist as a surname and as a badge of honour in yet another sense; I am very proud to possess this name which distinguishes me from all the rest of mankind. No one hitherto has felt Christian morality beneath him; to that end there were needed height, a remoteness of vision, and an abysmal psychological depth, not believed to be possible hitherto. Up to the present Christian morality has been the Circe of all thinkers—they stood at her service. What man, before my time, had descended into the underground caverns from out of which the poisonous fumes of this ideal—of this slandering of the world—burst forth? What man had even dared to suppose that they were underground caverns? Was a single one of the philosophers who preceded me a psychologist at all, and not the very reverse of a psychologist—that is to say, a "superior swindler," an "Idealist"? Before my time there was no psychology. To be the first in this new realm may amount to a curse; at all events, it is a fatality: *for one is also the first to despise.* My danger is the loathing of mankind.

7.

Have you understood me? That which defines me, that which makes me stand apart from the whole of the rest of humanity, is the fact that I *unmasked* Christian morality. For this reason I was in need of a word which conveyed the idea of a challenge to everybody. Not to have awakened to these discoveries before, struck me as being the sign of the greatest uncleanliness that mankind has on its conscience, as self-deception become instinctive, as the fundamental will to be blind to every phenomenon, all causality and all reality; in fact, as an almost criminal fraud *in psychologicis.* Blindness in regard to Christianity is the essence of criminality—for it is the crime *against* life. Ages and peoples, the first as well as the last, philosophers and old women, with the exception of five or six moments in history (and of myself, the seventh), are all alike in this. Hitherto the Christian has been *the* "moral being," a peerless oddity, and, *as* "a moral being," he was more absurd, more vain, more thoughtless, and a greater disadvantage to himself, than the greatest despiser of humanity could have deemed possible. Christian morality is the most malignant form of all falsehood, the actual Circe of humanity: that which has corrupted mankind.

It is not error as error which infuriates me at the sight of this spectacle; it is not the millenniums of absence of "goodwill," of discipline, of decency, and of bravery in spiritual things, which betrays itself in the triumph of Christianity; it is rather the absence of nature, it is the perfectly ghastly fact that *anti-nature* itself received the highest honours as morality and as law, and remained suspended over man as the Categorical Imperative. Fancy blundering in this way, *not* as an individual, *not* as a people, but as a whole species! as *humanity*! To teach the contempt of all the principal instincts of life; to posit falsely the existence of a "soul," of a "spirit," in order to be able to defy the body; to spread the feeling that there is something impure in the very first prerequisite of life—in sex; to seek the principle of evil in the profound need of growth and expansion—that is to say, in severe self-love (the term itself is slanderous); and conversely to see a higher moral value—but what am I talking about?—I mean the *moral value per se*, in the typical signs of decline, in the antagonism of the instincts, in "selflessness," in the loss of ballast, in "the suppression of the personal element," and in "love of one's neighbour" (neighbouritis!).

What! is humanity itself in a state of degeneration? Has it always been in this state? One thing is certain, that you are taught only the values of decadence as the highest values. The morality of self-renunciation is essentially the morality of degeneration; the fact, "I am going to the dogs," is translated into the imperative," Ye shall all go to the dogs"—and not only into the imperative. This morality of self-renunciation, which is the only kind of morality that has been taught hitherto, betrays the will to nonentity—it denies life to the very roots. There still remains the possibility that it is not mankind that is in a state of degeneration, but only that parasitical kind of man—the priest, who, by means of morality and lies, has climbed up to his position of determinator of values, who divined in Christian morality his road to power. And, to tell the truth, this is my opinion. The teachers and leaders of mankind—including the theologians—have been, every one of them, decadents: hence their transvaluation of all values into a hostility towards life; hence morality. *The definition of morality*: Morality is the idiosyncrasy of decadents, actuated by a desire *to avenge themselves with success upon life.* I attach great value to this definition.

8.

Have you understood me? I have not uttered a single word which I had not already said five years ago through my mouthpiece Zarathustra. The unmasking of Christian morality is an event which is unequalled in history, it is a real catastrophe. The man who throws light upon it is a *force majeure*, a fatality; he breaks the history of man into two. Time is reckoned up before him and after him. The lightning flash of truth struck precisely that which theretofore had stood highest: he who understands what was destroyed by that flash should look to see whether he still holds anything in his hands. Everything which until then was called truth, has been revealed as the most detrimental, most spiteful, and most subterranean form of life; the holy pretext, which was the "improvement" of man, has been recognised as a ruse for draining life of its energy and of its blood. Morality conceived as *Vampirism*.... The man who unmasks morality has also unmasked the worthlessness of the values in which men either believe or have believed; he no longer sees anything to be revered in the most venerable man—even in the types of men that have been pronounced holy; all he can see in them is the most fatal kind of abortions; fatal, *because they fascinate.*

The concept "God" was invented as the opposite of the concept life—everything detrimental, poisonous, and slanderous, and all deadly hostility to life, was bound together in one horrible unit in Him. The concepts "beyond" and "true world" were invented in order to depreciate the only world that exists—in order that no goal or aim, no sense or task, might be left to earthly reality. The concepts "soul," "spirit," and last of all the concept "immortal soul," were invented in order to throw contempt on the body, in order to make it sick and "holy," in order to cultivate an attitude of appalling levity towards all things in life which deserve to be treated seriously, *i.e.* the questions of nutrition and habitation, of intellectual diet, the treatment of the sick, cleanliness, and weather. Instead of health, we find the "salvation of the soul"—that is to say, a *folie circulaire*[124] fluctuating between convulsions and penitence and the hysteria of redemption. The concept "sin," together with the torture instrument appertaining to it, which is the concept "free will," was invented in order to confuse and muddle our instincts, and to render the mistrust of them man's second nature! In the concepts "disinterestedness" and "self-denial," the actual signs of decadence are to be found. The allurement of that which is detrimental, the inability to discover one's own advantage and self-destruction, are made into absolute qualities, into the "duty," the "holiness," and the "divinity" of man. Finally—to keep the worst to the last—by the notion of the *good* man, all that is favoured which is weak, ill, botched, and sick-in-itself, which *ought to be wiped out.* The law of selection is thwarted, an ideal is made out of opposition to the proud, well-constituted man, to him who says yea to life, to him who is certain of the future, and who guarantees the future —this man is henceforth called the *evil* one. And all this was believed in as *morality!—Ecrasez l'infâme!* [125]

9.

Have you understood me? *Dionysus* versus *the Crucified.* [126]

---

[124] "circular madness," manic-depressive psychosis

[125] "Crush the loathsome thing!"—A quotation from Voltaire, referring to the Catholic Church.

[126] See *The Will to Power* section 1052

www.ingramcontent.com/pod-product-compliance
Lightning Source LLC
Chambersburg PA
CBHW070904120626
46546CB00001B/129